Ghost in the Well

Ghost in the Well

The Hidden History of Horror Films in Japan

Michael Crandol

BLOOMSBURY ACADEMIC
LONDON • NEW YORK • OXFORD • NEW DELHI • SYDNEY

BLOOMSBURY ACADEMIC
Bloomsbury Publishing Plc
50 Bedford Square, London, WC1B 3DP, UK
1385 Broadway, New York, NY 10018, USA
29 Earlsfort Terrace, Dublin 2, Ireland

BLOOMSBURY, BLOOMSBURY ACADEMIC and the Diana logo are
trademarks of Bloomsbury Publishing Plc

First published in Great Britain 2021

Copyright © Michael Crandol, 2021

Michael Crandol has asserted his right under the Copyright, Designs and
Patents Act, 1988, to be identified as Author of this work.

For legal purposes the Acknowledgments on p. ix–x constitute an extension
of this copyright page.

Cover images: Frame from an unknown film based on the Dish Mansion legend. Courtesy
of the National Film Archive of Japan and Kobe Planet Film Archive
Film Strip © natasaadzic / Getty Images

All rights reserved. No part of this publication may be reproduced or
transmitted in any form or by any means, electronic or mechanical, including
photocopying, recording, or any information storage or retrieval system,
without prior permission in writing from the publishers.

Bloomsbury Publishing Plc does not have any control over, or responsibility for, any
third-party websites referred to or in this book. All internet addresses given in this
book were correct at the time of going to press. The author and publisher regret any
inconvenience caused if addresses have changed or sites have ceased to exist, but can
accept no responsibility for any such changes.

A catalogue record for this book is available from the British Library.

A catalog record for this book is available from the Library of Congress.

ISBN: HB: 978-1-3501-7874-8
PB: 978-1-3501-7873-1
ePDF: 978-1-3501-7876-2
eBook: 978-1-3501-7875-5

Typeset by Newgen KnowledgeWorks Pvt. Ltd., Chennai, India
Printed and bound in India

To find out more about our authors and books visit www.bloomsbury.com
and sign up for our newsletters.

Contents

List of Figures	vi
Acknowledgments	ix
Note on the Text	xi
Introduction	1
1 *Kaiki eiga*: Defining Classic Japanese Horror Films	19
2 Ghost Cats versus Samurai: Prewar *Kaiki* Cinema	63
3 The Dead Sleep Unwell: Wartime and Occupation Censorship and the Postwar Return of *Kaiki*	109
4 Uncanny Invasions: The Shintōhō Studio and Nakagawa Nobuo	145
5 Back from the Grave: The Death of a Genre and the *Kaiki* Legacy of J-horror	189
Afterword: The End …?	219
Bibliography	227
Index	237

Figures

1. An advertisement for the Shinkō Studio's *Ghost Story of Yotsuya* (*Iroha gana Yotsuya kaidan*, 1937) proclaims the film one of the studio's "unique *kaiki* films" — 25
2. Japanese advertisements for *Psycho* (1960), *Eyes without a Face* (*Les yeux sans visage*, 1960), and *House on Haunted Hill* (1959), all featuring similar depictions of female characters screaming in terror — 30
3. "Spooky forest" sets in *Mansion of the Ghost Cat* (*Bōrei kaibyō yashiki*, 1958), *The Wolf Man* (1941), and *The Vampire Lovers* (1970) — 38
4. Matte paintings and miniatures evoke Othered spaces. Castles atop foreboding hills in *The Ghost Cat of Okazaki* (*Kaibyō Okazaki sōdō*, 1954) and *Frankenstein* (1931) — 39
5. In this sequential series of shots from Nakagawa Nobuo's *Ghost Story of Yotsuya* (*Tōkaidō Yotsuya kaidan*, 1959), Oiwa's ghost appears to her sister Osode beautiful as she was in life, while simultaneously manifesting as the hideous *onryō* behind Naosuke. When Naosuke screams in fear, Osode looks but cannot see the source of his terror — 49
6. Okiku's double-exposure ghost in a frame from an unidentified production of the Dish Mansion legend (*c.* 1915) — 69
7. A samurai confronts a rather cuddly-looking *bakeneko* in a still from an unidentified film — 72
8. Beauty and danger combined in the person of vamp actress Suzuki Sumiko. Promotional image from Makino Studio's *Jokai* (1926) — 83
9. Suzuki Sumiko surrounded by a bevy of armed maidens in *The Cat of Arima* (*Arima neko*, 1937) — 94
10. Bela Lugosi in *Dracula* (1931) and Suzuki Sumiko in *The Cat of Arima* — 97

11	Publicity still from *The Ghost Cat and the Mysterious Shamisen* (*Kaibyō nazo no shamisen*, 1938), which showcases Suzuki Sumiko as well as the kaleidoscope technique used to portray the ghost cat. Such a shot that combines the ghost and the human characters in this fashion does not appear in the actual film	103
12	The "empty door" from Kinoshita Keisuke's *The Ghost Story of Yotsuya: A New Interpretation* (*Shinshaku Yotsuya kaidan*, 1949)	116
13	Poster for the Occupation-era film *The Iron Claw* (*Tetsu no tsume*, 1951). Despite no "real" monsters or themes of cosmic *osore*, the poster advertises it as one of "Daiei's unique *kaiki* pictures"	120
14	Irie Takako applying her makeup for *The Ghost Story of Saga Mansion* (*Kaidan Saga yashiki*, 1953)	123
15	Promotional image for *The Ghost Story of Saga Mansion* (*Kaidan Saga yashiki*, 1953)	123
16	*Obake yashiki* ("spook house") scares in *The Ghost Cat of Okazaki* (*Kaibyō Okazaki sōdō*, 1954)	127
17	Behind-the-scenes shot of Mōri Ikuko in the nude and covered in live snakes, for *Blue Snake Bath* (*Aoi hebi buro*, 1959)	131
18	Promotional image for *White Snake Beauty* (*Shirohebi Komachi*, 1958)	133
19	The cover of the 1969 issue of *Kinema junpō* devoted entirely to *kaiki* and *kyōfu*, featuring Christopher Lee as the face of the genre	141
20	The opening shot of *The Ghost Story of Kasane's Swamp* (*Kaidan Kasane ga fuchi*, 1957) with its painterly mise-en-scène, from which the camera cuts in at a fateful moment	153
21	The "third teacup" scene in *The Ghost Story of Kasane's Swamp*	156
22	Cursed walls in *The Ghost Cat and the Cursed Wall* (*Kaibyō noroi no kabe*, 1958) and *Mansion of the Ghost Cat* (*Bōrei kaibyō yashiki*, 1958)	161
23	Actress Satsuki Fujie as the *bakeneko* in the color *jidaigeki* sequence of *Mansion of the Ghost Cat* and as she appears in the monochrome *gendaigeki* sequences	162
24	Expressionistic shadows and point-of-view tracking movement in a series of successive shots from *Mansion of the Ghost Cat*	163

25	Promotional image for *Lady Vampire* (*Onna kyūketsuki*, 1959) showcasing the contemporary characters and setting plagued by Amachi Shigeru's vampire/werewolf hybrid	168
26	Publicity image of Wakasugi Katsuko as Oiwa from Nakagawa's *Ghost Story of Yotsuya* (*Tōkaidō Yotsuya kaidan*, 1959). Nineteenth-century woodblock print of Oiwa by Utagawa Kuniyoshi	178
27	Nakagawa's film favors long shots for the living Oiwa but brings the camera in close to depict the wrath of her vengeful ghost	180
28	Oiwa's ghost rises into frame in place of Iemon's new bride in a single take	182
29	The ghost's face completely revealed in the climax of *Ghost Actress* (*Joyūrei*, 1996) and completely hidden in the climax of *Ring* (*Ringu*, 1998)	199
30	Regan from *The Exorcist* (1973) and Samara from *The Ring* (2002)	204
31	The ghost as ambiguously ethereal and yet physically concrete in *Pulse* (*Kairo*, 2001)	206

Acknowledgments

The seeds of this work were planted what seems ages ago when I was working part-time in the music and video section of Barnes & Noble with vague aspirations of pursuing some kind of degree in Japanese studies. One day while stocking DVD shelves my fellow coworker, friend, and film buff Jared Hendrix asked if I had ever heard of a film called *Jigoku* and a director named Nakagawa Nobuo (I had not). My thanks must always first go to Jared and our little international film club for making me aware of Nakagawa's *kaiki* world.

Japanese film history might have remained nothing more than a private hobby had not Rachel DiNitto recommended making it a full-time academic pursuit, which I began under the guidance of her friend Christine Marran. I am forever indebted to both of them for putting me on the path. Thanks especially to Christine for fully embracing my decision to become "the horror guy" and never doubting I could do something interesting and meaningful with it.

While in Japan, the research required to do this project justice was carried out via a generous fellowship from the Japan Foundation, whose Fujimura Syuji was always available to help with matters pertaining to research as well as the day-to-day particulars of living in Japan. Fujiki Hideaki provided invaluable assistance and insight during my time as a research student at Nagoya University and has continued to be an enthusiastic supporter of me and my work. Various film archives around Japan allowed me to screen rare surviving prints of prewar *kaiki eiga*; I am indebted to the National Film Archive in Tokyo, Matsuda Films, and the Kobe Planet Film Archive for showing me these lost gems of Japanese horror movie history. My warmest appreciation goes to the members of Shutoki, particularly Miyata Haruo, Shimomura Takeshi, Suzuki Kensuke, and Nakagawa Shinkichi, who shared anecdotes and memories of Nakagawa Nobuo and his approach to filmmaking. Thanks also to Kurosawa Kiyoshi and Takahashi Hiroshi for taking time out of their schedules to discuss films that were not their own.

All of the fieldwork mentioned above would have been impossible to undertake were it not for the efforts of the excellent teachers at the Inter-University Center for Japanese Language Studies in Yokohama, especially Ohashi Makiko, who went above and beyond the call of duty to make sure I could read what I needed to read to succeed.

Friends and mentors at the University of Minnesota contributed constructive criticism and emotional encouragement in equal measure as this little history of *kaiki* took shape. Jason McGrath and Alice Lovejoy taught me how to think and write about film professionally without losing the enthusiasm of our inner movie lovers. To Jessica Chan, Devon Cahill, Farah Freyah Yazawa, Blair Williams, Saena Dozier, Tim Gitzen, Soo Hyun Jackelen, and Sravanthi Kollu, I am forever grateful for the camaraderie and commiseration. Most of all I must thank Paul Rouzer, without whose dear friendship and constant guidance I would have been lost before I ever truly began.

At Bloomsbury, Rebecca Barden and Veidehi Hans embraced this project immediately and enthusiastically, for which I am forever grateful. A grant from the Great Britain Sasakawa Foundation helped cover the costs of image permissions, and Okada Hidenori and Nakayama Akira provided invaluable assistance in procuring the best possible quality visual materials long-distance from Japan.

In a sense, my parents Donald and Jan Crandol wrote this book every bit as much as I did, from instilling in me a childhood love of Halloween and Vincent Price movies to supporting my decision to quit my job and become a full-time student in my mid-20s. Apart from leading ultimately to the volume you now hold in your hands, it also allowed me to hone my academic skills alongside my sister Katie. Reading *Frankenstein* and *Dracula* with her at the College of William and Mary made me want to keep on studying monsters forever.

I've worked on this manuscript, sometimes without hope it would ever see completion, over the course of almost a dozen moves across three continents. My wife Sayuri has been beside me every step of the way and made sure the quest was not in vain. She couldn't carry it for me, but she carried me.

Note on the Text

Research for this book was carried out in part via a grant from the Japan Foundation.

Funding for images provided by the Great Britain Sasakawa Foundation.

Material in this volume previously appeared in "The Ghosts of *Kaiki Eiga*," in *The Japanese Cinema Book*, ed. Alastair Philips and Hideaki Fujiki (London: BFI, 2020). Portions of Chapter 2 were previously published as "Beauty is the Beast: Suzuki Sumiko and Prewar Japanese Horror Cinema," in *The Journal of Japanese and Korean Cinema* 10, no. 1 (2018): 16–31.

For Japanese names I have followed the conventional Japanese order of family name first (e.g., Nakagawa Nobuo = Smith, John) except in the case of scholars whose work first appeared in English (e.g., Chika Kinoshita = John Smith).

Introduction

At the climax of the popular Japanese horror film *Ring* (*Ringu*, 1998), the ghost Sadako famously emerges from a well on a television screen. The scene frequently appears on lists of the scariest moments in horror movie history and has become an iconic image in the East Asian pop culture landscape.[1] Sadako and her cursed video, supposedly laid to rest by the film's protagonists, flash onto the TV screen without any apparent source as both the characters and the audience realize what they thought was dead, buried, and at peace still haunts the realm of the living.

For viewers familiar with traditional Japanese ghost stories, Sadako and her well embody an additional and extratextual uncanny return in their deliberate evocation of the "Dish Mansion at Banchō" legend. The centuries-old tale, still well known to today's Japanese schoolchildren, recounts the misfortunes of Okiku, a maid in a samurai lord's mansion murdered and tossed into a well for breaking one of ten precious dishes. Each night her ghost rises from the well to count out the nine remaining plates before shrieking and wailing over the tenth, her cries driving the lord who killed her to the brink of madness. In the guise of Sadako, Okiku's ghost transcends the reaches of time to haunt the world anew, and now her intended victim is not her cruel murderer, but all of us.

Sadako's well serves as a site of the uncanny in yet another way unknown to most audiences of *Ring*. The scene harkens back to the very earliest surviving footage from a Japanese horror film, an adaptation of the "Dish Mansion" story produced sometime before 1923. Only eleven minutes of the film remain, but they comprise all the best bits of the tale, including the seminal moment at the well. As Sadako would so famously do more than seventy years later, Okiku's

---

[1] See, e.g., Jordan Crucchiola, "The 100 Scares That Shaped Horror," *Vulture*, November 29, 2018, https://www.vulture.com/article/best-horror-movie-scenes.html. Accessed May 19, 2019.

ghost emerges from her watery depths to shock and terrify her victims, and in the process becomes the oldest extant "long-haired Japanese ghost" in the history of on-screen horror. Like the tip of an enormous iceberg, she represents a small fraction of the lost and forgotten plethora of Japanese horror films produced between the dawn of cinema and the rise to international prominence of "J-horror" pictures like *Ring* at the turn of the twenty-first century, in which the long dead and buried ghosts of Japanese horror cinema's formative years crawled out of the well once more to take the world by storm.

Sadako and her well were the return of something that once was—the return of a dead spirit, the return of Japan's traditional premodern ghost stories, the return of Japan's own horror film history—and this prompted a search for beginnings. Just as the protagonists of *Ring* embark on a quest to uncover the origins of Sadako's ghost, the global popularity of Japanese horror films at the dawn of the millennium spurred a wave of interest in the roots of Japanese horror cinema, an attempt to locate the ghost that haunted the creative well of the J-horror phenomenon. A flurry of publications appeared during the first decade of the twenty-first century grasping at possible origins for J-horror, positing everything from Noh theater to pornography as a potential ancestor of Sadako and her ilk. Many of these avenues inarguably make up integral parts of the tapestry that is Japanese horror history, but in attempting to pinpoint the cultural origins of J-horror it is easy to lose sight of the fact that the object in question remains a genre of popular film. If we seek an origin for popular Japanese horror films, we must consider the nature of transnational popular film genres, the public discourses that surround them across linguistic divides, and how such films are created in the global web of the commercial film industry.

It becomes necessary first to step back and ask a deceptively simple-seeming question:

What Is Japanese Horror Cinema?

Although we often debate the boundaries of the horror genre—where does horror end and science fiction begin? Is a Hitchcockian "thriller" the same thing as a supernatural "chiller"?—any casual film fan likely will tell you that *Dracula, Frankenstein, Psycho, The Exorcist, Alien, The Blair Witch Project, Friday the 13th Part XXXVII,* and *Saw 23* are, for all their vast differences in style and mode of production, horror films. The not-unreasonable assumption that a picture that features some horrific elements designed to elicit scares or dread from its audience is, in effect, a "horror film" has led many observers to apply the same breadth of generic classification when writing in English about Japanese cinema. Past studies of Japanese horror cinema have included art house films such as Mizoguchi Kenji's *Ugetsu* (*Ugetsu monogatari*, 1953) and Shindō Kaneto's *Onibaba* (1964), along with Fukusaku Kinji's hyperviolent survival film *Battle Royale* (*Batoru rowaiaru*, 2000) and rape-revenge exploitation pictures like *Freeze Me* (*Furiizu mii*, 2000), all under the generic umbrella of horror.[2] However, none of these pictures originally were conceived of as horror films in Japan, and such labeling divorces them from the cultural-historical context of their production, distribution, and reception in their home country.[3] Few if any Japanese film fans would imagine these pictures as belonging to the same generic category as *The Wolf Man* (1941) or *Night of the Living Dead* (1968).

The transnational popularity of the J-horror phenomenon at the turn of the millennium inspired much of this categorical confusion. "J-horror" became part of global vernacular in the wake of director Nakata Hideo's *Ring*, a landmark film in horror history that spawned numerous sequels, a big-budget Hollywood remake, and countless imitations in Japan, Greater East Asia, and the Western world. *Ring* and its spawn, of which Kurosawa Kiyoshi's *Pulse* (*Kairo*, 2001) and the myriad incarnations of the *Ju-On/The Grudge* franchise produced in both Japan and Hollywood are merely the highest-profile examples, were heralded at the time of their release for reinvigorating the horror genre with an emphasis on slow-burn psychological scares and creepy imagery over gruesome displays of gore. Western fans, critics, and distributors alike discussed and packaged these films as a savvy Asian alternative to the perceived dead end of Hollywood horror, which had become mired in self-referential sequels and remakes of tired slasher franchises.[4] By the middle of the first decade of the twenty-first century the contemporary Japanese horror film had become one of its nation's most successful "soft power" cultural exports, rivaling anime, manga, and video games in popularity. Yet the international discussion of Japanese horror cinema prior to the J-horror phenomenon remained largely confined to what had been commercially released in the West, resulting in a skewed view of Japanese horror film history weighted toward the art house cinema of auteurs like Mizoguchi

---

[2] See, e.g., Jay McRoy, ed., *Japanese Horror Cinema* (Honolulu: University of Hawaii Press, 2005).
[3] Mitsuyo Wada-Marciano discusses some of the reasons for this in "J-horror: New Media's Impact on Contemporary Japanese Horror Cinema," in *Horror to the Extreme: Changing Boundaries in Asian Cinema*, ed. Jinhee Choi and Mitsuyo Wada-Marciano (Hong Kong: Hong Kong University Press, 2009).
[4] Daniel Martin, "Japan's *Blair Witch*: Restraint, Maturity, and Generic Canons in the British Cultural Reception of *Ring*," *Cinema Journal* 48, no. 3 (2009): 35–51.

and Shindō, direct-to-video slasher films, and sadomasochistic pornography. Such accounts overlook the massive amount of popular B-cinema genre pictures produced in Japan during the prewar and early postwar decades that never received international distribution, instead identifying films like *Ugetsu*, *Onibaba*, and even Kinugasa Teinosuke's avant-garde silent film *A Page of Madness* (*Kurutta ippaigi*, 1926) as the ancestors of the contemporary Japanese horror film.[5]

These attempts at assembling a history of Japanese horror cinema within which to situate J-horror films like *Ring* seem based mainly on the presence of some ghostly supernatural element present in the cinematic text, regardless of the film's overall thematic mood or message and divorced from the context of its generic identity in Japan. A few of the characters in *Ugetsu* turn out to be ghosts, and *Onibaba* features a chilling climatic sequence tinged with hints of a supernatural curse at play in the characters' fate, yet the overall tone of both has little in common with what audiences in Japan or elsewhere would expect from the horror genre. Apart from their incidental ghostly elements, what most unites these films in a chronology with J-horror films like *Ring* and *Pulse* is that they are all internationally known examples of Japanese cinema, with the earlier films retroactively marketed as "classics" of Japanese horror.

The J-horror creators seldom if ever cite *Ugetsu* or *Onibaba* as predecessors to their own work. They do, however, frequently point to the B-pictures produced at the Shintōhō studio in the latter half of the 1950s as a major source of inspiration. In particular, contemporary Japanese horror filmmakers name the work of Nakagawa Nobuo, a contract director at Shintōhō who created several seminal horror films for the studio between 1957 and 1960, as a significant precursor to their own style. Nakagawa enjoys a modest cult following among global horror fans for his gruesome evocation of Buddhist hells in *Jigoku* (1960), often cited as one of the first gore films.[6] In Japan, Nakagawa's reputation rests as much on his adaptations of traditional ghost stories (*kaidan*) such as *The Ghost Story of Kasane's Swamp* (*Kaidan Kasane ga fuchi*, 1957), *Mansion of the Ghost Cat* (*Bōrei kaibyō yashiki*, 1958), and *The Ghost Story of Yotsuya* (*Tōkaidō*

---

[5] See, e.g., Jay McRoy's *Nightmare Japan: Contemporary Japanese Horror Cinema*, Contemporary Cinema Series, no. 4 (Amsterdam: Rodopi, 2008), as well as Ruth Goldberg's article "Demons in the Family: Tracking the Japanese 'Uncanny Mother' Film from *A Page of Madness* to *Ringu*," in *Planks of Reason: Essays on the Horror Film*, ed. Barry Keith Grant and Christopher Sharret (Oxford: Scarecrow Press, 2004), 370–85. Goldberg argues that Kinugasa Teinosuke's experimental silent film *A Page of Madness* (*Kurutta ippaigi*, 1926) "is the true predecessor of *Ringu*" (372).

[6] James Kendrick, *Film Violence: History, Ideology, Genre* (London: Wallflower Press, 2009), 57.

Yotsuya kaidan, 1959), all of which won rare critical praise for domestic horror films from critics of the day and anticipated much of what would come to be associated with the motifs and iconography of J-horror.[7] Kurosawa Kiyoshi, the most critically acclaimed contemporary Japanese horror filmmaker, has jokingly stated that he doesn't show his students Nakagawa's films because they would see from where he steals his ideas,[8] while *Ring* director Nakata Hideo paid homage to Nakagawa's *The Ghost Story of Kasane's Swamp* in 2007's *Kaidan*, complete with a nostalgic black-and-white recreation of the 1957 film's opening sequence. Nakagawa and his contemporaries at Shintōhō produced what many Japanese fans consider the pinnacle of domestic *kaiki eiga*—a term literally meaning "strange" or "bizarre films" that was the most commonly used generic label in Japanese for what we would call "horror films" in English until the 1970s, when the term fades from usage for reasons that will be discussed in the following pages. Yet despite Nakagawa's central position in the history of popular Japanese horror cinema, he remains a relatively unknown figure in Japanese film studies.

When I began the initial research for this book my intention was to rescue Nakagawa Nobuo from obscurity via a consideration of his *kaiki* work that would demonstrate both their technical and thematic sophistication as well as their influence on the later J-horror films, thus offering a fuller account of Japanese horror film history. I soon realized, however, that Nakagawa's half dozen or so *kaiki* films were themselves only part of a much larger story that needed to be told. If Nakagawa Nobuo's work has been largely ignored by Western scholarship, the massive amount of *kaiki* films produced in Japan during the prewar and early postwar decades (of which Nakagawa's films are merely the highest-profile examples) constitutes an utter black hole in English-language studies of Japanese cinema. Scholarship in Japanese is likewise sparse: Otherwise detailed histories of the nation's motion picture industry by Tanaka Jun'ichirō and Yomota Inuhiko omit discussion of the films of Nakagawa and the B-grade *kaiki* genre within which he worked. While a few scholars, notably Shimura Miyoko and Izumi Toshiyuki, have published several invaluable pieces on prewar and early postwar *kaiki eiga*, a robust Japanese-language theory of *kaiki* cinema has yet to emerge.

---

[7] Citing Kurosawa Kiyoshi, Wada-Marciano writes that the J-horror filmmakers' methods were "distinctly different from" the work of Nakagawa. While I agree that the content and style of J-horror often differ drastically from classic *kaidan* film adaptations, in the pages that follow I demonstrate the ways in which J-horror draws upon (and subverts) the conventions of *kaiki eiga*. See Wada-Marciano, "J-horror," 21.

[8] "Building the Inferno: Nobuo Nakagawa and the Making of *Jigoku*." *Jigoku* (Tokyo: Criterion, 2006), DVD.

For many years the most comprehensive primer of Japanese cinema history in English has been Joseph L. Anderson and Donald Richie's *The Japanese Film: Art and Industry*, first published in 1959 and again in an expanded and revised edition in 1982. Anderson and Richie's text cements the work of Golden Age auteurs like Kurosawa Akira, Ozu Yasujirō, and Mizoguchi Kenji at the top of their list of worthwhile pictures, while often dealing out harsh and dismissive value judgments against more popular modes of filmmaking. They predictably make no mention of Nakagawa Nobuo, and of *kaiki* films in general (which they deem the "ghost-film genre"), the authors have only this to say:

> The trouble with the ghost-film genre is that the stories are all alike. The audience knows precisely what to expect since they probably saw a different version of the same story a year before. The films are made cheaply and unimaginatively, yet the audience, responding to a well-known stimulus, is apparently thoroughly and delightfully chilled each summer.[9]

Anderson and Richie then resume their narrative of the great men of Japanese cinema, yet their dismissive comments suggest much regarding what truly is interesting about these "cheaply and unimaginatively" made pictures from a cultural perspective. The films are in fact often reworkings or outright remakes of the same story audiences had seen on-screen only a year or two prior. And they were indeed perennially popular, for as Anderson and Richie admit with some dismay, the audience kept coming back each summer to see them. Nakagawa's *The Ghost Story of Yotsuya* was released just three years after fellow Shintōhō director Mōri Masaki's version (*Yotsuya kaidan*, 1956); both were adaptations of a famous nineteenth-century ghost story that had been filmed more than twenty times by the late 1950s.

Yotsuya is one of the half dozen or so traditional Japanese ghost stories that filmmakers revisited repeatedly between the 1910s and the 1960s. Nakagawa's *Kasane's Swamp*—based on another nineteenth-century tale that borrows generously from *The Ghost Story of Yotsuya*—sits in the company of no less than eight competing film versions of the story. *The Peony Lantern* (*Botandōrō*) and *The Dish Mansion at Banchō* (*Banchō sarayashiki*) can each claim at least seventeen screen adaptations, while variations on the *bakeneko* or "ghost cat" legend had been lensed an incredible sixty-plus times by 1970. All of these tales treat with quite similar themes and motifs, notably the return from the grave

---

[9] Joseph L. Anderson and Donald Richie, *The Japanese Film: Art and Industry (Expanded Edition)* (Princeton, NJ: Princeton University Press, 1982), 262.

of a jilted, murdered, or otherwise wronged female spirit that exacts revenge on its still-living oppressors. *The Peony Lantern* has roots in Chinese literature, but these other archetypal Japanese ghost stories all originate in the premodern Edo period (1603–1868) as part of a cultural vogue for the ghostly, monstrous, and grotesque that manifested in the popular literary, visual, and performing arts. Ghost stories were annual fixtures of the kabuki theater by the end of the Edo period in the mid-nineteenth century. In the most obvious precursor to the ubiquitous *kaiki* films of the twentieth century, *The Ghost Story of Yotsuya* became a perennial hit of the popular stage, performed each year during the summer months coinciding with the *Obon* festival of the dead and playfully said to provide audiences a respite from the heat by giving them the shivers.

Anderson and Richie's complaint that "the stories are all alike" misses the true appeal of *kaiki* films as well as the venerable premodern traditions behind them. As film theorist Stephen Neale writes in *Genre*,

> The notion that "all westerns (or all gangster films, or all war films, or whatever) are the same" is not just an unwarranted generalisation, it is profoundly wrong: if each text in a genre were, literally, the same, there would simply not be enough difference to generate meaning or pleasure. Hence there would be no audience. Difference is absolutely essential to the economy of genre … Moreover, repetition and difference are themselves not separable … they function as a relation. There is hence not repetition *and* difference, but repetition *in* difference.

Neale then tweaks his statement slightly, adding that it would be more accurate to say that genres are about "difference *in* repetition."[10] So too with *kaiki* films, which like their stage ancestors in the Edo period drew in audiences who were not there for the stories (which, as Anderson and Richie note, they already knew), but to see what a particular rendition of them did with the material. Part of what made Nakagawa's films successful with both audiences and critics was their "difference in repetition," what they did differently with the old formulas—or in some instances, returning to the old formulas that had become diluted or discarded over time.

Therefore, a consideration of Nakagawa's work in the *kaiki* genre must be grounded in a history of the genre as a whole.

Was what drew audiences to the earliest film versions of *The Ghost Story of Yotsuya* in the 1910s the same thing that people were paying to see in 1927, 1937, 1949, and 1959? Colette Balmain, to date one of the only Western scholars to

---

[10] Stephen Neale, *Genre* (London: British Film Institute, 1980), 50.

address Nakagawa's films at any length, considers his 1959 version of *Yotsuya* mainly as a product of the postwar culture in which it was produced, a retelling of a traditional ghost story for a society struggling to come to grips with the defeat and devastation that followed in the wake of the Second World War. In this reading of the legend, the wicked samurai protagonist Iemon—a down-on-his-luck ronin who conspires to poison his wife, Oiwa, so that he may marry the daughter of a wealthy superior—becomes a warning against self-centered American-style individualism that threatened to overwhelm Japan in the wake of the Allied Occupation, while Oiwa's poison-disfigured face serves as a reminder of the victims of atomic radiation in Hiroshima and Nagasaki.[11] Certainly postwar Japanese audiences may have responded to Nakagawa's film in just such a way, but this of-the-moment interpretation leaves aside that the film's iconography and archetypal Japanese ghost story narrative incorporate the same elements that had been popular in prewar *kaiki* pictures, as well as the Edo period literature and drama from which it derives.

Balmain's topical reading of Nakagawa's postwar take on the *Yotsuya* legend has been taken up more recently by Valerie Wee in her book *Japanese Horror Films and Their American Remakes*, in which (following Balmain) she suggests "the Edo gothic horror film" first rose to prominence as a response to the supposed Allied Occupation ban on "samurai films" as a way to critique the postwar order of Western materialism.[12] The multiple historical inaccuracies in this claim aside, Balmain's and Wee's narrow historical readings are too lodged in a single cultural moment that ironically risks becoming too ahistorical as a catch-all explanation for a vaguely defined "Japanese horror" genre that makes no distinctions between premodern ghost stories, their mid-century film adaptations, and the drastic reworking of their certain elements in contemporary J-horror. Baryon Tensor Posadas, in his work on the doppelgänger in Japanese fiction, succinctly critiques a similar approach to "Japanese horror" in Jay McRoy's *Nightmare Japan*:

> The socio-cultural picture of Japan he paints is far too overly expansive and sweeping. Much of what he highlights in his analysis—fears of social change or critiques of the patriarchal structures—are not new themes in much of the existing commentary and discourse surrounding Japanese culture through the decades. His analysis tends to rely on a tired West/Japan binary as its starting

---

[11] Colette Balmain, *Introduction to Japanese Horror Film* (Edinburgh: Edinburgh University Press, 2008), 50–69.

[12] Valerie Wee, *Japanese Horror Films and Their American Remakes* (New York: Routledge, 2014), 41.

point with the effect of implicitly reifying an ahistorical notion of "Japan" or "Japanese culture."[13]

A fuller, more nuanced account of the history of *kaiki* cinema—and Nakagawa's proper place in it—must take into account shifting reasons for the genre's popularity through the decades and at the same time attempt to get at the enduring essence of centuries-old tales, all while sidestepping essentialist claims about "Japanese horror" in contrast to "Western horror." With this in mind I mostly have refrained from attempting sociopolitical readings of particular films and instead turn my attention to a more general consideration of the attractions of horror in the case of *kaiki* film and the formal markers of the genre as it was conceived in prewar and postwar Japan. The following chapters endeavor to chart the changing sites of on-screen appeal in the *kaiki* genre throughout the twentieth century, from the spectacle of early cinematic trick photography and the ambiguously sexy portrayals of female monsters in the 1920s and 1930s to the use of color and montage in the postwar work of Nakagawa. At the same time, I attempt via a consideration of both formal and thematic content to identify the connecting threads that brought prewar and postwar horror films together under the generic label of *kaiki*.

Unfortunately, any attempt to uncover the history of Japanese horror film prior to the end of the Second World War faces tremendous obstacles. The commercial Japanese film industry produced well over a hundred specimens of the *kaiki* genre before 1945, of which less than a dozen are known to survive. Only four exist in anything close to a complete print, and even these have suffered the effects of deterioration over the decades. They also remain haunted by the old critical hostilities toward the genre, as limited government and private funds for restoration invariably go toward more "worthy," A-list productions. Traces of the enormous prewar *kaiki* cinema culture endure primarily in secondary materials: magazine reviews, advertisements, and theater pamphlets. Even these can be difficult to come by, as the genre's low critical standing meant that publications such as *Kinema junpō*, Japan's longest-running and most prestigious film journal, typically gave B-grade *kaiki* films short shrift. To assemble the prewar history of Japanese horror cinema requires more than a little guesswork, and the puzzle will always contain missing pieces.

Kaiki as a genre encompassed not only domestic adaptations of traditional Japanese ghost stories but an almost steady stream of imported horror films

---

[13] Baryon Tensor Posadas, *Double Vision, Double Fictions: The Doppelgänger in Japanese Film and Literature* (Minneapolis: University of Minnesota Press, 2018), 188.

from America and Europe. Pictures like Universal's *Dracula* (1931) and *The Bride of Frankenstein* (1935) played just as central a role in defining the face of *kaiki* cinema in Japan as they did in establishing the genre of screen horror in the United States and elsewhere. American, British, and Italian horror films dominated the Japanese *kaiki* landscape at several points in the history of the genre, equaling and often eclipsing their domestic counterparts in popularity and critical repute. This book seeks to broaden the discussion of Japanese horror cinema via a positioning of American and European horror cinema in the discourse of *kaiki*. Its main topic of inquiry should not therefore be thought of as "the history of Japanese horror films," but more aptly "the history of horror films in Japan." While I reserve the bulk of attention for domestic examples of *kaiki* cinema, I ground my discussion in the genre's international identity in Japan, which included not just traditional *kaidan* ghost story adaptations but also Hollywood horror franchises like *Dracula* and *Frankenstein* and their progeny in both America and Europe. The result aims to provide an account of a popular film genre within a particular national context that takes into account the inherently transnational nature of popular commercial film in the global market.

Finally, there remains the curious fact that, while the Anglophone generic category of "horror film" remains as vigorous and visible today as it was almost ninety years ago, the *kaiki* label becomes an antiquated relic by the end of the 1970s in Japan. Horror film historians note the late 1960s and 1970s as an epochal period for the genre, the birth of "modern horror" when films like *Night of the Living Dead* (1968), *The Exorcist* (1973), *The Texas Chain Saw Massacre* (1974), and *Halloween* (1978) took horror out of its gothic and science-fiction settings and deposited it in the heart of modern, mundane middle America.[14] In the process, they jettisoned what Andrew Tudor has called the "secure horror" mode of previous decades—in which the heroes restore patriarchal authority and social normalcy at the conclusion of the picture—in favor of a new "paranoid horror" marked by cynicism and distrust of the traditional institutions that protected us in earlier horror efforts, with endings that were ambiguous at best in their defeat of the monster.[15] All of this dramatically reshapes the horror film landscape as the newly christened "slasher" subcategory comes to dominate the genre through the 1980s and 1990s. Although the "horror" label endures

---

[14] See, e.g., Peter Hutchings, *The Horror Film* (Harlow: Pearson, 2004).
[15] Andrew Tudor, "Why Horror? The Peculiar Pleasures of a Popular Genre," in *Horror: The Film Reader*, ed. Mark Jancovich (New York: Routledge, 2002), 47–55.

throughout all of these sea changes, in Japan the radical innovations coming from American commercial horror cinema coincide with an absolute dearth of domestic *kaiki* film production. The shuttering of the Daiei studio in the early 1970s and the Tōei studio's abandoning of the *kaiki* genre—as well as the genre's move to television—played roles in this, and for the future of the *kaiki* label their timing could not have been worse.

American films like *The Exorcist* and *Halloween* looked so different from the traditional *kaiki* fare that critics turned to transliterated English words like *okaruto* ("occult") and *spuratta* ("splatter") for generic categorization. By the middle of the 1980s *horā* ("horror") became the new Japanese appellation for the genre, with *kaiki* now used exclusively for older modes of horrific filmmaking. Yet it would be foolish to assume that the difference between *kaiki* films and *horā* films is merely chronological. Japanese fans, critics, and filmmaking professionals perceived a shift so cataclysmic in the style, content, and mode of production of horrific cinema that a new genre had to be christened to account for it. Therefore, we cannot simply say "*kaiki* film" equals "horror film," no more than we can say that *Ugetsu* and *Battle Royale* are horror films in a Japanese cultural context. I frame the following history in a theory of *kaiki* cinema that simultaneously distinguishes it from the Anglophone categorical construct of "the horror film" while accounting for *kaiki*'s encompassing of much Western horror cinema—for, if *kaiki* does not equate *en toto* to horror, it is undeniably horrific.

Overview of This Book

The first chapter of this book focuses not on particular films, studios, or directors but a history of the discourse of *kaiki* as it applied to both domestic and international films, followed by a consideration of *kaiki*'s defining features as a genre of popular cinema and how such features conform to or deviate from theories of horror film. I look not only at the term *kaiki eiga* but also competing and complimentary Japanese terminology for films featuring ghosts, monsters, and other motifs typically identified with the horror genre in English, such as *kaidan eiga* ("ghost story film"), *obake eiga* ("monster film"), and *kyōfu eiga* (literally, "horror film"). At certain points in history some of these terms are virtually interchangeable with *kaiki*, while at other times suggestive of alternatives to or niche subgenres of an overreaching *kaiki* label. After establishing some of the formal markers of *kaiki* cinema, I turn to the major academic theories of the horror genre, highlighting the differences between a Euro-American conceptualization of "horror film" and a Japanese conceptualization of *kaiki eiga*. Taking a cue from Rick Altman's syntactic/semantic approach to the study of genre, I consider why and how Japanese *kaiki* films that so obviously treat with motifs and themes associated with horror fail to meet the criteria established by many theorists for inclusion in the genre.

Film theory since 1990 has taken a turn toward more cognitive-based frameworks for understanding cinema, as in the work of David Bordwell, Noël Carroll, and Carl Plantinga, but the great flowering of horror film theory occurred largely in psychoanalytic studies like Robin Wood's seminal horror film essay "The American Nightmare" and Carol Clover's *Men, Women, and Chain Saws*, which continue to be influential in academic discussions of horror.[16] While Wood and Clover provide nuanced and convincing arguments for such an approach to Anglophone horror cinema, the limits of psychoanalysis become apparent when discussing genre across the cultural-linguistic divide of horror and *kaiki*. My work seeks to move the discussion of international horror theory beyond psychoanalysis, in the direction indicated by Noël Carroll's cognitive theory of horror, which he details in *The Philosophy of Horror* (although Carroll's definition of horror requires some adjustments to accommodate the parameters of *kaiki*), and developed by Mathias Clasen in his "biocultural" study of the genre, *Why Horror Seduces*.[17] I conclude by offering an attempted reconciliation between Western theories of horror and the Japanese concept of *kaiki* via a liberal use of Carroll combined with H. P. Lovecraft's concept of "cosmic fear" from his *Supernatural Horror in Literature*.[18] I ultimately choose the word *osore* ("terror") as the best Japanese term to describe the particular brand of fear ideally evoked by *kaiki* films, and subsequent chapters seek to employ this criterion in a historical discussion of the genre from its inception in the earliest days of commercial cinema through the 1960s, after which the term *kaiki* fades from usage as a category of popular film.

Carroll's theory of horror relies largely on Tzvetan Todorov's *The Fantastic: A Structural Approach to a Literary Genre*. Scholars such as Bliss Cua Lim have rightly pointed out the problems in applying Todorov's structuralist, Eurocentric

---

[16] See Robin Wood, "The American Nightmare: Horror in the 70s," in *Horror: The* Film *Reader*, 25–32; and Carol Clover, *Men, Women, and Chain Saws: Gender in the Modern Horror Film* (Princeton, NJ: Princeton University Press, 1992).

[17] See Noël Carroll, *The Philosophy of Horror: Or, Paradoxes of the Heart* (New York: Routledge, 1990); and Mathias Clasen, *Why Horror Seduces* (New York: Oxford University Press, 2017).

[18] Carroll deals with Lovecraft's theory in the pages of *The Philosophy of Horror*, 161–5.

theory to the film and literature of Asia.[19] Nonetheless (and partly for this very reason), I find Todorov's categories of fantastic literature useful for a discussion of the *kaiki* genre and for highlighting the limits of Anglophone horror theory in transcending cultural-linguistic divides. Todorov conceives three modes of the fantastic narrative: the "marvelous," in which entities like the ghosts and monsters associated with the horror genre are presented as a natural and known feature in the world of the narrative; the "uncanny," in which seemingly supernatural entities or occurrences ultimately receive a rational, mundane explanation; and the "pure fantastic," which hesitates between natural and supernatural explanations and remains ambiguous as to the existence of the supernatural.[20] Carroll rules out marvelous narratives from inclusion in the horror genre, but as we will see, applying Todorov's schema to Japanese *kaiki* films situates the vast majority of them within the category of the marvelous. I invoke Todorov's distinctions throughout my discussion to highlight the ways in which crossing cultural-linguistic borders upsets the boundaries of genre and forces us to rethink assumptions about categories of narrative often taken for granted.

The second chapter traces the history of *kaiki* cinema from its beginnings in early trick films of the first decades of the twentieth century through the establishment of the 1939 Film Act, which effectively turned the Japanese film industry into a war propaganda machine and shut down most genre fare in the process. Almost from its moment of inception the commercial Japanese film industry was busy making ghost and monster-filled adaptations of Edo period ghost stories. These now-lost, primordial *kaiki* pictures, like much early cinema, likely exemplified Tom Gunning's "cinema of attractions," which privileged the spectacle of the new medium of cinema over narrative continuity.[21] Evidence suggests scenes of spectacle like double-exposure see-through ghosts and stop-motion photography trumped narrative integration or any attempt to convey a sense of *osore* to the audience in the primordial *kaiki* film. However, by the mid-1920s changes in the mode of production of Japanese cinema largely supplant the cinema of attractions with a more narratively oriented mode of film. Themes of fear and suspense that lent the traditional Japanese ghost story much of its sense of *osore* now became

---

[19] Bliss Cua Lim, *Translating Time: Cinema, the Fantastic, and Temporal Critique* (Durham, NC: Duke University Press, 2009).
[20] Tzvetan Todorov, *The Fantastic: A Structural Approach to a Literary Genre*, trans. Richard Howard (Ithaca, NY: Cornell University Press, 1975), 41–57.
[21] Tom Gunning, "The Cinema of Attractions: Early Film, Its Spectators, and the Avant-Garde," in *Early Cinema: Space, Frame, Narrative*, ed. Thomas Elsaesser and Adam Baker (London: British Film Institute, 1990), 56–62.

part of the *kaiki* film equation. Spectacle remained important, however, and from the 1920s onward the site of attraction shifts from trick photography to the body of the actresses who portrayed the vengeful spirits and monsters of Edo ghost stories on film and the ambiguously sexualized and threatening sight of silver screen vamps (*vampu*) transformed into fearsome monsters before the audience's eyes. I organize much of this chapter around a discussion of vamp actress Suzuki Sumiko, Japan's first great horror star, whose portrayals of the *bakeneko* or "ghost cat" juxtaposed alluring femininity and monstrous physicality, shaping the public image of domestic *kaiki* film for most of the genre's lifespan.

By the early 1930s the *kaiki* genre becomes well established as a category of cinema comprised not only of domestic ghost stories but also Hollywood and European horror films, resulting in the emergence of a more cosmopolitan *kaiki* aesthetic in the years leading up to the Second World War. Japanese *kaiki* films began to incorporate much of the semantics of American horror cinema, but this should not be thought of as a simple case of Hollywood stamping out local difference. In her "vernacular modernism" theory of classical cinema, Miriam Hansen argues against the notion that Hollywood's dominance of the global film market in the 1930s wielded a top-down, hegemonic influence on local cinemas, but rather represented a more horizontal, adaptable model onto which native traditions could be grafted and reinterpreted in a contemporary, transnational medium.[22] Applying Hansen's idea not just to the 1930s, I consider the earliest Japanese ghost story films and their privileging of trick photography as being in dialogue with the pioneering special effects films of French filmmaker Georges Méliès. The great prewar boom of domestic *kaiki* films in the late 1930s, which saw the creation of the nation's first *kaiki* film star in the persona of Suzuki Sumiko, demonstrates an even more elaborate hybridity in its combination of Japanese conventions for portraying monsters on stage and screen with the techniques of Hollywood horror films from the Universal studio. This trend continues into the postwar work of Nakagawa Nobuo and reaches new levels of complexity in the J-horror phenomenon, which draws greater inspiration from American and British horror film but combines it with the motifs and iconography of domestic *kaiki* cinema, which in turn gets reinterpreted in American remakes of J-horror, a total reversal of Hollywood's role in Hansen's original model.

---

[22] Miriam Hansen, "The Mass Production of the Senses: Classical Cinema as Vernacular Modernism," in *Reinventing Film Studies*, ed. Christine Gledhill and Linda Williams (New York: Oxford University Press, 2000), 332–50.

Chapter 3 begins with a look at the interim years of war and occupation, amounting to a "lost decade" in which the *kaiki* genre was all but entirely suppressed by government censorship. Just two traditional Japanese ghost story adaptations appeared between 1941 and the end of the American Occupation in 1952: Kinoshita Keisuke's *Ghost Story of Yotsuya: A New Interpretation* (*Shinshaku Yotsuya kaidan*) and Watanabe Kunio's *Legend of the Nabeshima Ghost Cat* (*Nabeshima kaibyo-den*), both released in 1949. After examining the various political reasons for the suppression of *kaiki* film—first by the wartime Japanese government and then the American Occupation—I demonstrate how these two films scraped by the American censors via a massive diluting of their traditional *kaiki* elements, effectively erasing any sense of karmic vengeance embodied by their ghosts and monsters.

Kaiki cinema rebounds as soon as the Occupation ends, although much like its prewar ancestors continues to suffer from ill critical repute. For much of their history domestic *kaiki* films were held in contempt by critics, most often due to complaints that the films failed to properly integrate the themes of *osore*, leaving only the hollow spectacle of the actress's monstrous transformation. The Daiei studio's two notable attempts to create a second *kaiki* superstar along the lines of Suzuki Sumiko in the forms of Irie Takako and Mōri Ikuko exploited extratextual elements of the actresses' public personas over attention to narrative detail. In the case of Irie, her grotesque portrayals of the ghost cat depended for their impact on her status as a former screen beauty during the prewar era, while the studio's publicity department sold Mōri's willingness to appear nude on-screen while live snakes slithered over her flesh as a peek at the star's supposed erotic fetishes.

Reasons for the relative inattention to narrative themes of karmic retribution vary over time, including wartime and occupation-era censorship policies, the films' status as hastily produced, B-grade program pictures, and attempts to blend the genre with comedy and romance. Early postwar *kaiki* films also came to be dominated by what might be termed an *obake yashiki* or "spook house" mentality toward the presentation of the horrific, relying on simply achieved startle effects of a fleeting, momentary nature in the film's diegesis. At the same time, the blurring of science fiction and horror in American popular cinema and Japanese derivatives like *Godzilla* (*Gojira*, 1954) created a moment of existential crisis for the *kaiki* genre, resolved by the arrival of the British Hammer Films' color remakes of gothic horror classics like *Frankenstein* and *Dracula*, which reasserted the conventional markers of the genre and assured *kaiki*'s continued distinction from other horrific modes of popular film.

The fourth chapter turns its attention to the work and legacy of the Shintōhō studio and Nakagawa Nobuo, who brought the domestic *kaiki* film to its pinnacle of critical respect even as they laid the groundwork for new styles of horror filmmaking that would eventually see the *kaiki* label retired from usage. While I devote the bulk of the chapter to extended analyses of Nakagawa's three key *kaiki* works—*The Ghost Story of Kasane's Swamp*, *Mansion of the Ghost Cat*, and *The Ghost Story of Yotsuya*—I also consider the ways in which Shintōhō films by other directors such as Mōri Masaki's version of *The Ghost Story of Yotsuya* and Namiki Kyōtarō's *Vampire Bride* (*Hanayome kyūketsuma*, 1960) further contributed to this pivotal moment in the development of the *kaiki* genre. Most of the Shintōhō *kaiki* films draw much of their effectiveness from a sophisticated use of the uncanny, and the most radically progressive of them do this via a shattering of the old generic demarcations between period pictures and films set in the modern day, drawing monsters like the vengeful spirit and the ghost cat out of the Edo period ghost story adaptations to which they had previously been confined and unleashing them on modern Japanese society. And yet the film most widely held to be Nakagawa's masterpiece, *The Ghost Story of Yotsuya*, finds its "difference in repetition" via a fusion of innovative formal techniques with a return to the world of classic Edo ghost story narratives and the evocation of *osore* as an omnipotent arbiter of cosmic, karmic retribution.

My overview of *kaiki* cinema concludes in Chapter 5 with a dual examination of the genre's final years in the 1960s and eventual obsolescence in the 1970s, followed by its partial resurrection in certain motifs and iconographies of the J-horror movement in the late 1990s and early 2000s. J-horror continues to be a well-trod topic in academic writing, and it is not the aim of this book to dwell at length on films like *Ring*, *Pulse*, and *Ju-On* that have been subjected to exhaustive scrutiny elsewhere. Instead I offer a short consideration of the ways in which J-horror draws on and subverts *kaiki* film tropes like the vengeful ghost as depicted in the work of Nakagawa and others. J-horror takes the ghost in the well out of the stylized, gothic trappings of *kaiki* film, resituating her in a realist, modern aesthetic devoid of traditional cosmologies and rewriting the rules of how the vengeful ghost operates to create something freshly terrifying.

Due to restraints of time and considerations of length, I have left much interesting material aside. In particular, more could be said about the prolific *kaiki* output of the Japanese studios in the 1960s and the genre's move to television in the early 1970s. The concept of *osore* and the ways in which narrative functions to convey its essence might also prove to be worthy topics of more theoretically based inquiries into *kaiki* cinema. But first the social history of *kaiki* as a genre of popular film needs to be established. With this in mind, the following work seeks to locate the ghost in the well of Japanese horror, charting the weird, shifting topology of the *kaiki* genre and providing a map for those who would explore its shadowy corners in more detail.

1

Kaiki eiga: Defining Classic Japanese Horror Films

On February 12, 1931, Universal's *Dracula* premiered in New York, and no one knew quite what to call it. Today the Bela Lugosi classic is often identified as the first full-fledged specimen of the horror genre,[1] but distributors, exhibitors, and critics at the time of its release struggled to label the picture in generic terms for potential audiences. Not that *Dracula* had materialized, like its titular vampire, out of thin air. The nascent horror film genre it birthed had several important precursors in both America and Europe, notably the German Expressionist masterpieces *The Cabinet of Dr. Caligari* (*Das Cabinet des Dr. Caligari*, 1920) and *Nosferatu* (1922), John Barrymore's turn as *Dr. Jekyll and Mr. Hyde* (1920), and Universal's own releases of *The Phantom of the Opera* (1925) and *The Cat and the Canary* (1927). The German Expressionist films were presented and discussed as art films at the time of their release,[2] and *Dr. Jekyll and Mr. Hyde* was received as a filmographic record of the talents of a great stage actor preserved for posterity,[3] while the Universal pictures leading up to *Dracula* could be pegged into other already established genres by the invested parties. *The Phantom of the Opera* contained enough love-story elements to be labeled a romance, and the haunted house whodunit *The Cat and the Canary* was easily marketed as a mystery.[4]

---

[1] Andrew Tudor, e.g., begins his history of the horror film genre with the year 1931 and the release of *Dracula*. See *Monsters and Mad Scientists: A Cultural History of the Horror Movie* (Oxford: Basil Blackwell, 1989). See also Kendall R. Phillips, *A Place of Darkness: The Rhetoric of Horror in Early American Cinema* (Austin: University of Texas Press, 2018).
[2] Peter Hutchings, *The Horror Film* (Edinburgh: Pearson, 2004), 3.
[3] The *New York Times* review of the film from March 29, 1920, calls Barrymore a great stage actor but says "anything he does in 'the movies' must be totally unimportant to many … but [coming generations] may see *Dr. Jekyll and Mr. Hyde* and, in addition to enjoying something of Mr. Barrymore's art, they will receive a personal impression of the actor that will enable them to know and appreciate him."
[4] The film was directed for Universal by the German Expressionist filmmaker Paul Leni. Robert Spadoni discusses the film's large influence on *Dracula* (and, consequently, every subsequent film in

Dracula, however, seemed to be an entirely new beast. Exhibition campaigns tried to sell the film as a mystery, while much of the advertising material portrayed Bela Lugosi as something approaching a romantic lead. Several critics followed suit, calling the film a mystery or a romance in their reviews. But as Robert Spadoni points out in *Uncanny Bodies: The Coming of Sound Film and the Origins of the Horror Genre*, there is no mystery for the audience, who knows Dracula is the killer from the start, and Lugosi's coldly aloof portrayal of the Count lacks the romantic overtures that later Draculas would bring to the role.[5]

The reviews from 1931 are invariably aware that a sense of horror is a thematically unifying presence in *Dracula*, and most of them use the word "horror" at least once. *Variety* called it "a sublimated ghost story related with all surface seriousness and above all with a remarkably effective background of creepy atmosphere. So that its kick is the real emotional horror kick," while *Film Spectator* noted, "The dominant note of the production is eeriness, a creepy horror that should give an audience goose-flesh and make it shudder."[6] Still, they stop short of calling the film a "horror movie." Later the same year Universal followed up the success of *Dracula* with *Frankenstein*, by which time there seems to have been a consensus that a new film genre was emerging from a ghastly womb, and one can see the ongoing struggle to christen it in *Variety*'s prediction that *Frankenstein* would prove "whether nightmare pictures have a box office pull, or whether *Dracula* is just a freak."[7] The term "horror movie" does not appear to have been widely settled upon until after the release of *Frankenstein*, when Universal had fleshed out their cycle of "nightmare pictures" with such entries as *The Mummy* (1932), *The Invisible Man* (1933), and *Bride of Frankenstein* (1935), and rival studio Paramount threw their hats into the ring with *Dr. Jekyll and Mr. Hyde* (1931) and *Island of Lost Souls* (1932).[8]

Roughly two months before *Frankenstein* proved that "nightmare pictures" were here to stay, *Dracula* opened in Japan. Unlike their American counterparts, the Japanese critics knew exactly what to call it. In his review for *Kinema junpō*, Japan's longest-running and most prestigious film magazine, Murakami Hisao acknowledges the picture's novelty (as well as Universal's attempts to sell it as a mystery), but appears to be quite familiar with its generic species, opening with the line, "Now this is something novel these days, a mysterious *kaiki eiga*

---

the horror genre) in *Uncanny Bodies: The Coming of Sound Film and the Origins of the Horror Genre* (Berkeley: University of California Press, 2007).
[5] Spadoni, *Uncanny Bodies*, 49–51.
[6] Ibid., 47–8.
[7] Ibid., 97.
[8] Phillips, *Place of Darkness*, 180; Hutchings, *The Horror Film*, 3.

that deals with vampires."⁹ The term *kaiki eiga* is most commonly translated into English as "horror film," but as we have just seen, in 1931 the phrase had yet to take root in the English-speaking world. What had defied generic classification in its native country seemed to fit neatly into a preexisting category in Japan. The word *kaiki* reappears throughout Murakami's review: he praises director Tod Browning for "successfully brewing a *kaiki* atmosphere that catches hold of the audience's heart" and suggests cinematographer Karl Freund's camerawork is the likely source for much of the "*kaiki* flavor" of the production.¹⁰

The Japanese reception of *Dracula* upends assumptions about the Hollywood-centric origins of popular commercial film genres, throwing into the question the appropriateness of treating the phrase *kaiki eiga* as a mere analogue of the English "horror film" even as the former clearly encompasses much of the latter. Both terms have also shifted their meanings over time. At some points in history *kaiki* and horror have been treated as synonyms; at others they appear to be understood quite differently. *Kaiki* eventually fades into obsolescence as a generic category by the 1980s, subsumed into the English transliteration *horā*, an evolution that effaces a historically unique way of understanding a significant part of Japanese film culture. Instead of approaching *kaiki*, *horā*, and horror as interchangeable terms, this chapter seeks to illuminate the cultural and historical factors that make both Japanese and Western *kaiki eiga* unique in the global history of on-screen terror.

Kaiki as Film Genre

The word *kaiki* is composed of two characters, 怪 ("kai") and 奇 ("ki"), both of which mean "strange," "weird," or "bizarre." Variations on the word, all beginning with the character *kai*, recur throughout Japanese history to describe literature and drama featuring the weird, grotesque, and otherworldly. In his introduction to a collection of essays on *kaiki* cinema, Uchiyama Kazuki argues that *kaiki to gensō*, or "the weird and the fantastic," was an established literary subgenre by the Heian period (794–1185), as one classification of the short prose tales in such collections as the twelfth-century text *Konjaku monogatari-shū* ("Collection of Tales New and Old"),¹¹ although the Heian word used to describe prose tales

---

⁹ *Kinema junpō*, October 21, 1931, 28.
¹⁰ Ibid.
¹¹ Uchiyama Kazuki, "Nihon eiga no kaiki to gensō," in *Kaiki to gensō e no kairō*, ed. Uchiyama Kazuki (Tokyo: Shinwasha, 2008), 9.

with weird or fantastic themes is *kai-i* (怪異), another synonym for "strange" or "bizarre."

During the Edo period (1603–1868), the advent of cheap printing processes and an affluent urban merchant class with time and money to spare sees an explosion of another type of *kai* literature, *kaidan* (怪談). Literally meaning "strange tales" but frequently translated as "ghost stories," *kaidan* are narratives more often than not dealing with themes of revenge from beyond the grave or encounters with bizarre spooks, goblins, and monsters collectively categorized as *yōkai*. Urban Japanese of the seventeenth to nineteenth centuries delighted in reading collections of *kaidan* aloud at social gatherings as part of the "100 Ghost Stories" parlor game (*hyaku monogatari kaidankai*, "gathering of one hundred ghost stories"). These overnight, marathon recitations were playfully believed to have the power to summon real spirits, as one hundred candles doused one by one with the conclusion of each tale gradually plunged the gathering into darkness. As Michael Dylan Foster suggests in his study of *yōkai* culture, *Pandemonium and Parade*, the intersection of the horrific and the ludic in these ghost-story parties anticipates the same ambiguous enjoyment that horror films offer in the modern era.[12]

In addition to written collections printed for reading at "100 Ghost Stories" gatherings, the most popular *kaidan* tales further anticipated modern horror films in their adaptation to the kabuki theater (as well as the *kōdan* and *rakugo* oral storytelling formats), bringing grisly tales of terror to life in front of a paying audience. Kabuki playwright Tsuruya Nanboku IV's 1825 script for *The Ghost Story of Yotsuya* (*Tōkaidō Yotsuya kaidan*, literally "The Ghost Story of Yotsuya on the Tōkaidō Road," commonly shortened to *Yotsuya kaidan*), in which the vengeful ghost of a woman named Oiwa returns from the grave to torment her wicked samurai husband, Iemon, remains Japan's most famous ghost story to this day and a perennial presence on stage, film, and television, as well as the subject of a well-known belief that past productions of the story were cursed by Oiwa's spirit, resulting in the injury and even deaths of its performers.[13]

Following the arrival of motion pictures in Japan during the last years of the nineteenth century, the frequently performed *kaidan* of the kabuki stage soon found their way to Japanese cinema screens, with ghost stories being among the very first examples of commercial cinema in Japan. Adaptations of the most

---

[12] Michael Dylan Foster, *Pandemonium and Parade: Japanese Monsters and the Culture of Yōkai* (Berkeley: University of California Press, 2009), 52–5.

[13] Yokoyama Yasuko, *Yotsuya kaidan wa omoshiroii* (Tokyo: Heibonsha, 1997), 238.

popular *kaidan*, including *The Ghost Story of Yotsuya*, *The Dish Mansion at Banchō* (*Banchō sarayashiki*), and variations on tales of the popular *bakeneko* cat monster (felines that imbibe the blood of a murder victim and take on their form as a half-human, half-feline werecat) were remade on a semiannual basis from about 1910 onward, with all of the major studios frequently producing competing versions of the same story. Most were released during the summer months of the *Obon* festival of the dead. Not only was this an appropriately spooky practice akin to the Hollywood strategy of releasing horror films during the Halloween season, it also carried on a tongue-in-cheek tradition from the kabuki theater that ghost-story plays performed in the heat of summer provided free air conditioning for audiences by giving them the shivers.

Unfortunately, in most cases all that remains of these early pictures is their title, the name of the studio, and a release date. Several of the Nikkatsu studio's first *kaidan* adaptations were directed by Makino Shōzō and starred Onoe Matsunosuke, respectively, the first great director and actor of Japanese cinema. It is likely that their versions of *The Ghost Story of Yotsuya* (1912), *The Dish Mansion at Banchō* (1914), and *The Peony Lantern* (*Botandōrō*, 1914) were similar in style to the massive amount of samurai and ninja pictures the duo produced during this time, which were characterized by a one-scene, one-take setup in long shot, combined with camera tricks like stop-motion and double-exposure photography in the manner of French filmmaker and special effects pioneer Georges Méliès.[14] Méliès's legacy is clearly visible in the earliest surviving snippet of a Japanese *kaidan* film, which consists of eleven minutes of footage from an unidentified production of *The Dish Mansion* likely produced sometime in the latter half of the 1910s. In it, we see a samurai lord and his retainer sitting near a well. An audience familiar with the Dish Mansion legend would know the body of a murdered maid, Okiku, lies at the bottom of the well, and viewers would not be disappointed when Okiku's ghost rises from its depths to torment her murderer, the samurai lord. The effect is achieved with a simple double-exposure technique as Okiku's transparent form fades in atop the well, and her later appearance in the lord's bedchamber is marked by the use of stop-motion photography to illustrate her psychic manipulation of objects. Both scenes are framed in long shots that showcase the spectacular nature of Okiku's ghost, much like Méliès's early "horror" films like *The Haunted Castle*

---

[14] Kamiya Masako discusses the affinities between the trick photography techniques of Méliès and Makino in "Shoki nihon eiga no kaiki to torikku," in *Kaiki to gensō e no kairō*, 33–65.

(*Le Manoir du diable*, 1896), which are not about frightening the audience so much as enthralling them with the magic spectacle of early cinematic tricks.

By 1915 an average of at least half a dozen *kaidan* adaptations were being produced each year, and they remained a perennial fixture of Japanese cinema until the late 1930s, when a massive increase in the number of *kaiki* films is swiftly followed by their utter suppression at the hands of the government's 1939 Film Act, which forbade "frivolous" subjects in favor of nationalistic propaganda.[15] *Kaiki* was not the only term used at the time for what we would today be tempted to call "horror films" in English. Film adaptations of the most famous Edo period ghost stories were typically identified as *kaidan eiga*, though promotional materials and reviews from the 1920s show that the same works were sometimes called *obake eiga*, which literally means "monster" or "ghost movies" and would remain a synonymous term for *kaiki eiga* in Japan to the present day. Rather like "monster movie" or "creature feature" in English parlance, *obake eiga* seems to have had especially lowbrow implications. An advertisement for Makino Studios' 1927 take on *The Ghost Story of Yotsuya* (*Iroha gana Yotsuya kaidan*) says that the film is "no mere *obake* movie" (*tannaru obake eiga ni arazu*), suggesting the film is a more cultured affair than its generic brethren. Works featuring the perennial favorite *bakeneko* ghost cat were commonly referred to as *kaibyō eiga*, using an antiquated synonym for the mythical creature borrowed from kabuki traditions.

The word *kaiki*, however, featured in discourse surrounding all of these pictures. It appears in promotional material for films throughout the 1920s and 1930s that are otherwise identified as *kaidan* or *obake eiga*, frequently as part of a set phrase that promises audiences *kaiki to senritsu*, which means something like "bizarreness and trembling" but might be more deftly rendered as "thrills and chills." Advertising for the Japanese release of the prototypical Hollywood horror film *The Cat and the Canary* makes reference to the picture being adapted from the "great *kaiki* stage show" (*saidai kaiki geki*). As mentioned earlier, the *Kinema junpō* review for *Dracula* couldn't say enough about that film's *kaiki* qualities. By the late 1930s *kaiki* had become the all-encompassing generic umbrella for the subgenre of native *kaidan* adaptations of famous works such as *The Ghost Story of Yotsuya* as well as original *obake* stories featuring traditional monsters like the ghost cat and imported horror pictures such as the Universal *Dracula* and *Frankenstein* series. Just ten years after Makino Studios had insisted their version of *The Ghost Story of Yotsuya* was "no mere *obake* movie," the Shinkō Kinema Studio was proudly marketing its own *Yotsuya* vehicle in advertisements

---

[15] Shimura Miyoko, "Shinkō kinema no kaibyō eiga," *Eigagaku* 14 (2000): 58.

Figure 1 An advertisement for the Shinkō Studio's *Ghost Story of Yotsuya* (*Iroha gana Yotsuya kaidan*, 1937) proclaims the film one of the studio's "unique *kaiki* films." Courtesy of Matsuda Film Productions.

as "part of their unique series of *kaiki* films" (Figure 1). *Kinema junpō*'s preview article for the film names it one of the studio's scheduled "*kaiki* trilogy" for 1937, placing it alongside another *kaidan* adaptation, *The Ghost Story of the Mandarin Duck Curtain* (*Kaidan oshidori chō*, released 1938) and the *kaibyō eiga*, *The Cat of Arima* (*Arima neko*).[16]

So we see that while the English-speaking world found it necessary to posit a new film genre to accommodate the "nightmare pictures" that Hollywood began producing in earnest during the early 1930s, Japanese audiences and critics already had an established categorical niche waiting for such films across the Pacific. There seems to have been little question in Japan at the time that the Hollywood productions that came to be known as "horror films" in the West shared certain affinities with Japanese narrative traditions of *kai*, and that *Dracula*, *Frankenstein*, and *The Ghost Story of Yotsuya*, when adapted to film,

[16] *Kinema junpō*, June 11, 1937, 106–7.

all belonged to the same genre. *Kinema junpō*'s review from May 1932 of James Whale's *Frankenstein* is particularly struck by the film's affinities to Japan's classic *kaidan*. Film critic Shimizu Chiyota writes,

> The film has the flavor of a *kaidan*; indeed it is one of the most accomplished works of that genre. The desire to see something scary is something all people hold in their hearts to a degree. Here is a movie that expertly plays to this fact throughout.

The review concludes by suggesting that Japanese audiences, fond of seeing traditional *kaidan* such as *The Ghost Story of Yotsuya* performed year after year, will certainly find much to like in *Frankenstein*, and predicts the film will be a big hit.[17] When the sequel *Bride of Frankenstein* came to Japan in the summer of 1935, it significantly opened during the week of *Obon*, the traditional season for showing *kaidan* and *obake* fare.

It does not follow, however, that *kaiki* as a genre of popular cinema should be thought of as wholly and unproblematically equivalent to the Western "horror film." Neither does *kaiki* represent an understanding of genre utterly distinct from Western notions of horror. Alexander Zahlten is half-right when he argues against categorizing 1950s *bakeneko* movies as horror films because "that category possessed no relevance for film production or reception in Japan at the time these films were made or seen," and that this tendency reflects the overwhelming centricity of Hollywood-based models of genre.[18] The dominant position of Hollywood in the history of cinema as commercial entertainment makes it all too easy for studies of genre and national cinema to impose Anglophone generic categories on another culture's cinema, or else conceive of "national genres" essentially separate from Hollywood's hegemony. In practice, however, popular film genres more often consist of a commingling of domestic and international elements, with the generic corpus composed of foreign as well as domestic specimens. For example, Dudley Andrew points out that any study of 1920s French cinema "should take imports into account, because Hollywood films constituted 50 per cent of the images occupying the country's screens, that is, occupying the minds of those who made and watched films."[19] In the case of Japan, Wada-Marciano notes that discussions of Japanese genres like the *yakuza*

---

[17] *Kinema junpō*, May 11, 1932, 31.
[18] Alexander Zahlten, *The End of Japanese Cinema: Industrial Genres, National Times, and Media Ecologies* (Durham, NC: Duke University Press, 2017), 10.
[19] Dudley Andrew, "An Atlas of World Cinema," in *Remapping World Cinema: Identity, Culture, and Politics in Film*, ed. Stephanie Dennison and Song Hwee Lim (New York: Wallflower Press, 2006), 21.

("gangster") film tend to either introduce them as counterparts of Hollywood genres or else as "signs of cultural difference" defined by their opposition to a perceived Hollywood norm. Such an approach "reveals neither their meanings in the specific genre system nor their connections with the audience ... any discussion of the cultural specificity of cinema is often subsumed within the overriding narrative of Hollywood's dominant system."[20] A discussion of *kaiki* as a genre of popular cinema must bear in mind the particular Japanese cultural history and traditions that inform it while also dealing with the inextricable ties to Western horror cinema that shape much of its identity.

One must also not overlook that neither the Japanese *kaiki eiga* nor the English "horror film" possesses a fixed, unchanging definition over time. When Universal released *The Phantom of the Opera* in 1925, the horror genre had yet to be christened, yet today Lon Chaney's iconic Phantom is often presented alongside Lugosi's Count Dracula and Boris Karloff's Frankenstein's Monster as one of the studio's pantheon of horror movie all-stars. But in the 1950s—when science-fiction thrillers in the vein of *The Day the Earth Stood Still* and *The Thing from Another World* (both 1951) were in vogue—the Phantom, Dracula, and Frankenstein's Monster were rebranded by Universal as "Hollywood's Prize Science-Fiction Creatures."[21] Today this particular case of generic relabeling seems absurd. Though the case may be made for Frankenstein, it is hard to see the sci-fi in Count Dracula or the Phantom of the Opera. Yet the borders between horror and science fiction have never been satisfactorily established. Scholars, critics, and fans continue to debate the difference between "horror" and "science fiction" as the labels apply to films like *The Thing from Another World*, the giant-ants-versus-US-military opus *Them!* (1954), or to use a famous Japanese case, *Godzilla* (*Gojira*, 1954).

When the monster is not a ghost or vampire from traditional legend or gothic literature, but an alien from outer space or a giant radioactive lizard, does the work cease to be "horror" and become "science fiction"? Peter Hutchings opens his study of *The Horror Film* with this very issue, noting that the ontology of the genre is particularly vague "when attempts are made to separate out horror from the science fiction genre."[22] Similar questions have been raised in Japan over the use of the term *kaiki* as a generic label, and not always with the same willingness to acknowledge the vague boundaries of genre. In his overview

---

[20] Wada-Marciano, *Nippon Modern: Japanese Cinema of the 1920s and 1930s* (Honolulu: University of Hawai'i Press, 2008), 43–4.
[21] See Rick Altman, *Film/Genre* (London: British Film Institute, 1999), 78–9.
[22] Hutchings, *The Horror Film*, 1.

of the *kaiki* genre, Izumi Toshiyuki insists that *kaiki* demands a supernatural (*chōshizen*) origin for the monster free of any pseudoscientific explanation or human creation (intentional or otherwise), and explicitly rules out *Godzilla* and other sci-fi movie monsters from his definition of the genre.[23] The problem, of course, is that this also potentially precludes *Frankenstein* from the ranks of *kaiki* cinema. While it is easy to see why *Frankenstein* might be considered a sciencefiction movie, it is almost unthinkable to argue that it is not a horror film, and the *Obon* premieres and claims that the film out-*kaidan*s *Yotsuya kaidan* make it a representative *kaiki* film for many Japanese.

Godzilla, meanwhile, has seldom if ever been called a *kaiki* film. As part of *Kinema junpō*'s feature from July 1957, "The World of *Kaiki* Film" (*Kaiki eiga no sekai*), Izawa Jun says of Godzilla and his giant radioactive monster ilk, "These are not serious monsters (*obake*). They are no Oiwa," referring to the vengeful spirit at the center of *The Ghost Story of Yotsuya*.[24] Godzilla, Rodan (*Sora no daikaijū Radon*, 1956), *Mothra* (*Mosura*, 1961), and the other giant monster movies to come out of the Tōhō studio in the 1950s and 1960s were typically identified as *kaijū* (怪獣) films. Although we have here yet another *kai* prefix, *kaijū* signifies "strange beast," as opposed to the more generally atmospheric *kaiki*. Izawa posits that the typical giant radioactive monster narrative—most famously embodied by Godzilla but originating in American films such as *The Beast from 20,000 Fathoms* (1953)—depends on its resonance from a Judeo-Christian "Wrath of God" (*kami no ikari*) moral outlook, in which mankind is punished for its sins against the natural order by mutated agents of that order. As part of a society he considers lacking in (Western) religion, Izawa feels that Japanese *kaijū* films do not possess a spiritual dimension and are at best grim satires of the nuclear age. *The Ghost Story of Yotsuya*'s Oiwa, meanwhile, is deeply rooted in Buddhist notions of karmic cause and effect, returning from the grave to exact vengeance upon the adulterous husband who conspired to murder her.[25]

History would appear to disagree with Izawa that *Godzilla*'s nuclear narrative lacks any resonance for audiences, post–Second World War Japanese or otherwise, as the big green lizard has gone on to become Japan's most internationally recognized film star and often is included among the ranks of the all-time great movie monsters. What Izawa calls the "Wrath of God" motif in *kaijū* films largely conforms to what Noël Carroll identifies as one of the characteristic horror

---

[23] Izumi Toshiyuki, *Ginmaku no hyakkai: honcho kaiki eiga taigai* (Tokyo: Seidosha, 2000), 20–1.
[24] Izawa Jun, "Kaiki to wa? Nihon no obake to seiyō no obake," *Kinema junpō*, July 1, 1957, 44–6.
[25] Ibid.

genre plots, which he dubs the "overreacher plot." Typified by *Frankenstein*, the overreacher plot "is concerned with forbidden knowledge … the recurring theme of the overreacher plot is that there is some knowledge better left to the gods (or whomever)."[26] In *Godzilla*, nuclear experimentation creates a giant monster that threatens to destroy Japan, and the only way to stop it is to employ an even more potentially dangerous technology, Dr. Serizawa's oxygen destroyer, which the scientist uses to destroy both the monster and himself, intentionally taking the secret of the weapon's creation to his grave. The parallels with *Frankenstein*, while not exact, are enough to justify including *Godzilla* among the ranks of Carroll's typical horror plots. Izawa himself comments on the similarity between *Frankenstein* and nuclear giant monster movies in his article.[27] And yet there appears to be a consensus among scholars, critics, and fans in Japan that the former is a *kaiki* film while the latter are not. *Kinema junpo*'s special issue from 1969 devoted entirely to *kaiki* completely omits all *kaijū* movies from its pages, as do later works on *kaiki* cinema such as the abovementioned edited volume by Uchiyama Kazuki and works by Kurosawa Kiyoshi.[28] It would not seem enough, then, to locate the definition of *kaiki* cinema in the mere presence of a monster or even in the particular circumstances of the monster's encroachment into the human realm. Izawa's suggestion that it is an intrinsically religious element that gives a certain film a *kaiki* resonance for one culture but not another is also problematic, as this would essentially result in a nativist definition that would exclude most (if not all) foreign films from the genre.

Just a few years after the appearance of Godzilla, several films from America and Europe would pose further challenges to the generic identity of *kaiki*. The release of Alfred Hitchcock's *Psycho* in 1960 is a major turning point in the history of horror cinema in the West. Many historians and critics point to it as a transitional moment between "classic horror" in the tradition of *Dracula* and *Frankenstein* and the beginning of "new horror" typified by mundane contemporary settings, bloody on-screen violence, and an ambiguous ending in which the threat is not necessarily defeated. Noël Carroll explicitly rules it out of his conceptualization of the horror genre completely on the basis that there is no monster in the literal sense of the word, although he acknowledges that the film has many of the formal trappings of horror.[29] In Japan, promotional advertising

---

[26] Noël Carroll, *The Philosophy of Horror: Or Paradoxes of the Heart* (New York: Routledge, 1990), 118.
[27] Izawa, "Kaiki to wa?" 45.
[28] See Kurosawa Kiyoshi and Shinozaki Makoto, *Kurosawa Kiyoshi no kyōfu no eigashi* (Tokyo: Seidosha, 2003).
[29] Carroll, *The Philosophy of Horror*, 38–9.

Figure 2 Japanese advertisements for *Psycho* (1960, left), *Eyes without a Face* (*Les yeux sans visage*, 1960, center), and *House on Haunted Hill* (1959, right), all featuring similar depictions of female characters screaming in terror.

for *Psycho* featured graphics remarkably similar to films clearly identified as *kaiki* such as *House on Haunted Hill* (1959) (Figure 2). Advertisements for both films prominently feature an image of the female lead with a terror-struck expression frozen on her face. But while the ad for *House on Haunted Hill* proclaims it "a consummate bone-chilling *kaiki* film" (*hone made kōraseru kaiki eiga no iki*), the ad for *Psycho* avoids any generic terminology apart from naming its director as the master of the *surirā*, using the Japanese approximation of the English "thriller." *Kinema junpō*'s review of *Psycho*, meanwhile, significantly calls the film a *kyōfu eiga*, which quite literally means "horror film."[30] The word *kaiki* does not appear in promotional advertising or in the critical review for Hitchcock's film; however, the old phrase *kaiki to senritsu* or "thrills and chills" from the prewar heyday of *kaiki* pictures can be seen on the advertisement for *Eyes without a Face* (*Les yeux sans visage*, 1960), which appears in the same issue of *Kinema junpō* as the ad for *Psycho*. Often regarded as a spiritual sister of Hitchcock's film, its Japanese advertisement features similar imagery in a prominent shot of the film's female victim staring in abject terror. And despite the promise of good old-fashioned thrills and chills, the advert finally settles on branding *Eyes without a Face* an "art-horror film" (*kyōfu no geijutsu eiga*) (Figure 2).

At the time of their release in Japan, there seemed to be something about these pictures that evoked strong affinity to *kaiki* films yet precluded them from being listed among their ranks. While something like *House on Haunted Hill*

---

[30] *Kinema junpō*, October 15, 1960, 84.

(which like *Psycho* and *Eyes without a Face* features no "real" monsters) was pegged in the old generic terms, these new pictures warranted the appellation of a different genre label, *kyōfu eiga*, that semantically comes much closer to the Western term "horror film" than *kaiki*; yet several Western critics and theorists are reluctant to label them as horror films in English. Undoubtedly this has to do with Hitchcock's auteur status and *Eyes without a Face*'s French imported art film pedigree, which set them apart from an obvious pop culture confection like *House on Haunted Hill*. And yet the advertising for all three films betrays their generic affinities, which were implicitly if not explicitly acknowledged at the time of their release. Just as there are many people today who would disagree with Noël Carroll that *Psycho* and *Eyes without a Face* are not horror films, there are those in Japan who unquestionably conceive of them as, in fact, part and parcel of the *kaiki* genre. When asked about *kaiki* film, Kurosawa Kiyoshi explicitly mentions *Eyes without a Face* as a prime example.[31]

The phrase *kyōfu eiga* was used occasionally by film critics during the 1930s in discussions of Hollywood horror films and their Japanese imitations. The review for the 1937 film *The Avenging Corpse* (*Fukushū suru shigai*), a remake of the 1936 Warner Bros. picture *The Walking Dead*, starring Boris Karloff, calls the Japanese film a "Boris Karloff-style *kyōfu* movie."[32] However, by the end of the decade the term appears to have largely ceased being used for films that featured overtly monstrous or supernatural content. Today there is a strong sense among Japanese film aficionados that *kyōfu* denotes suspense thrillers in the vein of *Psycho* or Henri-Georges Clouzet's *Les Diaboliques* (1955), some of which might hint at supernatural elements but ultimately feature human murderers. When asked about the difference between *kaiki* and *kyōfu*, *Ring* screenwriter Takahashi Hiroshi had this to say: "What gets called *kaiki eiga* are mainly *kaidan eiga*, also foreign films like *Dracula* and *Frankenstein*. *Kyōfu eiga* are Western films like Hitchcock's *Psycho* and Clouzet's *Les Diaboliques*."[33]

Still, there may have been a sense in Japan during the late 1950s and early 1960s that many works of the now well-established English generic category of "horror" overlapped with *kaiki* and *kaidan* but that the words themselves did not mean the same thing, and the use of *kyōfu* as a generic label might have been a conciliatory gesture to the Western canon. Literary works translated from other languages that had previously been labeled *kaidan* were released in new editions

---

[31] Author's interview with Kurosawa Kiyoshi, June 3, 2013.
[32] Quoted in Izumi, *Ginmaku no hyakkai*, 115.
[33] Author's interview with Takahashi Hiroshi, June 18, 2013.

that rechristened them *kyōfu shōsetsu* ("horror novels").[34] Beginning in 1958 Tokyo Tsukamoto began publishing their "Collection of World Horror Novels" (*Sekai kyōfu shōsetsu-shū*). However, these were later reedited by the same publisher in 1969 as "Collection of *Kaiki* Novel Masterpieces" (*Kaiki shōsetsu meisaku-shū*), reverting to the more traditional use of a *kai*-derivative word. The slippage between the use of *kaiki* and *kyōfu* as generic labels and the ultimate futility of trying to sort them out into separate categories is made plain by the editor's preface, in which he claims that *kyōfu* as a literary genre "deals more than anything with the subject of fear inspired by supernatural occurrences."[35] Yet at least as far as cinema is concerned, *kyōfu* as a genre seems to delineate the exact opposite. Perhaps as a side effect of being used to distinguish films like *Psycho* and *Eyes without a Face* from more typical *kaiki* films, *kyōfu* ends up demarcating works in which the horror stems from an ultimately mundane source. Yet the distinction is hardly so neat, as both Western *kaiki* movies like *House on Haunted Hill* and domestic *kaiki* productions like *Diving Girls in a Haunted House* (*Ama no bakemono yashiki*, also 1959) also feature no "real" monsters (though admittedly both films' narratives more strongly hint at their possible existence than either *Psycho* or *Eyes*).

In the realm of cinema the term *kaiki eiga* continues to exist—if sometimes uneasily—alongside *kyōfu eiga* up through the early 1970s, after which a shift in production trends both within Japan and internationally finally sees *kaiki* fade from generic parlance. The *kaidan* and *obake* films derived from traditional dramatic and folkloric sources, which had been suppressed by both the wartime and subsequent Occupation governments for reasons that will be discussed later in this book, proved perennially popular for many years after their reappearance in the early 1950s, but by the 1970s this central subgenre of domestic *kaiki* cinema was all but extinct. This is no doubt in part due to the overall decline of the Japanese film industry. Shintōhō, the studio responsible for the most acclaimed *kaiki* pictures of the postwar years, collapsed at the end of 1961. Television, in Japan as elsewhere, took a heavy toll on box office attendance, and the families that went to the theaters on a weekly basis in the 1950s were by and large staying home by the close of the 1960s. Catering to the one demographic still buying movie tickets—young, single men—several of the major studios had turned to softcore pornography production.[36] Although the occasional porno version of

---

[34] Izumi, *Ginmaku no hyakkai*, 18–19.
[35] Ibid.
[36] Isolde Standish, *A New History of Japanese Cinema: A Century of Narrative Film* (New York: Continuum, 2005), 257–8.

a classic *kaidan* such as *The Peony Lantern* or the old *kaiki* staple, the *bakeneko* ghost cat tale, would appear, they were no longer being made with the intent to deliver "thrills and chills" to mainstream audiences.

Abroad, too, the decline of the British Hammer studios, the highest-profile producer of foreign *kaiki* films in the 1950s and 1960s, seemed to signal the death of the genre.[37] Apart from Tōhō's attempt at making a Japanese take on the Hammer vampire film with what are commonly referred to as the "Bloodthirsty Series" (*Chi o sū shiriizu*) of films released between 1970 and 1974, and a minor "occult boom" spurred by the international success of *The Exorcist* that resulted in what might be called a "Shinto *Exorcist*" with 1977's *Curse of the Inugami* (*Inugami no tatari*), there would be scant few domestic productions that warranted the label of *kaiki* going forward. Indeed, films in the vein of *The Exorcist*, with their striking content and stylistic departures from classic Hollywood horror, seemed especially ill-fitted to the *kaiki* label, being most often referenced in the press as *okaruto* or "occult" movies.[38] When newer versions of the old *kaidan* mainstay, *The Ghost Story of Yotsuya*, appeared in 1982 and 1994, they decidedly de-emphasized the *kaiki* elements. Since the 1970s there have been only a handful of pictures that have been presented or discussed in the context of *kaiki*, and these films, such as 2001's *Sakuya the Demon Slayer* (*Sakuya yōkaiden*) or 2007's *Kaidan*, are self-conscious, nostalgic throwbacks to the *kaiki* pictures of yesteryear.

Something else was happening in American cinema that would help render the term *kaiki* obsolete, as the seeds sewn by Hitchcock's *Psycho* began to come to bloody fruition in films like Tobe Hooper's *The Texas Chain Saw Massacre* (1974). Much has been written on the emergence of the "slasher" subgenre of horror that rose to prominence in the American cinema of the 1970s; two of the fundamental theoretical accounts of the horror genre, Robin Wood's "The American Nightmare" and Carol Clover's *Men, Women and Chain Saws*, deal almost exclusively with slasher films in the tradition of *Texas Chain Saw Massacre* and John Carpenter's *Halloween* (1978). As with Hitchcock's *Psycho*, these seminal slashers traded ghosts, vampires, and gothic castles for small-town America, mortal homicidal maniacs, and explicit acts of violence.[39] The slasher film enjoyed a huge boom in the 1980s, when major Hollywood studios

---

[37] See Marcus Hearn and Alan Barnes, *The Hammer Story: The Authorised History of Hammer Films* (London: Titan, 2007), 132–5.

[38] "Kaiki eiga montō," *Kinema junpō*, October 15, 1974. Reprinted in *Eiga kantoku Nakagawa Nobuo*, ed. Takisawa Osamu and Yamane Sadao (Tokyo: Riburopōto, 1987), 114–15.

[39] Though, as has been often remarked, later films in the slasher subgenre often call the mortality of the killer into question, and by Wes Craven's *A Nightmare on Elm Street* (1984), outright refute it.

successfully replicated the box-office success of the low-budget, independent slashers of the previous decade with the long-running *Friday the 13th* and *A Nightmare on Elm Street* series. When these films began to appear in Japan, the old *kaiki* label, having become muddled with *kyōfu* in the 1960s and antiquated by a decade of virtual dormancy in domestic production during the 1970s, was finally put in its grave. Advertising materials simply began to use the transliterated English word for horror, *horā* (ホラー).[40]

The arrival of the American slasher film in Japan coincided with the birth of the direct-to-video film market, which became a fertile learning ground for a new generation of young directors including Miike Takashi and Kurosawa Kiyoshi, who have since gone on to worldwide fame as filmmakers with a flair for the grotesque and horrific. Many of the V-cinema generation's earliest works are plainly inspired by the American slasher film, frequently exceeding their Western counterparts in explicit gore and scenes of depravity. Miike in particular proved to be an especially prolific director of direct-to-video cinema in the 1980s and 1990s. His bizarre, ultraviolent imagery was largely influenced by Ishii Teruo's *ero-guro-nansensu* adaptations of mystery writer Edogawa Rampo's canon made during the late 1960s and early 1970s. Eventually graduating to feature theatrical film production, Miike brought his bag of grotesque tricks with him, culminating in 1999's psychological slasher *Audition* (*Ōdishon*).[41] The film's global critical success and the subsequent international attention it brought to the V-cinema filmmakers cemented, for a brief while, the stereotype abroad that Japanese horror cinema's distinguishing feature was an excess of graphic violence. This proved a short-lived preconception however, as the arrival of the so-called "J-horror" films at the turn of the millennium—with their more atmospheric, psychological approach to scaring their audiences that was at least a partial return to the techniques of *kaiki* filmmaking—usurped the ultraviolent Japanese slasher film's place as the representative face of Japanese horror cinema.

The international popularity and influence of J-horror films like *Ring* and *Ju-On*, which were remade by Hollywood as successful film franchises, put international attention on Japan's horror film traditions, but with the passing of *kaiki* as an active genre of film in the 1970s and the retrograde application of the

---

[40] Uchiyama, "Nihon eiga no kaiki to gensō," 26. Anecdotes do exist that attribute the word's introduction to Alfred Hitchcock, who came to Japan to promote *Psycho* in 1960 and told the press that his new film was a "horror picture." Out of respect for the Master of Suspense, the term was supposedly left as-is in translation. However, I found no evidence in reviews or promotional materials to verify this account.

[41] For a discussion of Miike and V-cinema see Tom Mes, *Agitator: The Cinema of Takashi Miike* (Godalming: Fab Press, 2004).

horā label to films like *Dracula* and *The Ghost Story of Yotsuya*, discussions about the history of horror cinema in Japan risk losing the categorical distinctions between *kaiki*, *kyōfu*, and *horā* crucial to an understanding of the topic. The adoption of the English transliteration *horā* in the 1980s provided a way to talk about the now-defunct *kaiki* genre as part of an ongoing, unbroken continuum of filmmaking traditions, but brought with it a loss of specificity that obscures the true history of the genre.

Heart of Darkness: Toward a Theory of *Kaiki* Cinema

Horā's supplanting of *kaiki* as a category of popular film in Japan has significant consequences for the study of film genre and makes an excellent case study of how crossing cultural borders disrupts definitions of generic categories. Genre theorists such as Rick Altman have already shown how notions of genre can change over time with gothic horror's rebranding as science fiction in the 1950s, but the differences between "horror" and *kaiki* remind us that generic borders shift across cultural-linguistic lines as well as temporal ones. It is worth remembering the point S. S. Prawer raises in his study of horror film, *Caligari's Children: The Film as a Tale of Terror*: "In regarding the terror-film or the horror-movie as a genre one is not, of course, implying that there is some obligatory set of rules every work in that category must obey … What one is asking about, ultimately, is 'common consensus' *within a given society, a given culture*."[42] The English transliteration *horā* afforded Japanese film fans a means by which to place the now-defunct *kaiki* genre within a continuum of an ongoing, living tradition of popular film—the global genre of the horror movie. At the same time, it potentially effaces a more culturally particular way of conceptualizing and categorizing global film. *Horā* as a generic label belongs to the era of globalization. *Kaiki* is the "common consensus" of a given society, a given culture. While these two classifications of what we would deem "horror films" in English share many of the same formal and thematic markers, significant points of departure remain. An understanding of the difference between *kaiki* and *horā*—terms sometimes carelessly treated as synonyms—reveals how issues

---

[42] S. S. Prawer, *Caligari's Children: The Film as a Tale of Terror* (New York: Da Capo Press, 1980), 33. Emphasis added. Prawer echoes Andrew Tudor's point that film genres' definitions "depend on the particular culture within which we are operating." See Andrew Tudor, "Genre," in *Film Genre Reader III*, ed. Barry Keith Grant (Austin: University of Texas Press, 2004), 7.

of genre and language can intersect to rewrite (and in this case erase) cultural constructs often taken for granted.

The infiltration of the word *horā* into the Japanese film lexicon in the 1980s brought with it the same all-encompassing sense that the phrase "horror movie" held in English. Scholars, filmmakers, and critics in Japan now talk about director Nakagawa Nobuo's 1959 *The Ghost Story of Yotsuya*, widely regarded as the pinnacle of *kaiki* filmmaking, as a *horā* film, and seem willing to place all *kaiki* films within an even larger generic heading of *horā* that includes everything from silent-era *kaidan* adaptations to the most gruesome contemporary slasher movies.[43] This mirrors the situation in the English-speaking world, where F. W. Murnau's *Nosferatu*, the 1925 version of *Phantom of the Opera*, and other works that predate the advent of the horror film label are all today thought of as prime examples of the genre. Although they have been at times branded as mystery or science fiction, since the emergence of the term in the mid-1930s the "horror pictures" typified by Universal's *Dracula* and *Frankenstein* have almost unanimously been understood as cornerstones of the genre. While they are sometimes referred to as "gothic" or "classic" horror, they remain essentially inextricable from the broader generic term.

Press any Japanese film aficionado on the same subject, however, and one finds that *horā* has not so neatly absorbed the full meaning of *kaiki*. Just as *Dracula* was a *kaiki* film even before the category of "horror film" existed in English, most *horā* films produced since the adoption of the word *horā* in the 1980s are generally understood *not* to be *kaiki*. So, in effect, both *Dracula* and *A Nightmare on Elm Street* are horror movies and even both *horā* movies, but only one is a *kaiki* movie. *Kaiki eiga* therefore cannot properly be rendered into English as "horror film." As the various examples discussed in the previous section show, it is clearly a *certain kind* of horror film. It is not *Godzilla*, *The Exorcist*, or *Anabelle*, but it is *The Ghost Story of Yotsuya*; it is *Bride of Frankenstein*, it is *Eyes without a Face*. I devote the remainder of this chapter to an attempt at understanding what distinguishes a *kaiki* film from the rest of the *horā* genre.

---

[43] Zahlten, *End of Japanese Cinema*, 10. The retroactive application of the term *horā* to *kaiki eiga*, as well as the general slippage between the terms *kaiki*, *kyōfu*, and *horā* that has occurred with increasing ubiquity since the 1980s can be seen in a wide variety of material, from academic articles such as Yokoyama Yasuko's "Yotsuya kaidan eiga no Oiwatachi: kabuki to wakare, betsu no onna e," in *Kaiki to gensō e no kairō* to the popular volume edited by Haraguchi Tomō and Murata Hideki, *An Invitation to Japanese Horror Film* (*Nihon horā eiga e no shōtai*, Tokyo: Heibonsha, 2000), the title of which uses the characters for *kyōfu* with the phonetic gloss of *horā*. Kurosawa Kiyoshi and Shinozaki Makoto also devote much of their book *Kurosawa Kiyoshi's Horror Movie History* (*Kurosawa Kiyoshi no kyōfu no eiga-shi*) to discussion of both *kaiki* and modern slasher *horā eiga*.

Othered Spaces and Places: Formal Aspects of *Kaiki* and the Question of Fear

On a very rudimentary level, one of the things that sets a *kaiki* film apart from other *horā* films is merely its age. Today the phrase *kaiki eiga* carries an antiquated, nostalgic value. They quite simply "don't make 'em like that anymore." Even when they do—as in the case of Nakata Hideo's *Kaidan*—it is at best a one-off homage to a dead genre rather than a genuine revival. So the difference between *kaiki* and *horā* is in part a temporal one, but the very fact that the old generic label needed to be retired and replaced by a new one indicates that the difference between *kaiki* and *horā* is not just chronological. According to J-horror director Sasaki Hirohisa, it is impossible to make a *kaiki* movie today. It is not just the fact that true *kaiki* films belong to an earlier era. Sasaki believes there is a lost art involved in their making:

> When filming something otherworldly, the artistry of making the thing itself [via makeup and special effects] is important, but how do you go about filming it? If you film it out in the open, you lose the feeling of it. The truth is location shooting, realism, things like that are a hindrance, I think.[44]

For Sasaki, a crucial component of *kaiki* is the sense of "super-realism" (*sūpā riarizumu*) that came with shooting on indoor studio sets, a practice now all but extinct in the Japanese film industry. Praising the 1960 *kaiki* film *The Ghost Cat of Otama Pond* (*Kaibyō Otama ga ike*), Sasaki says,

> Even the exterior scenes were shot on-set. It's an all-set movie ... For example, the opening scene in the forest ... It's scary because it's unnaturally impenetrable. There are no skinny pine trees, intentionally there are only fat, broad-leafed trees. Nowadays you can't film a spooky, impenetrable forest like that. In Japan only coniferous forests grow naturally. To show the fear of an impenetrable forest, where one can lose their way, requires tremendous power of art direction. Also, the low-lying fog that hangs on the ground cannot be done today. The fog machine smoke is bad for the actors' health, and is no longer allowed.

He goes on to lament the impossibility of shooting such a scene today because the contemporary Japanese film industry has neither the money nor the talent to build such sets.[45] Although Sasaki seems to have only Japanese

---

[44] Q&A with Sasaki Hirohisa, April 13, 2013.
[45] Ibid. *The Ghost Cat of Otama Pond* was the directorial debut of *kaiki* master Nakagawa Nobuo's assistant director, Ishikawa Yoshihiro, and along with Nakagawa's work is widely considered one of the finest examples of Japanese *kaiki* filmmaking.

Figure 3 "Spooky forest" sets in *Mansion of the Ghost Cat* (*Bōrei kaibyō yashiki*, 1958, above), *The Wolf Man* (1941, below left), and *The Vampire Lovers* (1970, below right).

kaiki films in mind when he goes on to attribute the stylized hyperrealism of constructed sets as growing out of kabuki theater traditions,[46] much the same argument can be made for Western *kaiki* pictures, which often feature exterior scenes shot on stylized interior sets largely owing to the influence of German Expressionism. The "spooky forests" of Japanese *kaiki* films recall virtually identical interior forest sets featured in Universal's *The Wolf Man* (1941) and Hammer's *The Vampire Lovers* (1970), to name just two examples (Figure 3).

Other examples of the "super-realism" created by the obvious artificiality of *kaiki* films include the well-known Gothic castle interiors of any given Dracula or Frankenstein movie, which have parallels in the Japanese castles, Buddhist temples, and samurai mansions wherein the action of most domestic *kaiki* films transpires, as well as the matte paintings and miniatures used for the establishing shots of such nonexistent locales (Figure 4). Kurosawa Kiyoshi, a core creator of the J-horror phenomenon and one of Japan's few academic authorities on the *horā* genre, echoes Sasaki's sentiments in his discussion of the Italian-French

---

[46] Ibid.

Figure 4 Matte paintings and miniatures evoke Othered spaces. Castles atop foreboding hills in *The Ghost Cat of Okazaki* (*Kaibyō Okazaki sōdō*, 1954, left) and *Frankenstein* (1931, right).

coproduction *Mill of the Stone Women* (*Il mulino delle donne di pietra*, 1960), which he names as one of his personal favorite *kaiki* pictures:

> Even if I wanted to, I couldn't make a film like *Mill of the Stone Women*. It would take an impossible amount of money to build sets like that today. Even if I could somehow, audiences probably wouldn't come to see it … because of all this I intentionally make a different kind of *horā* film—not "*kaiki*" films but "*horā*" films.[47]

Both Sasaki and Kurosawa stress the sense of the stylized, anti-realistic atmosphere evoked by the artificial sets of both Japanese and foreign *kaiki* films as one of the elements that distinguish them from the rest of the *horā* genre. Unlike horror or *kyōfu* cinema, which is defined by the emotion it is meant to produce in its audience, the word *kaiki* by definition points to an atmosphere of the strange and bizarre, rather than the emotional affect of horror. When asked about this distinction between *kaiki* and *horā*, Kurosawa responded thusly:

> *Kaiki*'s nuance might be termed "gothic horror" in English. It's things like Hammer movies and *The Ghost Story of Yotsuya*, period pieces in which ghosts or mysterious figures like Dracula appear, and the whole movie has a sense of taking place "not now," but "long long ago." I suppose that's very similar to gothic horror. Those films aren't mainly about horror, the ones I want to call *kaiki*. They're atmospheric, moody. Even if they're provisionally set in the modern day, the action will take place in some old mansion, like in *Eyes Without a Face*. It's

---

[47] Kurosawa and Shinozaki, *Kurosawa Kiyoshi no kyōfu no eigashi*, 40, emphasis added.

actually "the present" yet it has a very old, period feel to it … I would say fear isn't even a necessary element of *kaiki* cinema.[48]

In other words, an essential ingredient of *kaiki* is its evocation of an Othered time and place, a world spatially alien or removed from our own mundane, contemporary existence. On the most obvious level this is achieved by the period settings that characterize many Western and Japanese *kaiki* films, but for Sasaki and Kurosawa, this otherworldly atmosphere finds expression primarily in the set work and production design, which reject location shooting and other elements of realism. That the resulting ambiance need not necessarily be horrific also partially explains how many Japanese *kaiki* pictures warrant their generic appellation when their monsters often do not appear until the third act of the film. While most Western horror films tend to introduce their monsters early and make them the central focus of the plot, typical Japanese *kaiki* pictures such as *The Ghost Story of Yotsuya* will not even hint at the ghost's existence until the final act of the film.

However, it is perhaps too much to suggest that an evocation of the emotion of fear is not a necessary component of *kaiki*. Delivering scares to the audience was obviously another crucial element of the *kaiki* formula and appears to have been the main source of *kaiki*'s appeal for viewers. As discussed previously, advertising for *kaiki* films typically featured images of the female lead with a terror-struck expression on her face alongside the picture's title in wobbly, "shivering" characters. The poster for the 1958 film *The Ghost Cat of Yonaki Swamp* (*Kaibyō Yonaki numa*), to cite one example, promises the film is "delightfully scary!" (*kowai ga tsukai!*), blatantly peddling the same intersection of fear and delight that "100 Ghost Stories" parties provided for Edo period aficionados of *kaiki*.

Furthermore, the most common criticism of the more poorly reviewed specimens of the genre was that the films were not genuinely frightening. Professional critics in Japan often proceeded from the bias that the *kaiki* genre (at least the domestically made product) was a disreputable breed of filmmaking in general, but their reviews suggest they might have been inclined to take a more positive view of the pictures if only they succeeded in truly thrilling the audience. *The Legend of the Saga Ghost Cat* (*Saga kaibyō den*, 1937), the film that touched off the immediate prewar *kaiki* boom and made its lead actress, Suzuki Sumiko, the nation's first monster movie star, was trounced by *Kinema*

---

[48] Author's interview with Kurosawa Kiyoshi.

junpō primarily for being a "*kaiki* movie that's not scary."⁴⁹ The magazine's negative review of Daiei's postwar *kaiki* film, *The Ghost Cat of Arima Palace* (*Kaibyō Arima goten*, 1953), perhaps best illustrates the all-too-common complaint, finding the film's attempts at frightening imagery to be worthy of ridicule: "The filmmakers didn't have a single truly creepy (*kai-i*) idea … before it would frighten the children in the audience, it would more naturally induce howls of laughter."⁵⁰

The public plainly went to see these pictures desiring to be scared. Audience research for prewar and early postwar *kaiki* films in Japan is virtually nonexistent, making Yanagi Masako's 1957 *Kinema junpō* article "*Kaiki* Films and the Audience" (*Kaiki eiga to kankyaku*) an invaluable resource, and worth summarizing its data in detail. Yanagi notes that the audience for *kaiki* films in the postwar years was overwhelmingly young, and largely female. Seventy percent of the audience for *The Ghost Cat at Ōma Crossing* (*Kaibyō Ōma ga tsuji*, 1954) was under the age of 25, and 50 percent female. For *The Ghost Cat of the 53 Way Stations* (*Kaibyō gojusan-ji*, 1956) the audience was 60 percent female, and 65 percent female for the same year's *The Ghost Story of Plover Pond* (*Kaidan chidori ga fuchi*). Following a screening of the Shintōhō studio's 1956 version of *The Ghost Story of Yotsuya*, Yanagi polled audience members on their reasons for attending the film. The most common response was "to see something scary" (*kowai mono mita sa*).⁵¹ Commenting on the actual screening itself, Yanagi is struck by the nervous laughter in the theater as the film plays, along with lots of chattering, pointing at the screen, and screams from the audience when something startling occurs, followed by raucous laughter. All of this indicates that the *kaiki* moviegoing experience was indeed rather like similarly boisterous screenings of horror films in the West, and recalls the observation of cultural historian Marina Warner that "the squealing laughter that erupts during horror movies … expresses an attempt not to be touched, not to be moved, to overcome the more usual response of fear."⁵² Yanagi concludes that "if it can just startle the audience and make them scared, that alone lets us say this kind of movie is eighty-percent successful."⁵³

---

[49] *Kinema junpō*, February 21, 1937, 118. The movie's influential success indicates audiences thought otherwise.
[50] *Kinema junpō*, February 15, 1954, 65.
[51] Yanagi Masako, "Kaiki eiga to kankyaku," *Kinema junpō*, July 1, 1957, 51.
[52] Marina Warner, *Monsters of Our Own Making: The Peculiar Pleasures of Fear* (Lexington: University of Kentucky Press, 2007), 258.
[53] Yanagi, "Kaiki eiga to kankyaku," 51.

The Limits of Horror Film Theory in the Case of Japanese *Kaiki* Cinema

Rather like its horror/*horā* counterparts, a *kaiki* film's perceived success depended more than anything on evoking a sense of fear. Here one might be tempted to conclude that, as a genre, *kaiki* can be defined simply as a horror film set in a space marked-off from the everyday modern world, be it a Transylvanian castle, a samurai mansion, a spooky forest, or merely "long, long ago." We should then be able to apply the major academic theories of filmic horror—most of which focus on the ways in which these films create the sense of horror that lends the genre its name—to *kaiki* cinema without much difficulty. However, one finds that many of the most influential and accepted works of horror film theory rule out the brand of fear featured in Japanese *kaiki* pictures as incompatible with the genre.

Applying Rick Altman's two-pronged "semantic/syntactic" approach to film genres locates the failure of theories of horror cinema to fully account for *kaiki* films in a difference between the syntactic elements of Japanese and Western films that share a common semantics. In other words, Japanese *kaiki* films contain many of the same surface features as Western horror film (monsters, haunted castles, thunderstorms, and sequences designed to scare the audience) but deviate on much of their themes (the nature of the Other, rationality vs. supernatural, karmic retribution). This is why anyone looking at a Japanese *kaiki* film would be hard-pressed to disagree that they are part of the horror genre, even though many syntactically centered theories of horror film disqualify them from inclusion. As Altman points out,

> For every film that participates actively in the elaboration of a genre's syntax there are numerous others content to deploy in no particular relationship the elements traditionally associated with the genre. We need to recognize that not all genre films relate to their genre in the same way or to the same extent.[54]

Altman also points out a general tendency to treat genres "as if they spring full-blown from the head of Zeus," without paying proper attention to the shifting historical and cultural circumstances of their conception.[55] It is absurd to disqualify *kaiki* films from the horror genre purely on the grounds of their syntax. It is equally absurd to assume no difference between *kaiki* and horror in light of their distinct historical and cultural contexts.

---

[54] Altman, *Film/Genre*, 221.
[55] Ibid., 218.

Since most of the of the horror films produced in America and Europe from the 1930s through the 1960s were classified as *kaiki* in Japan, it is not surprising that the major theories of film horror also neatly account for most non-Japanese examples of *kaiki* cinema, but we run into trouble when trying to apply them to many of the most famous and representative works of domestic *kaiki* film. In his landmark study of American slasher cinema of the 1970s, Robin Wood identifies the distinguishing theme of *all* horror film as "Normality threatened by the Monster":

> The very simplicity of this formula has a number of advantages. It covers the entire range of horror films, being applicable whether the monster is a vampire, a giant gorilla, an extraterrestrial invader, an amorphous gooey mass, or a child possessed by the Devil, and this makes it possible to connect the most seemingly heterogeneous movies.[56]

Wood defines his Monster as a symbolic Other, an abject externalization of what has been repressed in humanity by society and whose presence poses a threat to the dominant social order or "normality." It is important here to note that this definition of the Other is not the same as the "Othered spaces" I suggest are a key component of *kaiki* films. While I use the term to describe the hyperrealism of stylized, constructed sets, Wood defines his Other as "that which bourgeois ideology cannot recognize or accept but must deal with ... it functions not simply as something external to the culture or the self, but also as what is repressed in the self and projected outward in order to be hated and disowned."[57] Barbara Creed's work on the monstrous-feminine in horror cinema, which draws largely on Julia Kristeva's theory of the abject as "what disturbs identity, system, order,"[58] supports Wood's conclusions. Creed asserts that "horror film attempts to bring about a confrontation with the abject ... in order finally *to eject the abject* and redraw the boundaries between human and non-human."[59] Both Wood and Creed view the horror film as promoting an essentially conservative social agenda that privileges "normal," established society. In the case of Western horror this often means white bourgeoisie heterosexual Christian patriarchy, with the monster either an implicit or explicit

---

[56] Robin Wood, "The American Nightmare: Horror in the 70s," in *Horror, The Film Reader*, ed. Mark Jancovich (New York: Routledge, 2002), 32.
[57] Ibid., 27.
[58] Julia Kristeva, *Powers of Horror: An Essay on Abjection*, trans. Leon S. Roudiez (New York: Columbia, 1982), 4.
[59] Barbara Creed, "Horror and the Monstrous-Feminine: An Imaginary Abjection," in *Horror, The Film Reader*, 75. Emphasis added.

embodiment of one or more societal elements in opposition to the dominant mode (nonwhite, proletariat, queer, Godless, female, etc.).

Obviously the societal "normal" looks different in the cinema of non-Western nations like Japan—with one prominent exception. Since all societies that produce horror films are historically patriarchal, the feminine becomes the most ubiquitously used symbol of the Other, abject, or monstrous in global horror cinema, in opposition to the posited normalcy of the social order in which the spectator is assumed to be a part. Wood lists "Woman" as one of the primary categories of "Other," in horror film, writing, "The dominant images of women in our culture are entirely male created … on to women men project their own innate, repressed femininity in order to disown it as inferior."[60] The very title of Creed's work, "The Monstrous-Feminine," indicates its central project, an analysis of portrayals of the feminine as abject, monstrous threats to society, aligning the monstrous-feminine with the nonhuman in its violation of social norms.

A quick survey of prominent monsters in Japanese *kaiki* films reveals that the vast majority are indeed feminine, the two most oft-recurring monsters of the genre being the almost always female *bakeneko* cat spirit and the *onryō* or vengeful ghost, which traditionally takes the form of a wronged woman seeking vengeance upon her still living oppressors. In Nakagawa Nobuo's version of *The Ghost Story of Yotsuya*, to cite the flagship example, the "good wife" Oiwa is poisoned, disfigured, and left for dead by her husband, but in death she returns to punish the man who wronged her in life. Yet it can be argued that Oiwa's ghost *restores* the normality that has been threatened by the lawless behavior of her husband Iemon, who flouts the moral code of the samurai for personal wealth and gain. Her wrath remains relentlessly fixed upon the social transgressor, Iemon, until at last he begs forgiveness for his crimes in the moment when Oiwa's spirit engineers his ultimate demise. By destroying the wicked Iemon, Oiwa's ghost restores order and social harmony, her spirit shedding its hideous appearance and returning to its former beauty in the final moments of the film.

Wood's horror movie monsters must be annihilated for the good of society, but the monsters of Japanese *kaiki* films often annihilate *on behalf of* society. If the point is, as Creed suggests, to eject the abject and reestablish the boundaries of the human and nonhuman, *The Ghost Story of Yotsuya* and many other *kaiki* films emphasize that the ghosts are often possessed of more humanity than their oppressors, who sacrifice their own humanity for selfish or otherwise unscrupulous motives and are finally ejected from the world via the ghosts'

---

[60] Wood, "The American Nightmare," 27.

deadly vengeance. Kristeva writes "[that] which is subjectively experienced as abjection, varies according to time and space," but that the goal of demarcating the abject always involves "no other goal than the survival of both group and subject."[61] In the world of *Yotsuya*, the survival of "the group" (Edo society) depends on the removal of the wicked Iemon, not the morally righteous Oiwa. Kristeva's theory of abjection works in this reading of *Yotsuya*'s archetypal Japanese ghost story narrative, but only by inverting the places of the monster and its victim in the role of the abject.

It might be possible to view Oiwa herself as a social aberration when considered in a Buddhist context. Her intense, unchecked emotions and desire for vengeance bind her spirit to the mortal realm even after death; in Buddhism this intense state of *shūnen* or "fierce attachment" hinders the soul's attainment of Enlightenment and often requires the interventional prayers of a monk to set the wayward spirit back on the proper path. But here one finds themes of rehabilitation and reincorporation into the whole, rather than the motifs of expulsion and extermination that characterize the diegetic worlds of classic Hollywood horror films operating in a Judeo-Christian cosmology. And while the explicitly Buddhist problem of the monster's *shūnen* is frequently a component of traditional ghost stories from the Edo period, this aspect is typically downplayed in *kaiki* film adaptations, which focus more on the punishment of the wicked, socially transgressive human characters at the hands of vengeful spirits.

The preponderance of female monsters in Japanese *kaiki* cinema might seem to lend itself better to feminist psychoanalytic readings of horror film, yet these monstrous females operate in ways that often conflict with psychoanalytic notions of the monstrous-feminine. A fundamental link between femaleness and the monster concerns issues of the maternal, which Barbara Creed has written about extensively in "The Monstrous-Feminine." As stated previously, Creed's work depends largely on Kristeva's theory of horror as abjection: that which horrifies us is what we have rejected from our own selves. Because all individuals have experienced abjection in their earliest attempts to free themselves from dependency on the figure of the mother, Creed sees a distinguishing feature of horror film as the construction of the maternal as abject, an issue rendered doubly horrifying by the mother's desire to retain a hold over her child:

> We can see abjection at work in the horror text where the child struggles to break away from the mother, representative of the archaic maternal figure …

---

[61] Kristeva, *Powers of Horror*, 68.

constructed as the monstrous-feminine. By refusing to relinquish her hold on her child, she prevents it from taking up its proper place in relation to the Symbolic.[62]

Creed clearly has a certain strain of horror film in mind in regard to the monstrous-feminine (one that seems to privilege the work and influence of Alfred Hitchcock), though she does argue that confrontation with the abject—so often symbolized by the mother—is "the central ideological project of the popular horror film" in general.[63] Yet it is worth considering her comments on monstrous-feminine mothers in particular regard to Nakagawa Nobuo's *kaiki* works, which are in no small measure concerned with issues of the monstrous in relation to the maternal.

Reluctance of the mother to part with her child is a key element in the creation of the monster in Nakagawa's *Ghost Story of Yotsuya*. Dying from the poison Iemon has slipped into her drink, Oiwa cradles their infant son in her arms, refusing to part with the child even in death. "You poor child! How could I leave you with a man like Iemon?" Oiwa laments, "Die with your mother! I could never enter paradise if I left you behind!" With her dying breath Oiwa's body falls on the child, presumably smothering him. Although such action might seem reprehensible out of context, Iemon has already made plain his intention to abandon the baby to starvation. By taking the child with her to the land beyond, Oiwa demonstrates her undying love as a mother. Oiwa's ghost frequently appears to Iemon holding their son in her arms, and her vengeful spirit's presence is announced in the climactic scene of the film by the child's cries, making Oiwa's vendetta a mission to punish the sins of the father as much as those of the husband.[64]

Colette Balmain has identified this valorization of the maternal as a key recurring component of Nakagawa's *kaiki* films.[65] The elderly ghost cat of Nakagawa's *Mansion of the Ghost Cat*, much like Oiwa, returns from the dead in large part to avenge the murder of her grown son, and the mother-daughter team of spirits in Nakagawa's *Snake Woman's Curse* (*Kaidan hebi-onna*, 1968) work together to destroy the wicked landlord who raped the younger woman in life. As in Western horror cinema, maternal attachment gives rise to monstrous

---

[62] Creed, "Horror and the Monstrous-Feminine," 72.
[63] Ibid., 75.
[64] Actress Wakasugi Katsuko discusses the filmmaking decisions to place emphasis on the infant in *Yōen gensō kaiki jiai Waksugi Katsuko*, ed. Maruo Toshiō (Tokyo: Wise, 200), 170.
[65] Colette Balmain, *Introduction to Japanese Horror Film* (Edinburgh: Edinburgh University Press, 2008), 62.

mothers in Nakagawa's filmic universe; however, the victims are not the children but those who would do them harm. Although Nakagawa's *kaiki* films develop the theme of the "valorous maternal monster" most fully, it is not unique to his own work in the genre. Films like Kato Bin's *The Ghost Cat of Okazaki* (*Kaibyō Okazaki sōdō*, 1954) also feature mothers who transform into monsters in part to protect their children.

Along with the monstrous and the maternal, the most oft-written-about incarnation of the feminine in horror is the victim, whose torment at the hands of the monster is considered the result of transgressing traditional gender roles and the theory of the gaze. The act of looking is central to the horror genre as well as *kaiki* film, as the audience has come, presumably, to "see the monster" and come face-to-face with the source of fear. In American and European horror films, the audience often experiences their view of the monster via the gaze of a female victim, for patriarchal society permits the female horror movie victim to enact responses to the monstrous deemed inappropriate for the traditional male hero. As Carol Clover notes in her discussion of gender and horror film, *Men Women, and Chain Saws*, "Angry displays of force may belong to the male, but crying, cowering, screaming, fainting, trembling, begging for mercy belong to the female. Abject terror, in short, is gendered feminine."[66] But what are the consequences of this gendered, terrified look at the monster? Mary Anne Doane expands on Laura Mulvey's theory of the female gaze in classical cinema as essentially passive (women are there to be looked at, not to do the looking),[67] theorizing that a woman's active gaze "can only be simultaneous with her own victimization" in the world of motion pictures.[68] Woman is, in effect, punished for appropriating the active male gaze. Linda Williams applies this idea to the horror genre when she suggests "the horror film offers a particularly interesting example of this punishment in the woman's terrified look at the body of the monster." Citing the famous and influential scene from Rupert Julian's *The Phantom of the Opera* in which the hideous face of Lon Chaney's phantom is unmasked by the curious young opera singer Christine (Mary Philbin), Williams writes,

---

[66] Carol J. Clover, *Men, Women, and Chain Saws: Gender in the Modern Horror Film* (Princeton, NJ: Princeton University Press, 1992), 51.
[67] See Laura Mulvey, "Visual Pleasure and Narrative Cinema," in *The Film Theory Reader: Debates and Arguments*, ed. Marc Furstenau (New York: Routledge, 2010), 200–8.
[68] Mary Anne Doane, "The 'Woman's Film': Possession and Address," in *Re-vision: Essays in Feminist Film Criticism*, ed. Mary Anne Doane, Patricia Mellencamp, and Linda Williams (Los Angeles: American Film Institute, 1983), 72.

Everything conspires here to condemn the desire and curiosity of the woman's look ... It is as if she has become responsible for the horror that her look reveals, and is punished by not being allowed the safe distance that ensures the voyeur's pleasure of looking.[69]

The Phantom of the Opera is perhaps the first of innumerable films in which the viewer's initial glimpse of the monster is afforded by the curiosity of a female character subsequently punished for wielding the active, male gaze. This also holds true for Nakagawa's "Western-style" *kaiki* film, *Lady Vampire* (*Onna kyūketsuki*, 1959), in which hapless female victims fall prey to the clutches of Amachi Shigeru's tuxedo-wearing Dracula knockoff after gazing in abject terror upon his vampiric form. But the female victims of Nakagawa's period ghost story films are the monsters themselves, who have not been punished for wielding the male gaze but are formerly passive souls driven to seek redress beyond the grave against their male oppressors. Orui, the vengeful ghost antiheroine of Nakagawa's *Ghost Story of Kasane's Swamp*, returns in death to avenge herself upon her husband Shinkichi and his young lover Ohisa, as well as the villainous Omura, a ronin with designs on Orui who has goaded Shinkichi into eloping with Ohisa. Although Ohisa is the first to fall prey to the vengeful spirit's wrath, only the two male characters actually see Orui's ghost. As Shinkichi gazes upon his mistress, her guise suddenly transforms to that of Orui's deformed spirit. The terrified Shinkichi strikes at the monster with a sickle, only to find he has fatally wounded Ohisa. The ghost's lone female victim thus dies without ever laying eyes upon the monster. The viewer's revelatory glimpses of the monster's form are afforded only via the male gaze, first by Shinkichi and then Omura, who, after murdering Shinkichi, is relentlessly assaulted by Orui's spirit in the final moments of the film. If the typical American or European horror film codes the act of gazing upon the monster as female, frightened, and transgressive, Japanese films like *Kasane's Swamp* present the act as male, frightened, and reactionary.

Even more interesting is a scene in Nakagawa's *Ghost Story of Yotsuya* in which Oiwa's ghost appears in the eyes of the female gaze as beautiful while simultaneously appearing monstrous in the male gaze. Oiwa's sister Osode has been forced into marrying Naosuke, a coconspirator of Iemon's who provided the disfiguring poison used to bring about Oiwa's death. Unaware of her sister's demise, Osode is overjoyed when Oiwa appears one night outside their door. Apart from her pale complexion and inability to speak, Oiwa appears to her

---

[69] Linda Williams, "When the Woman Looks," in *Horror, The Film Reader*, 62.

Figure 5 In this sequential series of shots from Nakagawa Nobuo's *Ghost Story of Yotsuya* (*Tōkaidō Yotsuya kaidan*, 1959), Oiwa's ghost appears to her sister Osode beautiful as she was in life, while simultaneously manifesting as the hideous *onryō* behind Naosuke. When Naosuke screams in fear, Osode looks but cannot see the source of his terror.

sister as the beautiful woman she was in life. Osode excitedly runs to greet her, but Nakagawa keeps the camera behind Osode and gives no view of her reaction to her sister's appearance. The reaction shot is instead focused on the terrified Naosuke, who knows Oiwa is dead, and behind Naosuke the disfigured, hideous version of Oiwa's ghost lurks ominously.[70] Nakagawa then cuts back and forth between Osode, happily reunited with the beautiful visage of her sister, and the increasingly panicked Naosuke, who finally shrieks in terror when the disfigured version of Oiwa lays her hand upon his shoulder. This is followed by a quick reaction shot of Osode, gazing in perplexity at the spot where previously the hideous ghost of her sister had lain, but when the camera cuts back there is only Naosuke wailing in fear (Figure 5).

If anyone is punished for looking at the monster in Nakagawa's period ghost story films, it would seem to be the male characters. The women are spared

---

[70] Note that the reveal of Oiwa's hideous ghost does not replicate Naosuke's literal point of view, but is nonetheless associated with Naosuke's *perception* of Oiwa's ghost. For Osode there is no terror; but for Naosuke, Oiwa is terror incarnate, and that is how the audience sees her as well in the shots of Naosuke (see Figure 5).

the consequences of the gaze. In the case of Osode, she is not even capable of exercising it, a fact that a feminist reading may interpret as even more misogynist than much Western horror cinema. And yet even the male characters are not truly punished *for* looking at the monster. Rather, their ability to see the monster is the punishment itself—punishment for their crimes against oppressed women who attain in death and monstrous transformation the justice denied to them in life. However, I would argue that this upsetting of gender norms does not constitute a "threat to normality" that would neatly reconcile domestic *kaiki* cinema with Wood's definition of horror cinema. In life Oiwa and Orui remain filial and devoted wives, subservient to the demands of their husbands. The social transgressors are the men who flout the rules of traditional society, and their deaths at the hands of the empowered female ghosts merely restore normalcy to the patriarchal world. After their vengeance is complete both Oiwa and Orui return to their beautiful, ideally feminine selves and cease to haunt the realm of the living.

Marvelously Terrifying: Evoking Cosmic Fear in a Fantasy Setting

We might ask ourselves at this point, are the "monsters" of Japanese *kaiki* cinema even monsters at all? They have the audience's sympathy, act as defenders of the social norm, are selflessly devoted mothers, and confound theories of the gaze. Surely the real monster of *The Ghost Story of Yotsuya* is not the physically repellant ghost of Oiwa, but the morally repellent human villain, Iemon. Likewise, the standard ghost cat film concerns the efforts of the cat spirit to do justice upon the wicked samurai who pose a threat to the peaceful, harmonious lives of the other characters. The syntax of the Japanese *kaiki* monster confounds the expectations of horror film theory, but semantically speaking there can be little doubt that these creatures are fundamentally monstrous. In *The Philosophy of Horror*, probably the most influential work of horror theory in the past thirty years, Noël Carroll defines the horror monster as a categorically interstitial being—neither one thing nor another but something "in-between"—which produces a sense of repulsion in the beholder.[71] Vampires, zombies, and ghosts are all "un-dead" (as is Frankenstein's Monster, most often depicted as a reanimated patchwork of corpses); normally tiny ants grow as big as tanks in *Them!*; the Wolf Man and

---

[71] See Carroll, *The Philosophy of Horror*, 17–24, 40–52. Although he rules out a metaphoric use of the term "monster," thereby excluding films like *Psycho* from his conceptualization of the genre, it is easy enough to see how a more liberal use of Carroll's definition could apply to the schizophrenic transvestite Norman Bates, as well as other human serial killers featured in slasher films.

the Creature from the Black Lagoon are half-human, half-animal. Japanese *kaiki* films are dominated by two iconic figures likewise repulsive in their categorial interstitiality: the vengeful revenant epitomized by the rotting corpselike figure of Oiwa in *Yotsuya* and the part-woman, part-feline ghost cat. That the Japanese word for the general category of beings these creatures belong to, *bakemono*, literally means "changing thing" makes the point indisputable—here also be monsters.

As Carroll points out, however, monsters alone do not a horror movie make:

> Even if a case can be made that a monster or monstrous entity is a necessary condition for horror, such a criterion would not be a sufficient condition. For monsters inhabit all sorts of stories—such as fairy tales, myths, and odysseys—that we are not inclined to identify as horror … we will have to find a way to distinguish the horror story from mere stories with monsters in them, such as fairy tales. What appears to demarcate the horror story … is *the attitude of the characters in the story to the monsters they encounter.*[72]

In ruling out "fairy tales, myths, and odysseys" from the horror genre, Carroll draws upon the work of Tzvetan Todorov and his distinction between "marvelous," "uncanny," and "fantastic" narratives. Simply put, Todorov breaks fantastic literature into three categories—tales in which seemingly supernatural occurrences ultimately receive a rational explanation (uncanny), tales in which the existence of the supernatural is an accepted part of the narrative diegesis (marvelous), and tales that hint at the existence of the supernatural while holding out the possibility of a rational explanation (what Todorov calls the "pure fantastic").[73] Carroll notes that most horror films would fall into Todorov's subcategory of the "fantastic/marvelous," which are "stories that entertain naturalistic explanations of abnormal incidents but conclude by affirming their supernatural origins."[74] Although Carroll finally rejects Todorov's category as too general to define the horror story, his own conception of the genre greatly depends on the idea of "entertaining naturalistic explanations" for the monsters encountered in any given horror narrative.

If the ultimate definition of the horror genre lies in "the attitude of the characters in the story to the monsters they encounter," Carroll gives two related but distinct

---

[72] Ibid., 16, emphasis added.
[73] Tzvetan Todorov, *The Fantastic: A Structural Approach to a Literary Genre*, trans. Richard Howard (Ithaca, NY: Cornell University Press, 1975), 41–57
[74] Carroll, *The Philosophy of Horror*, 16–17. Carroll notes that the fantastic/marvelous encompasses nonhorror works as well, such as *Close Encounters of the Third Kind* (1977), in which the supernatural is portrayed as beatific, not horrific.

components of that attitude. The first is revulsion. The human characters in the horror narrative react to the monsters with "shuddering, nausea, shrinking, paralysis, screaming, and revulsion," and, Carroll argues, this sense of revulsion comes from the "impurity" of the monster's categorically interstitial nature.[75] This recalls Creed's theories of the abject in horror film. However, shorn of the ideological dimension, it is more applicable to the case of *kaiki*. *The Ghost Story of Yotsuya*'s human villain Iemon may be the ideological impurity that needs to be ejected from the boundaries of society, but his trembling, terrified fear of the physically impure Oiwa mirrors the reactions of the morally upright human heroes of Western horror cinema. By itself, however, repulsion is not enough to define the horror genre. The monsters of marvelous "fairy tales, myths, and odysseys" also induce fear and revulsion. Hansel and Gretel are terrified of the hideous witch that imprisons them in the gingerbread house, but we are not inclined to call Grimms's fairy tales "horror stories," despite their frequently gruesome and horrific content.

For Carroll, the other essential half of the horror formula is that "the monsters are not only physically threatening, they are *cognitively threatening*. They are *threats to common knowledge* ... what horrifies is that which lies outside cultural categories and is, perforce, unknown."[76] "Hansel and Gretel" is not a horror story because, in this and other "pure marvelous" narratives, the existence of monsters like the witch is a known part of the diegetic world. Hansel and Gretel's fear stems not from the mere fact of the witch's existence, which is presented as an accepted feature of the fairy-tale landscape rather than a cosmological aberration, but from the physical threat she poses to them. In other words, Hansel and Gretel's fear is more akin to the fear Jane experiences at being cornered by a savage lion in the jungle before Tarzan swings to her rescue. Much the same can be said of the monsters that populate "myths and odysseys" as well as examples from contemporary fantasy films and novels such as *The Lord of the Rings*, which is loaded with horrific and repulsive ghosts and monsters that are depicted as quite natural features of J. R. R. Tolkien's marvelous Middle-Earth.

The real "horror" of the horror genre is an encounter with something truly *super*natural and which "should not exist." Carroll notes that many horror narratives follow what he calls "the complex discovery plot," in which the monster's existence is initially revealed only to a select individual or group, who must confirm the monster's existence in the face of rational skepticism.[77]

---

[75] Ibid., 18–32.
[76] Ibid., 34–5, emphasis added.
[77] Ibid., 99.

Much of the attending shock and repulsion inspired by the monster springs accordingly from the realization that it merely exists, confounding the characters' rational assumptions about reality. The particular brand of fear that distinguishes the horror genre, then, is a type of Freudian uncanny, which "arises when the boundary between fantasy and reality is blurred, when we are faced with the reality of something that we have until now considered imaginary," and, Freud notes, finds ultimate representation for many people in "anything to do with death, dead bodies, revenants, spirits, and ghosts"—or more simply put, monsters.[78]

Izumi Toshiyuki largely shares Carroll's ideas about the necessity of the monster being "cognitively threatening" in his own attempts to define *kaiki* when he says that the supernatural element of *kaiki* film must come from "beyond the limits of human comprehension" and "represent a threat to human understanding." Japanese *kaiki* productions such as *Lady Vampire* and *Diving Girl's Ghost* (*Kaidan ama yūrei*, 1960) that are set in the present day fit comfortably in Carroll's and Izumi's schema, but the majority of domestic *kaiki* cinema takes place in the premodern Edo period. This is a world in which, rather like Grimms's fairy tales and other "pure marvelous" narratives, the appearance of a vengeful wraith or a ghost cat may instill fear but not disbelief among the other characters. Most Japanese *kaiki* films are adaptations of Edo *kaidan* ghost stories, which were created by and for members of a society that had yet to draw clear distinctions between natural and supernatural phenomena.[79] Although perhaps not everyone in Edo Japan believed the existence of ghosts and goblins was an uncontestable fact, none of the characters in the representative *kaidan* of the era treat such beings as anything less than an accepted (if fearsome) part of their world.

Both Katarzyna Marak and Valerie Wee have observed in their respective work on Japanese horror film that "the mere presence of a ghost … is not a problem in itself"[80] and "Japanese *kaidan* treat the supernatural as an accepted aspect of reality and do not undermine or question its existence."[81] The filmmakers who adapted these works into the *kaiki* films of the twentieth century preserve

---

[78] Sigmund Freud, *The Uncanny*, trans. David McLintok (New York: Penguin, 2003), 150, 148.
[79] For a discussion of belief in the supernatural during the Edo period see Noriko T. Reider, "The Appeal of *Kaidan*: Tales of the Strange," *Asian Folklore Studies* 59, no. 2 (Nagoya: Nanzan University, 2000): 272–4.
[80] Katarzyna Marak, *Japanese and American Horror: A Comparative Study of Film, Fiction, Graphic Novels, and Video Games* (Jefferson: McFarland, 2015), 14.
[81] Valerie Wee, *Japanese Horror Films and Their American Remakes*. Routledge Advances in Film Studies (New York: Routledge, 2014), 39.

this naturalistic attitude to the supernatural in their own work, and as a result, such *kaiki* pictures take on a "pure marvelous" quality for modern audiences. In these fanciful evocations of a society that has yet to deal with the European Enlightenment, no one wastes any time trying to convince the other characters that monsters "don't exist." For Freud, this naturalistic attitude toward the monstrous absolutely negates the potential for an uncanny effect:

> The imaginative writer may have invented a world that, while less fantastic than that of the fairy tale, differs from the real world in that it involves supernatural entities such as demons or spirits of the dead. Within the limits set by the presuppositions of this literary reality, such figures forfeit any uncanny quality that might otherwise attach to them.[82]

Although Carroll's theory of horror is not quite as unbending as Freud's declaration (which strictly applied would deny many "fantastic/marvelous" horror stories the ability to inspire a sense of the uncanny), at first glance it does appear to rule out Japanese *kaiki* films as "stories with monsters in them" as opposed to true horror stories. But to discount the sense of fear evoked in Japanese *kaiki* cinema as such requires two suppositions—first, that the feelings of fear experienced by the human characters in the face of a vengeful spirit or ghost cat is the same type of fear felt by Hansel and Gretel in the face of the witch (or Jane when confronted by the jungle lion, or Frodo Baggins pursued by goblins and Ringwraiths); and second, that the audience vicariously experiences that fear in the same manner, which is devoid of any uncanny quality.

I wish to address the second supposition first. Noël Carroll's "thought theory" of audience reaction to horror is important here, and indeed Carroll's work on this particular aspect of horror has proven usefully applicable outside the horror genre in dealing with the paradox of the pleasure attendant to experiencing negative emotions in viewing cinema. In regard to the particular problem of why the obvious fictions of the horror story induce a real sense of fear in the viewer, thought theory provides an answer to the following question: If we all know that there are no such things as vampires, then why does Count Dracula frighten audiences? Because movies allow us to safely imagine what it would be like to be in a situation wherein Dracula exists. That is, the viewer need not believe that he or she is in actual danger to experience the actual emotion of fear. Fictional narratives suggest scenarios that produce

---

[82] Freud, *The Uncanny*, 155–6. Note Freud's use of the word "fantastic" differs from Todorov's, just as Todorov's "uncanny" is not the same as Freud's.

real emotional responses since "actual emotion can be generated [merely] by entertaining the thought of something horrible"[83] and, as Mathias Clasen elaborates in *Why Horror Seduces*, "our imaginations [have] evolved to enlist appropriate emotional responses when we cognitively entertain hypothetical scenarios."[84] Carl Plantinga succinctly sums up the argument in *Moving Viewers: American Film and the Spectator's Experience* when he declares that "belief is not essential to emotion."[85] Plantinga makes the further argument that, as an audiovisual medium that is *perceived* rather than *read*, film prompts more visceral, spontaneous emotional reactions than literature. Reading about a man being suddenly bitten by a cobra typically does not produce the same startled, flinching reaction exhibited by moviegoers upon seeing a sudden close-up of a cobra on-screen.[86]

Carroll's thought theory, coupled with the spontaneous, visceral response to cinema that Plantinga calls the "direct affect" of film, offers a way of explaining how Japanese *kaiki* films can instill a sense of uncanny horror in the audience even if its diegetic world belongs to the wholly marvelous. While audiences are often cued to experience emotions similar to the characters on-screen, their cognitive perception of the diegetic world on-screen remains separate. The viewer, existing outside the text, may be afraid for characters utterly unaware they are in any danger. Or they may be at moral odds with a character like Iemon in *The Ghost Story of Yotsuya* and experience his fear of Oiwa's ghost while simultaneously desiring to see him punished for his wicked deeds. This cognitive dissonance also means that just because a vengeful spirit or ghost cat may be a known and accepted entity in the marvelous Edo landscapes of the *kaiki* diegesis, it does not preclude the real-world contemporary audience from responding to the monster with the same sense of incredulous, uncanny horror that the post-Enlightenment characters of Western *kaiki* films like *Dracula* exhibit. We can spin Plantinga's phrase on its head and it still holds true—if belief (on the part of the audience) is not essential to emotion, then *dis*belief (on the part of the characters) is not essential to emotion, either. If *The Ghost Story of Yotsuya* prompts us to imagine what it would be like to be haunted by a vengeful spirit, and the immediate, spontaneous emotional responses characteristic of the perceived medium of cinema prove effective, then it is perhaps more relevant

---

[83] Carroll, *The Philosophy of Horror*, 79–81.
[84] Mathias Clasen, *Why Horror Seduces* (New York: Oxford University Press, 2017), 30.
[85] Carl Plantinga, *Moving Viewers: American Film and the Spectator's Experience* (Berkeley: University of California Press, 2009), 65.
[86] Ibid., 117.

that the monsters represent an uncanny anomaly for the viewer's understanding of reality, rather than the other characters.

Of course, we can extend this logic to other examples like the film version of *The Lord of the Rings*, wherein sequences featuring the ghostly, undead Ringwraiths might easily produce a horrific response in the viewer, and yet we would not name the overall work as part of the horror genre. Genre-mixing is ubiquitous in film, and filmmakers often insert recognizable "genre cues" from a variety of well-known generic motifs so that one sequence of *The Lord of the Rings* may be obviously horrific in its presentation of the monstrous, while the next may be utterly devoid of anything we are inclined to identify with the horror genre. But is it merely the quantity of such scenes that separates such films from the *kaiki* genre? As mentioned previously, many Japanese *kaiki* films withhold the monster's entrance into the narrative until the final act of the film. What then sets such films apart from other works of fantasy in which ghosts or monsters make limited appearances?

The difference is, in part, a formal one. Both *kaiki* and other types of horror/*horā* film emphasize the fear experienced by the human characters in the face of the monstrous to a greater degree than analogous scenes in films like the *Lord of the Rings* or *Pirates of the Caribbean* series, most often via lingering close-ups of the victim's terrified face. Such scenes often delay the ultimate result of the monster's presence (is it successfully defeated/evaded, or does it have its way with the victim?) and draw out the sense of suspense. I believe, however, that there is a deeper component to the brand of fear presented in *kaiki* cinema, which brings us back to the first supposition that would seemingly disqualify Japanese *kaiki* films as horrific. Just because the human inhabitants of the marvelous worlds of *kaiki* cinema believe in ghosts and monsters and take their existence at face value, is their fear of such creatures truly the same as the fear of the monstrous exhibited in other marvelous narratives such as the fairy tale or fantasy novel?

As discussed previously, the targets of the monster's wrath in Japanese *kaiki* films are often the true villains of the piece, in contrast to most Western *kaiki* films. The victims were once the victimizers, and the monster their onetime victim. The spirit of Oiwa is the jilted wife of the heartless Iemon, and the myriad ghost cats of *kaiki* cinema all act on behalf of abused wives, maids, and concubines who were either murdered or else driven to suicide by callous lovers or jealous rivals. Powerless in life, the victims become all-powerful in death. While a noble retainer occasionally succeeds in dispatching the ghost cat, somehow he never manages to do it before the monster enacts its revenge on the villain(s) of the piece. An outstanding example of this fact can be seen in the climax of *The Ghost Cat of Arima Palace*, when the virtuous samurai character beheads the *bakeneko* only to witness the monster's decapitated head fly through the air and fatally bite its target, the wicked matron who had murdered the cat's mistress. Vengeful wraiths like Oiwa or Orui of *Kasane's Swamp* are even more omnipotent and unstoppable. The villains of Japanese *kaiki* cinema dig their own graves, the monsters they create licensed cosmological agents of their destruction—karmic retribution incarnate. The repetition of this formula, which stretches all the way back to the Edo-period *kaidan* tales, ensures that the audience knows the transgressor is utterly doomed from the outset. Interviewing a young lady about her reasons for liking *kaiki* movies in 1957, Yanagi Masako recorded the following response: "Female wraiths and ghost cats are somehow sympathetic. They have no choice but to become monsters … and the people they go after are unequivocally evil, which is gratifying,"[87] implying Japanese *kaiki* films appeal in part because they play out the drama of karmic vengeance. The fear provoked by these monsters, then, is not simply the fear of an encounter with the monstrous, but the fear of inexorable, inescapable fate—do wrong, and monsters will come to get you. Vengeful wraiths and ghost cats may be "knowable" and even natural in the context of a *kaiki* film's diegesis, but this does not diminish the awesome and sublime quality of their cosmic omnipotence as agents of karmic retribution.

This element of terrible awe recalls H. P. Lovecraft's theory of "cosmic fear." Seeking to differentiate what he calls the "weird tale" from "the literature of mere physical fear and the mundanely gruesome," Lovecraft identifies in the weird tale's evocation of fear an attendant sense of wonder and awe at "spheres of existence whereof we know nothing and wherein we have no part":

> The true weird tale has something more than secret murder, bloody bones, or a sheeted form clanking chains according to rule. A certain *atmosphere* of breathless and unexplainable dread of outer, unknown forces must be present … Atmosphere is the all-important thing, for the final criterion of authenticity is not the dovetailing of a plot but the creation of a given sensation … The one test of the really weird is simply this—whether or not there be excited in the reader a *profound sense of dread*, and of contact with unknown spheres and powers.[88]

---

[87] Yanagi, "Kaiki eiga to kankyaku," 51.
[88] H. P. Lovecraft, *The Annotated Supernatural Horror in Literature*, ed. S. T. Joshi (New York: Hippocampus Press, 2012), 26–8, emphasis added. Lovecraft's theory builds on Burke's idea of the Sublime, in particular its relation to the emotion of terror. See Edmund Burke, *A Philosophical Enquiry into the Sublime and Beautiful* (Oxford: Oxford University Press, 2015), 47–9.

Lovecraft's emphasis on "atmosphere" reminds us that, as a generic label, *kaiki* too signifies atmosphere over emotion. Horror can be invoked by any multitude of "mundanely gruesome" things, but cosmic fear, like *kaiki*, depends on a particular ambiance, an impression of "profound dread" at being confronted with vast forces at the limits of human comprehension. Attempting to unpack Lovecraft's idea, Noël Carroll writes,

> This kind of awe responds to or restores some sort of primordial or instinctual human intuition about the world … cosmic fear is not simply fear, but awe, fear compounded with some sort of visionary dimension which is said to be keenly felt and vital.[89]

Carroll goes on to argue rightly that this definition of cosmic fear is too narrow to account for the entirety of the horror genre. Cosmic fear is just one kind of horror; but *kaiki*, it will be recalled, is also just one kind of *horā*. Significantly, Lovecraft's theory works well with most of the Western works of horror cinema that get classified as *kaiki* in Japan. Count Dracula, Frankenstein's Monster, and the ghosts that haunt such films as *The Uninvited* (1944) or *The Haunting* (1963) all induce a "profound sense of dread" in the other characters and suggest the existence of powers beyond human understanding. Even Western *kaiki* films with no corporally present monster, such as Roger Corman's Edgar Allan Poe adaptations starring Vincent Price, warrant inclusion via the omnipresent sense of predetermined destiny that pervades the narratives of these pictures. Like Iemon in *The Ghost Story of Yotsuya* or the villains of the many ghost cat pictures, Vincent Price is doomed from the outset, and he is keenly, profoundly aware of it. The very cosmos seems to be arrayed against the human characters of *kaiki* cinema. Kurosawa Kiyoshi calls this sense of a "machine of fate" (*unmei no kikai*) the "fundamental feeling of *kaiki* film."[90]

The problem with Lovecraft's theory as applied to Japanese *kaiki* film is, of course, his emphasis on the "unknown" aspect of cosmic fear, which leads us back to an insistence that the monster be an entity that "should not exist." It is true that the particular variety of fear present in Japanese *kaiki* cinema may not be "cosmic fear" in the strictest Lovecraftian sense of the term, but it is nonetheless an inarguably sublime and awe-inspiring form of terror. When pressed about his earlier-quoted statement that fear is not a necessary requirement for a *kaiki* film, Kurosawa Kiyoshi responded thusly:

---

[89] Carroll, *The Philosophy of Horror*, 163.
[90] Kurosawa and Shinozaki, *Kurosawa Kiyoshi no kyōfu no eigashi*, 35.

The idea that something already died away, and yet here it still exists, is a big theme [of *kaiki* film], and you can establish that without so-called "fear" (*kowasa*), I think. It's not merely "scary" but a feeling of *terror* (*osore*), the nervousness provoked by something still existing that should have faded away 100 years ago and the dread of still-living humans coming into contact with it is absolutely essential to *kaiki* cinema.[91]

By drawing a clear distinction between something that is "merely scary" (*tada kowai*) and the terror (*osore*) of coming into contact with something that should have long since departed this plane of existence, Kurosawa echoes Lovecraft's point about cosmic fear almost exactly. For even if the vengeful wraiths and ghost cats are knowable and understood forces, they are nonetheless beings that *should have* moved on from the world of humanity but are held back by their fierce emotional attachment (*shūnen*), which compels them to seek vengeance on those who oppressed them in life before they can rest. As the young woman attending the screening of *The Ghost Story of Yotsuya* in 1957 said, "They had no choice but to become monsters," and the "bad guys" have no recourse but to succumb to their wrath. The machine of fate moves ever on.

Lovecraft's particular brand of cosmic fear hinges on the hinted existence of forces beyond the pale of human understanding, while the *osore* of Japanese *kaiki* cinema is the dread of upsetting or otherwise running afoul of the cosmic order and provoking forces against which there is no defense. As Clasen observes, "Perhaps the most horrifying thing about ghosts, apart from the fact that they should not exist, is that there is no way to escape them. There is no way to have a fair fight with a ghost."[92] Both the Hollywood horror monster and the Japanese *kaiki* ghost instill the same sense of terrible awe in the human characters via their seeming omnipotence.[93] One could even argue that there is in fact an unknown element to the monsters of Japanese *kaiki* cinema in that, as far as their deserving victims are concerned, no one knows how to stop them.

Definitions of cosmic fear, profound dread, and *osore* recall a centuries-old discourse regarding the difference between "horror" and "terror," a topic that has been taken up by literary figures from Samuel Taylor Coleridge and

---

[91] Author's interview with Kurosawa Kiyoshi. Kurosawa expresses similar sentiments in *Eiga wa osoroshii* (Tokyo: Seidosha, 2001).
[92] Clasen, *Why Horror Seduces*, 48.
[93] This applies even to classical Western *kaiki eiga* such as *Dracula*. Although the audience may know garlic and wooden stakes can defeat the vampire, the characters themselves are typically ignorant of such methods at the outset of the narrative, and the vampire terrorizes his victims unchecked until the second-act appearance of the Van Helsing figure, himself usually presented as an "Other" with affinities to the supernatural.

Anne Radcliffe to Stephen King. Critics have long championed "terror" while condemning "horror" as crass and vulgar.[94] Summarizing the arguments of Coleridge and Radcliffe, D. P. Varma writes, "Terror creates an *intangible atmosphere of spiritual psychic dread*, a certain superstitious shudder at the other world. Horror resorts to a cruder presentation of the macabre, by an exact portrayal of the physically horrible and revolting."[95] This distinction has long informed criticism of the horror genre, where a "less is more" aesthetic that merely implies horrific beings and deeds is said to evoke this prized "intangible atmosphere" of dread, while gory displays of blood and grotesquely made-up monsters shown in shocking close-ups are often deemed to be artlessly offensive.

Of course most horror films feature a combination of both terror and horror, and on the whole Japanese critics seem to have been much less worried about the distinction between the two forms and any attendant value judgments. Still, the typical *kaiki* film's keen sense of *osore*, the very fact that the genre's name stresses "intangible atmosphere" over emotion, and its affinities with Lovecraft's cosmic fear all suggest that *kaiki* traffics more in terror than horror. If we recall the *Film Spectator* review of *Dracula* quoted at the beginning of this chapter, we find it may be suitably applied to the entirety of the *kaiki* genre: "The dominant note of the production is *eeriness*, a creepy horror that should give an audience goose-flesh and make it shudder." This, perhaps more than any other reason, explains why the *kaiki* label was never able to be comfortably applied to *kyōfu* films such as *Psycho* or *Les Diaboliques* with contemporary, mundane settings and mortal murderers, and finally faded from usage with the rise of the slasher film, after which the more all-encompassing term *horā eiga* became the norm.

Conclusion

Although *kaiki eiga* will no doubt continue to be rendered in English as "horror film" in general discussions of Japanese cinema for convenience's sake, the term properly applies only to a certain strain of horror/*horā* filmmaking, demonstrating

---

[94] In his famous review of Matthew Lewis's *The Monk* (1796), Coleridge disparaged the novel's penchant for displays of "the horrible" as betraying a "low and vulgar taste," while Radcliffe theorized the difference between horror and terror in "On the Supernatural in Poetry," first published in *New Monthly Magazine* in 1826. More recently, popular horror author Stephen King discusses the differences between terror, horror, and repulsion (finding terror to be "the finest" of the three) in *Danse Macabre* (New York: Simon and Schuster, 2010).

[95] Quoted in Julian Petley's "'A Crude Sort of Entertainment for a Crude Sort of Audience': The British Critics and Horror Cinema," in *British Horror Cinema*, ed. Steve Chibnall and Julian Petley (New York: Routledge, 2002), 28. Emphasis added.

how issues of translation potentially mask disruptions of generic categories that occur when crossing historical, cultural, and linguistic boundaries. This is an especially thorny problem when dealing with the topic of transnationally popular specimens of commercial cinema. We should attempt to understand *kaiki eiga* as neither "the Japanese word for horror movies" nor as a category that exists in a kind of hermetically sealed cultural vacuum like "Japanese horror movies," but as something at once culturally distinct and inherently transnational. *Kaiki* is a Japanese way of understanding films from around the world during a particular era in modern Japanese history, a lesson that can and should be applied more broadly to international studies of popular film genres.

The use of the word *kaiki* as a genre of film both predates the coinage of the phrase "horror movie" in English and falls out of usage following several industrial, formal, and thematic shifts in international horror film production. *Kaiki* was the dominant mode of filmic horror in both Japan and the West until the dawn of the atomic age, when American science-fiction horrors such as *The Beast from 20,000 Fathoms* and Japanese imitations like *Godzilla* begin to articulate distinctly postmodern fears. Nonetheless *kaiki* films endure through the 1960s, after which the severe decline of the Japanese film industry, the closure of Hammer Film Productions in Great Britain, and the rise of the American slasher film all conspire to bring about the death of the genre. The adoption of the English transliteration *horā* in the 1980s provided a way to talk about the now-defunct *kaiki* genre as part of an ongoing, unbroken continuum of filmmaking traditions, but brought with it a loss of cultural specificity and historical context.

What might be deemed "gothic horror movies" in vernacular English, a *kaiki* film is defined by its evocation of spaces physically and/or temporally removed from present-day reality, accomplished via a period setting or else stylized art direction, often relying on elaborate set work. Attendant to this Othered space is an evocation of *osore* or cosmic terror most often embodied in the figure of the monster, which differs from mere horror or *kowasa* in the sense of awe it provokes in the human characters and (ideally) the audience. In the case of Western *kaiki* films this sense of terrific awe stems from the cognitive threat the monster represents as a being whose existence cannot be rationally explained and violates our understanding of the natural world. Japanese *kaiki* films, most often set in a "pure marvelous" envisioning of the Edo period, tend to treat their monsters as more naturalistic features of the fantasy landscape, yet nonetheless invoke a similar sense of cosmic terror in their presentation of the monster as an omnipotent arbiter of karmic retribution.

Of course, whether or not a film successfully realized the *kaiki* potential inherent to its material is an entirely separate matter. The reviews for a vast majority of *kaiki* pictures produced in Japan up through the early postwar era were overwhelmingly negative, most often complaining that the films were "not scary," suggesting that for many years the Japanese *kaiki* film failed to tap fully into the sense of cosmic *osore* that ideally distinguished the genre. The following chapter more closely examines the production of *kaiki* film in Japan from the dawn of cinema through the outbreak of the Second World War, tracing the genre's development from simple trick films to the coalescence of an *osore* aesthetic informed by the spectacle of star actresses' on-screen monstrous transformations and a comingling of native *kaiki* traditions with the influence of Hollywood horror.

2

Ghost Cats versus Samurai: Prewar *Kaiki* Cinema

A case could be made that the oldest narrative film made in Japan, 1899's *Momijigari* ("Maple Viewing"), is also the nation's first *kaiki eiga*. Shot by Shibata Tsunekichi of the Mitsukoshi department store's photography division, the film records six minutes of kabuki actors Ichikawa Danjūrō IX and Onoe Kikugorō V performing a scene from the play *Momijigari* in which a female demon attacks a samurai admiring autumn maple leaves. One wants to imagine that *Momijigari* is proof that from Japanese cinema's moment of inception filmmakers were keenly attuned to the medium's potential for conveying *kaiki* narratives. In truth, though, *Momijigari*'s origin has more in common with the early, plotless films of the Lumière Brothers such as *Workers Exiting a Factory* (*La Sortie des usines Lumière à Lyon*) and *Train Arriving at a Station* (*L'arrivée d'un train en gare de La Ciotat*, both 1895) than with something like the Edison Studio's *Frankenstein* (1910), which employed special effects unique to the medium to bring to a fantastic story to life. Shibata had been taking his camera around Tokyo, filming street scenes in Ginza and geisha in Shimbashi, and a kabuki performance was another obvious choice for his filmic records of urban culture in the late Meiji era (1868–1912). Nonetheless, in it we can see several of the seeds of the nascent Japanese commercial filmmaking industry, including those that would bear *kaiki* fruit.

While he conceived his work as a filmographic record of a theatrical production, Shibata shot no "behind the scenes" footage of the actors out of character or makeup. The viewer sees no more than what a spectator in the audience would see of an actual performance. The film preserves the fictional world of the drama, even when the edges of the stage or onstage assistants are clearly visible in-frame. Although Shibata seems to have thought of himself as a mere recorder and not as any kind of active creative agent akin to what we would now identify as a "film director," his choice to photograph *Momijigari* in the manner that he did means the film does convey a wholly diegetic world unto itself. The incorporation of theatrical stage traditions in commercial Japanese film did not become widespread until 1908,[1] but *Momijigari* demonstrated from the outset that the medium could be utilized to convey the existence of a fictional universe, and that an already existing and popularly familiar storehouse of theatrical stage scripts could be adapted for such a purpose. The development of narrative *katsudō shashin* or "moving pictures" in Japan during the first fifteen years of the twentieth century soon split into two broad generic classifications, which drew from two distinct theatrical traditions—the contemporarily set *shinpa* or "new school" dramas that were based on recent, Western-influenced stage melodramas and the *kyūha* or "old school" period pictures, which drew on kabuki.[2]

Ironically, the modern spirit of "civilization and enlightenment" (*bunmei kaika*) that molded the Meiji era inadvertently helped to ensure that many of these earliest productions wound up being adaptations of premodern *kaidan* ghost stories. At the end of the Edo period, when kabuki performances of Tsuruya Nanboku IV's *Ghost Story of Yotsuya* were all the rage, another grotesque form of flourishing popular entertainment was the *misemono* or sideshow. These open-air carnival spaces featured freak shows, haunted houses, and other playful representations of the monstrous, much like the traveling American carnivals of the nineteenth and twentieth centuries. However, following the Meiji Restoration of 1868, government unease about Japan appearing backward and primitive in the eyes of the West led to the active discouragement of such "unenlightened" displays, and by the mid-1870s authorities had banned most of the traditional *misemono* acts. Into the place of the old monstrous curiosities stepped new, technological curiosities imported from abroad and deemed more appropriate to the modernizing Meiji spirit.[3] Edison's Kinetograph being one such marvel, by the turn of the century cinema had supplanted the monsters of the Edo freak shows and haunted houses as the premier sideshow attraction, and indeed the earliest Japanese commentators on the new medium quite deliberately ascribed it the status of *misemono*.[4] But the old Edo *misemono* monsters were never far

---

[1] Aaron Gerow, *Visions of Japanese Modernity: Articulations of Cinema, Nation, and Spectatorship, 1895–1925* (Berkeley: University of California Press, 2010), 99–100.

[2] By the 1920s these early terms were replaced by the still-used *gendaigeki* ("modern production") and *jidaigeki* ("period production"), just as *katsudō shashin* fell out of usage in favor of *eiga*. See Gerow, *Visions of Japanese Modernity*, 18.

[3] Gerald Figal, *Civilization and Monsters: Spirits of Modernity in Meiji Japan* (Durham, NC: Duke University Press, 1999), 21–6.

[4] Gerow, *Visions of Japanese Modernity*, 50.

away, and were almost literally waiting in the wings to leap back into the public eye via motion pictures.

Kabuki's wealth of ghost story material had also fallen victim to the Meiji effort to purge Japanese culture of perceived superstitious belief in ghouls and goblins. The major theatrical troupes, eager to portray themselves as sophisticated and erudite entertainment, began writing the ghosts out of their productions. New plays in which ghosts were explained away as psychological hallucinations were performed, and traditional ghost stories like *The Dish Mansion at Banchō* were revised to downplay their *kaiki* content.[5] Some kabuki superstars like Ichikawa Danjūrō continued to perform the old ghost story material, but it largely fell to the minor troupes to carry on the Edo traditions of spooks and specters onstage. Denied access to the larger theater stages and officially recognized as a form of *misemono*, the minor troupes were at first condemned as low-class, crass amusement,[6] but by the beginning of the Taishō period (1912–26) many theater aficionados came to appreciate these performances as preserving many of the cast-off traditions abandoned by the more modernized major troupes.[7] Foremost among such attractions was the spectacle of the split-second costume changes, as actors would transform into ghost cats or vengeful spirits onstage. Meiji and early Taishō audiences flocked to see the minor troupes not from any interest in the stories (which were already well known), but from a desire to see the spectacle of the actor's performance, further aligning them to the phenomenon of *misemono*.[8]

When that newest of *misemono*, the cinema, looked to the stage for material, the major troupes had little interest in ongoing commercial collaboration, leaving it to minor troupe performers like Onoe Matsunosuke and Sawamura Shirōgorō to step in front of the cameras and bring their repertoire of *kaidan* traditional ghost stories with them. Yoshizawa, the nation's first commercial motion picture studio, released *Kaidan yonaki iwa* during its initial year of operation in 1908.[9] In 1910 *kaidan* film production got underway in earnest, as Yoshizawa released the first film version of the *kaidan* classic *The Peony Lantern* (*Botandōrō*) in June, then promptly released the second, *New Peony Lantern* (*Shin-botandōrō*) in July. Newly formed competitor Yokota debuted the first film version of the *Yotsuya* legend, *Oiwa inari*, directly opposite *New Peony Lantern*, and the M. Pathe

---

[5] Izumi Toshiyuki, *Ginmaku no hyakkai: honchō kaiki eiga taigai* (Tokyo: Seidosha, 2000), 66.
[6] Ibid.
[7] See Shimura Miyoko, "'Misemono' kara 'eiga' e: Shintōhō no kaibyō eiga," *Engeki eizō* 43 (2002): 19–20.
[8] Ibid.
[9] This may have been a retitled release of a foreign film. See Izumi, *Ginmaku no hyakkai*, 209.

studio gave Japan one of the first of what would be many ghost cat pictures with *The Evening Cherry Blossoms of Saga* (*Saga no yozakura*) in November. The following year would see competing versions of the third great stage *kaidan*, *The Dish Mansion at Banchō*, and another *Ghost Story of Yotsuya* adaptation, before the three studios would merge to form Nikkatsu in 1912.

This chapter traces the emergence of *kaiki* as a film genre during the silent and early sound eras of commercial cinema in Japan. With their emphasis on trick photography to portray the magical quality of vengeful spirits and ghost cats, the earliest *kaidan* adaptations of the 1910s belong—like the films of French film pioneer Georges Méliès—to film historian Tom Gunning's "cinema of attractions," which he posits as the dominant mode of the earliest commercial cinema.[10] Films produced in the mode of the cinema of attractions centered on displays of pure spectacle such as the special effects of Méliès and Japan's early *kaidan* films. Narrative continuity was of minor importance, and what little story there may have been in these films served primarily as a way to string the moments of spectacle together. By the middle of the 1910s the cinema of attractions in Europe and America had begun to give way to a more narrative-centric filmmaking Gunning names the "cinema of narrative integration," with special effects subordinated to the primacy of telling a story. Japanese cinema, meanwhile, experienced a protracted dominance of the cinema of attractions, only fully transitioning to a cinema of narrative integration in the 1920s,[11] when the marvel of trick photography ceased to be the centerpiece of *kaidan* adaptations. However, moments of spectacle continued to be of crucial importance to the emerging *kaiki* genre. The main site of attraction shifted from special photographic effects to the body of the actresses who portrayed ghosts and goblins on-screen, and the emphasis on the metamorphosis of Japanese cinema's first screen sex symbols into grotesque monsters reintroduced the element of *osore* to the *kaidan* adaptation. This crucial development, which crystalized in the canonization of vamp actress Suzuki Sumiko as Japan's first *kaiki* star, coupled with the rise of Hollywood horror and its popularity and influence in Japan, provides much of the framework for discussion of the *kaiki* film genre from the mid-1920s until its demise in the early 1970s.

---

[10] Tom Gunning, "The Cinema of Attractions: Early Film, Its Spectators, and the Avant-Garde," in *Early Cinema: Space, Frame, Narrative*, ed. Thomas Elsaesser and Adam Baker (London: British Film Institute, 1990), 56–62.
[11] See Laura Lee, "Japan's Cinema of Tricks: Optical Effects and Classical Film Style," *Quarterly Review of Film and Video* 32, no. 2 (2015), 141–61.

Playing Tricks: The Primordial *Kaiki* Film

We can only conjecture as to the content of the very earliest screen adaptations of Edo *kaidan* like *The Ghost Story of Yotsuya*. Even going so far as to identify them as primordial specimens of the *kaiki* genre requires something of a leap of faith, and must be based solely on the pictures' titles, which suggests they were—like other period films of the day—straightforward adaptations of the stage plays that would go on to be mainstays of the *kaiki* genre in subsequent decades. Less than a third of all films made in Japan prior to the end of the Second World War still exist, and virtually nothing from the first decade of commercial studio film production in Japan survives. The situation is even more woeful for *kaiki* films, which even today are haunted by the legacy of their poor critical standing and remain a low priority for restoration efforts. Of the hundreds of *kaiki* pictures made in Japan before 1945, less than a dozen are known to survive, and even these exist mostly in fragmented, incomplete states. Barely a frame of anything that could be grouped with the *kaiki* genre remains from these earliest years of studio filmmaking in Japan.

Many of these prototypical *kaiki* pictures were created by director Makino Shōzō and actor Onoe Matsunosuke, part of the approximately eight hundred period pictures the duo made at Nikkatsu during the 1910s. Makino and Onoe's unprecedented financial and popular success was matched only by the disdain they received from the intellectual film critics of the day. The proponents of the Pure Film Movement (*Juneiga geki undō*), a group of intellectuals desiring a Japanese cinema that mirrored what they saw as the more sophisticated filmmaking techniques of Europe and America, lambasted the Makino/Onoe pictures for being little more than canned theater. Shot in a one-scene, one-take tableaux style that replicated the viewpoint of a theater spectator, the screening of such films relied on live, in-house narrators known as *benshi* for any sort of narrative comprehensibility. Film aficionados Kaeriyama Norimasa and Shigeno Yukiyashi, two of the founders of the Pure Film Movement, numbered among the first Japanese to develop theories of the cinematic medium as an art form distinct from other modes of performance and storytelling, and Kaeriyama eventually became a filmmaker himself, putting his principles into practice. At the same time, newly founded studios like Shōchiku embraced the Pure Film Movement's vision of a Japanese cinema that made more thorough use of techniques like the close-up and continuity editing. While the question of whether the Pure Film Movement's ideals constituted a superior form of cinema to the "canned theater" of Makino and Onoe remains debatable, the tastes of the Kaeriyama and Shigeno's circle came to dominate critical discourse of Japanese cinema for decades, informing much of the discussion surrounding *kaiki* films through the prewar era.

Aaron Gerow has suggested that these early pictures may have included more so-called "filmic" techniques than their critics were prepared to give them credit for, but notes the lack of surviving examples makes it difficult to verify the conjecture.[12] Although it appears that in many ways early Japanese filmmakers were content to present their work in much the same manner it would be seen on stage, in the case of stories like *The Ghost Story of Yotsuya* and *The Peony Lantern* they swiftly realized the new medium's potential for portraying *kaiki* special effects in a fashion quite different from kabuki's established repertoire of stage tricks. While films like the 1915 version of *Yotsuya* evidently clung to such obvious trappings of the traditional theater as casting a female impersonator in the role of Oiwa, evidence suggests that the stage methods of portraying the otherworldly nature of her vengeful spirit via trap doors and split-second costume changes were supplanted by trick photography unique to the cinematic medium. The brief review of the 1915 version of *The Ghost Story of Yotsuya* in *Kinema Record*, the mouthpiece of the Pure Film Movement, notes, "The spectacle of simple trick-photography, such as the double-exposure ghost, creates a sense of mystery for the audience."[13]

Despite their well-known hostility to Makino and Onoe, the Pure Film Movement critics were more favorably disposed to the duo's work when it made use of such essentially filmic techniques as double exposure, reverse filming, and stop-motion photography. These tricks featured most prominently in their tremendously popular ninja pictures as well as the many adaptations of *kaidan* and *bakeneko* (ghost cat) stage plays produced at the same time.[14] *Kinema Record* atypically praises the pair in its review of the early ghost cat picture *The Cat of Okazaki* (*Okazaki no neko*, 1914), saying, "The cat trick effects are in truth admirably done. Only Matsunosuke's group can pull off this kind of production."[15] The magazine is equally generous to their follow-up effort, *The Ghost Cat of Sannō* (*Sannō no bakeneko*, 1914), declaring that "from first to last it is crammed with incredibly interesting tricks."[16] The surviving footage from the

---

[12] Gerow, *Visions of Japanese Modernity*, 94–117.
[13] *Kinema Record*, November 10, 1915, 25.
[14] See Kamiya Masako, "Shoki nihon eiga no kaiki to torikku," in *Kaiki to gensō e no kairō: kaidankara J-horā e*, ed. Uchiyama Kazuki (Tokyo: Shinwasha, 2008), 38–40; as well as Lee, "Japan's Cinema of Tricks," 151.
[15] *Kinema Record*, May 10, 1914, 30.
[16] *Kinema Record*, August 3, 1914, 27.

Figure 6 Okiku's double-exposure ghost in a frame from an unidentified production of the Dish Mansion legend (*c.* 1915). Courtesy of the National Film Archive of Japan and Kobe Planet Film Archive.

pre-1923 *Dish Mansion* film discussed in Chapter 1, which depicts the double-exposure ghost of Okiku dissolving atop her well and playing stop-motion tricks on the sleeping samurai, confirms that such uniquely filmic tricks were the likely centerpiece of these formative *kaiki* pictures (Figure 6).

Trick photography was also being employed in the *rensa* or "chain drama" performances, a hybrid of film and theater in which live actors performed the interior-set scenes, then cleared the stage to make way for the silver screen, where the same actors would be seen on film performing exterior scenes or, in the case of more *kaiki* material, scenes featuring double-exposure ghosts. Izumi Toshiyuki quotes an audience member's recollection of one such *rensa* performance:

> An actress named Shikishima Hanaeda, who always played ruffians and scoundrels, portrayed a thief who sneaks into a temple and murders a priest in one scene. The priest was played by an actress from Nakano, Abe Nobuo, who's since passed away. It was a simple scene but lasted about ten minutes, after which was a scene in which the ghost appears … Via an incredibly primitive technique

the ghost floated out, the thief tumbled over, surprised, and the curtain fell. That was it. This was at the Mitomo Theater in Asakusa.[17]

Although it is unclear from the audience member's recollection which part of the performance was live and which was filmed, it is highly likely that the scene featuring the ghost involved some manner of filmed trick photography. Since studios like Yoshizawa and Tenkatsu produced straightforward cinema intended to be screened with *benshi* narration as well as the film components of *rensa*, it is uncertain from the records of film titles how many of these primordial *kaiki* films were actually part of a *rensa* show.[18]

Interestingly, Makino Shōzō claimed to have independently discovered several of the trick photography techniques seen in earlier foreign films that were widely screened in Japan like Edison's *The Execution of Mary Stuart* (1895) and the work of Méliès, such as starting and stopping the camera to make actors disappear.[19] Whether or not Makino learned such tricks from watching European and American cinema or developed them on his own, the utilization of them shows the ways in which early cinema developed an international common vernacular of expression. Makino's films adapt native material—in this case the Edo-period ghost stories—to the screen by discarding the theatrical stage conventions for depicting ghosts and monsters and instead utilizing techniques seen in Méliès's pioneering films. And much like Méliès's whimsical phantoms and devils, early Japanese *kaidan* adaptations became showcases for spectacular tricks at the expense of de-emphasizing the inherently horrific features of the ghosts and goblins they depict. The narrative intertitles in the surviving silent footage discussed above identify it as an adaptation of *The Dish Mansion at Banchō*, but the footage has little to do with the narrative of Okiku's revenge on her murderer, instead dwelling on the spectacular appearance of her see-through ghost, her ability to appear and disappear in a cloud of smoke, and to psychically manipulate objects. Such tricks invoked a sense of wonder and awe in early audiences, but there is nothing particularly grotesque, repulsive, horrific, or terrifying about their execution.

---

[17] Izumi, *Ginmaku no hyakkai*, 72.
[18] *Rensa* rivaled more conventional films as popular entertainment until the practice was swiftly extinguished by the Tokyo Moving Picture Regulations in 1917, which banned the practice on the grounds that the small, wooden theaters in which they were performed represented a major fire hazard. See J. L. Anderson, "Spoken Silents in the Japanese Cinema; or, Talking to Pictures: Essaying the *Katsuben*, Contextualizing the Texts," in *Reframing Japanese Cinema: Authorship, Genre, History*, ed. Arthur Nolletti Jr. and David Desser (Bloomington: Indiana University Press, 1992), 271–2.
[19] Kamiya, "Shoki nihon eiga no kaiki to torikku," 41–2.

I have been somewhat reluctant to use the term *kaiki* when discussing these films, since it is clear from the reviews in *Kinema Record* that—among the early film critics, at least—if films featuring ghosts or monsters belonged to a particular subgenre, it was the trick film. As the short reviews quoted above show, interest in these films was entirely due to their use of cinematic tricks, or *torikku*. Shigeno Yukiyashi may have (almost) coined the phrase *kaiki eiga* in 1914 when he writes in *Kinema Record* that *torikku* can greatly enhance the enjoyment of certain films such as *kikai naru eiga* (奇怪なる映画, using an inversion of the two characters that comprise the word *kaiki*), but Shigeno positions this fleeting observation in a larger discussion of "trick films," bestowing the status of genre on the term by giving his article the English title "Trick Pictures and Illusion Pictures."[20] For the authors—and presumably the readers—of *Kinema Record*, the ghost story pictures were not generically defined by any sense of *kaiki* or cosmic terror/*osore*, but the same special effects that could also be found in Onoe Matsunosuke's ninja films, or the comic "tanuki exterminator" (*tanuki taiji*) pictures that depicted the antics of the shape-shifting Japanese raccoon dogs.

The scant bit of visual evidence surviving from this era—while not enough to make any sweeping conclusions about the content of Taishō-era *kaidan* films—supports the hypothesis that many of these pictures were made with the intent to dazzle audiences with the spectacle of cinema rather than frighten them with themes of *osore*. A still frame in the collection of Misono Kyōhei from an unidentified Taishō-era film shows what appears to be a samurai confronting a ghost cat (Figure 7). Battles between samurai and ghost cats are a commonplace sight on the kabuki stage, and the Shinkō studio's *kaiki* films of the 1930s and their 1950s Daiei counterparts also regularly feature such scenes, leading Misono to surmise that the still in his collection comes from an early ghost cat picture such as *The Cat of Okazaki* or *The Evening Cherry Blossoms of Saga* (both adapted from the stage and remade in the sound era by Shinkō, and later Daiei).[21] It is all the more striking, then, that the ghost cat is not an actor with disheveled hair and grotesque makeup, as actresses Suzuki Sumiko and Irie Takako would perform the role in decades to come. Instead the cat monster appears to be an

---

[20] Shigeno Yukiyashi, "Trick Pictures and Illusion Pictures," *Kinema Record* 2, no. 6 (January 1, 1914): 12. Shigeno inverts the characters for *kaiki* to "*kikai*" (奇怪), a synonym with an identical meaning. Directly analogous to the classical Chinese *zhiguai*, Shigeno's word choice has a more archaic flair to it. *Kaiki* appears to have become standard by 1926, when the word appears in Kawabata Yasunari's *Dancer of Izu* (*Izu no odoriko*).

[21] Misono Kyōhei, ed., *Misono korekushon: Meiji, Taishō, Shōwa eiga shiryōshū taisei* (Tokyo: Katsudō shiryō kenkyūkai, 1970).

Figure 7 A samurai confronts a rather cuddly-looking *bakeneko* in a still from an unidentified film.

actor in a large plush costume, looking like nothing so much as a character one would expect to meet wandering around Tokyo Disneyland.

Horror (and *kaiki*) films tend to lose much of their ability to scare with age. Today some people have a hard time believing anyone ever found Boris Karloff frightening in *Frankenstein*, yet audience members reportedly fled the theater in terror in 1931.[22] But it is difficult to imagine that anyone in the audience for this film would have been scared by the frankly adorable *bakeneko* seen in this image, or that the filmmakers intended it to be frightening.

Misono's plush ghost cat may in fact come not from a straightforward *kaidan* adaptation like *The Cat of Okazaki*, but one of the many "Seven Wonders" (*nana fushigi*) films made at the same time, which were based on the folklore motif of the *tanuki ongaeshi*, or "The Tanuki Who Returns a Favor." Films about the magical, shape-shifting tanuki were another popular topic of Taishō-era trick films. Although tanuki tales tended to be more whimsical than the ghastly narratives of otherworldly revenge typical of *kaidan*, they shared much of the same *kaiki* imagery, as tanuki were fond of taking on the guise of more gruesome

---

[22] Robert Spadoni, *Uncanny Bodies: The Coming of Sound Film and the Origins of the Horror Genre* (Berkeley: University of California Press, 2007), 94.

monsters like vengeful wraiths and ghost cats to play pranks on unwitting human victims. In a typical Seven Wonders story, a tanuki who has been aided by the human protagonist will take on the form of seven *kaidan*-esque monsters to frighten and punish the villain of the piece, usually a wicked samurai or even the shogun himself. Although this is thematically quite close to other tales of marvelous karmic comeuppance such as the *Yotsuya* legend or the typical ghost cat narrative, tanuki tales most often dilute the horrific dimension of the act of vengeance. In Shintōhō's *Seven Wonders of Honjo* (*Kaidan honjo nana fushigi*, 1957), for example, the film significantly undercuts any sense of horrific *osore* by portraying the tanuki in human form as cute young women and including fanciful shots of the humanized creatures dancing merrily after playing their ghostly tricks on the villains. Presumably this sense of whimsy would have figured into the Taishō-era Seven Wonders films as well, and the plush ghost cat in Misono's still could quite conceivably come from such a production.

Director Yoshino Jirō was something of a specialist in Seven Wonders films, making at least five versions for three different studios between 1917 and 1922. A quick look at his oeuvre also turns up productions of *The Ghost Story of Yotsuya* (1921) and *The Dish Mansion at Banchō* (1922); *bakeneko* pictures such as *The Ghost Cat of Arima Palace* (*Kaibyō Arima goten*, 1919) and *The Cat of Nabeshima* (*Nabeshima no neko*, 1923); a slew of ninja pictures starring Onoe Matsunosuke's rival, Sawamura Shirōgorō; and Tenkatsu's two-part special effects extravaganza *Journey to the West* (*Saiyūki*, 1917), also starring Sawamura.[23] With *kaidan*, ghost cat, tanuki, ninja, and Monkey King pictures all to their credit, Yoshino and Sawamura—like Makino and Onoe at Nikkatsu—laid much of the foundation for the eventual genre of *kaiki*, and it was a foundation wholly intertwined with and probably largely indistinguishable from other trick films of the day.

Yoshino and Sawamura's move to the new Shōchiku studios in 1921 demonstrates the ongoing importance of the trick film's uniquely cinematic special effects to certain strains of the continually popular *kyūha*—which by now were beginning to be called by the still-used appellation for period pictures, *jidaigeki*. Shōchiku famously entered the film production business in 1920 with the intention of making movies that would showcase the latest innovations in style and technique, hiring several Hollywood-trained filmmakers to realize their goal, which seemed to be the fulfillment of the Pure Film Movement's calls for a Japanese cinema that would not merely replicate the kabuki or

---

[23] Izumi examines records of *Journey to the West*'s use of special effects in *Ginmaku no hyakkai*, 80–1.

shinpa theatergoing experience.²⁴ But despite Shōchiku's stated purpose of "the production of artistic films resembling the latest and most flourishing styles of the Occidental cinema,"²⁵ that had long since transitioned from the cinema of attractions to a cinema of narrative integration, the studio hired Yoshino and Sawamura to create the same sort of presumably trick-heavy period pictures they had been making for the Tenkatsu and Kokkatsu studios. Shōchiku would become famous for its contemporarily set *gendaigeki* productions, but their early release slate includes Mori Kaname's *Ghost Cat of Nabeshima* (*Nabeshima neko sōdō*, 1921), *The Peony Lantern* (also 1921), and *The Ghost Story of Yotsuya* (1923), as well as Yoshino's *Dish Mansion at Banchō*, *The Seven Wonders of Honjo* (*Honjo nana fushigi*), *The Seven Wonders of Fukugawa* (*Fukugawa nana fushigi*, all 1922), and his own version of *The Cat of Nabeshima* (1923).

Unfortunately, it is difficult to ascertain much about these early Shōchiku *kaidan* adaptations and how they were received. *Kinema Record* ceased publication in 1917, and although its spiritual successor, *Kinema junpō*, appeared just two years later, it only reviewed foreign films until 1922. Even then its coverage of Japanese cinema was selective and tended toward pictures that more fully exemplified the ideals of the Pure Film Movement and eschewed genre cinema aimed at a mass audience. It was not until the beginning of the Shōwa era (1926–89) that the magazine began to offer more comprehensive coverage of domestic releases.²⁶ The competing publication *Eiga hyōron* ("Film Review") also did not appear until the last year of Taishō, making the first half of the 1920s something of a black hole of critical information about *kaidan* pictures, which appear to have no longer been garnering praise solely by virtue of their special effects.

Although the critics in *Kinema Record* had been initially indulgent of the trick-heavy *kaidan* and ghost cat films, by the end of the journal's run the novelty seems to have been wearing off. An editorial from the October 1917 issue of *Record* commenting on Tokyo's recently established rating system for movies (A for adults-only, B for general audiences) groups *kaidan* among the "vulgar" entertainment of children and the uneducated, saying, "if the films [made in Japan] remain at the level of ghost stories or *shinpa* tragedy, they will not interest an adult, whether grade A or even grade B films."²⁷ The *kaidan* trick films were

---

[24] Joseph L. Anderson and Donald Richie, *The Japanese Film: Art and Industry*, 2nd ed. (Princeton, NJ: Princeton University Press, 1982), 40–1.
[25] Quoted in Gerow, *Visions of Japanese Modernity*, 172.
[26] Izumi, *Ginmaku no hyakkai*, 91.
[27] "Shinchōrei tai gyōsha mondai," *Kinema Record* no. 50 (October 1917): 1–3. Quoted in Gerow, *Visions of Japanese Modernity*, 125.

of course never the Pure Film Movement's ideal cinema, the group desiring a more comprehensive marshaling of various techniques including close-ups and the use of actresses in place of female impersonators in addition to the use of essentially filmic, in-camera effects and trick photography. After a few years of double-exposure ghosts appearing and dissolving on-screen, the *kaidan* pictures may have begun to feel like one more variation of the old *misemono* spectacles that according to critics represented a primitive precursor to the "mature" cinema of narrative integration. *Kinema junpō* inherited the bias against *kaidan* adaptations expressed in the 1917 *Record* piece, and coverage of such pictures before the late 1920s is scant. By this time Shōchiku had mostly abandoned its early interest in trick-heavy *kaiki* productions. Yoshino Jirō would leave the company in 1927 to join Makino Shōzō's self-titled studio, formed in 1921 after parting ways with Onoe Matsunosuke. Makino's former employer Nikkatsu also appears to have lost interest in traditional ghost stories by the beginning of the Shōwa era. Although Shōchiku would continue to produce the occasional *kaidan* adaptation into the 1930s, the genre would remain mainly the province of minor studios until the government's 1939 Film Act effectively shut down all production of *kaiki* film.

It was at Makino that Yoshino directed his sole surviving *kaidan* film, 1929's *Kaidan: Fox and Tanuki* (*Kaidan kitsune to tanuki*), and although it appears to be an atypical specimen of the genre in several respects, it suggests that the spectacle of special photographic effects had ceased to be the main site of attraction in such films. At thirty-three minutes, *Kaidan: Fox and Tanuki* also represents the only substantial extant footage from a silent-era *kaiki* film apart from the eleven minutes of *Dish Mansion* footage discussed in Chapter 1. The *kaidan* in the picture's title, however, is tongue-in-cheek, as the film follows not the antics of actual shape-shifting foxes and tanuki but comical intrigue among a family of thieves, who in an isolated sequence attempt to frighten each other by disguising as ghosts and rigging mock *hi no tama* floating fireballs onto fishing poles.

Yoshino may be spoofing his earlier, presumably more earnest depictions of *kaiki* at Tenkatsu and Shōchiku, or mimicking Hollywood haunted house mysteries like *The Cat and the Canary*, wherein the "ghosts" are actually criminals in disguise. In any case, *Fox and Tanuki* feels like an atypical *kaidan* production. It does, however, demonstrate that many of the developments in film style championed by the Pure Film Movement had by this time infiltrated even the "vulgar" *kaidan* productions of the minor studios. Comparing *Fox and Tanuki* to the surviving footage from the unidentified *Dish Mansion at Banchō* picture, one sees a greatly diminished emphasis on trick photography for pure spectacle's sake. Whereas the centerpiece of the *Dish Mansion* footage is the extended scene in which Okiku's ghost magically manipulates *shōji* curtains via stop-motion photography, the fleeting ghost imagery in *Fox and Tanuki* is achieved with simpler, on-set lighting and shadow effects, and their presence is more definitely tied into the narrative flow of events, as the ghosts and goblins are revealed to be human pranksters. Yoshino's film also makes use of close-ups, parallel editing, and more detailed intertitles—though it should be noted that the *Dish Mansion* footage also includes the occasional medium close-up and intertitles, supporting Gerow's conjecture that early Japanese cinema could be more dynamic than its reputation suggests.

Although I was unable to locate a review for Yoshino's *Fox and Tanuki*, *Kinema junpō*'s coverage of other *kaidan* films that do not survive from the same period, including Makino Studio's *Ghost Story of Yotsuya* from 1927, Shōchiku's *Autumn Flower Lantern* (*Akisaku dōrō*, 1927), and the Kawai studio's version of *Yotsuya* from 1928, tellingly make little to no mention of trick effects, corroborating the assumption that by this time spectacular displays of trick photography had indeed ceased to be the defining element of such films. The *Junpō* reviews strike a sharp contrast to the ones found in *Kinema Record*. Admittedly, they are much longer and more in-depth than the one or two sentences that appeared in *Record*, but the tricks were the *only* thing worth mentioning for the *Record* reviewers. Discussing Makino Studio's *Ghost Story of Yotsuya*, critic Yamamoto Ryōkuyō is more concerned with the film's fidelity to the narrative and spirit of Nanboku's kabuki text and the performance of the actors than being dazzled by special effects.[28] While the films themselves almost certainly continued to make use of tricks like double-exposure ghosts, such displays had undoubtedly become commonplace, ceasing to even be worthy of mention as a potential draw for audiences.

Beauty Is the Beast: Vamp Actresses and Monstrous Transformations

Trick photography was no longer a novelty in Japanese cinema of the 1920s, but *Fox and Tanuki* featured a new draw for audiences in the person of "vamp" actress Izumi Kiyoko. Actresses had been a part of Japanese cinema almost from its inception, especially in the *rensa* chain dramas and select *shinpa*

---

[28] *Kinema junpō*, August 1, 1927, 54.

productions, but—in another holdover from traditional theater—*onnagata* female impersonators played the majority of on-screen female roles until the early 1920s. Although it has been suggested that *onnagata* became obsolete because they precluded the use of close-up shots, Hideaki Fujiki has shown that close-ups of *onnagata* did exist (even if they were heavily criticized), instead arguing the eventual phasing out of *onnagata* in cinema was a result of the actresses' sexual allure eclipsing the appeal of the female impersonators' virtuosic performances.[29] The advent of the female movie star as an object of sexual desire brought a new site of attraction to the Japanese film industry, one that could be seamlessly injected into the cinema of narrative integration and, in the case of the *kaidan* adaptations, supplant the extended trick photography set pieces that belonged more conspicuously to the cinema of attractions. The spectacle of *kaidan* films would no longer revolve primarily around protracted displays of stop-motion and double exposure, but instead the sight of Japan's newly minted screen sex symbols transformed into hideous monsters before the audience's eyes.

In 1925, the same year Izumi Kiyoko made her film debut, another vamp actress, Satsuki Nobuko, became the first woman to portray *The Ghost Story of Yotsuya*'s famous vengeful wraith Oiwa on-screen. By the end of the decade the role of the monster in domestic *kaiki* film had become the exclusive province of the vamps. The etymology of the term "vamp," or *vampu* in Japanese, makes the connection seem almost fated. Originating in the 1915 Hollywood film *A Fool There Was*, in which Theda Bara appears as a femme fatale nicknamed "The Vampire Woman," the term in English was quickly shortened to "vamp" and applied to actresses who specialized in playing bad-girl roles, divesting the term of any overtly horrific or supernatural association. Erudite Japanese cinema aficionados, always eager to adopt the latest film terminology from abroad, imported the word almost as soon as actresses began appearing in analogous roles in Japanese films. In 1922 *Kinema junpō* first applied the term to none other than future Oiwa Satsuki Nobuko, but left it in its original, longer form as "vampire" (*vampaiyā*).[30] As late as 1980 old filmmaking hands like Nakagawa Nobuo were still using the elongated term "vampire" to describe femme fatale actresses.[31]

---

[29] See Hideaki Fujiki, *Making Personas: Transnational Film Stardom in Modern Japan* (Cambridge: Harvard University Press, 2013), 192–202.
[30] Quoted in Izumi, *Ginmaku no hyakkai*, 105.
[31] Nakagawa Nobuo refers to actress Suzuki Sumiko as a "*vampaiyā*" in a piece he wrote for *Kinema Junpō* in 1980 on "Five Outlaw Women of Japanese Film History." See "Wa ga nihon eigashi ue no shiranami gonin onna," reproduced in *Eiga kantoku Nakagawa Nobuo*, 126–8.

While Hollywood vamps in the Theda Bara mold typically featured in contemporarily set urban noirs, many of the most popular Japanese *vampu* first rose to popularity appearing in period samurai and ninja action films in the stock role of the *yōfu* or "seductress," the beautiful yet dangerous female criminals and bandits who appeared as foils to the male heroes popular with younger audiences of the day.[32] Although not literal monsters, the *yōfu* (like vamps) had an etymological connection to the monstrous, the character *yō* (妖, "bewitching") being the same one that appears in the word for goblin, *yōkai* (妖怪). And like many *kaiki* monsters, *yōfu* possessed an ambiguously attractive and frightening, Othered quality to them, sexually desirable yet physically formidable and threatening.[33] Deadly fighting women were another pre-cinematic holdover from the kabuki stage, but the spectacle of seeing actual women perform these intensely physical roles made the *vampu* some of Japan's first and most popular female film stars. Shimura Miyoko, who has published several articles on the *bakeneko* subgenre of *kaiki* film, notes that the vamps were among the first female players in an emerging star system of production in commercial Japanese cinema during the 1920s:

> Based on the "star system," *jidaigeki* originally had an aspect of heroism, and under that system big stars like Bandō Tsumasaburō, Arashi Kanjūrō, Kataoka Chiezō, and Ichikawa Utaemon became the heroes of children [in the audience]. Arrayed against these hero actors were the so-called vamp actresses like Tōa's Hara Komako, Nikkatsu's Sakai Yoneko and Fushimi Naoe, Teikine's Matsueda Tsuruko, and Makino's Suzuki Sumiko, who were ubiquitous in the mid-1920s. Billed as putting the male actors to shame in grand *tachimawari* (fight scenes), the vamps were incredibly popular, in what could be called the female version of the star system. In contrast to the straightforward symbols of heroism the male actors were for the youngsters that made up the bulk of the audience, the vamp actresses' alleged mixture of allure and fearsomeness was likely a complex symbol of eroticism. Outwardly feminine while being able to partake in the exceedingly masculine physical activity of the *tachimawari*, audiences were startled and captivated by the unlikely appeal of the vamps' bewitching figure combined with her contrary physicality.[34]

---

[32] Writings in Japanese on cinema often will use the characters for *yōfu* with the phonetic gloss of *vampu*.

[33] Isolde Standish sees this same combination of allure and threat in Japanese cinema's portrayals of *modan gāru* or "modern girls" in the *gendaigeki* of the 1930s. See *A New History of Japanese Cinema: A Century of Narrative Film* (New York: Continuum, 2005), 57.

[34] Shimura Miyoko, "Shinkō kinema no kaibyō eiga," *Eiga gaku* 14 (2000): 54.

Like Noël Carroll's horror monsters, which are often "fusion figures" that compound "ordinarily disjoint or conflicting categories" of being,[35] the Japanese vamp actress constituted a categorically interstitial entity, possessing feminine beauty and masculine physical strength. Shimura ascribes much of Suzuki Sumiko's later emergence as Japan's first *kaiki* star to her place of prominence in Japanese film culture as a liminal figure in whom sexual allure coexisted alongside a fearsome physical aggressiveness.[36] The two conflicting aspects of the vamp's star persona—sensually appealing yet physically threatening—found externalized expression when the same actresses began to be cast as the hideous ghosts and half-feline *bakeneko* that had heretofore been played on-screen by female impersonators.

As the most representative works of *kaidan* drama and literature featured female ghosts and monsters, the decision to cast the fearsome vamps in the screen versions of these stories was in some ways a quite obvious and natural one. Had Western gothic horror literature contained a similar preponderance of iconic female monsters instead of the male Count Dracula, Mr. Hyde, and Frankenstein's Monster, Hollywood vamps might also have found themselves typecast as more literal vampires. However, not everyone found vamp actresses like Suzuki Sumiko suitable for the role of monsters like *Yotsuya*'s Oiwa. Prior to her poisoning Oiwa is an attractive beauty who only in the second half of the story becomes a wrathful destroyer of men. The living Oiwa is the archetypical virtuous woman or *teijo*, loyal to her unfaithful husband and sacrificing all to protect her child.[37] Some critics in the 1920s were keenly aware of the contradiction of having bad-girl vamps play good-girl characters like Oiwa. About Suzuki Sumiko's performance in the 1927 adaptation of *Yotsuya*, *Kinema junpō*'s review complains that the vamp actress is miscast as the *teijo* Oiwa, failing to convincingly convey the character's inherent virtue in a role unsuited to her talents.[38]

Nonetheless, throughout the mid to late 1920s the monsters of *kaidan* were played on-screen almost exclusively by vamp actresses like Suzuki, Satsuki, and Matsueda Tsuruko, the latter earning a more favorable review for an effectively frightening performance in the Teikine studio's *Ghost Story of Kasane's Swamp* (*Kaidan Kasane ga fuchi*, 1924) and going on to appear in versions of *The Dish*

---

[35] Noël Carroll, *The Philosophy of Horror: Or Paradoxes of the Heart* (New York: Routledge, 1990), 44.
[36] Shimura, "Shinkō kinema no kaibyō eiga," 55.
[37] Yokoyama discusses the *bijo/teijo* dichotomy in "Yotsuya kaidan no Oiwa-tachi: kabuki to wakare, betsu no onna e," in *Kaiki to gensō e no kairo: kaidan kara J-horā e*, ed. Uchiyama Kazuki (Tokyo: Shinwasha, 2008), 152.
[38] Quoted in Yokoyama, "*Yotsuya kaidan no Oiwatachi*," 152–3.

Mansion at Banchō (1926), *The Ghost Story of Yotsuya* (1927), and *The Peony Lantern* (1930).[39] Like Oiwa in *The Ghost Story of Yotsuya*, *Kasane*'s Orui, *The Dish Mansion*'s Okiku, and *The Peony Lantern*'s Otsuyu are all virtuous female archetypes, and in terms of personality are diametrically opposed to the vamps that the actresses who portrayed them were identified with by critics and audiences of the day. There is, however, an interesting affinity between the vamps and the virtuous ghosts. Keeping in mind that the Japanese word for monster, *bakemono*, literally means "changing thing," one finds that the portrayals of Oiwa, Orui, and their ilk are marked by a stark physical transformation, from attractive living lover to hideous undead revenant, typically occurring at about the halfway point of the narrative. The two contradictory halves of the *kaidan* female monster, Beauty and Beast, alluring and repellent, offer a concrete, physical separation of the ambiguously feminine-yet-fearsome qualities that coexist in the person of the vamp. In this sense, the appeal of the female *bakemono* and the vamp function in a quite similar manner, the former being a visual sorting out of the commingled natures of the latter.

The physical transformation of Beauty into Beast was what had supplanted the by-now commonplace trick effects as the main site of spectacle in 1920s *kaidan* films, despite Yokoyama Yasuko's suggestion that once monsters like Oiwa began to be portrayed by actresses on-screen the roles lost much of their sense of carnival. On the traditional kabuki stage, the male actor cast in the role of Oiwa typically also appears as the male ghost Kohei and (perhaps more importantly) Yomoshichi, the handsome hero of the piece and the character who actually kills the villainous Iemon in the play's climax, making him a thematic counterpart to Oiwa's ghost. This lends the otherwise grim and ghastly *Yotsuya* a carnivalesque quality that lightens the proceedings, as audiences delight in watching the actor pull off the split-second costume changes, alternating between the hideous female ghost and the dashing male hero. The part of Oiwa/Yomoshichi was, accordingly, a choice role for kabuki actors, and presumably for the male actors who played the characters in the earliest film versions of the story. Conversely, Yokoyama suggests that Oiwa was not an attractive part for actresses, as the performance became separated from Yomoshichi, leaving only a hideous transformation that was unrelentingly grim.[40]

---

[39] Izumi, *Ginmaku no hyakkai*, 106.
[40] Yokoyama, "*Yotsuya kaidan* no Oiwatachi," 153. Satoko Shimazaki discusses the history of male actors' performance of Oiwa onstage in *Edo Kabuki in Transition: From the Worlds of the Samurai to the Vengeful Female Ghost* (New York: Columbia University Press, 2016), 182–9.

I would argue, however, that the sense of carnival merely became extratextual in the case of the vamp actresses' portrayal of Oiwa and other monsters, a result of the newly emerging star system in Japanese cinema. Such a system had been lacking in the previous decade, when the main selling points of a film were the *benshi's* live narrative accompaniment,[41] and in the case of the formative *kaiki* films, the trick effects. Although the star system in the 1920s was institutionally organized around promoting the image of male action heroes like Bandō Tsumasaburō, as Shimura Miyoko points out the vamp actresses rivaled their male counterparts in actual popularity. The cult of personality surrounding figures like Matsueda Tsuruko and Suzuki Sumiko certainly was being exploited by casting these "complex symbols of eroticism" in roles that would throw their seductive and sexy personas into sharp relief by transforming them into grotesque monsters right before the audience's eyes. The sense of spectacle and carnival, then, relied not on the actor's taking on multiple personas within a single text, as in the stage versions of *The Ghost Story of Yotsuya*, but on the actress's established star persona as an object of sex appeal being playfully inverted by rendering her temporarily hideous.

Most importantly, the idea that the *kaidan* adaptations ought to convey a sense of fear enters the discourse surrounding the emerging *kaiki* genre in response to the vamps' taking over of the role of the monster from the female impersonators. Instead of dwelling on the ways in which the special effects of the earlier trick-centric films would delight audiences, now the critics were discussing how the performances of vamps like Matsueda Tsuruko instilled a sense of horror in the viewer. *Kinema Record*'s brief review of the 1915 film version of *The Ghost Story of Yotsuya* focused entirely on how "the spectacle of simple trick-photography, such as the double-exposure ghost creates a sense of mystery (*fushigi*) for the audience."[42] Nine years later, *Record*'s successor publication *Kinema junpō* made no mention of trick photography in another adaptation of a classic ghost story, *Kasane's Swamp* (*Kasane ga fuchi*, 1924). Instead of the "sense of mystery" created by the trick effects, now the attention centered on the figure of Matsueda as the ghost, whose "performance and makeup are more than adequate to instill a sense of *horror* (*kyōfu*) in the audience."[43] Fear had finally become part of the *kaiki* equation, and it would remain the central criterion in determining the success of films that made up the genre by audiences and critics alike.

---

[41] See Hideaki Fujiki, "The Advent of the Star System in Japanese Cinema Distribution," *Jōhō bunka kenkyū* 15 (2002): 1–22.
[42] *Kinema Record*, November 1915, 25.
[43] Quoted in Izumi, *Ginmaku no hyakkai*, 106. Emphasis added.

Suzuki Sumiko

Although other vamps like Matsueda initially seem to have been better received in the role of the vengeful wraith, it was Suzuki who would eventually become the vamp most associated with playing monsters on-screen. The movement of the site of spectacle in Japanese *kaiki* films during the 1920s from trick photography to the body of the female performer—which relied on an established, extratextual star persona—would find its ultimate expression a decade later with the minting of Suzuki Sumiko as the *bakeneko joyū* or "ghost cat actress," Japan's first great *kaiki* star.

Born in Tokyo in 1904 to an affluent merchant family, as a child Suzuki took lessons in dance, shamisen, and koto. After performing with various *shinpa* theatrical troupes, she made her rather prestigious film debut at the age of 15 in a supporting role in Hollywood-trained director Thomas Kurihara's *Lust of the White Serpent* (*Jasei no in*, 1921). Foreshadowing her later association with the *kaiki* genre, the film was an adaptation of a tale in author Ueda Akinari's eighteenth-century ghost story collection *Tales of Moonlight and Rain* (*Ugetsu monogatari*), which would later serve as source material for Mizoguchi Kenji's renowned *Ugetsu* (1953). Following the destruction of the Tokyo film studios in the Great Kantō Earthquake of 1923, Suzuki relocated along with the rest of the Japanese film industry to Kyoto, where she achieved star status appearing in vamp roles for the Makino, Teikine, and Kawai studios. Her breakthrough role as the titular vamp in Makino's 1926 period action film *Jokai* ("Weird Woman") made Suzuki into the premiere vamp of her day by taking advantage of her background in dance to create what has been put forward as "the first female swordplay film" (Figure 8). [44]

Jokai appears to have been the catalyst in marrying the image of the Japanese vamp with the choreographed *tachimawari* action set pieces that were a crucial component of the vamps' popularity, and Suzuki's star persona would continue to be bound up with *tachimawari* fight scenes even after graduating from vamp roles to demonic ghost cats in later years.[45] In 1930 the publication *Film All-Stars* (*Eiga sutā zenshū*) named her "the quintessential vamp. ... Hara Komako and Fushimi Naoe are fine as vamps go, but no one can hold a candle to Suzuki Sumiko."[46] Although she made the occasional appearance in contemporarily

---

[44] Hasebe Toshio, ed., *"Shihan" Kawai, Daito eiga 2: Kawai eiga no danyū joyū.* (Tokyo: Takei Kikaku, 1994), 17.

[45] Lisa Spalding notes that fight choreography by the 1920s had become more realistic than the slow-paced *tachimawari* of the kabuki stage in "Period Films in the Prewar Era," in *Reframing Japanese Cinema*, 132. In its indebtedness to the theatrical tradition, however, the term endured.

[46] Kondō Keiichi, ed., *Eiga sutā zenshū 10* (Tokyo: Heibonsha, 1930), 114.

Figure 8 Beauty and danger combined in the person of vamp actress Suzuki Sumiko. Promotional image from Makino Studio's *Jokai* (1926).

set *gendaigeki* (modern dramas) like Teikine's *Madam Knockout* (*Madamu KO*, 1931), she overwhelmingly appeared in period *jidaigeki* pictures as assorted vamps, ne'er-do-wells, and female criminals who embodied the sexy-yet-deadly image upon which Suzuki's fame was first built. Her sex symbol status arguably reached its epitome in 1935 when she starred as the infamous murderess Takahashi Oden in *The Hell of Oden* (*Oden jigoku*), in which her backside appeared naked from the waist up to reveal Oden's fearsome underworld tattoo. Never before had a domestically made film bared so much female flesh, and *The Hell of Oden* was a watershed moment in the history of on-screen sexuality in Japanese cinema.[47]

During this period Suzuki wound up under contract to Shinkō, the studio that would become the home of Japanese *kaiki* production in the years leading up to the Second World War. Shimura Miyoko suggests that Suzuki—already at the unforgivably old age of 32 in 1936—was finding it increasingly difficult to continuing banking on her reputation as a sexy vamp. When Shinkō decided to make the first all-talkie *bakeneko* picture, *The Legend of the Saga Ghost Cat* (*Saga kaibyō-den*), for release in early 1937, the fading sex symbol was offered the chance to reprise her monstrous Beauty-to-Beast performances from the previous decade, and the resulting popularity of Suzuki's performances as a monster in the late 1930s depended upon audience's memories of the former vamp's initial stardom in the late 1920s.[48] Considering *Saga Ghost Cat* and Suzuki's later *bakeneko* films incorporated elements like the *tachimawari* fight scenes for which the actress previously had been renowned, this was undoubtedly the case. That her marketability as a sex symbol was on the wane seems unlikely, however, given that only a year prior she had stripped to the waist for Shinkō in *The Hell of Oden*, causing a sensation that suggests her sex appeal was still very much alive. Neither was casting Suzuki in the role of the monster a novel consequence of her advancing age, as the spectacle of Suzuki's monstrous transformations was clearly already happening concurrently with the height of her popularity as a sexy vamp in the late 1920s, when she appeared in multiple productions of *The Ghost Story of Yotsuya*. Seen in this light, Suzuki's subsequent fame as the "ghost cat actress" becomes the inevitable culmination of the marriage between the sexual vamp and the horrific monsters of Japanese *kaiki* cinema. Nonetheless, Suzuki herself initially resisted the decision as a potentially unflattering development in

---

[47] Hasebe, *"Shihan" Kawai, Daito eiga* 2, 17.
[48] Shimura, "Shinkō Kinema no kaibyō eiga," 54–5.

her career, agreeing to role only after studio boss Nagata Masaichi promised to pay her a bonus for the gig.[49]

The Daitō studio had actually beaten Shinkō to the punch with their own version of *The Saga Ghost Cat* (*Kaibyō Saga no yosaku*) in 1936, which received a rare favorable review from *Kinema junpō* for a domestic *kaiki* picture.[50] Shinkō's *Legend of the Saga Ghost Cat*, meanwhile, received a chilly critical reception, with *Kinema junpō* succinctly condemning the picture as "a *kaiki* film that's not the least bit scary."[51] But if Shinkō's version lacked the "successful *kaiki* atmosphere" of Daitō's earlier effort,[52] it possessed a far more lucrative asset in the star figure of Suzuki Sumiko. Daitō's film failed to ignite the renewed interest in the genre that Shinkō and Suzuki's version created, which led to a *kaiki* boom among the minor studios that would see almost forty films produced between 1937 and 1940.

Seeking to replicate Shinkō's formula, Daitō and other competing B-studios like Zenkatsu began casting star actresses like Miki Teruko and Miyagawa Toshiko as ghost cats. Shinkō even tried to create their own second *bakeneko* star in the person of Yamada Isuzu, who finally refused to accept the role.[53] And despite being branded the "ghost cat actress," Suzuki, along with the other leading ladies of the small studios, also began appearing once again as Oiwa and other vengeful spirits from the famous ghost stories of the Edo period. Shōchiku even got partially back into the *kaiki* act with their own star actress Tanaka Kinuyo, in that most genteel of the great *kaidan* tales, *The Dish Mansion of Banchō*, in 1937.[54] At the center of it all was Suzuki, whose continued portrayals of *bakeneko* in Shinkō productions like *The Cat of Arima* (*Arima neko*, 1937), *The Ghost Cat in the Red Wall* (*Kaibyō akakabe Daimyōjin*, 1938), and *The Yellow Rose Cat* (*Yamabuki neko*, 1940) cemented her place as Japan's first bona fide *kaiki* superstar, as synonymous with playing movie monsters as Bela Lugosi and Boris Karloff. That her *kaiki* films were almost universally trashed by the critics seems to have had little effect on their popularity with audiences. Perhaps even more so than the films of the previous decade, the Japanese *kaiki* boom of the late 1930s was a star-driven phenomenon.

---

[49] Tanaka Jun'ichirō, *Nagata Masaichi* (Tokyo: Jiji Press, 1962), 75.
[50] *Kinema junpō*, February 1, 1936, 149. Quoted in Shimura, "Shinkō kinema no kaibyō eiga," 52.
[51] *Kinema junpō*, February 21, 1937, 118.
[52] Shimura, "Shinkō kinema no kaibyō eiga," 52.
[53] See Daisuke Miyao, "A Ghost Cat, a Star and Two Intertexts: A Historical Analysis of *a Cat, Shozo, and Two Women* (1956)," *Journal of Japanese and Korean Cinema* 8, no. 2 (2016): 89–103.
[54] The majority of this film survives, although incomplete. Okiku's ghost does not appear in any of the extant footage.

Hollywood Horror and Sound-Era *Kaiki* Cinema

The 1930s brought other important developments in the ongoing emergence of the *kaiki* genre, not the least of which was the advent of Hollywood horror. Miriam Hansen's theory of the vernacular modernism of classical cinema puts forward the argument that Hollywood in the 1930s was globally successful "not because of its presumably universal narrative form but because it meant different things to different people and publics, both at home and abroad," and that American film genres were "dissolved and assimilated into different generic traditions, different concepts of genre."[55] Applying this approach to Japanese *kaiki* film, we see that—with the introduction of Hollywood's Universal monster movies—the *kaidan* adaptations were now understood to be native manifestations of a larger, transnational genre of film, and Hollywood's impact can be seen in both the content and reception of late-1930s domestic *kaiki* cinema.

Ironically, it was a lull in the domestic production of *kaidan* pictures that precipitated the final coalescence of the *kaiki* genre. After enjoying a boom prompted by the showcasing of the vamp actresses and their monstrous transformations, which saw three competing versions of *The Ghost Story of Yotsuya* produced in 1927 and three more in 1928 (along with other usual suspects like *The Peony Lantern*, ghost cat pictures, and Yoshino's *Fox and Tanuki*), production severely declined in the early 1930s. Izumi Toshiyuki suggests several reasons for the sudden dearth of films that had been perennially popular, including the onset of the Great Depression and the beginnings of national militarization with the Manchurian Incident of 1931, though the most immediate cause was certainly the burning down of Teikine's Kyoto studio in September 1930, which had been one of the main producers of *kaidan* films.[56] What little remained of Teikine would be folded into the newly formed Shinkō Kyoto studio the following year. Secretly funded by Shōchiku capital, Shinkō would ultimately come to be the prewar studio most closely linked with the *kaiki* genre in the public eye. The studio's formative years, however, were plagued by violent strikes and walkouts, and it would not be until the latter half of the decade before Shinkō would find its *kaiki* voice.

Fortunately for Japanese fans of ghosts and monsters, this domestic dry patch corresponded exactly with the coming of the Hollywood horror movie,

---

[55] Miriam Bratu Hansen, "The Mass Production of the Senses: Classical Cinema as Vernacular Modernism," in *Reinventing Film Studies*, ed. Christine Gledhill and Linda Williams (New York: Oxford University Press, 2000), 341.
[56] Izumi, *Ginmaku no hyakkai*, 111.

set off by the worldwide successes of Universal's *Dracula* and *Frankenstein* in 1931–2 and prompting a plethora of similar productions from the studio, as well as from rivals Paramount and Metro-Goldwyn-Mayer. The Universal pictures in particular were very well received in Japan, and Izumi's conjecture that the newly minted American horror movie genre sated the Japanese filmgoer's taste for *kaidan* during this period is borne out by the *Kinema junpō* review of *Frankenstein* quoted in the previous chapter, which explicitly compares the work to a *kaidan* and predicts the film will be a hit with Japanese audiences.[57] As a generic label, however, *kaidan* was evidentially too inextricably linked to a discourse of Edo culture to be applied to foreign films, however appropriate the comparison may have seemed to some critics.

Another word was needed. In 1914 Shigeno Yukiyashi introduced the phrase *kikai naru eiga*, which by the late 1920s had become standardized as *kaiki eiga*. *Kaiki*, a more general term for a certain atmosphere than an established, native category of literature like *kaidan*, was now applied to prototypical horror movies from abroad like *The Cat and the Canary*. Although the term *kaiki eiga* predates the coinage of the term "horror movie" in English, it is not until the proliferation of Hollywood horror films in Japan during the first half of the 1930s that *kaiki* becomes more ubiquitous as a generic label. Film scholar Ōsawa Jō has even suggested that, until the coincident critical and commercial success in Japan of Hammer Films' color remakes of *Frankenstein* and *Dracula* alongside Shintōhō's color *kaidan* pictures in the late 1950s, the term *kaiki* was only applied to foreign horror films.[58] While it is true that up through the 1950s Japanese films like *The Ghost Story of Yotsuya* and the ghost cat pictures were most commonly called *kaidan*, *kaibyō*, or *obake eiga*, advertising and reviews from the late 1930s discussed in the previous chapter clearly show that all three terms were by this point understood to be subgenres of *kaiki*. Hollywood horror in this period was not received as a generically distinct, alien form of filmmaking, but conceptually repositioned in a local context.

In light of this embracing of the nascent Hollywood horror films as kith and kin to domestic ghost story adaptations, it is not at all surprising that they would come to impact the public's perception of domestic *kaiki* pictures. American horror seems to have increased a demand among critics and audiences that domestic *kaiki* films be even more frightening than the vamps had previously

---

[57] Izumi proposes the taste for *kaidan eiga* in the early 1930s was satisfied by Universal horror movies in *Ginmaku no hyakkai*, 112.
[58] Ōsawa Jō, "Shintōhō no obake eiga to *Tōkaidō Yotsuya kaidan*: jyanru no fukkatsu to kakushin," in *Kaiki to gensō e no kairō*, 78.

been able to affect via their grotesque transformations. When production of *kaidan* adaptations finally resumes in earnest from about 1936 onward, one begins to notice for the first time what would remain a common refrain among critics well into the postwar years—that Japanese *kaiki* films "weren't the least bit scary" (*kowaku mo nai kaiki eiga*) compared to their American counterparts.

That the films were not frightening enough was only one of many complaints levied at domestic *kaiki* films in the 1930s. Sea changes in the Japanese film industry such as the advent of sound made the low-budget genre pictures made at places like Shinkō look all the more backward in the eyes of the critics. Talkies had finally become the norm at the major studios by 1936, but the smaller studios like Shinkō, Kyokutō, and Daitō were still making "part talkies" with limited sound sequences as late as 1939.[59] Contentwise, too, there was little hope of successfully competing with Shōchiku's and Tōhō's big-budget *gendaigeki* productions, which were being directed by avid students of foreign cinema like Ushihara Kiyohiko. Instead, small-studio heads like Shinkō's Nagata Masaichi turned to the perennially popular yet critically unfashionable *jidaigeki* genres—specifically ninja pictures, tanuki fantasies, and, of course, *kaiki* films—something critics saw as perpetuating the outdated Onoe Matsunosuke *kyūha* traditions. These were certainly more cinematic efforts than the old "canned theater" films of the early Taishō era.[60] As Yoshino's *Fox and Tanuki* demonstrates, it was not that the B-studio *jidaigeki* failed to adopt more sophisticated filmmaking techniques like the close-up and parallel editing. If the films were derided for being throwbacks to the Onoe era, it had more to do with their thematic content—and, ironically enough, the presence of trick effects, which by the late 1930s had long lost all the novelty that once earned them the praise of the Pure Film Movement critics and were now viewed as something that would only amuse the small children in the audience. An article from the February 1939 edition of *Eiga hyōron* sums up the general critical hostility to *jidaigeki*:

> If [*jidaigeki*] are low-class affairs, it's because they don't give a damn about human psychology and are only about violence and cutting down people. On top of that, there are ninja tricks to divert the kiddies; even ghost cats show up. Things like this are, in a word, utterly unnecessary.[61]

---

[59] Shimura, "Shinkō kinema no kaibyō eiga," 52.

[60] Daisuke Miyao considers the change in terminology for period pictures from *kyūgeki* to *jidaigeki* in the early 1920s as indicative of fundamental changes in formal technique, noting that *jidaigeki* of the 1920s were often considered more sophisticated in their technique than *gendaigeki*, though clearly by the end of the 1930s this attitude seems to have changed. See Daisuke Miyao, *The Aesthetics of Shadow: Lighting and Japanese Cinema* (Durham, NC: Duke University Press, 2013), 68–9.

[61] "Jidai eiga ni nozomu," *Eiga hyōron*, February 1, 1939, 35.

Other criticism from the era complains that period pictures lacked the relevancy of contemporarily set films and totally missed the point of cinema as an art form at the forefront of modernity.[62] It would be fairer to say the *jidaigeki* of the small studios were quite simply B-grade genre pictures, following proven conventions and formulas, turned out quickly for a fast profit and with no aspirations of competing artistically with the majors. Still, it would be remiss to suggest that the filmmakers responsible for these pictures were incapable or unwilling to innovate when the opportunity arose. Looking at the few surviving domestic *kaiki* films from this period, one sees not simply a retread of the old familiar material but an emerging mode of *kaiki* filmmaking that begins to incorporate a more cosmopolitan style, conscious of its *kaiki* cousins from Hollywood and laying much of the foundation for the truly groundbreaking *kaiki* films the Shintōhō studio would produce in the postwar era.

Michael Raine has called the 1930s a time of great "transcultural mimesis" in Japanese cinema, when the omnipresent popularity of Hollywood film resulted in parodic borrowings and reworkings of American cinema in Japanese contexts, most obviously in films with titles like *King Kong: Made in Japan* (*Wasei Kingu Kongu*, 1933). Rather than dismiss the phenomenon as "naïve copying," Raine suggests that transcultural mimesis partly entailed an "Aristotlian sense of learning by imitation" and that the practice

> aimed, simultaneously, at *re-creating* Hollywood film in Japan, *parodying* the absurdities of American cinema (eg., heterosexual romance, strong female characters) and even *learning* from the gap between Japanese and American cinema something of the invisible but nonetheless real "geopolitical incline" between Japan and the United States.[63]

Japanese critics (and presumably audiences) lauded such pictures for their ability to approximate and recontextualize familiar Hollywood product, for example calling Shimazu Yasujiro's *First Steps Ashore* (*Joriku daiippo*, 1932) a "splendid imitation" of Sternberg's *Docks of New York* (1928).[64] The practice extended to horror films as well, as evidenced by pictures like *The Avenging Corpse* (*Fukushū suru shigai*, 1937), the no-longer extant "Boris Karloff-style *kyōfu* film" that, judging from surviving synopses, was a scene-for-scene remake of the 1936 Karloff vehicle *The Walking Dead*.

---

[62] Shimura, "Shinkō kinema no kaibyō eiga," 57.
[63] Michael Raine, "Adaptation as 'Transcultural Mimesis' in Japanese Cinema," in *The Oxford Handbook of Japanese Cinema*, ed. Daisuke Miyao (New York: Oxford University Press, 2014), 115.
[64] Ibid., 114.

However, while something like *The Avenging Corpse* lays bare Japan's position on the "geopolitical incline" vis-à-vis the United States, the Japanese reviews of *Dracula* and *Frankenstein* quoted previously suggest a more complex relationship with American popular cinema, one in which the local takes a preeminent position over the global. *First Steps Ashore* appealed to Japanese filmgoers in its approximation of Hollywood themes and motifs, but *Frankenstein*'s most admirable quality was its approximation (however unintentional) of a traditional Japanese narrative form—the *kaidan*. Hollywood's gothic horror pictures, which in the early 1930s were only just beginning to coalesce into a recognized genre, found themselves subsumed into the already established *kaiki* genre in Japan. By the latter half of the decade, their influence on venerable *kaiki* institutions like *The Ghost Story of Yotsuya* and the ghost cat pictures was clearly present, yet less overtly mimetic. For if *kaidan* adaptations were an integral part of the *kaiki* genre, they also belonged inextricably to the *jidaigeki* megagenre of period films with their own native filmmaking traditions, many of which originated in the performative and spectacular aspects of the kabuki theater.

Recalling their old affinities with the ninja trick films of previous decades, the last great prewar flowering of Japanese *kaiki* cinema grew directly out of a series of ninja pictures Nagata Masaichi put into production at Shinkō upon taking over the studio in 1936. The studio's first ghost cat picture, *Legend of the Saga Ghost Cat*, was originally intended to be the third part of a trilogy of ninja films, following the previous year's *Ninja of Osaka Castle* (*Ninjutsu Osaka-jō*) and *Jiraiya: The Stormcloud Scroll and the Transformation Scroll* (*Jiraiya: yōun no maki/hengen no maki*). The filmmakers originally planned to incorporate the famous "Ghost Cat of Nabeshima" legend into a genre hybrid ninja/*bakeneko* picture. One of the studio's production managers, coincidentally a descendent of the Saga family that features prominently in the legend, decided a ghost cat was entertainment enough in itself, and the project became a straightforward *bakeneko* picture.[65] Suzuki Sumiko, an old hand at portraying ghosts and goblins and fresh off her sensational nude appearance as Takahashi Oden, naturally was cast at the title monster. Directing duties were entrusted to the newly signed Mokudō Shigeru, a former actor and protégé of Mizoguchi Kenji. *Legend of the Saga Ghost Cat* was Mokudō's first directorial effort in four years, and the film's

---

[65] Shimura cites an article from the newspaper *Miyako shimbun* that contains this anecdote. See "Shinkō kinema no kaibyō eiga," 52.

popular success ensured that he would spend the remainder of his career at Shinkō as the studio's go-to director for *kaiki* projects. Likewise, Suzuki found herself labeled as the "ghost cat actress" from this point forward. As mentioned previously, the now-lost film was drubbed by critics but scored a hit with audiences that launched the late-1930s *kaiki* boom among the minor studios and minted Suzuki as the "ghost cat actress."

To Suzuki's credit, *Junpō* blames the failure of *Legend of the Saga Ghost Cat* to be properly frightening not on the actress's performance, but on the fact that the title monster only appears in the penultimate scene of the film. This is typical of the plot structure for many traditional *kaidan* narratives, wherein the monster does not appear until the third act to visit karmic vengeance upon the human villains of the piece. Critics in the late Taishō and early Shōwa years, it will be recalled, found the 1924 adaptation of the traditional *kaidan* narrative *The Ghost Story of Kasane's Swamp* starring Matsueda Tsuruko more than adequately frightening, and one can assume that it followed the typical pattern of withholding its monster until the final act. But after several years of being fed a steady diet of Universal horror movies in which the monster appears early in the film and remains the central focus of the plot, Japanese film critics repeatedly fault domestic *kaiki* films like *Saga Ghost Cat* and *The Cat of Arima* for not featuring enough monster and—in effect—not being frightening enough.[66]

The reviewers generally fail to acknowledge that the cause of this lies primarily in the Edo-period source material, necessitating that any reasonably faithful adaptation of *kaidan* narratives will be structurally quite different from a Hollywood horror movie. On the other hand, the films were by this time being quite consciously marketed by the studios as part of the same *kaiki* genre that included *Dracula*, *Frankenstein*, and *The Mummy*. When the monsters do finally show up, the growing influence of Hollywood can be seen in their presentation, but even then these scenes owe as much to the *chambara* (swordplay) aesthetic of the ninja films, especially in their retention of Suzuki's signature *tachimawari* fight scenes. In the following section I examine the surviving Suzuki Sumiko *kaiki* films and the ways in which they constitute a meeting of domestic and foreign traditions of the strange and horrific in Japanese cinema.

---

[66] *Junpō* critic Murakami Tadahisa's review of *The Cat of Arima* echoes his complaint levied against *The Legend of the Saga Ghost Cat*. See "Arima neko," *Kinema junpō*, January 13, 1938, 274.

Three Case Studies: *The Cat of Arima*, *The Ghost Story of the Mandarin Duck Curtain*, and *The Ghost Cat and The Mysterious Shamisen*

Three surviving films from the late-1930s heyday of Japanese *kaiki* pictures demonstrate the continuing place of prominence held by the conventions of *chambara* alongside motifs inherited from stage productions of *kaidan*, as well as the ways they share the screen with moments influenced by Hollywood horror in an emerging transnational style of *kaiki* cinema. Unlike previous decades, we have multiple surviving specimens from this era to examine, although what exists today constitutes only a fraction of the substantial *kaiki* output from the Japanese studios between 1936 and 1940, after which the government Film Act of 1939 stamped out *kaiki* film production and mobilized the studios for the total war effort. Shinkō alone made at least thirteen *kaiki* pictures during this period, and records indicate the total domestic *kaiki* output from all the studios topped forty productions in less than four years.

Three Japanese *kaiki* films from this period survive almost in their entirety, and they are all Shinkō efforts: 1937's *The Cat of Arima* (*Arima neko*) and two pictures from 1938, *The Ghost Story of the Mandarin Duck Curtain* (*Kaidan oshidori chō*) and *The Ghost Cat and the Mysterious Shamisen* (*Kaibyō nazo no shamisen*). That each is an "all-talkie" (*āru tōkii*) shows that while the genre was generally held in critical contempt, these were prestige pictures for the B-studio. All three star Suzuki Sumiko, and both *Arima* and *Mandarin Duck Curtain* were directed by Mokudō Shigeru, who by the end of 1938 was the most prolific director of *kaiki* films in the country. The combination of Suzuki and Mokudō makes it reasonable to assume we have here two representative examples of the genre to examine. The third film, *Mysterious Shamisen*, was overseen by the acclaimed former Shōchiku director Ushihara Kiyohiko, who was undoubtedly given the project by Shinkō in an effort to elevate the artistic standing of their stock-in-trade, B-grade *kaiki* pictures.

Ushihara's film contains several stylistic flourishes and departures from Mokudō's work, providing a useful counterpoint for determining the breadth of formal and thematic material domestic *kaiki* cinema allowed. But even Ushihara's more experimental genre piece—which unlike Mokudō's films is not based on a classic ghost story—adheres to a rather conventional revenge narrative arc typical not only of *kaidan* but many non-*kaiki jidaigeki* as well. The problem of the monster's presence is not the crux around which the plot turns, as in a Universal horror movie. In all three pictures, the monster is an avenging agent injected into the narrative to exact retribution upon the villains for the murder of the heroine, its monstrous status almost incidental to the main story. While it is the literal ghost of the main protagonist in *Mandarin Duck Curtain*, the other two films utilize a *bakeneko* cat spirit acting on the victim's behalf. In both *Mandarin Duck Curtain* and *Mysterious Shamisen*, the monster assumes a supporting function in the final act of revenge, which is ultimately achieved by the victim's still-living younger sister, further marginalizing the monster from the centrality of the narrative. *The Cat of Arima* allows its monster to carry out the actual act of punishment itself, but of the three films withholds its appearance the longest, only revealing the ghost cat in the final climatic moments and with virtually no prior foreshadowing that a *kaiki* conclusion is in store to what is otherwise a pretty mundane *jidaigeki* tale. Although the narrative structures of these three films stand in contrast to the more monster-centric Hollywood horror films, stylistically they constitute a blend of Japanese and Western approaches to cinematic depictions of *kaiki*.

The Cat of Arima

Arima's climatic confrontation, during which the ghost cat uses her marvelous powers to battle a small army of armed maidens single-handedly, demonstrates obvious affinities with the *chambara* swordplay pictures, which feature an extraordinarily masterful (yet human) swordsman who can take on a multitude of opponents at once. To many contemporary viewers these spectacular action set pieces may seem more akin to films like the *Zatoichi* series than anything we would be inclined to associate with horror, but the *tachimawari* fight scenes grew out of the obligatory onstage battles between ghost cats and samurai heroes that were a mainstay of the kabuki theater while simultaneously harkening back to the cinematic *tachimawari* Suzuki Sumiko performed in her early vamp roles. The climax of *The Cat of Arima* represents a stellar specimen of *tachimawari*. Throughout most of the picture's runtime Suzuki appears as the human maid Onaka, whose mistress, Otake, is bullied into committing suicide by the wicked matron of Arima Palace. When the loyal Onaka tries and fails to avenge her mistress herself, Otake's pet cat assumes the form of Onaka and massacres the matron along with the complicit harem of Arima.

Although director Mokudō Shigeru arms his star actress with only her *bakeneko* cat claws, he stages Suzuki's fight with the maidens in a manner that emphasizes her ability to engage her opponents in a physical, concrete fashion,

Figure 9 Suzuki Sumiko surrounded by a bevy of armed maidens in *The Cat of Arima* (*Arima neko*, 1937).

much like the human vamp antiheroines Suzuki first rose to fame portraying in the 1920s (Figure 9). Mokudō places Suzuki in the center of the frame, surrounding her with her adversaries and undercranking the camera to film the fight at high speed, a convention of prewar swordplay pictures. The sequence employs other trick photography effects typical of *kaiki* films, but emphasis remains on creating a spectacle of action and excitement over a sense of horror. A brief shot of Suzuki crawling upside down on the ceiling, achieved by flipping the camera, might evoke a sense of otherworldly horror in a different context, but by placing the shot amid the chaos of the ghost cat's battle against the maidens, it instead adds to the thrilling excitement of the *tachimawari* fight, a flourish akin to Errol Flynn swinging from a rope during a swordfight aboard a pirate ship (Suzuki, incidentally, also swings from a rope during the sequence). There are no double-exposure shots of Suzuki fading in and out of the frame, and no stopping the camera to have her instantly traverse the space of the shot in a more ethereal, ghostly fashion. *The Cat of Arima*'s most impressive expression of the *bakeneko*'s superhuman ability involves no trick photography at all beyond undercranking the camera to accelerate the pace of a single long take in which the monster rapidly ascends a series of winding staircases, all the while fighting off her pursuers. This sequence would not be at all out of place in a non-*kaiki*, action *chambara* film, and overall seems aimed at instilling a sense of heart-pounding excitement in the audience more so than bloodcurdling dread.

Yet the thrilling spectacle of the *tachimawari* remains thoroughly entwined with the chilling spectacle of Suzuki's monstrous transformation. The Japanese vamps' sexual allure was founded largely upon their ability to perform the *tachimawari*, and the climactic battle of *The Cat of Arima* becomes an uncanny encore performance by the acknowledged queen of the martial vamps, her former figurative monstrosity now rendered literal in the persona of the *bakeneko*. Shimura concludes that the Shinkō's studio's success with the ghost cat pictures rested upon "a return to the primordial appeal of the extraordinary Suzuki Sumiko's use of *chambara* and *ninjitsu*," a marriage of *tachimawari* "with the enjoyable elements of fear and surprise in the process of the *bakeneko* actress's transformation."[67]

Mokudō does include a few fleeting shots that take a break from the otherwise relentless *chambara* action and speak to an emerging *kaiki* aesthetic at least partially informed by Hollywood horror (and its roots in German Expressionism). An effectively creepy shot of Suzuki as the ghost cat emerging from the shadows and walking slowly, straight on toward the camera recalls similar shots of actor Max Schreck as the vampire Count Orlock in *Nosferatu*. A more complex sort of *kaiki* cosmopolitanism can be seen in *Arima*'s obligatory *neko jarashi* ("cat toying") scene, a holdover from the kabuki stage in which acrobats performing as the ghost cat and their human victim(s) would leap about the stage in a pantomime of a cat toying with a mouse. In the postwar Daiei ghost cat films of the 1950s the protracted *neko jarashi* becomes an explicitly marked-off moment of spectacle, with acrobatic stunts that increased in length and complexity from film to film, and traditional kabuki musical accompaniment that breaks sharply with the otherwise Western orchestral scores. In the postwar years critics singled them out as detracting from the sense of fear found in a more ideal *kaiki* picture, but the conclusion of *The Cat of Arima*'s *neko jarashi*, in which Suzuki hypnotically compels her victim into complacency before sinking her teeth into her neck in vampiric fashion, represents the single most chilling moment of the film.

A casual observer at first glance might take this as nothing more than an homage to Bela Lugosi's Count Dracula. Suzuki stalks silently straight toward

---

[67] Shimura, "Shinkō Kinema no kaibyō eiga," 58–9.

the audience, her victim rendered stunned and helpless by her wide, unblinking, piercing stare. One cannot help but note the parallels with Lugosi's hypnotic count. Writing in 1993 about his impressions of *The Cat of Arima*, film historian Satō Tadao could just as easily be describing Lugosi's performance in *Dracula* when he recalls being impressed by the image of "Suzuki Sumiko's ubiquitously piercing, seductive look in her eyes that followed you everywhere … lunging at her prey and chewing at their necks like a vampire."[68]

But the moment is neither a mere pastiche nor a thoughtless grafting of the Hollywood vampire motif onto the Japanese *bakeneko* tale. The notion of the *bakeneko* "going for the jugular" predates the introduction of the suave Victorian vampire to Japan, as evidenced by nineteenth-century illustrations that depict the monster not as the humanoid costumed performers of the kabuki stage, but as the fearsome, giant cat creature of legend, gripping its victim by the throat in its jaws in the manner of a vicious beast. Suzuki's demurer, vampiric attack to her victim's neck represents a blending of traditional and modern *kaiki* visual iconography in the synergy of popular cinema. The neck-biting scene in *The Cat of Arima* thereby invokes Lugosi's Dracula not only as an acknowledgment of generic affinity between Universal monster movies and Japanese *kaiki* film but also as a way of conveying an element of traditional ghost cat depictions in the terms of modern cinema. Moreover, Suzuki does not simply ape Lugosi but uses an established asset of her star persona for a horrific effect suggested by her male American counterpart. The striking eyes of Suzuki's ghost cat simultaneously recalled Lugosi's piercing stares in *Dracula* while also being long associated with Suzuki herself (Figure 10). Her wide-eyed, hypnotic gaze was a well-known feature of the actress from her days as a sexy vamp. Satō describes them as *adappoi* or "coquettish,"[69] and Shimura Miyoko notes that, even under the monstrous feline makeup, Suzuki's femininity shines through in her eyes, recalling her earlier vamp and *anego* ("big-sis") roles in non-*kaiki* productions.[70]

In truth, the amount of makeup Suzuki wears in *The Cat of Arima* is minimal compared to the much more elaborate makeup her successor Irie Takako would don in the Daiei studio's *bakeneko* films of the 1950s, or—judging from surviving advertising materials and critical reviews—what Suzuki herself wore in her various portrayals of Oiwa's ghost. Suzuki instead sells the

---

[68] Satō Tadao, Sumigawa Naoki, and Marubi Sadamu, ed., *Shinkō kinema: senzen goraku eiga no ōkoku* (Tokyo: Firumuātosha, 1993), 126.
[69] Ibid.
[70] Shimura, "Shinkō kinema no kaibyō eiga," 55.

Figure 10 Left: Bela Lugosi in *Dracula* (1931). Right: Suzuki Sumiko in *The Cat of Arima*. Courtesy of the National Film Archive of Japan.

performance primarily with her expressions and mannerisms, mewling with a trickle of blood from her lips and sporting disheveled, unkempt hair. *The Cat of Arima* being the oldest extant example of a *bakeneko* film, it is hard to say if this represents a significant departure from earlier cinematic portrayals. Yet whether the monstrous transformation was effected primarily via makeup or by the performance of the actress, it is still in the body of the female star that the main site of spectacle lies in domestic *kaiki* films of the late 1930s. That Suzuki became known as the "*bakeneko* actress" instead of the "*bakemono* (monster) actress" suggests, however, that there was something more memorable about her performances in pictures like *The Cat of Arima* for audiences than, for example, her more makeup-heavy appearances as the ghost of Oiwa. Speaking of Suzuki's ghost cat performances, Satō Tadao echoes Shimura Miyoko's observations about the vamp actresses being "complex symbols of eroticism" when he says,

> Of course, the performance of [Suzuki] taking on the form of a cat may be thought of as frightening to the point of inducing shivers, but at the same time, wrapped up in that fear is an intense element of eroticism which is also important. For youngsters of the time, we could say the fear of eroticism was driven home most intensely by Suzuki Sumiko's ghost cat.[71]

In the more restrained makeup of the ghost cat, Suzuki retains her feminine beauty even as she performs the horrific acts of the beast, giving these performances in particular an uncanny quality very similar to the same beautiful-yet-dangerous appeal of the vamp.

---

[71] Satō et al., *Shinkō kinema*, 125.

The Ghost Story of the Mandarin Duck Curtain

Suzuki's makeup is similarly restrained in 1938's *Ghost Story of the Mandarin Duck Curtain*, in which she portrays a facially scarred vengeful wraith in the Oiwa mold. Unlike *The Cat of Arima*, this time Suzuki plays the suffering heroine herself. Having witnessed in childhood her mother's murder at the hands of yet another wicked matron (a stock figure of *kaidan* revenge narratives), as an adult Suzuki falls victim to the same woman's evil machinations while searching for her missing younger sister, whom the matron had raised as her own. Suzuki's discovery of this fact results first in having her face slashed with a needle, and then finally her murder at the hands of the matron and her attendants, who attack her while wearing various bestial Noh masks. Suzuki's ghost then appears to her younger sister, asking to be avenged and leaving behind the *hannya* female demon costume the matron wore during the murder. The matron is then tormented by both Suzuki's ghost and the still-living younger sister who, wearing the *hannya* mask, avenges Suzuki's death by killing the matron and her attendants.

Directed by Mokudō Shigeru, *Mandarin Duck Curtain* continued the duo's trend of poor critical reception. Utterly forgotten today, the film's depiction of multiple murders offended critics of the time, who called the film "excessively sadistic, and too much to swallow as simple entertainment. It's hard to call the mass murder of women entertaining."[72] Ethical viewing matters aside, *Mandarin Duck Curtain* showcases several accomplished *kaiki* sequences that anticipate the work of Nakagawa Nobuo at Shintōhō in the latter 1950s, which would be acclaimed by critics for its masterful conveyance of *kaiki* atmosphere. *Mandarin Duck Curtain* proves that Mokudō and Suzuki's work deserves at least some of the credit attributed to Nakagawa for establishing the idealized aesthetic of Japanese *kaiki* films.

Suzuki's facially disfigured ghost has obvious affinities with *Yotsuya*'s Oiwa and *Kasane*'s Orui, but unlike Suzuki's multiple appearances as Oiwa's ghost, here Mokudō keeps her makeup to a minimum, allowing the actress to retain her feminine beauty even after her "monstrous" transformation. The truly grotesque Oiwa represents an obvious externalization of the vengeance-consumed monster into which the virtuous woman becomes, but Mokudō conveys the transformation more subtly in *Mandarin Duck Curtain*. As her slight facial scar inexplicably swells and worsens, Suzuki sits in bed, wailing and

---

[72] *Kinema junpō*, April 12, 1938, 79.

clutching her face. Mokudō films these scenes in long shots that make use of low-key lighting and heavy shadows, much like the German Expressionist films and the Universal horror movies. When he finally brings the camera in closer, Suzuki turns so that the scarred side of her face cannot be seen. After delaying the reveal of Suzuki's disfigurement in such a manner over two nonconsecutive sequences, Mokudō finally gives the audience their first glimpse of Suzuki's entire face in a point-of-view shot of her reflection in a bowl of water, her own horrified reaction ideally mirroring the audience's own state. The fact that the scar itself is quite small compared to other vengeful ghosts like Oiwa and does not compromise Suzuki's natural beauty is irrelevant. The protracted, suspenseful buildup and the starkly terrified reactions of both Suzuki and the other characters to the unnatural disfigurement drive home the cosmic, karmic implications of a vengeful spirit in the making, lending the sequences a deeper sense of *osore* than a simpler reveal of more exaggerated makeup might provoke. Significantly, Nakagawa Nobuo would stage his own reveal of Oiwa's facial disfigurement in a very similar manner in 1959's *Ghost Story of Yotsuya*, which—unlike the derided and forgotten *Mandarin Duck Curtain*—was almost immediately hailed as a masterpiece of the *kaiki* genre.

These scenes also demonstrate another important element of an emerging transnational style of *kaiki* filmmaking in their use of sound. Complimenting the dark, shadowy shots of Suzuki wailing in bed are the sounds of a temple bell tolling in the distance over the wind howling ferociously. The sounds of a dark and stormy night were first introduced to the *kaiki* genre in the work of director James Whale in *Frankenstein* and *The Old Dark House* (1932), and as in those pictures, in *Mandarin Duck Curtain* they act as an otherworldly harbinger, giving voice to the notion that dangerous cosmic forces of *osore* are on the verge of being unleashed. The temple bell underscores a popular religious dynamic, as Suzuki's transformation into a vengeful spirit plays into Buddhist conceptions of both karmic retribution and the unchecked *shūnen* or rage that affects her spirit. Thus the sound of the bell belongs to the traditional world of Edo-period *kaidan*, even as it resonates with the modern transnational style of *kaiki*, where Western church bells also toll on dark and stormy nights to warn of ghouls and vampires. Of the few surviving talkie *kaiki* films made in Japan before the Second World War, only *Mandarin Duck Curtain* features such extensive use of sounds that would become horror movie clichés, although the Daiei ghost cat films made in the first half of the 1950s would make similar use of howling wind, driving rain, and crashing thunderstorm sound effects.

Mokudō continues to imply Suzuki's monstrous transformation via subtle means, having her hair become unkempt and disheveled (part of the iconography of vengeful wraiths and ghost cats) as a matter of course during her final struggle with the Noh mask murderers. Once Suzuki's character has been killed and the transformation is complete, the film still relies on low-key lighting and Expressionistic shadows to convey a sense of *kaiki* atmosphere around her spirit. Rather than have her ghost magically appear via a double-exposure effect, Mokudō merely underlights Suzuki during the scene in which her ghost visits her younger sister, lending a sense of creepy ambiguity as to whether she is truly dead, until she tells her sister that she is no longer of this world. The film does resort to the old double-exposure technique for the scenes in which Suzuki's ghost becomes a more invasive presence, haunting the wicked matron by appearing suddenly in her bedchamber.

Like *The Cat of Arima*, an action-heavy, *chambara*-style fight sequence concludes the picture, but with the younger sister taking on the physical action, Suzuki's character is freed up to become the locus of the film's expressions of *kaiki* in the climax. In the most striking moment of the film, the matron's cronies are disposing of the body of yet another of their mistress's victims, when suddenly they all drop the corpse in horror. Mokudō then cuts to an empty shot, into which Suzuki suddenly flies up from the bottom of the frame in an extreme close-up, from the position of the dropped corpse. This quite effective "startle" moment would become a hallmark of *kaiki* and horror moviemaking conventions, and the shot in *Mandarin Duck Curtain* may well be the first of its kind in the genre's history. Like the protracted reveal of Suzuki's facial scar, this shot would be echoed in Nakagawa's *Ghost Story of Yotsuya*, as would the film's increasingly rapid cutting during the climax. In her final moments the matron seems to be haunted by the film itself, as Mokudō employs a series of swift cuts depicting both Suzuki's ghost and the *hannya* mask now worn by the sister, who finally stabs the matron to death. While Nakagawa's later film would feature a more extreme and experimental montage, it has a clear antecedent in Mokudō's work on *Mandarin Duck Curtain*.

The Ghost Cat and the Mysterious Shamisen

Experimental cinematography is on even greater display in Ushihara's *Ghost Cat and the Mysterious Shamisen*, which employs a method of filming its monster unique in the history of the genre. Likely because of its director's reputation, more prints of this film survive than of Mokudō's work, and in 2011 it became only the second prewar Japanese *kaiki* film known to have screened outside of Japan, after Mizoguchi Kenji's now lost version of the *Kasane's Swamp* legend,

Passion of a Female Teacher (*Kyōren no onna shisō*), was favorably received in France in 1926.[73] While *Mysterious Shamisen* remains an obscure film little seen both in Japan and abroad, its comparatively high profile vis-à-vis the two more conventional surviving Mokudō films has the potential to result in a somewhat skewed perception in regard to domestic prewar *kaiki* cinema. Unsurprisingly, Ushihara demonstrates far less interest in the emerging generic conventions of *kaiki* cinema than Mokudō. The screenplay by Hata Kenji—who scripted several of Shinkō's *kaiki* films, including *The Cat of Arima* and *Mandarin Duck Curtain*—suggests some of the departures. Since the domestic *kaiki* boom got underway in early 1937 the various B-studios had by this time adapted most of the traditional ghost cat tales to the screen, and Hata crafted an original story for Ushihara's film. The *kaiki* elements appear much earlier in the film's runtime than in those based on Edo-period ghost stories, though they remain isolated segments in Hata's screen treatment, which adheres to a revenge arc narrative typical of both *kaiki* and non-*kaiki jidaigeki*.

This time out Suzuki appears in the role of the villainous kabuki actress Mitsue, deviating from the established pattern of casting her in the role of the sympathetic monster. After she murders the pet cat of her lover, Seijiro, as well as a young rival for his affections named Okiyo, her victims' two spirits become merged into a vaguely defined entity that alternately appears as a cat and as the ghost of her rival. The most significant appearance of this hybrid vengeful wraith/ghost cat occurs at the start of the second act, as the shamisen gifted to Okiyo by Seijiro passes through the hands of a variety of owners, all of whom are haunted by the ghost of Okiyo and/or the cat. Seeking a novel way of presenting his monster, Ushihara uses a kaleidoscope lens to alternately photograph the face of a stuffed cat and the face of actress Utagawa Kinue as Okiyo, creating a multifaceted image in which multiple visages swirl about the frame.

As a consequence of this technique, virtually all of the footage of the ghost results in surreal, hallucinogenic point-of-view shots from the perspective of the character currently being haunted by the spirit, which suggests a more ambiguous reading of the ghost as potentially existing only in the mind of the character. Ushihara resorts to filming his ghost in a more conventional manner in only one scene, itself a convention of the genre by this point, in which Okiyo's spirit visits her younger sister, reveals the identity of her murderer, and begs to

---

[73] Mizoguchi's film was praised at the time of its release by *Kinema junpō* for "brimming with passion and power that exquisitely captured the lives of the lower Edo classes," but appears to have downplayed the *kaiki* elements. Kawabe Jūji discusses Mizoguchi's film and its reception in *B-kyū kyoshōron: Nakagawa Nobuo kenkyū* (Tokyo: Shizukadō, 1983), 114, 123.

be avenged. Here the ghost can be seen cohabitating the same physical space of the scene as the human character, fading in via the familiar double-exposure technique. Although Okiyo's ghost imparts information it would be otherwise impossible for her sister to know, Ushihara pointedly concludes the scene by showing the sister rouse from sleep, implying the sequence was a dream and reinforcing the same ambiguity that his more experimental shots of the ghost create.

The kaleidoscope effect returns with some modification in the climax, when Okiyo's sister conspires with Mitsue's now-jilted lover Seijiro to murder her onstage during her farewell performance with the theater troupe to which she and Seijiro belong. Now it is the haunted who appears in the center of the swirling multitude of ghostly visages, as Suzuki appears surrounded by infinite manifestations of her victims (both feline and human). In a montage even swifter and more delirious than the one that concludes Mokudō's *Mandarin Duck Curtain*, Ushihara juxtaposes these shots with close-ups of the masked younger sister, disguised as a fellow performer portraying a monkey onstage and advancing upon Mitsue with dagger in hand, as well as with shots of Seijiro ever more intensely strumming the titular shamisen, which constitutes the sole musical accompaniment of the scene. As in the earlier scenes that employed the kaleidoscope effect, Ushihara never shows the ghost inhabiting the same physical space as the other characters, and the rapid montage adds to the impression that the ghost exists merely as a hallucination on the part of Suzuki's character (Figure 11).

All of this roots *Mysterious Shamisen* more firmly in what Tzvetan Todorov calls the "pure fantastic" mode of fiction typified by the work of Edgar Allan Poe, wherein the existence of supernatural forces remains thoroughly ambiguous, as opposed to the "pure marvelous" worlds more typical of Japanese *kaiki* films and exemplified in the late 1930s by the work of Mokudō, which presents the monsters' existence as a matter of fact. Pure fantastic narratives allow for a wholly psychological interpretation of *kaiki* phenomenon. The murderer in Poe's "The Tell-Tale Heart" may be haunted by nothing more than a guilty conscience, and Roderick Usher in "The Fall of the House of Usher" not cursed but merely insane. Likewise, the semiabstract kaleidoscope images of the ghost that swirl about Suzuki in the climax of *Mysterious Shamisen* lend themselves to being read as a manifestation of Mitsue's repressed guilt, or else an expression of the sister's and Seijiro's burning desire for revenge, as the shots are juxtaposed in montage with close-ups of their intense expressions while Seijiro strums the shamisen with mounting fervor.

Figure 11 Publicity still from *The Ghost Cat and the Mysterious Shamisen* (*Kaibyō nazo no shamisen*, 1938), which showcases Suzuki Sumiko as well as the kaleidoscope technique used to portray the ghost cat. Such a shot that combines the ghost and the human characters in this fashion does not appear in the actual film. Courtesy of the National Film Archive of Japan.

Since the Meiji Restoration this "pure fantastic" mode of *kaiki* had been the preferred model of many literary and social critics, conforming as it did to the Western ideal of the genre popularized by Poe (whose work was incredibly popular in Meiji Japan)[74] and allowing the audience to fancifully indulge in entertaining the possibility of supernatural forces while simultaneously disavowing an unquestioning belief in their existence. As mentioned at the beginning of this chapter, the Meiji government of the late nineteenth and early twentieth centuries was insistent in dissuading any "backwards" traditional belief in the supernatural, to the extent that classic, "pure marvelous" *kaidan* were revised to present their *kaiki* incidents as psychological allegory. San'yūtei Enchō's late Edo tale *Kasane's Swamp*—one of the most often filmed *kaidan*

---

[74] J. Scott Miller discussed Poe's popularity in Meiji Japan as part of his presentation "The Feline as Agent of Karmic Retribution: Poe's *Black Cat* in Japan," given at the annual conference of the American Comparative Literature Association held in Vancouver, Canada, March 31–April 3, 2011.

narratives—was republished in 1888 under the title *Shinkei Kasane ga fuchi* or "The Neurosis of Kasane's Swamp," complete with a new tongue-in-cheek preface by the author explaining that stories that presented the unambiguous existence of ghosts were out of fashion.[75] "Superstitious" thematic content had ceased to be a significant cause of alarm in political and intellectual corners by the end of the Meiji era, with figures such as anthropologist Yanagita Kunio and writer Izumi Kyōka arguing for the cultural legitimacy of traditional marvelous tales in their own work.[76] Yanagita and Kyōka having made it safe to tell the old stories in their original, pure marvelous modes under the mantle of cultural heritage, the movie versions that came in later decades most often reverted to a variation of Enchō's original title, *Kaidan Kasane ga fuchi*.[77] But Shinkō's *Mysterious Shamisen*, with its obvious attempts to raise the artistic pedigree of the *kaiki* genre in the hiring of Ushihara, the film's unique cinematography, and its atypically "pure fantastic" presentation of the material, reveals the lingering sentiment that such approaches carried more cultural sophistication.

That *Mysterious Shamisen* aspired to an even more narrative-driven evocation of karmic *osore* than the typical genre fare that Mokudō (and presumably other *kaiki* directors of the day) were turning out can also be seen in the fact that the film features no spectacle of monstrous transformation built around a star persona. Genre star Suzuki Sumiko of course still receives top billing, and Shinkō's marketing wing built the advertising campaign around her image, as they did for all of the *kaiki* films in which the "ghost cat actress" appeared. But here alone among Shinkō's *kaiki* films does Suzuki forego the role of the monster. The film instead engages in an alternative, more highbrow showcase of spectacle in its protracted scenes of Suzuki performing kabuki theater, recalling similar interludes of traditional theater that disrupt the narrative flow in Mizoguchi's works like *Osaka Elegy* (*Naniwa eregi*, 1936) and *Ugetsu* (1953). Stepping into the role of the monster usually occupied by Suzuki, Utagawa Kinue wears not even the restrained makeup her predecessor displays in *The Cat of Arima* or *Mandarin Duck Curtain*, and she undergoes no grotesque transformation on-screen. The ghost appears either as the cat or as Utagawa, but never as the categorically interstitial werecat of more typical ghost cat films, nor as the

---

[75] Figal, *Civilization and Monsters*, 27–8.
[76] Gerald Figal discusses Yanagita's and Izumi Kyōka's reappraisal of traditional marvelous narratives in Chapters 4 and 5 of *Civilization and Monsters*.
[77] Enchō first performed the tale in 1859 as an oral *rakugo* under the title *A Latter-Day Kaidan of Kasane's Swamp* (*Kasane ga fuchi gojitsu kaidan*).

repellently disfigured wraith in the Oiwa tradition. Its sense of *kaiki* derives mainly from the film's Todorovian fantastic hesitation, which allows for an interpretation of events as a manifestation of *osore* cosmic vengeance, even as it holds out a possible psychological interpretation of its unique *kaiki* imagery. Nakagawa Nobuo would perfect his own *kaiki* approach to filmmaking along similar lines twenty years later at Shintōhō, grounding his films more firmly in the traditional marvelous mode of *kaidan* while infusing the imagery with an allegorical level that made his monsters both literal and figurative symbols of fear and guilt.

The stigma that had built up around domestic *kaiki* cinema was perhaps insurmountable by this time, and the critics lamented that a talented director like Ushihara would stoop to make a ghost cat movie, regardless of the fact that here was a *bakeneko* film that did not feature Suzuki Sumiko running about performing *tachimawari* acrobatics in monster makeup.[78] The same year Shinkō put another of its critical darling directors, Mori Kazuo, to work on *The Ghost Cat and the Red Wall*, which restored Suzuki to the role of the ghost cat, but was nonetheless expected to raise the prestige of the genre in the same way it was hoped *Mysterious Shamisen* might have done. The film was reasonably better received than Ushihara's,[79] but forces external to the film industry insured this was not the beginning of a *kaiki* renaissance.

In 1939 Japan's increasingly fascist government instituted the Film Act (*Eigahō*), effectively drafting the studios into service of the propaganda machine. The film industry was now under the direct control of the Cabinet Propaganda Office (*Naikaku jōhōkyoku*), which instituted government censorship at the preproduction level and began rationing film stock.[80] *Kaiki* pictures, along with other pure entertainment genres like the ninja films with which their history was so entwined, while not outright banned, were effectively forced out of production. Films that were already in the pipeline still sneaked out. During the week of *Obon* in 1940 Suzuki Sumiko made her final appearance in a Shinkō *kaiki* film as the titular *Golden-Tailed Fox* (*Kinmō kitsune*), a role probably similar in many respects to her ghost cat performances, but once this last batch of *kaiki* pictures wrapped, the genre would vanish from Japanese cinema screens amid a decade of war and occupation.

---

[78] Shimura Miyoko, "Kōgeki no kōzō: *Kaibyō nazo no samisen*, *Kyatto piiporu* o megutte," *Eiga gaku* 16 (2002): 29.
[79] See the review in *Kinema junpō*, January 14, 1939, 82.
[80] Standish, *New History of Japanese Cinema*, 142–3.

Conclusion

Like the horror film genre in the West, *kaiki* did not emerge fully formed on cinema screens but gradually coalesced over the course of the silent and early sound eras. Ghosts, monsters, and other semantic markers of *kaiki* were present almost from the moment of Japanese cinema's inception, but the aesthetics of *osore* would only manifest after moves toward a more narratively integrated mode of cinema and the introduction of actresses. The female body became the vehicle through which visual spectacle and thematic terror were wed to create the genre of *kaiki eiga*.

The primordial domestic *kaiki* pictures of the early twentieth century had begun as trick films in the tradition of Georges Méliès, part of the "cinema of attractions" whose purpose was to dazzle and amaze early cinema audiences with the spectacle of special effects, not chill them to the bone in the manner of the Edo *kaidan* ghost stories from which they were frequently adapted. This initially earned them a modicum of respect among the reformers of the Pure Film Movement, who otherwise disdained works adapted from traditional theater for not making proper use of techniques specific to the medium. In the early 1920s, after the novelty of trick photography had worn off, the Japanese film industry began to universally embrace more so-called cinematic methods such as the close-up and the use of actresses in place of female impersonators. The predominantly female monsters of traditional ghost stories were now portrayed on-screen by women, and the site of spectacle shifted from the special effects themselves to the body of the star actress, around whom they effected a monstrous transformation from Beauty into Beast.

Popular screen vamps like Suzuki Sumiko, already Othered by their interstitial combination of feminine sex appeal and masculine physicality, found a literal expression of their fearsomeness in the on-screen mutation of the beautiful and virtuous heroine into grotesque, facially disfigured vengeful wraiths and half-human, half-feline ghost cats. Fear, too, returned to the equation, as reviewers began to talk about the frightening aspects of the actresses' performances (or else their failure to be effectively frightening), and as with their stage antecedents these *obake eiga* or "monster movies" began to be expected to scare audiences instead of merely dazzle them with trick photography.

In the 1930s, the critical and commercial popularity of Hollywood horror movies brought an even greater demand for pictures deemed truly frightening, as well as an awareness of Japan's own *obake* movies as existing within a global vernacular of popular genre filmmaking, the overarching label of which informally became *kaiki*. Japanese *kaiki* films produced in the mid- to late 1930s exhibit a partial assimilation of Hollywood horror style and techniques (themselves owing much in turn to German Expressionism), innovating ways to capture a sense of *kaiki* and *osore* on-screen. That said, many prewar domestic *kaiki* films continued to differ markedly from their Hollywood counterparts in the narrative structure inherited from the Edo *kaidan*, often withholding the appearance of the monster until the final act and assigning it a secondary role in the act of karmic retribution. This, combined with the *tachimawari* action swordplay sequences inherited from its *chambara* cinematic cousin, could render the film structurally and tonally more similar to a non-*kaiki jidaigeki* action picture than a Hollywood horror movie. When *kaiki* filmmaking resumed in earnest in the mid-1950s, the Shintōhō studio and director Nakagawa Nobuo would refine the genre along more uniformly horrific lines, bringing domestic *kaiki* cinema unprecedented critical acclaim and laying the groundwork for the eventual shift from *kaiki* to *horā*. This would only be possible, however, following a period of tremendous upheaval in the Japanese film industry as the nation struggled to forge a new identity in the aftermath of the Second World War.

3

The Dead Sleep Unwell: Wartime and Occupation Censorship and the Postwar Return of *Kaiki*

Ring screenwriter Takahashi Hiroshi compares the presentation of the monstrous in many early postwar *kaiki* films to the *obake yashiki* or "spook house" rides common at Japanese amusement parks. Echoing his colleague Kurosawa Kiyoshi's comments about the primacy of mood and atmosphere, Takahashi believes the ideal *kaiki* films "have a psychological sense of value to them. They're aesthetic things," but goes on to suggest the "spook house" mode of *kaiki* film lacks a true sense of terror:

> The way things like Oiwa are depicted in representative *kaidan* films like *The Ghost Story of Yotsuya*—ghosts with swollen faces, hanging from the ceiling and appearing with a surprise—is a traditionally Japanese thing. They're like carnival spook house gimmicks that pop out at you, but they've been around a long time, and are also in kabuki … Actually, they're not that frightening … What a lot of people call "scary" (*kowai*) is really just a surprise or startle. It's the same as a spook house ride. The frightening feeling you get when you return home late at night and are alone in your room is a completely different thing.[1]

The "completely different thing" Takahashi describes is *osore*, the feelings of terror and dread that we find in Lovecraft's cosmic fear and in Japanese *kaiki* films' dramas of omnipotent karmic vengeance (the "psychological aesthetic thing"), but not in the momentary startles of the carnival spook house ride.

Moments of shocking spectacle had been a fundamental component of the *kaiki* genre ever since actresses' grotesque portrayals of ghosts and monsters replaced trick photography as the main site of attraction in silent-era *kaidan* adaptations. While such moments litter early postwar *kaiki* films, the narrative

---

[1] Author's interview with Takahashi Hiroshi.

themes of karmic vengeance often come across muted, underdeveloped, or even outright absent. In the case of the very few *kaiki* films made in Japan under the American Occupation, this was primarily an issue of censorship policies, which prohibited themes of revenge being depicted on-screen. When the genre returned in force following the end of the Occupation in 1952, paradigm shifts had occurred in the commercial Japanese film industry that had seen the elimination of minor studios like Shinkō, which relied on popular genre films for survival. Major studios like Daiei produced *kaiki* films as program pictures to fill out production slates in-between A-list projects. This resulted in an inattention to narrative detail that, like the Occupation-era censorship policies, diluted the themes of *osore*—Takahashi's "psychological, aesthetic thing"—leaving only the hollow spectacle of spook house scares and ensuring the genre's continued low critical repute.

The immediate postwar period was a particularly volatile moment in the history of *kaiki* cinema. As the world entered the postmodern epoch, competing visions for the future of the *kaiki* genre unsettled its identifying markers. In the 1950s an era of censorship gave way to increasingly explicit spectacles of sexuality surrounding the female body, while the dawn of the atomic age threatened not just global security but also the very existence of *kaiki* as it was traditionally known. Some filmmakers tried to replicate prewar formulas while others experimented with the limits of the form. Meanwhile the critics questioned the relevance of genre altogether in the face of new forms of cinematic horror that dealt with the uniquely modern terrors of a post-Hiroshima world. The decade would close, however, with an unlooked-for return of the *kaiki* genre's traditional hallmarks that serves to further illuminate its distinct position in the global discourse of horror cinema.

Silencing the Dead: Wartime and Occupation Censorship

In the wake of the 1939 Film Act, the combination of the Cabinet Propaganda Office's discouragement of "vulgar" subjects like ghosts and monsters,[2] along with a limited, government-rationed supply of film stock and the injunction that all studios must produce a quota of "national policy films" (*kokusaku eiga*) each month,[3] eradicated domestic production of *kaiki* films. Foreign *kaiki* pictures

---

[2] Kawabe Jūji, *B-kyū kyoshōron: Nakagawa Nobuo kenkyū* (Tokyo: Shizukadō, 1983), 115.
[3] Isolde Standish, *A New History of Japanese Cinema: A Century of Narrative Film* (New York: Continuum, 2005), 143–4.

like the Universal horror pictures also were subject to censorship, and exhibition of international films was severely curtailed.[4] Hollywood horror had completely vanished from Japanese theaters by the outbreak of war with the United States in December 1941.

The nation's defeat and subsequent occupation by the Supreme Command of Allied Powers (SCAP) in 1945 might have been expected to prompt a return to the production of escapist entertainment like *kaiki* movies for the war-weary masses—and in part it did, with the MacArthur government actively seeking to purge the film industry of the nationalism and militarism that had permeated it under the wartime administration. In its effort to do so, however, SCAP instituted a censorship program of its own that was in some ways even stricter than its predecessor. *Kaiki* cinema was once again virtually banned from production, albeit for reasons utterly different from those of the wartime government. In order to pass the Occupation censors, the very few examples of the genre that managed to make it to theaters in the years from 1945 to 1952 had to discard the thematic elements of karmic retribution that made them *kaiki* in the first place.

The Film Act was not the last measure the wartime government had adopted to control the output of Japan's commercial film studios. Shortages of film stock due to the war effort, coupled with the desire to streamline the process of preproduction censorship, prompted the government in 1941 to demand the merger of the ten largest commercial studios into just two companies, each limited to producing two films per month. Minor studios like Shinkō would, in effect, be swallowed up by the industry's two biggest players, Shōchiku and Tōhō, while the government's plan was to dissolve the assets of third major, Nikkatsu, among the other two.[5] Only Shōchiku, which came out of the proposed restructuring stronger than Tōhō, liked the plan. Shinkō head Nagata Masaichi presented an alternate, three-studio solution to the government's orders to consolidate the industry, which saw Shōchiku and Tōhō each absorb some of the minor studios in a fashion that put them on more equal footing. Shinkō notably was not one of the minors in question, but would instead merge with Nikkatsu and Daitō to form a new major studio. The government approved of Nagata's solution. Nikkatsu, owning a considerable stake in its own chain of theaters, agreed to surrender its production and distribution wings to Nagata on the condition that it could remain its own exhibition company. The result was the

---

[4] Ibid.
[5] Joseph L. Anderson and Donald Richie, *The Japanese Film: Art and Industry*, 2nd ed. (Princeton, NJ: Princeton University Press, 1982), 142.

creation of Daiei, with Nagata at the helm.⁶ The head of a minor studio infamous for its disreputable *kaiki* pictures had maneuvered both himself and the Shinkō talent responsible for filling Japanese movie screens with vengeful ghosts and cat monsters into the position of a major studio comparable to Shōchiku and Tōhō in size and distribution power.

The actress and the director most responsible for the ghosts and monsters, however, did not join in this new era of Japanese film studio history. Suzuki Sumiko, the face of the *kaiki* genre, abruptly retired from the film world in 1941, devoting herself full-time to performing in live stage productions where she appeared in many of the same roles (including ghost cats) she had played on-screen for Shinkō. The move reportedly infuriated Nagata, though Suzuki's decision was not a radical one among *jidaigeki* film stars of the time. With *chambara* and *kaiki* films no longer being produced, many actors who built their fame on playing ninjas and ghost cats found live theater a way to circumvent the government's suppression of these genres on-screen. After the end of the war Suzuki continued to appear onstage in her trademark ghost cat roles, and at the height of the postwar *kaiki* craze she made a momentary return to cinema screens in Tōei's *The Ghost Cat and the Clockwork Ceiling* (*Kaibyō karakuri tenjo*, 1958). *Kaiki*'s chief creative talent behind the camera, Mokudō Shigeru, also left Shinkō in 1941 and retired from directing. His last work for the studio was a production of *Momijigari*, whose maple-tree demoness had been featured in Shibata Tsunekichi's pioneering 1899 film. Thus the industry's attempts to return to *kaiki* filmmaking after the war ended in 1945 would represent something of a fresh start, bereft of the duo that arguably had defined the genre in terms of domestic production and brought it to its first flowering of maturity.

It might be more accurate to call these initial efforts a "false start" rather than a "fresh start" in light of the obstacles the Occupation's own film censorship program presented for *jidaigeki* period productions. Into the place of the wartime Cabinet Propaganda Office stepped the Civil Information and Education Section (CIE) and the Civil Censorship Detachment (CCD), which, seeking to undo the work of their predecessor, maintained much of its practice.⁷ Films initially continued to be subject to censorship at the preproduction level, with the CIE and CCD examining screenplays and demanding rewrites of anything that smacked of militarism or feudal loyalty in the eyes of the American occupiers.⁸

---

⁶ Ibid., 143–4.
⁷ See Hiroshi Kitamura, *Screening Enlightenment: Hollywood and the Cultural Reconstruction of Defeated Japan* (Ithaca, NY: Cornell, 2010), 33–8.
⁸ Anderson and Richie, *The Japanese Film*, 162.

In November 1945—just two months after Japan's surrender—the CIE issued a list of thirteen themes that were deemed "problematic" and would be unlikely to pass censorship. Number two, "showing revenge as a legitimate motive,"[9] guaranteed that the archetypal Edo *kaidan* narrative—which was all about the bloody, wrathful vengeance of sympathetic monsters from the grave against those who had defeated them in life—would not pass the censors.

This presented a crisis not only for any return to *kaiki* filmmaking but also for many of the most popular *jidaigeki* subjects like *Chūshingura*, the famous tale of the loyal forty-seven *rōnin* who sacrifice their own lives to avenge the death of their master. The most oft-filmed story in Japanese cinema history, screen versions of *Chūshingura*, had continued to appear with the Cabinet Propaganda Office's blessing during the war years, unlike its sister narrative, *The Ghost Story of Yotsuya*, which takes place in the same fictionalized world as the forty-seven *rōnin* and features some of the same characters.[10] With Japan's military defeat, however, it was not only the "vulgar" *jidaigeki* projects like ninja and *kaiki* films that were a problem. Film histories sometimes erroneously state that the CIE forbade the production of *jidaigeki* outright, despite obvious and high-profile exceptions like Kurosawa Akira's *Rashōmon* (1950), but any filmmaker wishing to make a traditional *jidaigeki* picture had to traverse a minefield of possible censorship. Not surprisingly, most chose not to even try, sticking to the contemporarily set *gendaigeki* projects that promoted the Occupation's stated "desirable subjects" such as "showing Japanese in all walks of life co-operating to build a peaceful nation" and "promoting tolerance and respect among all races and classes."[11] This new, peaceful Japan where democracy and the rule of law would always prevail held no room for vengeful ghosts of the past like Oiwa, though a few filmmakers would brave the attempt to resurrect the spirits of *kaiki* cinema during the Occupation years.

The first was Kinoshita Keisuke, the director who would become internationally renowned for films like *A Japanese Tragedy* (*Nihon no higeki*, 1953) and *Twenty-Four Eyes* (*Nijūshi no hitomi*, 1954) that depicted the terrible cost of the war and its aftermath on everyday Japanese. It might have been felt that if anyone could get a *kaiki* picture past the Occupation censors, it was the great humanist

---

[9] Standish, *New History of Japanese Cinema*, 156–7.
[10] Tsuruya Nanboku's kabuki version of *The Ghost Story of Yotsuya* (*Tōkaidō Yotsuya kaidan*) was conceived as a side story to *Chūshingura*, with Oiwa's husband Iemon being the would-be forty-eighth *rōnin* who instead throws his lot in with their lord's enemies. His eventual slayer, Yomoshichi, is one of the loyal forty-seven. *Tōkaidō Yotsuya kaidan* was originally performed in 1825 over the course of two evenings on a double bill with *Chūshingura*.
[11] Standish, *New History of Japanese Cinema*, 155–6.

Kinoshita, who had managed even to subtly critique the war effort in his 1944 national policy picture *The Army* (*Rikugun*). In 1949 Shōchiku got approval to release his two-part *The Ghost Story of Yotsuya: A New Interpretation* (*Shinshaku Yotsuya kaidan*). Shōchiku and Kinoshita only got the film made, however, by virtually eliminating the *kaiki* elements. In Kinoshita's version of the famous ghost story, Oiwa's spirit makes only the briefest of appearances in fleeting, point-of-view shots from her husband/killer Tamiya Iemon's perspective, constituting less than a minute of screen time in a two-part picture that runs almost two-and-a-half hours.

The film compensates in small part by including two "dark and stormy night" sequences full of howling wind, driving rain, thunder crashes, and lightning flashes. Such scenes were by now established tropes of both foreign and domestic *kaiki* pictures thanks to the work of James Whale and Mokudō Shigeru, and as in their films, here Kinoshita uses the motif to suggest omnipotent, cosmic forces of *osore* arrayed against the human characters. Kinoshita also retains some of the original story's sense of inevitable karmic comeuppance by depicting the uncanny recurrence of Oiwa's facial scar afflicting other characters such as her sister Osode, Iemon's new bride Oume, and finally Iemon himself.

All of this works to suggest that Iemon's ultimate demise is divine karmic justice, but in order to prevent his death from being depicted as karmic *vengeance* (which would not pass censorship), the desire for his punishment cannot be given expression in the persona of Oiwa's wrathful ghost. Being the oldest extant *Yotsuya* film, it is impossible to say how Kinoshita's version compares to what had come before, but actor Uehara Ken portrays Iemon as a far more remorseful figure than any subsequent performer would on-screen. Badgered by the truly villainous Naosuke into poisoning his wife, Uehara's Iemon regrets the decision almost instantly and spends the remainder of the film plagued with guilt, making the split-second, point-of-view appearances of Oiwa's ghost easily read by the audience as a hallucinatory manifestation of Iemon's tormented conscience.[12] This recalls Ushihara Kiyohiko's use of point-of-view shots in *The Ghost Cat and the Mysterious Shamisen* to suggest an ambiguous interpretation of the ghost, but unlike Suzuki Sumiko's poker-faced Mitsue, Uehara's Iemon

---

[12] Both Gregory Barrett and Yokoyama Yasuko argue for this interpretation. See Gregory Barrett, *Archetypes in Japanese Film: The Sociopolitical and Religious Significance of the Principal Heroes and Heroines* (Cranbury, NJ: Associated University Press, 1989), 99–100; and Yokoyama Yasuko, "*Yotsuya kaidan* eiga no Oiwa-tachi: kabuki to wakare, betsu no onna e," in *Kaiki to gensō e no kairō: kaidan kara J-horā e*, ed. Uchiyama Kazuki (Tokyo: Shinwasha, 2008), 156.

vocally expresses his sense of guilt to the point of raving madness, which more unequivocally implies Oiwa's ghost is a mere psychological hallucination.

Other directors like Nakagawa Nobuo who would subsequently tackle the *Yotsuya* legend would follow Kinoshita's lead in using Oiwa's ghost in part as a symbol of Iemon's internalized feelings of guilt, but would also retain a sense of her as a character in her own right, with the omnipotent agency to exact revenge on her hated husband/murderer. Oiwa typically voices her *onnen*—the uncontainable rage that gives birth to her vengeful spirit—in plain terms to Iemon. Nakagawa's 1959 version adapts original lines from Nanboku's 1825 kabuki script such as "I will visit my hatred upon you—be sure of that!" and "I will make an end to the blood of the Tamiya line!" Only in Kinoshita's film does Oiwa's ghost remain utterly silent. In her momentary appearances she gazes impassively at Iemon, without even so much as a look of anger or judgment on her face. Robbing Oiwa's ghost of her voice divests the narrative of any personal, vindictive dimension to Iemon's karmic punishment, but it also robs *The Ghost Story of Yotsuya* of much of its *kaiki* potency, as no fearsome monster drives the machine of fate toward its inevitable, horrible end.

Kinoshita's reworking of one of the most iconic scenes from the *Yotsuya* legend perfectly illustrates the diminished presence of Oiwa's ghost and its impact on the tone and themes of this "new interpretation." A highlight of the tale since the heyday of its nineteenth-century kabuki renditions has been the gruesome sequence in which Iemon, fishing by the river's edge, encounters the bloody reanimated corpses of Oiwa and the murdered servant Kohei nailed to either side of a door that he and his henchmen previously threw into the river in order to dispose of the bodies. On stage the scene embodies the height of kabuki spectacle, as a single actor portrays both Oiwa and Kohei in split-second costume changes that occur when the door flips over. In Nakagawa's 1959 film version the scene becomes a masterpiece of horror, the water turning blood-red before Oiwa and the door emerge from the depths amid a cacophony of thunder, flutes, and drums to declare her vengeful curse upon an awestruck Iemon. Kinoshita's film retains the iconic door-in-the-river, but the object of its ghostly visitation becomes Kohei's distraught mother, searching for what's become of her missing son. It thereby serves not as a harbinger of karmic vengeance but as an elegiac farewell to a parent from a departed child, resonating with the climactic scene in the director's wartime picture *The Army* that depicted the final separation of mother and son. The most obvious change from traditional versions of *Yotsuya*, however, is the conspicuous absence of Oiwa's and Kohei's ghosts, their presence only hinted at by the bloodstained but empty door floating downriver and,

Figure 12 The "empty door" from Kinoshita Keisuke's *The Ghost Story of Yotsuya: A New Interpretation* (*Shinshaku Yotsuya kaidan*, 1949).

in a single brief shot, shown spinning in the water under the influence of an apparently otherworldly power (Figure 12). Kinoshita's "empty door" embodies the essence of his "new interpretation," which either through political necessity or the director's own interests required that Oiwa's vengeful ghost be absent from the screen. Without the theme of her grave-transcending hatred there is no act of revenge to upset the censors, but neither is there any sense of *osore*. Critics have remarked that, as a result, *The Ghost Story of Yotsuya: A New Interpretation* works as one of Kinoshita Keisuke's humanist tragedies, but fails to satisfy as a work of *kaiki*.[13]

The film's reveal of Oiwa's disfigured face—another iconic moment in the *Yotsuya* legend—further illustrates the ways in which Kinoshita trades *kaiki* and otherworldly horror for human tragedy. As Mokudō did in *The Ghost Story of the Mandarin Duck Curtain* and Nakagawa would do in his own version of *Yotsuya*, Kinoshita withholds the reveal as long as possible, creating suspense by having another character react in horror to Oiwa's appearance while obscuring her face

---

[13] Yokoyama, "*Yotsuya kaidan* no Oiwatachi," 156–7.

from the camera.[14] The musical accompaniment, however, is not ominous as it is in more typical *kaiki* film, but melancholic and wistful, emphasizing tragedy over horror or *osore*. Mokudō and Nakagawa both finally reveal the ghastly disfigurement in point-of-view shots that replicate the woman's own horrified, initial glimpse of herself in the mirror. Kinoshita, meanwhile, first shows us Oiwa's disfigured face in a shot that replicates Iemon's point of view, underlining the sense of guilt and remorse he feels over his misdeed, rather than Oiwa's own sense of shocked horror, which triggers her need for revenge.

Kinoshita as a director seems to have been little interested in themes of vengeance regardless of censorship policies, and he seizes upon the element of the original story—the tragic breakdown of the family unit—that both complements his own recurring themes as a filmmaker and would appease the censors' desire for films that promoted social harmony. Accordingly, Kinoshita's *New Interpretation* concludes not with Oiwa's ghost completing a vendetta against the husband who betrayed her, but with her sister Osode and her husband Yomoshichi happily awaiting the birth of a child, reaffirming both Kinoshita's and the Occupation censors' notion of the ideal family unit that Iemon had cast aside.

One month after *The Ghost Story of Yotsuya: A New Interpretation* premiered during the *Obon* season of 1949, director Watanabe Kunio's *Legend of the Nabeshima Ghost Cat* (*Nabeshima kaibyōden*) also passed CIE censorship and made it to cinema screens. Unlike Kinoshita, Watanabe had been labeled a C-class war criminal by SCAP for his participation in national policy filmmaking in Manchuria.[15] This made his production of the Nabeshima ghost cat legend—a feudalistic tale of revenge if there ever was one, in which the titular monster wreaks its vengeance on the hotheaded *daimyō* who murdered its master over a game of *go*—all the more remarkable. The film was made at a relatively new studio, Shintōhō (or "New Tōhō"), founded in 1947 by defectors from Tōhō following a series of violent strikes. By the mid-1950s Shintōhō would become Japan's "grindhouse" studio, devoted to the production of B-genres like *kaiki*, but in its formative years its aim was the production of quality cinema at a studio by and for artists. Like *The Ghost Story of Yotsuya: A New Interpretation*, Watanabe's *Legend of the Nabeshima Ghost Cat* focuses more on the human drama than on *kaiki to senritsu* thrills and chills, and while this represents Shōchiku's

---

[14] It should be noted that Nanboku's original stage directions also call for this delayed reveal, and although it is impossible to say with any certainty, at least some of the prewar film versions of the *Yotsuya* story likely also incorporated such a setup.
[15] Anderson and Richie, *The Japanese Film*, 164.

and Shintōhō's interest in refined cinema over genre formula, it also was an unavoidable consequence of Occupation censorship.

As in Kinoshita's revamped version of *Yotsuya*, Watanabe's film weights the interpretation of the *kaiki* elements toward a purely psychological symbol of guilt, rather than the wrath of cosmic forces. *The Legend of the Nabeshima Ghost Cat*, like Kinoshita's film, features a totally silent ghost that appears exclusively in brief, subjective point-of-view shots. Once again silencing the ghost effaces any overtly expressed theme of revenge from the narrative. Only the wicked lord of Nabeshima and his crony, Hanzaemon, ever see the ghost of the murdered *go* player, Mata'ichirō. There is no scene equivalent to the ones in the *kaiki* work of Mokudō Shigeru or Ushihara's *Ghost Cat and the Mysterious Shamisen* in which the ghost appears to a loved one to reveal the crime and plead for vengeance. Other film versions of the *Nabeshima* story typically include multiple monsters, not only the vengeful spirit of the murdered *go* player but also a ghost cat that acts on behalf of his entire family, who all subsequently fall victim to the cruelty of the Nabeshima lord. Watanabe's version includes ample talk of "ghost cat rumors" (*bakeneko uwasa*) among the townsfolk who live in the shadow of Nabeshima Castle, but the creature never makes an appearance in any form save as a small, real kitten—hardly the stuff of *kaiki*. Of course, had the title monster actually appeared in the film as a full-fledged werecat *a la* Suzuki Sumiko, its presence would signal karmic vengeance incarnate. The climax of *The Legend of the Nabeshima Ghost Cat*, accordingly, includes no ghost cat at all, and only a single brief shot of Mata'ichirō's ghost holding the black kitten before the authorities invade the castle to arrest the lord and Hanzaemon. Truth and Justice prevail in place of vengeance from beyond the grave, which no doubt pleased the purveyors of the American Way in the CIE and CCD.

Daiei and the Return of the Ghost Cat

Daiei tried an alternative workaround to the problem of producing *kaiki* films under the American Occupation by turning to the *shinpi* or "mystery" genre, which at least as far back as Universal's *The Cat and the Canary* in 1927 had shared an often blurry boundary with *kaiki* in Japanese filmgoers' imaginations. Nagata's new studio was the undisputed king of the period film in the few years it existed prior to the end of the war, comprised of the *jidaigeki* talent of Shinkō, Daitō, and Nikkatsu. But rather than try and squeeze the feudal worlds of samurai and ghost cats past the censors like Kinoshita and Watanabe did at Shōchiku and

Shintōhō, Daiei opted to switch focus to production of *gendaigeki*. To satisfy the market for *kaiki*, this meant looking not to the Edo-period *kaidan* ghost stories that traditionally formed the backbone of domestic *kaiki* production but to the popular mystery novels of the era that often featured horribly disfigured murderers, or else criminals posing as ghosts and monsters—a trope established by American *kaiki* haunted house whodunits like *The Cat and the Canary*. Human criminals without the cosmic license of *osore* and karmic retribution on their side invited the audience's revulsion without the attendant sense of awe inspired by truly inhuman monsters like the sympathetic Oiwa and the ghost cat, and both Japanese filmgoers and the censors could agree on their unequivocal condemnation when they are brought to justice at the conclusion of the picture.

Daiei's Occupation-era films like *Ghost Train* (*Yūrei bessha*, 1949) and *The Iron Claw* (*Tetsu no tsume*, 1951) always conclude with a rational explanation for the *kaiki* goings-on, but as Uchiyama Kazuki notes, the pictures overall emphasized the horrific and *kaiki*-inflected elements over detective work and mystery. For example, Nakagawa Nobuo's postwar *shinpi-kaiki* hybrid for Tōhō, *The Vampire Moth* (*Kyūketsuki ga*, 1956), adapts one of mystery novelist Yokomizo Seishi's "Kindaichi Kōsuke" stories, the Japanese equivalent of Sam Spade or Philip Marlowe. *Vampire Moth*, however, only introduces Detective Kindaichi halfway into the picture's runtime, and instead of his dogged investigation mainly follows the point of view of the title "monster's" terrified—and clueless—female victims, stalked through shadowy corridors, foggy graveyards, and gothic mansions. The elaborate makeup and special effects employed to create the "fake monsters" and malformed criminals—much of it done by special effects wizard Tsuburaya Eiji, famous for his work on Tōhō's *Godzilla* series—also invited comparisons to the makeup-heavy Universal horror pictures.[16]

The focus on the "monster" and the other characters' horrified reactions to it rather than the process leading to its eventual unmasking aligns such films more closely to Tzvetan Todorov's conception of the fantastic/uncanny rather than his definition of the mystery genre. Commenting on the similarities and differences of the horror story and the murder mystery, Todorov writes, "The emphasis differs in the two genres: in the detective story, the emphasis is placed on the *solution* to the mystery; in the texts linked to the uncanny (as in the fantastic narrative), the emphasis is on the *reactions* which this mystery provokes."[17] Genuine ghosts

---

[16] Uchiyama Kazuki, "Nihon eiga no kaiki to gensō," in *Kaiki to gensō e no kairō*, ed. Uchiyama Kazuki (Tokyo: Shinwasha, 2008), 15–16.

[17] Tzvetan Todorov, *The Fantastic: A Structural Approach to a Literary Genre*, trans. Richard Howard (Ithaca, NY: Cornell University Press, 1975), 50 (emphasis added).

and monsters would return to Japanese theater screens following the end of the Occupation in 1952, but modern-day *shinpi-kaiki* hybrids like Nakagawa's *Vampire Moth* also continued to appear, and the Shintōhō studio would throw a third genre into the mix—the skin flick—with the epically titled *Diving Girls in a Haunted House* (*Ama no bakemono yashiki*, 1959). Although today's *kaiki* film authorities like Takahashi Hiroshi and Izumi Toshiyuki hesitate to include these pictures in their definitions of *kaiki*, the Occupation-era advertising reveals that, at the time, they were intended to fill the demand for *kaiki* created by the CIE censorship policies: the poster for *The Iron Claw* explicitly calls it one of "Daiei's unique *kaiki* pictures" (*Daiei ishoku kaiki eiga*) (Figure 13).

When the Occupation ended in 1952 and sovereignty was once again officially in Japanese hands, Nagata wasted no time in getting Daiei back into the business of more traditional *kaiki* film production that had been the hallmark

Figure 13 Poster for the Occupation-era film *The Iron Claw* (*Tetsu no tsume*, 1951). Despite no "real" monsters or themes of cosmic *osore*, the poster advertises it as one of "Daiei's unique *kaiki* pictures." ©KADOKAWA.

of the studio's prior incarnation, Shinkō. Once more Japanese cinema screens would be filled with monsters like the ghost cat and vengeful spirit that explicitly operated as agents of karmic retribution, potentially restoring the themes of *osore*, which lent weight to their spectacular imagery. Unlike its predecessor studio, however, Daiei was able to compete head-on with Shōchiku and Tōhō in the production of prestige pictures, and after the Daiei-produced *Rashōmon* won the Golden Lion at the Venice Film Festival and an Honorary Oscar at the American Academy Awards, Nagata set the studio on a two-pronged course of production.[18] On one side were high-profile, A-list pictures designed to win awards at foreign film festivals, and on the other were B-list "program pictures" (*puroguramu pikuchua*), which could be dashed off between prestige projects—sometimes using leftover sets and costumes from the A-pictures—and filled the domestic demand for popular genre fare.[19] As a result, Daiei's post-Occupation *kaiki* films demonstrate less concern with innovation than Shinkō pictures like *The Ghost Cat and the Mysterious Shamisen* or *The Ghost Cat and the Red Wall*, which employed acclaimed directors and experimental filmmaking techniques in an effort to elevate the genre in the eyes of the critics. Instead, Daiei simply sought to replicate the old, profitable Shinkō formula. Most prominent among its first efforts to do so were direct remakes of two Shinkō ghost cat films: *The Ghost Story of Saga Mansion* (*Kaidan Saga yashiki*, 1953), which was a reworking of Shinkō's first *kaiki* hit, *The Legend of the Saga Ghost Cat*, and *The Ghost Cat of Arima Palace*, a new version of *The Cat of Arima*. But to recapture the prewar ghost cat successes, the most visible and bankable component of the formula—Suzuki Sumiko—would first have to be replaced.

Irie Takako

Irie Takako, recently arrived at Daiei following her departure from Tōhō, was drafted to step into Suzuki Sumiko's paws and, like her predecessor, the "ghost cat actress" moniker would become inextricably attached to her legacy. Both women had previously been renowned as silver screen vamps in the silent era, although Irie was a breed apart from the typical *jidaigeki* villainesses typified by Suzuki and other vamps under contract to the minor studios. In the prewar era Irie commanded leading roles in major studios' A-list *gendaigeki* productions,

---

[18] See Yoshiharu Tezuka, *Japanese Cinema Goes Global: Filmworkers' Journeys* (Hong Kong: Hong Kong University Press, 2012), 40–51, for *Rashomon*'s impact on Daiei's production strategy.
[19] Anderson and Richie, *The Japanese Film*, 228.

becoming one of the most popular stars of her day for her striking beauty. While Suzuki Sumiko had cultivated an image of dangerous sexuality marked by formidable physical prowess, Irie's more sympathetic vamp characters hewed closer to those of the great actress of silent Shanghai cinema Ruan Lingyu, a wholly feminine "good girl" forced to do bad things by dire circumstance.[20] The fearsome acrobatics and monstrous eroticism of the ghost cat were a natural extension of Suzuki's established star persona, but the role was a comparatively awkward fit for the aging and ill Irie. Forty-two years old in 1953, Irie was a decade older than Suzuki had been when she became typecast as a "ghost cat actress." Having left the Tōhō studio unceremoniously after contracting Graves' disease, which caused her eyes to unnaturally bulge, many people—including Irie herself—saw Daiei's decision to cast her as their new *kaiki* star as a humiliating fall from grace.[21]

As a result of all of these factors, Irie's performances as the ghost cat do not hinge as much on the ambiguity of monstrous sex appeal, although the pleasurable tension between the desirable body of the actress and the horrific nature of her *bakeneko* form remains implicit. Suzuki's limited makeup in *The Cat of Arima* let the vamp's large, coquettish eyes shine through the feline façade, the monstrosity conveyed primarily through the actress's performance. Irie's portrayals relied more on the makeup itself, which was more generously applied to the older woman's features (Figure 14). Heavy lines around the mouth and eyes, prosthetic cat ears, and masculine fur-covered forearms almost completely obscure any traces of the actress's femininity. While the 1953 films *The Ghost Story of Saga Mansion* and *The Ghost Cat of Arima Palace* adhere to the convention of showing Irie as a desirable woman prior to her monstrous transformation, the metamorphoses are completer and more spectacular than Suzuki's vampish ghost cat. In a masterful shot from *The Ghost Story of Saga Mansion*, Irie morphs from her normal human appearance to the grotesque cat creature in a single, unbroken take that lasts thirty seconds in duration, achieved via subtle lighting effects that disguise her makeup for the first half of the shot.

On posters and promotional images, however, potential audiences usually only saw the ghastly visage of Irie in her monstrous persona (Figure 15). The sense of beauty-into-beast spectacle surrounding a once-popular silver screen starlet still undoubtedly remained the films' main selling point, but even

---

[20] Irena Hayter discussed Irie's vamp image in "Mannequins, Movies, and Mass Culture in the 1920s" at the Association for Asian Studies annual conference held in Denver, Colorado, March 21–24, 2019.
[21] Irie Takako, *Eiga joyū* (Tokyo: Gakufushoin, 1957), 226.

Figure 14 Irie Takako applying her makeup for *The Ghost Story of Saga Mansion* (*Kaidan Saga yashiki*, 1953). ©KADOKAWA.

Figure 15 Promotional image for *The Ghost Story of Saga Mansion* (*Kaidan Saga yashiki*, 1953). ©KADOKAWA. Courtesy of the National Film Archive of Japan.

more so than Suzuki's prewar pictures that spectacle became extratextual. Japanese film scholar Daisuke Miyao, building on Shimura Miyoko's work on the *bakeneko* subgenre of *kaiki* genre, suggests the appeal for these pictures lay in exploiting the disparity between Irie's past image and her present fallen state as a screen beauty who was no longer beautiful.[22] Thirtysomething Suzuki Sumiko had still been able to trade on her sex symbol status, while fortysomething (and physically ill) Irie Takako became instead a figurative and literal ghost of her former image. Yet, within the context of the films' narratives, Irie still plays the desirable woman up until the moment of her transformation. In the case of Suzuki her sexual allure straddled the divide of the beauty-to-beast spectacle, but for Irie desirability and monstrosity became more clearly divided while also relying to a greater extent on the audience's memories of Irie's past stardom.

The Daiei ghost cat films relied a little *too* much on the audience's memories in other regards, for as the series progressed, the conventions and iconography of the archetypical ghost cat legend continued to appear, but not always accompanied by coherent narrative explanations for them. Postwar audiences, not as familiar with the old kabuki stories as previous generations, questioned why some of the pictures were even about cats in the first place, and indeed some of Daiei's *kaiki* films such as *The Ghost Cat at Ōma Crossing* (*Kaibyō Ōma ga tsuji*, 1954) and *The Ghost Cat of Yonaki Swamp* (*Kaibyō Yonaki numa*, 1957) are simply *kaidan* tales of vengeful ghosts who inexplicably sport cat ears and perform *neko jarashi* feline pantomimes. Shimura Miyoko observes the tacked-on feeling of the cat motif in these pictures actually preserves the ad-hoc approach to the ghostly and fantastic that characterized the kabuki and *kōdan* oral storytelling formats from which the films were descended.[23] Nonetheless, Daiei's first two ghost cat pictures, perhaps influenced by the Hollywood preference for tight continuity, carefully foreshadow the presence of the cat monster, establishing the pet cat of the murder victim early in the picture and including the crucial shot of the animal imbibing the blood of its master, which enables it to assume its half-human monstrous form. Later entries in the series assumed the audience knew the formula well enough and, as in *Ghost Cat at Ōma Crossing*, barely acknowledge the pet cat and omit the blood-lapping scene. Irie's makeup in *Ōma Crossing* looks more like the ghost of Oiwa than her prior ghost cat appearances (indeed other characters in the film comment on the resemblance between Irie's character and "Oiwa-sama"); yet her appearances are heralded by the mewling of a cat, and she faithfully performs the *neko jarashi* on one of the villains during the climax.

---

[22] Miyao, "A Ghost Cat, a Star, and Two Intertexts: A Historical Analysis of *A Cat, Shozo, and Two Women* (1956)," *Journal of Japanese and Korean Cinema* 8, no. 2 (2016): 89–103.

[23] Shimura Miyoko, "'Misemono' kara 'eiga' e: Shintōhō no kaibyō eiga," *Engeki eizō* 43 (2002): 14.

The narrative ellipses evidentially led to confusion among casual viewers of the *kaiki* genre. In his review of the Shintōhō studio's 1958 *Mansion of the Ghost Cat*—which reestablished the narrative connection between cat and ghost cat—critic Tada Michitarō happily remarked that he had seen several ghost cat movies, but until viewing *Mansion of the Ghost Cat* had never understood why a vengeful spirit would take the form of a werecat.[24] Yet even in Daiei's first ghost cat outings, *The Ghost Story of Saga Mansion* and *The Ghost Cat of Arima Palace*, the real biological cat and the human actress portraying the *bakeneko* serve two distinct and somewhat dislocated functions. As Shimura explains, the symbolic role of the cat-turned-*bakeneko* can be divided into two phases:

> "Phase One" is the *neko* (cat), which symbolizes loyalty [to its murdered master] … "Phase Two" is the *bakeneko* (ghost-cat), which symbolizes revenge. The *bakeneko* film's story develops from Phase One to Phase Two, with the great feelings of loyalty in the *neko* giving rise to the vengeful behavior of the *bakeneko* … [but] there is no onscreen transformation of the *neko* into a *bakeneko*, as in a werewolf movie, and thus the two have an onscreen presence independent of each other. Additionally, conventional *bakeneko* films that emphasize the actress place a much greater emphasis on Phase Two. The loyal relationship of Phase One is there merely to foreshadow the later appearance of the *bakeneko* actress.[25]

In other words, the filmmakers treated the *osore*-inflected narrative of the actress-driven ghost cat vehicle as negligible compared to the spectacle of Suzuki Sumiko or Irie Takako prancing around in feline makeup. In the case of the Daiei films this privileging of performance over the script clearly reflects their status as program pictures produced quickly between prestige projects. It also remains in line with theatrical performances of previous eras, in which the story was merely a shaky skeleton upon which to showcase the actors' craft.

The emphasis on spectacle over tight narrative cohesion went beyond the physical appearance of Irie Takako, as the Daiei *kaiki* pictures gradually became more and more crowded with ghosts and ghouls that would pop out at the unwitting human characters in set pieces that Takahashi Hiroshi compares to the *obake yashiki* spook house rides at Japanese amusement parks. Director Kato Bin's trio of ghost cat pictures for Daiei, *The Ghost Cat of Okazaki* (*Kaibyō Okazaki sōdō*, 1954), *The Ghost Cat at Ōma Crossing*, and *The Ghost Cat of the 53 Way Stations* (*Kaibyō gojūsan tsugi*, 1956), best exemplifies this spook house

---

[24] Tada Michitarō, "*Bōrei kaibyō yashiki*," *Kinema junpō*, September 1, 1958, 75.
[25] Shimura, "'Misemono' kara 'eiga' e," 15.

approach to *kaiki* filmmaking. Kato's first *kaiki* film for Daiei, *The Ghost Cat of Okazaki*, opens *in media res* to give the audience a momentary glimpse of Irie already transformed into the ghost cat before flashing back to tell the film's story in a more conventional order. The establishing matte-painting shot of Okazaki Castle atop a hill in the gloom of night evokes affinities with Hollywood *kaiki* films—notably *Frankenstein*—but the subsequent shot replicates the effect of riding a car through a carnival spook house. Kato employs a point-of-view tracking shot gliding straight-ahead through the halls of Okazaki Castle, although the film has yet to introduce any characters to which the point of view might be identifiably attached in the audience's imagination. In effect the audience itself is the one traveling through the haunted castle, and the camera conveniently comes to a halt right in front of a wall that begins to crumble on cue. Irie flies out from behind the wall in full ghost cat regalia accompanied by a swell of music until her grotesquely painted visage fills the frame—and the audience ideally squeals in pleasurable terror.

Perhaps because director Arai Ryōhei's attempt at innovative *kaiki* special effects to depict Irie Takako's still-living decapitated head flying through space in the previous year's *The Ghost Cat of Arima Palace* had been met with such derision,[26] Kato's *kaiki* efforts stick to comparatively simple fun-house setups like the opening of *Okazaki*. Kato has Irie glide out from behind shōji curtains while the frightened human characters are looking in the opposite direction, turning in time to see the ghost cat standing over them and shriek in terror. In one effective shot from *Okazaki*, the camera tracks left to follow a fear-stricken woman creeping backward along a castle wall until she bumps right into the form of Irie standing still where she had been waiting out of frame (Figure 16). The director's favorite trick, however, involved nothing more elaborate than to position his ghosts behind a closed door, which would slide open of its own accord at the moment the monster's victim approaches. Variations on the technique appear in *The Ghost Cat at Ōma Crossing*, such as a scene in which Irie hangs concealed in the branches of a tree until her murderer walks under the boughs and she descends floating on wires to startle him. All of this is not to say that Kato's *kaiki* films did not make use of other established tropes of the genre like double exposure, thunderstorm sound and lighting effects, and the *neko jarashi* pantomime sequences—or that the spook-house startle moments that feature in his work fail to produce the desired effect. But more so than Arai

---

[26] *Kinema junpō*'s damning review of *The Ghost Cat of Arima Palace* quoted in Chapter 1 specifically mentions the effect when it proclaims the film more likely to make the children in the audience howl with laughter before it would frighten anyone.

Figure 16 *Obake yashiki* ("spook house") scares in *The Ghost Cat of Okazaki* (*Kaibyō Okazaki sōdō*, 1954).

Ryōhei's earlier ghost cat efforts for Daiei and Suzuki Sumiko's surviving prewar work, Kato's films perpetuate the lingering notion that domestic *kaiki* films prior to the work of Nakagawa Nobuo were little more than amusement park spook house rides transferred to the silver screen.

The *obake yashiki* gimmicks themselves are not the problem. Indeed, without them the *kaiki* genre would be bereft of one of its main attractions for audiences. The jump scare, as it has come to be known among horror film fans, has long been an integral part of the genre, although traditionally critics have held it in the same derision Takahashi Hiroshi expresses for the "not that scary" *obake yashiki* moments of *kaiki* film: a momentary startle rather than a lingering sense of terror. Recently Adam Charles Hart has argued for a more appreciative consideration of what he calls the "sensational address" of horror film, one that sees the jump scare not as cinematic excess in opposition to narrative form but integral to the structure of the genre.[27] The best horror and *kaiki* films marry the sensational address to compelling characters and well-developed narrative themes. To recall the age-old debate begun by Coleridge and Radcliffe, they traffic in horror *and* terror/*osore*.

Therein lies the weakness of the later Daiei ghost cat films' inattention to narrative detail. Emphasizing the startling moment while neglecting the themes of *osore* dilutes the power of the work in much the same way the Occupation censorship of those same themes had done. Unlike Kinoshita's and Watanabe's muted monsters, Irie was free to express her cosmic rage vocally; but even though her presence is undeniably portrayed as no mere guilt-induced hallucination, inflicting bodily harm and engaging in *tachimawari* fight scenes with hordes of samurai, Irie's performances as the ghost cat were still largely silent. Omitting the

---

[27] Adam Charles Hart, *Monstrous Forms: Moving Image Horror across Media* (New York: Oxford University Press, 2020), 22–31.

themes of loyalty in the pet cat that enable the act of cosmic revenge by failing to establish the blood-lapping motif further robs the text of its *kaiki* potency. The Daiei films frequently succeed in crafting startling spook house moments, but—to paraphrase Takahashi's comments quoted at the beginning of this chapter—they do not follow you home from the theater to your empty room at night.

Mōri Ikuko and *Kaiki* Eros

As the 1950s wore on, so too did Daiei's commitment to at least one annual *kaiki* program picture, though as the decade neared a close the tiredness of Irie's ghost cat series became increasingly apparent. Rival studio Shintōhō (discussed in detail in the next chapter) began scoring unprecedented positive reviews for domestic *kaiki* films by devoting its top talent and resources to adaptations of the most popular *kaidan* ghost stories like *Kasane's Swamp* (*Kaidan Kasane ga fuchi*, 1957) and *The Ghost Story of Yotsuya* (*Tōkaidō Yotsuya kaidan*, 1959), as well as a novel reinterpretation of the *bakeneko* material in *Mansion of the Ghost Cat* (*Bōrei kaibyō yashiki*, 1958). Meanwhile, Daiei's ghost cat formula inherited from the prewar heyday of Shinkō and Suzuki Sumiko continued to receive the usual critical drubbing, and eventually lost ground at the box office to the studio's competitors.[28] Irie Takako made her fifth and final appearance as the *bakeneko* in 1957's *Ghost Cat of Yonaki Swamp* (*Kaibyō Yonaki numa*).

Daiei would thereafter cease its strategy of crafting its *kaiki* fare around the star persona of Irie as the second great "ghost cat actress" and instead turn to a new breed of celebrity, the "glamour actress" (*gurāma joyū*), whose fame was constructed entirely around a newly opened horizon for exploitation in Japanese commercial cinema: on-screen nudity. Although the studio's attempt to sell its glamour star Mōri Ikuko as the new face (or perhaps more accurately, the new body) of *kaiki* met with no great success, the novel fashion in which Daiei combined Mōri, her willingness to bare her flesh for the camera, and her supposed fondness for snakes with the themes and motifs of the *kaiki* genre stands in unique contrast to the rest of the genre as it existed in Japan during the latter 1950s, particularly in its reliance on crafting Mōri's off-screen persona as monstrous.

---

[28] Ōsawa Jō, "Shintōhō no obake eiga to *Tōkaidō Yotsuya kaidan*: jyanru no fukkatsu tokakushin," in *Kaiki to gensō e no kairō: kaidan kara J-horā e*, ed. Uchiyama Kazuki (Tokyo: Shinwasha, 2008), 71.

Female nudity was largely taboo in prewar Japanese film. In 1935 Suzuki Sumiko raised eyebrows when her backside appeared nude from the waist up in Shinkō's *The Hell of Oden*, and while this prefigured her sexualized portrayals of the ghost cat the following year, it was hardly the start of a sexual revolution in Japanese cinema. Nothing more daring appeared before the Film Act in 1939, and by 1940 any films dealing with "sexual frivolity" were prohibited.[29] After the war ended in 1945 the sexualized portrayal of women's bodies in cinema manifested in tandem with the proliferation of *nikutai bungaku* or "literature of the flesh," meant to titillate male audiences hungry for distractions under the cloud of defeat and occupation.[30] Two years after the end of the Occupation in 1954 the industry's newly established self-regulating censorship body, Eirin, introduced the *seijin* or "adult" classification for film ratings, and films like Nikkatsu's influential "Sun Tribe" pictures of 1955–6, with their focus on swimsuit-clad young stars embracing in the throes of passion, began to nudge the door open for more explicit displays of flesh on-screen.

In 1956 Shintōhō, which by this point was almost totally committed to the production of exploitation genres such as *kaiki* and *yakuza* gangster pictures, discerned an opportunity in the newly created *seijin* rating and pioneered the *ama* genre, capitalizing on the sex appeal of Japan's traditional female pearl hunters, famous for diving without scuba gear—or swimsuits. The first *ama* film, *Revenge of the Pearl Queen* (*Onna shinju ō no fukushū*, 1956) owed its box office success to the buzz around its previously unknown star, Maeda Michiko, whom Donald Richie and Joseph Anderson dismissively described as "an actress comprised almost entirely of mammary glands."[31] Although the film contains no scenes of simulated sex and conveniently positioned mise-en-scène always obscures her nipples and genital area, the hitherto fore unseen display of female nudity in a mainstream commercial release caused a sensation. Shintōhō promptly built up a stable of aspiring actresses with no compunction about baring it all for the camera and heavily promoted its roster of "flesh actresses" (*nikutai joyū*). The other major studios also in the business of producing B-genre pictures, notably

---

[29] Hirano Kyoko, *Mr. Smith Goes to Tokyo: Japanese Cinema under the American Occupation, 1945–52* (Washington, DC: Smithsonian Institute, 1992), 16.

[30] Ayako Saito, "Occupation and Memory: The Representation of Woman's Body in Postwar Japanese Cinema," in *The Oxford Handbook of Japanese Cinema*, ed. Daisuke Miyao (New York: Oxford University Press, 2014), 331–3.

[31] Anderson and Richie, *The Japanese Film*, 267.

Tōei and Daiei, soon followed suit with their more respectable sounding but no less titillating "glamour actresses."[32]

Mōri Ikuko, a newly signed glamour actress under contract to Daiei, debuted in a supporting role as an exotic dancer in *The Invisible Man Meets the Fly* (*Tōmei ningen to hae otoko*, 1957) the same year Irie Takako made her final appearance as the ghost cat. Mōri initially posed a problem for the studio's press department. Already at the atrociously old age of 25 when she made her acting debut, she was several years older than her fellow glamour stars and considered late for a sexy new find.[33] Meanwhile the studio was struggling to find a new direction for their *kaiki* output in the face of diminishing returns. A potential solution for both dilemmas presented itself when Mōri, sensing she needed a gimmick to distinguish herself, began bringing her pet snake with her to the studio.

In June 1958 Daiei launched an ad campaign for *White Snake Beauty* (*Shirohebi Komachi*), the first in a rapidly produced trio of erotic *kaiki* films that would showcase the studio's sensational new "serpent actress." *Serpent's Wrath* (*Shūnen no hebi*) followed less than three months later, and the trilogy wrapped up with *Blue Snake Bath* (*Aoi hebi buro*) in early 1959. Press releases quoted Mōri saying it was "a dream come true" to appear on-screen with her beloved snakes,[34] and publicity images featured both in-character shots of a semi-clad Mōri shrieking in terror as they wind and slither about her body and out-of-character photos in similar setup with Mōri striking sexy, sultry poses. Most revealing were candid behind-the-scenes shots of Mōri calmly letting stagehands drape live snakes over her bare shoulders and chest (Figure 17).

As we have seen, the combination of sexuality and monstrosity was a crucial component of Japanese *kaiki* cinema going back to the silent era and continued to be implicit even in Irie Takako's unflattering portrayals of the ghost cat, but the decision to place the snake-loving glamour star Mōri Ikuko into a series of period *kaiki* films dramatically rewrote the formula. Previously, the top-billed female role had almost always gone to the innocent heroine/victim, whose bodily transformation into a grotesque monster was the main site of attraction. Mōri also received top billing, but in all three films stars as a villainous femme fatale. The switch-up appears to have been motivated entirely by Mōri's status as a glamour star. Female villainous roles in Japanese *kaiki* film to this point, if they

---

[32] For further discussion of the rise of nudity in commercial Japanese cinema of the 1950s, see Jasper Sharp, *Behind the Pink Curtain: The Complete History of Japanese Sex Cinema* (Godalming: Fab Press, 2008), 31–42.

[33] Shimura Miyoko, "Kaibutsu ka suru joyū-tachi: neko to hebi wo meguru hyōshō," in *Kaiki to gensō e no kairō*, 186.

[34] Ibid., 187.

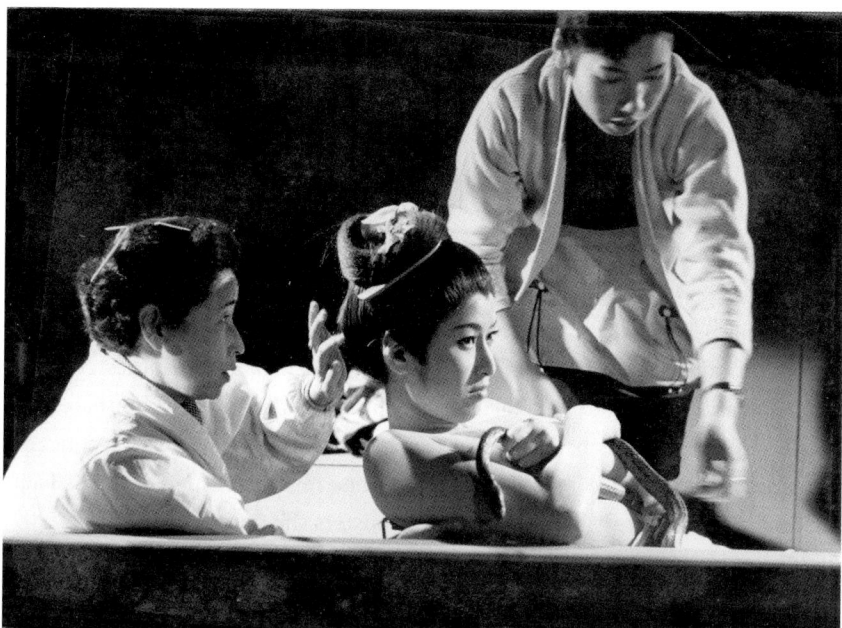

Figure 17 Behind-the-scenes shot of Mōri Ikuko in the nude and covered in live snakes, for *Blue Snake Bath* (*Aoi hebi buro*, 1959). ©KADOKAWA.

featured at all, were usually minor and portrayed by elder actresses, appearing as the wicked matrons or jealous romantic rivals who are haunted by the monstrously transformed heroine. In the Daiei snake films the villain, in the considerably more voluptuous figure of Mōri, takes center stage, while the role of the monstrously transformed heroine diminishes. Mōri's body takes over from the heroine/victim as the primary site of spectacle, but hers is not a body transformed. In the first film of the series, *White Snake Beauty*, Mōri plays a sideshow performer who in a gratuitous scene fondles, caresses, and kisses her pet snakes in a state of undress after a bath, expressive of her character's sexual perversity as well as supposedly showcasing the actress's own fetishistic predilection for snakes. In the second and third films of the series Mōri's characters do not share the actress's supposed fondness for snakes, so hers instead becomes a body punished, in macabre fashion, as the vengeful spirit of the heroine summons hordes of serpents to assault her conveniently exposed flesh.

The fact that Mōri never undergoes any sort of bodily monstrous transformation is significant. Like previous *kaiki* stars, her appeal lies in a juxtaposition of desirability and grotesque monstrosity, but in the case of her immediate predecessor Irie Takako, these two aspects were starkly sorted out from each other on-screen. Although Irie's body was the site of spectacle, desirability and repulsion are kept distinct by the elaborate visual metamorphosis undergone by the actress. Mōri, meanwhile, undergoes no such physical change. As a glamour star, her nude body is already the main attraction, and rendering it bloody and repulsive under heavy make-up would cancel out the spectacle. The snake films accordingly render their displays of the macabre and the grotesque concurrent with the spectacle of Mōri's bare flesh, combining sexuality and monstrosity even more thoroughly than Suzuki Sumiko's prewar portrayals of the vampish ghost cat. Shimura notes that Mōri's on-screen sexuality is at its most explicit at the exact moment of monstrosity, as her clothes come off to exploit the voyeuristic spectacle of live snakes slithering over her bare skin. Mōri's desirability thus becomes inextricably entwined with the grotesque and the macabre, unlike Irie Takako, whose intricate makeup helped to disassociate the image of the actress herself from the monsters she portrayed.[35]

Mōri was different in one other obvious way: she didn't play the monster. Daiei compensated by constructing Mōri Ikuko herself as monstrous. Off-screen at least, Mōri might not have been perceived as macabre in the public consciousness were it not for the aggressive push of Daiei's advertising wing to convince moviegoers that letting snakes slither over her body was something the actress enjoyed doing in her spare time as well. The snake films are, it must be said, not very good. Although intended to replace the Irie Takako ghost cat series, which were declining in popularity, the studio rushed out these B-grade program pictures with the same *obake yashiki* spook house approach to the *kaiki* material, neglecting to develop the themes of *osore* that underpin the narrative. It was likely felt that an additional hook beyond Mōri's nudity was needed to help pull in audiences, hence the behind-the-scenes images of the star at ease in the buff with hordes of snakes on her and sensational quotes about this "curiously creepy actress" (*kimyō joyū*) who kept her home full of snakes.[36] The obvious intention was to convince audiences that Mōri was not acting in the scene from *White Snake Beauty* in which her character fondles and kisses the snakes draping her flesh, but rather that viewers were getting an authentic, voyeuristic peek at her kinky fetish in action. But perhaps the most evocative promotional image for the series was a headshot of Mōri, eyes closed in a deathlike repose with a venomous serpent coiled about her throat (Figure 18). Thusly was her off-screen persona crafted to be even more creepily alluring than

---

[35] Ibid., 188–9.
[36] Ibid., 187.

Figure 18 Promotional image for *White Snake Beauty* (*Shirohebi Komachi*, 1958). ©KADOKAWA.

her on-screen performances. Daiei would have Japan believe that the woman herself held an implicitly perverse and potentially dangerous erotic fascination with the macabre.

Although they wielded no great lasting impact on the genre, Mōri Ikuko's snake films and the advertising campaign built around them represent the ultimate example of the extratextuality that went into the making of a *kaiki* star. Suzuki Sumiko's fame as the first great horror star of Japanese cinema rested largely upon her prior reputation for athletic physicality. Irie Takako, Suzuki's successor to the ghost cat mantle, was the compelling fallen star, whose monstrous appeal lay in the audience's memories of her former stature. But Mōri Ikuko was herself monstrous in the public eye. In truth, Mōri held no fetishistic obsession with snakes. She merely was unafraid of them and sought to capitalize on the point. When her father expressed concern about the studio's portrayal of her off-camera lifestyle, she assured him, "It's a harshly competitive world, and you have to be unusual to succeed in this business. Don't worry!"[37] Her reputation as a hypersexual, "curiously creepy" woman with an affinity for the macabre would, however, come back to haunt her, as we will see in Chapter 5.

Blurring and Redrawing the Boundaries: Tōei's "Chinese-Style Romances," Atomic-Age Science Fiction, and Hammer Horror

Even before Daiei traded its ghost cats for erotic snake women, other developments both in Japan and abroad contributed to a moment of existential crisis in the critical imagination regarding the boundaries of the *kaiki* genre. Studios like Shōchiku and the newly formed Tōei had begun to experiment with blending the domestic *kaiki* film with elements from other genres like comedy and romance. While the combining of motifs from supposedly disparate genres was nothing new in commercial cinema, many felt that comedy and romance were antithetical to the narrative themes of *osore* that defined the ideal *kaiki* film. Meanwhile, Japanese critics seemed willing to embrace the blurring of the boundaries between horror and science fiction that was occurring in 1950s Hollywood cinema. By 1957 leading voices in film criticism like Satō Tadao were proclaiming science fiction to be the future of the *kaiki* genre. The same year, however, the release of the British Hammer Films' *The Curse of Frankenstein* would reassert the original conception of *kaiki* cinema as belonging to what might be termed the gothic mode of horror filmmaking.

The Daiei ghost cat and snake films lacked attention to narrative detail that undermined the themes of *osore* their monsters ideally represented, but another place where the absence of *osore* was keenly felt was in the recently formed Tōei Studio's initial forays into the *kaiki* genre. Created in 1949 and occupying the former facilities of Shinkō, Tōei also occupied the place in the Japanese film industry that Shinkō had vacated upon becoming Daiei: home of the B-grade *jidaigeki* period film. Tōei employed much of Shinkō's prewar talent, and by the middle of the decade was "making money hand over fist" with *jidaigeki* double bills.[38] This could lead one to suppose that Tōei's *kaiki* films might be truer successors to the Shinkō spirit than Daiei's ghost cat pictures. Tōei eventually would produce some of the more horrific latter-day *kaiki* films in the 1960s, but

---

[37] Ibid., 194.
[38] Anderson and Richie, *The Japanese Film*, 239.

their earliest efforts in the genre tended to resemble the occasional Shōchiku romantic *kaidan* production like Tanaka Kinuyo's appearance in the 1937 *Dish Mansion at Banchō* more than anything else. Although Tōei films like the *bakeneko* spoof *The Ghost Cat and the Chicken* (*Kaibyō koshinuke daisōdō*, 1954) clearly respond to Daiei's series, more typical entries in the studio's 1950s *kaiki* output include a version of *The Peony Lantern* (1955) that emphasizes the ghostly romance between the hero and his departed lover and discards the gruesome consequences of a man copulating with a corpse that feature prominently in the original version of the tale.

The following year's color production *The Ghost Story of Plover Pond* (*Kaidan chidori ga fuchi*) continued Tōei's romantic *kaiki* bent, as did 1957's production of *The Dish Mansion at Banchō* starring Misora Hibari. Japan's favorite on-screen sweetheart of the 1950s, it was unthinkable that Misora's turn as the ghost of Okiku would draw inspiration from the earliest, horrific versions of the Dish Mansion legend, in which the murdered maid's ghost rises each night from the well in which she was drowned to torment her killer Aoyama with her incessant wailing. Instead, like Tanaka Kinuyo before her, Misora appears in an adaptation of Okamoto Kidō's romantic reworking of the legend, which reconceived Okiku and Aoyama as star-crossed lovers. While the results no doubt pleased Misora's throngs of adoring fans, critics with an appetite for *kaiki to senritsu* "thrills and chills" found it lacking:

> There's none of the *urami* (hatred) and curses [typical of the genre] ... Even after becoming a ghost Okiku still adores Aoyama. It feels like some kind of Chinese-style romance, while interesting Japanese-style ghouls and goblins are nowhere to be found. The whole thing's got a watered-down feeling to it ... you'd expect Misora Hibari's *obake* to burst into some insipid song.[39]

Condemning the film as a "Chinese-style romance" and lamenting the absence of "Japanese-style ghouls and goblins" draws an explicit contrast between two East Asian ghost story traditions. On the Chinese side the reviewer appears to have in mind the ghostly love stories of Pu Songling (1640–1715). The Qing dynasty author wrote many tales of ghouls and goblins that equal or surpass Japanese *kaidan* in gruesomeness, but his most popular stories feature human men who marry ghosts or fox spirits and live happily ever after. Pu Songling's collected writings are considered by many the epitome of Classical Chinese strange fiction, and as such the Chinese cultural conception of *kai(ki)* carries

---

[39] Tada Michitarō, "*Kaidan Banchō sarayashiki*," *Kinema junpō*, September 15, 1957, 68.

a more romantic flavor than the representative Japanese ghost stories, which tend toward the grotesque and horrific. Of the "Big Three" Japanese *kaidan* (*The Ghost Story of Yotsuya*, *The Dish Mansion at Banchō*, and *The Peony Lantern*), only *The Peony Lantern* has a clear Chinese antecedent. While Okamoto Kidō and Misora Hibari eventually turned *The Dish Mansion* into a love story, the earliest versions of the legend featured no such romance between Okiku and Aoyama, in contrast to the Chinese-derived *Peony Lantern*, which had love story elements intact from its inception. Thus, while a Chinese conception of *kaiki* might allow for Misora Hibari to profess her love for her paramour and burst into song, the above-quoted review shows that Japanese critics expected their *kaiki* films to come with *urami* and curses.

If Tōei's "Chinese-style" ghostly love stories and the continuation of the occasional *shinpi-kaiki* mystery hybrids like Shintōhō's *The Man Who Vanished in the Black Cat Mansion* (*Kuroneko-kan ni kieta otoko*, 1956) began to blur the boundaries of the *kaiki* genre, Hollywood horror faced a similar existential crisis in the 1950s with the proliferation of the science fiction/horror hybrid. As noted in Chapter 1, debating the boundaries of sci-fi and horror became one of the central projects of film critics, genre theorists, and movie aficionados after the gothic horrors of Universal gave way to films like *Earth vs. the Flying Saucers* and *Invasion of the Body Snatchers* (both 1956). The differences went beyond merely replacing traditional folkloric monsters like the vampire, ghost, and werewolf with distinctly twentieth-century creatures like space aliens and radiation-mutated lizards and insects. The individualized, personal terror engendered by Count Dracula, Frankenstein's Monster, or even Irena Reed from *Cat People* (1942) stalking their few chosen victims through shadowy corridors found itself supplanted by depictions of mass panic on a societal level. Often read as expressing Cold War fears of nuclear Armageddon, many science fiction horrors of the 1950s feature hordes of people fleeing whole cities that fall victim to the monsters' rampage of destruction. Such depictions of mass panic afford little chance for either the characters or the audience to reflect upon the nature of the monsters' violation of our rational understanding of the natural world—which Noël Carroll and other horror theorists deem a necessary component of the horror movie formula. There is only enough (screen) time to flee for one's life.

The most famous example of such a film is of course a Japanese one, though it must be remembered that the original 1954 *Godzilla* took its inspiration largely from a Hollywood release of the previous year, *The Beast from 20,000 Fathoms*. *Godzilla* was part of the Tōhō studio's attempts to avoid more traditional *kaiki* fare like the period ghost story adaptations and ghost cat pictures produced by the other major studios in favor of a more urbane, modern type of horror along the lines of the sci-fi horror hybrids of 1950s Hollywood.[40] Although eclipsed in global visibility by the endlessly enduring Godzilla franchise, Tōhō's "transforming man" pictures of the 1950s and 1960s include classic oddities like *Matango* (1963). The film's hokey-sounding plot about a group of castaways who mutate into giant mushroom creatures prefigures both the pessimistic critiques of society that horror film historians identify as a key feature of the turn to "modern horror" in 1970s Western film and the "body horror" motif of 1970s and 1980s American horror in works like Ridley Scott's *Alien* (1979) and the films of David Cronenberg.

Interestingly, while Japanese critics of the day seemed willing to consider American and European science fiction horror hybrids as *kaiki*, they were less inclined to view Tōhō's efforts as serious entries in the genre, considering them hollow parodies of Hollywood sci-fi. By 1957, the undeniable global popularity of what were in Japan known as *kaiki* films prompted *Kinema junpō* to commission a series of feature articles by several of the most prominent film critics of the day, published under the umbrella title of "The World of *Kaiki* Film" (*Kaiki eiga no sekai*).[41] In "The Appeal of *Kaiki* Films" (*Kaiki eiga no miryoku*), Satō Tadao doubts that traditional *kaidan* tales of vengeance from beyond the grave retain relevance for a contemporary audience, finding them unable to address the particular fears of a postwar society in which the personal vendetta of an angry ghost seemed trivial compared to the possibility of nuclear holocaust and human extinction, writing, "Actually, what must be considered as the modern-day *kaidan* is the science fiction film (*kūsō kagaku eiga*)."[42] One might think the obvious case study for Satō's argument would be *Godzilla*'s homegrown nuclear narrative, but instead he goes on to discuss an American film, *The Incredible Shrinking Man* (1957), praising the film's use of special effects to depict spectacles like a miniaturized human battling an enormous housecat. Echoing somewhat the formalist sentiments of the Pure Film Movement critics from four decades earlier, Satō considers these uniquely filmic techniques far more frightening than the "theatrical" (*gekijoteki*) tricks of Japanese ghost cat pictures and *kaidan* adaptations.[43]

---

[40] Ōkubo Tomoyasu, "Henshin ningen no tokuisei: Tōhō 'henshin ningen shiriizu' o megutte," in *Kaiki to gensō e no kairō*, 102–4.
[41] The feature appeared in the July 1, 1957, edition of *Kinema junpō*.
[42] Satō Tadao, "Kaiki eiga no miryoku," *Kinema junpō*, July 1, 1957, 47.
[43] Ibid.

Meanwhile Izawa Jun, in his piece "What Is *Kaiki*?" (*Kaiki to wa?*), finds traditional Japanese *kaidan* more relevant than the science fiction films, at least for a domestic audience. He draws a clear line from what he argues are the roots of the Western sci-fi/horror hybrid in *Frankenstein* to the giant radioactive ants and spiders of contemporary Hollywood science fiction films, identifying a "Wrath of God" (*kami no ikari*) motif that expresses fears of reprisal for overreaching scientists tampering in God's domain that Izawa says carries a special resonance for Western Judeo-Christian society. But it will be recalled from Chapter 1 that Izawa finds the Japanese versions of the giant radioactive monster narrative nothing more than pale imitations, lacking the religious dimension for Japanese audiences. Instead, what speak to a Japanese sense of horror are Oiwa-*sama* and tales of karmic comeuppance that mark the traditional *kaidan*.

While Satō and Izawa disagree about the value of *kaidan* movie adaptations in 1950s Japan, they both give the domestic radioactive *kaijū* genre short shrift ("These are not serious monsters"),[44] while perhaps unfairly finding their Hollywood counterparts seriously frightening and worthy of discussion as *kaiki* cinema. However, a decade later when the magazine published an entire issue devoted to "*Kaiki* and Horror Film" (*Kaiki to kyōfu eiga*) in the summer of 1969, not only were Japanese *kaijū* movies like *Godzilla* omitted from discussion, so too were the foreign sci-fi horror hybrids that Satō Tadao found so compelling.[45] After a few years of mild identity crisis, *kaiki* was once again the exclusive domain of vampires, werewolves, ghost cats, and vengeful spirits.

What had happened in ten years that caused *Kinema junpō* to rethink their inclusion of science fiction in its conception of the *kaiki* genre? A glance at the 1957 "World of *Kaiki* Film" feature shows portents of things to come. A picture of actor Peter Cushing in the just-released *The Curse of Frankenstein* appears on the first page of the feature, directly above Izawa Jun's title "What is *Kaiki*?"—a prophetic placement in hindsight. The film's release was apparently too recent to allow much discussion of it in the articles that made up the feature, apart from a brief mention in Shimizu Akira's "*Kaiki* Movies A-to-Z," in which the author comments that the film's emphasis on the doctor over his monstrous creation hews closer to Mary Shelley's original novel than James Whale's 1931 version.[46] *The Curse of Frankenstein*'s worldwide commercial success and subsequent

---

[44] Izawa Jun, "Kaiki to wa? Nihon no obake to seiyō no obake," *Kinema junpō*, July 1, 1957, 45.
[45] For further discussion of *Godzilla*'s and the Hammer horror films' contrastive places in Japanese film discourse, see Michael Crandol, "Godzilla versus Dracula: Hammer Horror Films in Japan," *Cinephile* 13 no. 1 (2019): 18–24.
[46] Shimizu Akira, "Kaiki eiga no arekore," *Kinema junpō*, July 1, 1957, 48–9.

impact on global horror (and *kaiki*) film production would, however, be enormous.

The UK-based Hammer Film Productions' first of many remakes of 1930s Universal horror movies, *The Curse of Frankenstein* appeared in the midst of the sci-fi/horror craze to inaugurate a revival of the gothic mode of horror filmmaking, a return to crumbling castles, traditional monsters like the vampire and werewolf, and a sense of dread in place of the mass panic of the sci-fi disaster epic. The movement was not limited to the Hammer studio, although their long-running *Frankenstein* and *Dracula* series starring Cushing and Christopher Lee, respectively, remain the highest-profile examples. The success of *The Curse of Frankenstein* and especially Hammer's follow-up, *Dracula* (1958) formed part of a global zeitgeist of gothic horror in the late 1950s and 1960s, which included Roger Corman's eight-film cycle based on the works of Edgar Allan Poe for American International Pictures, Italian director Mario Bava's bold experimentation with color in pictures like *Black Sabbath* (*I tre volti della paura*) and *The Whip and the Body* (*La frusta e il corpo*, both 1963), and—in Japan—the critically acclaimed work of Nakagawa Nobuo at Shintōhō.[47]

Very few of these films were merely clones of Hammer product. In the case of Nakagawa, his work appears contemporaneously with the first Hammer horror movies, ruling out the possibility of trying to copy the "Hammer horror" formula that had yet to coalesce. Rather than mere imitation, the late 1950s/early 1960s zeitgeist of gothic horror represents vernacular modernism at its best, as different filmmaking industries seized upon a common stylistic movement to tell their own stories with their own sets of cultural particulars, be it the American gothic work of Poe in Roger Corman's Hollywood or a Japanese *kaidan* from Shintōhō. The gothic horror revival did not kill the *kaijū* or science fiction horror hybrids: Tōhō's *Godzilla* and *Mothra* (*Mosura*) series flourished during the 1960s, and filmmakers like Mario Bava did not limit themselves to gothic pictures like *Kill, Baby, Kill* (*Operazione paura*, 1966) but also directed science fiction horrors like *Planet of the Vampires* (*Terrore nello spazio*, 1965) and prototypical slasher films (*giallo*) like *Blood and Black Lace* (*Sei donne per l'assassino*, 1964).[48] But

---

[47] For a discussion of Hammer's global impact on the gothic horror film see Kevin Heffernan's *Ghouls, Gimmicks, and Gold: Horror Films and the American Movie Business, 1953–1968* (Durham, NC: Duke University Press, 2004), 61. Roberto Curti discusses Hammer's impact on Italian horror in *Italian Gothic Horror Films, 1957–1969* (Jefferson, MO: McFarland, 2015), 1–16.

[48] Also worth noting is *The Manster*, a B-grade, 1959 US-Japanese coproduction in which an American journalist in Tokyo falls victim to the experiments of a deranged Japanese scientist who keeps among his mutated creations a woman who bears a striking resemblance to the ghost of Oiwa—likely the first time the classic *kaidan* iconography of the vengeful ghost appeared on foreign movie screens.

what the gothic horror revival did do was reestablish and strengthen the original Japanese conception of *kaiki* as a genre that dealt with themes of *osore*—be it the terror of the existence of vampires or the cosmic, karmic vengeance of Oiwa and the ghost cat—in settings removed from the modern, everyday world. The special issue of *Kinema junpō* devoted exclusively to *kaiki* and *kyōfu* (horror) attests to Hammer's central role in reasserting the original markers of the *kaiki* genre in Japan, featuring a large illustration of Christopher Lee as Dracula on the cover and including a translation of the complete screenplay for 1958's *Dracula* as one of two "Horror Scenario Classics" alongside Nakagawa Nobuo's *Ghost Story of Yotsuya*.[49] As far as *Kinema junpō* was concerned, Christopher Lee was the face of *kaiki* (Figure 19).

Such pictures largely had vanished from American and European screens during the 1950s until Hammer brought them back in vogue with more overt depictions of sexuality and violence presented with lurid, bright-red blood and widescreen cinematography, qualities that won them praise in Japan even as censors, watchdog groups, and conservative critics in the Western world recoiled in outrage. The early Hammer horror films routinely faced heavy censorship from the British and American film regulatory bodies. It was not the violence visited on the human characters by the monsters that caused an uproar, but the bloody dispatching of the monsters at the hands of the heroes. Images of female vampires in low-cut nightgowns being staked through the heart were especially met with disapproval by conservative sectors of Anglophone society as coded portrayals of sexual assault. A famous anecdote recounts how the climactic scene of the Count's destruction in 1958's *Dracula*, in which actor Christopher Lee's flesh appears to boil and melt in the sunlight, was thought lost for over half a century until it was discovered in Japan's National Film Archive vaults in 2012. The scene had been removed by the British and American censors and remained intact only in the Japanese release. Hammer's forays into horror may have been transgressive and taboo-shattering in the West, but Mōri Ikuko's nude displays of flesh in Daiei's erotic *kaiki* snake series were far more revealing than Hammer's sexualized content, while the Shintōhō studios own increasingly lurid depictions of graphic violence (which will be examined in the next chapter) similarly met with no social backlash. In Japan, Hammer was in bloody good company.

The disparity between the British and Japanese film critics' assessment of the same formal elements of Hammer's *Dracula* reveals that, while Japanese *kaiki* films historically suffered low critical repute just as Western horror films were

---

[49] *Kinema junpō*, August 20, 1969. The phrase is rendered in English in the magazine.

Figure 19 The cover of the 1969 issue of *Kinema junpō* devoted entirely to *kaiki* and *kyōfu*, featuring Christopher Lee as the face of the genre.

long derided as trash cinema by Anglophone critics, the reasons for their bad reputations could be quite different. The review of *Dracula* that appeared in the UK's *Daily Worker* sums up the backlash in the English-speaking world:

> I went to see *Dracula*, a Hammer film, prepared to enjoy a nervous giggle. I was even ready to poke gentle fun at it. I came away revolted and outraged … Laughable nonsense? Not when it is filmed like this, with realism and with the modern conveniences of colour and wide screen … This film disgusts the mind and repels the senses.[50]

Compare this to the review of *Dracula* that appeared in *Kinema junpō*, which commends the film for the very same reasons the British publication condemned it:

> Scenes that will likely cause weak-willed women and children to spontaneously scream and throw both hands over their eyes appear one on the heels of another. The reasons for this are exceedingly simple—Technicolor, and special effects … The script, the performances, the cinematography, every aim and effort is put entirely toward the single focus of creating a sense of gloom and instilling terror, and on this account, we can say the film is a total success.[51]

Western film critics hostile to the horror genre most frequently attack the pictures on moral grounds. They are, according to their detractors, at best vulgar, exploitative displays of violence—and at worst, dangerously subversive in their indulgence of the horror aficionado's latent sadomasochistic desires. As Linda Williams has theorized in her influential piece on the so-called "body genres" (horror, melodrama, and pornography), the critical unease with horror may ultimately lie in the way it seeks to provoke in its audience "an apparent lack of proper esthetic distance, a sense of over-involvement in sensation and emotion."[52] Yet this is exactly what Japanese critics of domestic *kaiki* film deride the pictures for failing to accomplish, complaining that the results "weren't scary" and "laughable" while Hammer horror could admirably make the audience "spontaneously scream" and cover their eyes.

The Japanese critical admiration for the Hammer pictures stood in contrast to most domestic *kaiki* films based on traditional *kaidan* and ghost cat tales,

---

[50] Nina Hibbin, "*Dracula*," *The Daily Worker*, May 24, 1958. Quoted in Peter Hutchings, *Hammer and Beyond: The British Horror Film* (New York: St. Martin's Press, 1993), 9.
[51] Sugiyama Shizuo, "*Kyūketsuki Dorakyura*," *Kinema junpō*, Fall Special, 1958, 120.
[52] Linda Williams, "Film Bodies: Gender, Genre, and Excess," in *Film Theory and Criticism: Introductory Readings*, ed. Leo Braudy and Marshall Cohen (New York: Oxford University Press, 1999), 705.

which had reappeared several years before *The Curse of Frankenstein* with the end of the American Occupation in 1952. Like their prewar ancestors, they were generally held to be not frightening, be it due to laughable special effects, the irrelevance of Edo-period ghost stories to contemporary postwar Japan, or the presence of Misora Hibari—all elements deemed to dilute the themes of *osore* inherent in the *kaidan* narrative. However, at the same time Hammer horror was redefining Count Dracula and Dr. Frankenstein for a new generation of theatergoers, the Shintōhō studio and its senior director, Nakagawa Nobuo, were doing the same for the ghosts and werecats of domestic *kaiki* cinema.

Conclusion

The decade following Japan's defeat in the Second World War was a period of transition and uncertainty for both the production of *kaiki* films as well as the discourse surrounding them.

Navigating censorship gave rise to new forms of *kaiki* and experimentations with the content of the genre. The postwar order called into question the relevance of the older form of both Japanese *kaiki* films and Hollywood's classic horror films. Invaders from outer space and radioactive giants like Godzilla threatened to unleash instant death and destruction on a massive scale that made some critics opine nineteenth-century gothic holdovers like Oiwa's personal vendettas as ill-suited to express the societal terrors of the nuclear age. Despite predictions that the traditional *kaiki* film's days were numbered, the close of the 1950s instead saw old and new monsters cohabiting on cinema screens. While Godzilla and other sci-fi monsters found themselves incorporated into the horror genre umbrella in Anglophone cultures, the rise of Hammer served to reinscribe the differences of the *kaiki* genre as separate from these newer forms of on-screen horror, further marking *kaiki* as a distinct historical and cultural way of approaching transnational genre cinema.

When *kaiki* film production in Japan resumed in earnest following an almost twelve-year moratorium imposed by wartime and occupation censorship, the Japanese film industry was a very changed business from the late 1930s. The government-mandated consolidation of the industry into three major studios in 1941 eliminated smaller outfits like Shinkō, which relied on popular genres like *kaiki* for survival and strove to make horror pictures that would both please the crowds and the critics with innovative techniques like those seen in *The Ghost Cat and the Mysterious Shamisen*. This was a moot point, however, as first the wartime Japanese government and then the ensuing American Occupation both suppressed the production of *kaiki* films for different reasons. The studios attempted a few workarounds to the problem of censorship in regard to the production of traditional *kaidan* adaptations, although in the bargain had to remove most of the themes of *osore* cosmic revenge that made the films *kaiki* in the first place.

After the Occupation ended in 1952, former Shinkō head Nagata Masaichi, now head of Daiei, reinstated annual production of ghost cat pictures. However, no longer reliant on cheaply produced genre pictures for its survival, Nagata's new studio did not lavish the same level of attention on their *kaiki* productions, which were quickly filmed during breaks between more ambitious, A-list pictures. Daiei's attempts to diversify their *kaiki* content while also taking advantage of relaxed attitudes toward on-screen nudity in the snake films of Mōri Ikuko likewise failed to capture audience's imaginations. The newly founded Tōei studio also began an annual production schedule of *kaki* films, though these tended to either be comedic parodies of the Daiei films or else romantic reworkings of classic *kaidan* that emphasized undying love between man and ghost over ghastly tales of revenge from beyond the grave. Not surprisingly, domestic *kaiki* films of the immediate post-Occupation years continued to receive the same critical drubbing their prewar counterparts had received: either through lack of innovation or detours into comedy and romance, the films still "weren't scary."

They were, however, still perennially popular with audiences, and in 1957 *Kinema junpō* acknowledged this with their "World of *Kaiki* Film" feature, in which top critics of the day debated the essence of *kaiki*. Some found the spark of the genre in the karmic omnipotence of traditional Japanese monsters like the ghost of Oiwa, while others felt the Hollywood science fiction/horror hybrids of the 1950s were the true successors to the outdated wraiths and ghost cats of premodern Japan. By the end of the decade, the former seems to have won out, as the tremendous popularity of Hammer Films' gothic revivals of *Frankenstein* and *Dracula* reasserted the primacy of period costumed horror to the *kaiki* label, and—perhaps even more importantly in the Japanese case—the Shintōhō studio and director Nakagawa Nobuo brought Oiwa and her undead ilk back to Japanese theater screens with a frightful vengeance.

4

Uncanny Invasions: The Shintōhō Studio and Nakagawa Nobuo

Critics and fans alike unanimously consider the Shintōhō *kaiki* films of director Nakagawa Nobuo the most accomplished domestic examples of the genre. Although he frequently professed to have no personal interest in such material, having been assigned all of his *kaiki* projects at the studio by executive producer Ōkura Mitsugi, Nakagawa brought his decades-honed expertise as a filmmaker to bear on the world of vengeful spirits and ghost cats. Films like *The Ghost Story of Kasane's Swamp* (*Kaidan Kasane ga fuchi*, 1957), *Mansion of the Ghost Cat* (*Bōrei kaibyō yashiki*, 1958), and *The Ghost Story of Yotsuya* (*Tōkaidō Yotsuya kaidan*, 1959) exhibit a sophistication of camerawork, staging, and mise-en-scène not seen in a domestic *kaiki* film since the prewar heyday of the Shinkō studio and more typically associated with the films of renowned auteurs like Kurosawa Akira, Ozu Yasujirō, and Mizoguchi Kenji.

A remarkably strong consistency of vision underlies the films' technical excellence. Nakagawa's *Ghost Story of Yotsuya*, generally regarded as the best of the more than thirty screen adaptations of the tale, dwells on the psychology of its two main characters—the stoically self-serving Iemon and the rage-consumed ghost of Oiwa—reflecting the director's professed interest in story over spectacle.[1] His *kaiki* films demonstrate a mastery of both and show that he understood startling moments of sensational address in horror film need not be mere excess but work in tandem with the narrative, lending each other weight. A careful depiction of Oiwa's hatred is essential to establish the narrative themes of *osore* that inform the spectacular imagery of *kaiki* films, as Oiwa's ghost enacts the terrible drama of karmic retribution against the husband who betrayed her.

---

[1] When asked about how he approached his *kaiki* filmmaking assignments, Nakagawa replied, "Whatever kind of movie you're making, it's the same. If the scenario is no good, it's hopeless" (Nakagawa Nobuo, "Obake eiga sono hoka/watashi no kiroku eiga ron," in *Eiga kantoku Nakagawa Nobuo*, ed. Takisawa Osamu and Yamane Sadao (Tokyo: Riburopōto, 1987), 106).

Nakagawa revisited the notion of karma again and again in his pictures, his characters becoming trapped by inexorable fate brought on by past misdeeds, from the star-crossed lovers of *Kasane's Swamp* to the cursed protagonists of *Mansion of the Ghost Cat* and the doomed antihero of his idiosyncratic horror film *Jigoku* (1960). In spite of his professed lack of interest in the genre, Nakagawa's sensibilities as a storyteller lent themselves extraordinarily well to a powerful depiction of *osore* that critics felt had been sorely lacking in Japanese *kaiki* films almost from their inception. At the same time, his skill in formally depicting the symbols of psychological terror in ways that delivered pleasurable scares to the audience meshed the spook-house mode of sensational address with narrative sophistication to achieve the elusive equilibrium of spectacle and *osore*.

Nakagawa would be the first to point out that his films were not the work of one man. Both he and commentators on his work like Kurosawa Kiyoshi give much of the credit for the films' success to art director Kurosawa Haruyasu's expert conveyance of the *kaiki* themes and imagery:

> Kurosawa [Haruyasu's] art direction was rather like old German Expressionism, with a psychological, spiritual effect. Psychological expressions and images that heightened the drama would appear directly onscreen. He once said that he would think about how, without any money in the budget, he could pack in things from reality that would convey a mental, spiritual meaning.[2]

The contributions of cinematographer Nishimoto Tadashi, as well as screenwriter and assistant director Ishikawa Yoshihiro, also should not be overlooked. Furthermore, the industrial-commercial circumstances in which Nakagawa and his crew created these films played an important role in elevating the *kaiki* genre at Shintōhō. While I take these factors into consideration, in particular discussing the role of studio head Ōkura Mitsugi and the business decisions that resulted in these films at some length, the results are nonetheless also the work of a director with a distinct vision and style. In the discussion that follows "Nakagawa" often becomes an implied author, shorthand for the collective of talent behind Shintōhō's best efforts in the *kaiki* genre. However, the consistency of vision discernable in the director's work across differing crews and projects—from his first true *kaiki* film, *Kasane's Swamp*, to post-Shintōhō projects like *Snake Woman's Curse* (*Kaidan hebi onna*, Tōei, 1968, discussed in Chapter 5)—makes it clear that Nakagawa undeniably left his personal stamp on *kaiki* film history.

---

[2] Author's interview with Kurosawa Kiyoshi.

Close examination of Nakagawa's three key *kaiki* works for Shintōhō, along with other innovative pictures made at the studio by other directors under Ōkura's mandate, illuminates both Nakagawa's and his contemporaries' pivotal role in creating a new type of *kaiki* film. The Shintōhō pictures represent the pinnacle of the classic *kaiki* style while at the same time pioneering techniques that look forward to what might be deemed a more *horā*-esque approach to traditional material. They employ all the familiar hallmarks of the genre such as Othered spaces, themes of karmic retribution, and of course spook-house scares and startles. Innovations in both form and content, meanwhile, give them a fresh immediacy that allows the old-fashioned *kaiki* film to speak to fears of the postwar generation. Shintōhō pointed the way forward for Japanese horror with new approaches to filming the monster, widening the scope of its karmic wrath, and removing the action to modern-day Japan. Nakagawa's *kaiki* films in particular planted seeds of the J-horror movement that would flower decades later all over the globe.

Ōkura Mitsugi, Nakagawa Nobuo, and Shintōhō's *Kaiki* Revolution

Shintōhō underwent sea changes in management during the years following Watanabe Kunio's Occupation-era release of *Legend of the Nabeshima Ghost Cat* discussed in the previous chapter. Its commitment to high-end artistic works reached an apex with Mizoguchi Kenji's *Life of Oharu* (*Saikaku ichidai onna*, 1952), one of the acknowledged masterpieces of world cinema, but the studio's lack of capital and inability to procure sufficient booking venues kept the company perpetually on the verge of collapse.[3] Unlike its competitors, Shintōhō owned none of its own theaters, a problem almost overcome when Nikkatsu decided it wanted back into the production business and considered a merger with the struggling studio. Realizing that such a proposal would see the company completely swallowed up by Nikkatsu, the Shintōhō stockholders objected, and ultimately Nikkatsu resumed film production by itself.[4] In late 1955 the Shintōhō board turned to Ōkura Mitsugi, a former *benshi* and business mogul with a reputation for revitalizing struggling theater chains, and offered

---

[3] Kawabe Jūji, *B-kyū kyoshōron: Nakagawa Nobuo kenkyū* (Tokyo: Shizukadō), 89–90.
[4] Joseph L. Anderson and Donald Richie, *The Japanese Film: Art and Industry*, 2nd ed. (Princeton, NJ: Princeton University Press, 1982), 242.

him the position of chief executive in hopes that he could turn their fortunes around.

His successful career as a *benshi* narrator of silent cinema and his hands-on approach to theater management gave Ōkura a keen appreciation for the value of pandering to the tastes of a mass audience, and with absolute authority over the studio he put Shintōhō on a path diametrically opposed to its previous filmmaking philosophy. Author and Ōkura expert Yamada Seiji elaborates,

> [The first studio head's] belief was if time and money were risked on top-notch directors who produced work that could compete with the most popular stars, the result would surely be a hit, and the studio's booking contracts would increase. Ōkura's policy was the exact opposite. He thoroughly slashed the budgets and the shooting schedules, promoted young directors and actors from within the studio, and implemented a "Planning First" production strategy that targeted a young, twentysomething audience.[5]

Under Ōkura's management the studio that produced *Life of Oharu* became Japan's grindhouse factory, and projects that could not be produced cheaply, quickly, and pegged into a genre that had proven mass appeal did not make it past Ōkura's desk.[6] The studio's new dedication to popular but seedy genres like *yakuza* crime dramas and pioneering exploitation skin flicks like Maeda Michiko's *Revenge of the Pearl Queen* soon gave Shintōhō a lurid reputation in the industry. Central among the lurid genres was *kaiki*, and much like the Hammer studio in Great Britain, Shintōhō would take its *kaiki* efforts to new levels of gruesomeness that—uniquely among the studio's otherwise infamous reputation for "inferior films for delinquents"[7]—would attract praise in equal measure from critics and audiences.

No doubt recalling its popularity during the days of the *benshi*, one of the first *kaiki* projects Ōkura put into production was a revival of *The Ghost Story of Yotsuya* (*Yotsuya kaidan*, 1956), directed by Mōri Masaki. More than twenty versions of this most famous and gruesome Japanese ghost story were made before the war, but with Daiei focusing on ghost cats and Tōei devoting its attention to more

---

[5] Yamada Seiji, *Maboroshi no kaidan eiga o ōtte* (Tokyo: Yōsensha, 1997), 48. Mark Schilling also discusses Ōkura's strategy in *Nudes! Guns! Ghosts!: The Sensational Films of Shintoho* (Udine: Udine Far East Film Festival, 2010), 14–25.

[6] A notable exception would be *The Meiji Emperor and the Russo-Japanese War* (*Meiji tennō to Nichi-Rō sensō*). Upon assuming leadership of Shintōhō, Ōkura sunk the studio's last yen into this ultranationalistic, widescreen color epic in a go-for-broke attempt to save the company from bankruptcy. The gamble paid off spectacularly. When the film was finally released in April 1957 it wound up being the highest grossing film of the year and single-handedly got Shintōhō out of the red. See Anderson and Richie, *The Japanese Film*, 250–1.

[7] Nachi Shirō and Shigeta Yoshiyuki, ed., *Ayakashi Ōkura Shintōhō* (Tokyo: Wise, 2001), 20.

romantic *kaidan* adaptations, Mōri's picture was only the second *Yotsuya* film to appear in the postwar era, after Kinoshita Keisuke's *The Ghost Story Yotsuya: A New Interpretation* in 1949. Although quickly forgotten in the wake of Nakagawa Nobuo's superior version three years later, Mōri's *Yotsuya* remains important for several reasons. Unlike Kinoshita's "new interpretation," Mōri's film marked the true return of Oiwa—Japan's most iconic *onryō* or "vengeful ghost"—to Japanese theater screens after an almost twenty-year absence. Not counting Tanaka Kinuyo's genteel, silent ghost in Kinoshita's film, the last time Oiwa had vented her fury on-screen was in the form of Suzuki Sumiko, in Mokudō Shigeru's now-lost 1937 version of *Yotsuya*. Interestingly, this two-decade gap roughly corresponds to the period between the end of the Universal studio's first cycle of gothic horror movies in the late 1930s and their British remakes by Hammer beginning in 1957. Thusly did actress Sōma Chieko's Oiwa serve as a reintroduction of a classic monster to a new generation of film fans in much the same way Christopher Lee brought Frankenstein's Monster and Count Dracula back from their cinematic crypts to haunt movie theaters once again. And just as the popularity of *The Curse of Frankenstein* and *Dracula* forever transformed the Hammer studio into a factory of horrors, Shintōhō's financial success during the *Obon* season of 1956 with *The Ghost Story of Yotsuya* and Watanabe Kunio's *The Vengeful Ghost of Sakura* (*Onryō Sakura daisōdō*) prompted Ōkura to institute a policy of producing at least two new *kaiki* films each year in time for the summer festival of the dead.[8]

Shimura Miyoko observes that although these films often lacked even the production value of Daiei B-pictures like the Irie Takako ghost cat series, by Shintōhō's standards many of their *kaiki* productions received A-list treatment.[9] Daiei produced its *kaiki* films as program pictures made to fill out the studio's quota and mark time between more "serious" productions, and they were treated as such by most of the staff. Shintōhō's *kaiki* films, meanwhile, were vital to the studio's continued existence under Ōkura's system. He assigned the studio's top talent to their production, and beginning in 1958 the top-billed feature of the annual "monster cavalcade" (*obake daikai*) was made in widescreen and color—an extravagance a studio like Daiei rarely deigned to bestow upon the disreputable *kaiki* genre. Color and widescreen were of course another innovation of the Hammer gothic horror remakes, furthering the affinities between Shintōhō's domestic *kaiki* product and their imported counterparts from Great Britain.

---

[8] Suzuki Yoshiaki, *Shintōhō hiwa: Izumida Hiroshi no sekai* (Osaka: Seishinsha, 2001), 204.
[9] Shimura Miyoko, "'Misemono' kara 'eiga' e: Shintōhō no kaibyō eiga," *Engeki eizō* 43 (2002): 14.

Most of the creative talent at Shintōhō, remembering the days when the studio mantra was to make films by and for artists, resented Ōkura and his "one-man system" (*wan man taisei*), under which all projects were genre pictures mandated from the top.[10] Watanabe Kunio, the studio's most renowned filmmaker under contract, resigned in 1958. This left Nakagawa Nobuo as Shintōhō's senior director under contract, having made his directorial debut in 1934, unlike the majority of Ōkura's directors who had only begun making pictures after the war. Trusting him with key projects, Ōkura gave Nakagawa the job of realizing the studio's first two annual color widescreen *Obon* releases—1958's *Mansion of the Ghost Cat* and the following year's revisiting of *Yotsuya*.

In later years, when these pictures began to be acknowledged as classics of the genre, Nakagawa frequently spoke of his irritation at being forced by Ōkura to churn out *kaiki* fare. In a 1974 interview, Nakagawa was asked if he had any particular interest in the *kaiki* genre, to which he replied, "Not especially … It was simply work assigned to me by the studio, nothing more … when the order came to make *The Ghost Story of Yotsuya* my honest reaction was to say a bit wearily, 'What, another monster movie?'"[11] His talent for the genre, however, was undeniable, and even if Watanabe had remained at the studio Nakagawa likely still would have been given the task. Shintōhō's 1957 *kaiki* triple bill had consisted of a rerelease of Mōri's *Yotsuya* along with two short, black-and-white features—Kadono Gorō's *Seven Wonders of Honjo* (*Kaidan Honjo nana fushigi*) and Nakagawa's first full-blown *kaiki* effort, *The Ghost Story of Kasane's Swamp*.[12] Kadono's picture was a throwback to the "seven wonders" tanuki films Yoshino Jirō had specialized in during the silent era, and following the "seven wonders" pattern attributes the *kaiki* phenomena depicted in the film to the adorably whimsical, shape-shifting tanuki, undercutting any frightening sense of *osore*. Nakagawa's *Kasane*, meanwhile, won rare praise from the critics at *Kinema junpō*, who to this point had been almost universally hostile to domestic *kaiki* film. Despite his insistence that he had no interest in the genre, Nakagawa's

---

[10] Yamada, *Maboroshi no kaidan eiga o ōtte*, 126–8.

[11] "Kaiki eiga montō," *Kinema junpō*, October 15, 1974, 114–15. Nakagawa remained dismissive of all his *kaiki* work save *Yotsuya* and *Jigoku* until his death in 1984. However, when the Art Theater Guild (ATG) gave him free reign to make a final picture of his choosing in 1984, the result was *The Ghost Story of Undead Koheiji* (*Kaidan ikiteiru Koheiji*), suggesting Nakagawa had finally come to embrace his legacy as the nation's foremost director of *kaiki* film.

[12] Nakagawa had flirted with *kaiki* material in his 1949 comedy *Enoken: Tobisuke's Vacation Adventure* (*Enoken no Tobisuke bōken ryokō*), his freelance *shinpi-kaiki* mystery hybrid for Tōhō, *Vampire Moth* (*Kyūketsuki ga*, 1956), and a short sequence in his 1956 *jidaigeki* for Ōkura and Shintōhō, *The Ceiling at Utsunomiya* (*Utsunomiya no tenjō*), but *Kasane* was his first unequivocal *kaiki* work.

accomplished work on *Kasane* assured he would become Ōkura's go-to director for *kaiki* until Shintōhō's collapse in 1961.

The Ghost Story of Kasane's Swamp (1957)

Junpō critic Tada Michitarō's review of *Kasane* explicitly compares it to both the Tōei *kaidan* romances and Daiei's ongoing ghost cat cycle, taking the other studios' films to task for compromising the genre's sense of *insan* or "doom and gloom," which Tada admiringly finds ample amounts of in Nakagawa's work:

> We can call this an orthodox (*ōsodokkusu*) *kaidan* story, which is to say there is a consistent tone of doom-and-gloom (*insan*) permeating throughout. It does away with heresies like using Misora Hibari to make a "beautiful monster movie" (as seen in last year's Tōei production—a "beautiful monster" makes about as much sense as a "beautiful hydrogen bomb"), or crafting themes of heroic salvation (as in this year's Daiei production), or injecting Achako-style laughs (this year's Shōchiku production); *Kasane's* single-minded purpose is *insan*. That's why, when it comes to monster movies, to my mind Shintōhō's are the most impressive. These are old-fashioned, fearsome kabuki monsters, whose grasp reaches beyond lifetimes, wreaking vengeance on the children for the sins of the parents, and from which there is no hope of salvation. The thought that such dreadful enmity (*enkon*) is not something that ends after a single lifetime strikes a deep chord.[13]

The word *insan*, which I translate as "doom and gloom," conveys the nuance of inevitable tragedy, making it an apt choice to describe the themes of inescapable karmic fate found in domestic *kaiki* cinema and aligning Tada's use of the term closely with my own usage of *osore* to describe the horrific affect of the genre. *Kasane* establishes this atmosphere of *insan* from the very first frames of the title sequence, with the credits superimposed over a series of successive images of a beautiful woman gradually dissolving into a rotten corpse, then finally a pile of bones. This is explicitly Buddhist imagery, the visual depiction of a beautiful woman-turned-skeleton having long been used as didactic tool to convey the impermanence of all things. As Tada notes in his review, the mood is maintained

---

[13] Tada Michitarō, "*Kaidan Kasane ga fuchi*," *Kinema junpō* September Special, 1957, 91. Misora Hibari's "beautiful monster movie" of the previous year is of course Tōei's *Dish Mansion at Banchō*. Daiei's "heroic" production is most likely a reference to *The Ghost Cat of Yonaki Swamp* (*Kaibyō Yonaki numa*). "Achako-style laughs" refers to popular comedian Hanabishi Achako's supporting role in Shōchiku's *Kaidan of Repentance: Passion of a Jealous Teacher* (*Kaidan iro zange: kyōren onna shishō*).

for the subsequent entirety of the picture, without any detours into sentimental romance, samurai heroics, or comedy relief, resulting in an "orthodox" *kaidan* adaptation that was welcomed for its generic purity.

The film's prologue sequence showcases Nakagawa's technical mastery of his craft and sets the stage for a new direction in domestic *kaiki* filmmaking. *Kasane*'s lengthy opening shot and its careful mise-en-scène invite comparisons to the films of Mizoguchi, though the techniques came to be associated with Nakagawa as well.[14] On a snowy night out front of the dwelling of the blind masseur Minagawa Sōetsu, the narrative begins to unfold in a long take over one minute in duration. Sōetsu's housekeeper and his young daughter Orui see him off at the door as he ventures out to pay a visit on the samurai Fukami Shinzaemon, to whom he has loaned some money. The camera at last cuts in on a key moment as Sōetsu trips on his way out into the snow. The housekeeper takes it as a bad omen and implores her master to remain at home. Sōetsu laughs off the warning and asks Orui what she would like him to buy for her once he collects the debt. She asks for a shamisen, and Sōetsu continues off into the night. Two important elements of foreshadowing warrant Nakagawa's termination of the initial long take and motivate the cut to a medium shot of the father, daughter, and housekeeper. Sōetsu's stumble and his dismissal of the housekeeper's warning not only tip off viewers that his attempt to collect the money will end in tragedy but also suggest that the subsequent tale of what befalls his daughter Orui becomes predestined as a result of his decision to scoff at fate. The shamisen Orui asks for also becomes central to the fated drama that plays out (Figure 20).

As the prologue sequence continues, *Kasane's Swamp* effectively frontloads the monstrous elements that earlier domestic *kaiki* films typically withheld until much later in their running times. On average, the monster first appears in surviving prewar and early postwar *kaiki* pictures around the fifty-minute mark, sometimes with little foreshadowing that a *kaiki* third act follows the heretofore mundane *jidaigeki* drama. By contrast, Nakagawa gives his audience the full *kaiki* experience at the twelve-minute mark of *Kasane*, more akin to foreign *kaiki* films from America and Europe that introduce the horrific elements

---

[14] In an interview with Nakagawa for *Movie Magazine* in 1981, Katsura Chiho observes that from the production of *Kasane's Swamp* onward we can see the emergence of a "one scene, one take" style in Nakagawa's work reminiscent of Mizoguchi, with which Nakagawa concurs. The interview is reprinted in its entirety in *Eiga kantoku Nakagawa Nobuo*, pp. 193–220 (The comparison to Mizoguchi appears on page 214). In the same volume Yamane Sadao argues the hallmark of Nakagawa's style is the "fluidity" (*ryūdōsei*) of his camera, citing the opening long take of *The Ghost Story of Yotsuya* as the quintessential example. See page 296 of *Eiga kantoku Nakagawa Nobuo*.

Figure 20 The opening shot of *The Ghost Story of Kasane's Swamp* (*Kaidan Kasane ga fuchi*, 1957) with its painterly mise-en-scène (left), from which the camera cuts in at a fateful moment (right).

early in their runtimes. Sōetsu's efforts to collect the loan from Shinzaemon end in the predictable tragedy, further foreshadowed by the incessant crying of Shinzaemon's infant son Shinkichi during the masseur's visit. The arrogant, hot-headed Shinzaemon—unable to repay the money he owes to a man beneath his caste—murders Sōetsu and has his body dumped into Kasane's Swamp. The masseur's ghost soon returns to haunt Shinzaemon, driving the samurai to accidentally murder his own wife before stumbling into Kasane's Swamp himself, plagued by visions of Sōetsu's ghost as he drowns. The film's prologue thus stands as a complete mini-*kaidan* of its own, the fifteen-minute sequence hitting all of the familiar plot points of the typical Japanese ghost story: the unjust death of an innocent, followed by their return from the grave and ghostly revenge against their oppressor, who unwittingly kills his loved one before meeting his own end.

It will be recalled that Kato Bin's 1954 *Ghost Cat of Okazaki* also included a monster-filled prologue in the form of a brief flash-forward sequence of Irie Takako's ghost cat emerging from behind a crumbling wall, but devoid of any narrative context the sequence becomes a pure *obake yashiki* spook-house moment, startling but without any lingering sense of dread. *Kasane*'s prologue has its flourishes of sensational address as well, with Sōetsu's ghost popping out at Shinzaemon at opportune moments, but the sequence also invokes a strong sense of the uncanny in its implication that cosmic forces of predestination are in play. Sōetsu's failure to heed the bad omen, the infant Shinkichi's inexplicable wailing—and in hindsight, Orui's fateful request that her father buy her a shamisen—all serve to evoke the uncanny when the murder and subsequent haunting occur. The uncanny themes established in the prologue become even more pronounced by having the tragedy repeat in more elaborate fashion over the course of the main narrative, which concerns the fate of Sōetsu's and Shinzaemon's grown children.

Writing about the doppelganger in the fiction of E. T. A. Hoffmann, Freud could just as easily be discussing Nakagawa's *Kasane's Swamp* when he locates its uncanny affect in "the constant recurrence of the same thing, the repetition of the same facial features, the same characters, the same destinies, the same misdeeds, even the same names, through successive generations."[15] Orui and Shinkichi grow up only to replicate the tragedy of their parents. Taken in as an infant by a family friend of the Fukami clan, the adult Shinkichi falls in love with his adopted sister Ohisa, whom he accompanies to her weekly shamisen lessons under the tutelage of the now-grown Orui. Ohisa's parents disapprove of the young man's affections for their daughter, and believing his true love forever beyond his reach, the weak-willed Shinkichi finds himself goaded into a romantic liaison with Orui, who uses him to deflect the unwanted advances of a villainous admirer, Omura. Meanwhile, Sōetsu's aged housekeeper learns that Shinkichi is the son of Fukami Shinzaemon and that Orui has become romantically involved with the child of her father's murderer. She implores Orui to end the relationship lest she invite the wrath of her father's spirit, but the young woman stubbornly defies fate, declaring, "I shall do as I please!" (*atashi wa sukina yōni surunda!*) and spurning the warnings of the housekeeper just as her father had in the film's opening. The shamisen, first mentioned in the prologue sequence and later the vehicle through which she became acquainted with Shinkichi, then recurs in the narrative once again, this time acting as the agent of Orui's inevitable karmic doom. The shamisen pick tumbles from the shelf where it rests, striking Orui across the eye and inflicting her with a disfiguring facial scar.

Such a wound is of course a primary trope of Japanese ghost stories, most famously seen in the person of *Yotsuya*'s Oiwa but also familiar from Enchō's original version of *Kasane's Swamp*, as well as Suzuki Sumiko's performance in 1938's *Ghost Story of the Mandarin Duck Curtain*. Kinoshita Keisuke utilized the motif to uncanny effect in his *Ghost Story of Yotsuya: A New Interpretation*, lending the picture what little sense of *osore* it possesses in the uncanny reappearance of Oiwa's scar afflicting the other characters. In Nakagawa's film the trope signals that Orui is now fated to die and return as a vengeful spirit, not only because the audience recognizes the generic cue but also because the wound uncannily recalls the cut her father received to his own face at the hands of Shinzaemon in the prologue, which prefigured his own death and ghostly

---

[15] Sigmund Freud, *The Uncanny*, trans. David McLintok (New York: Penguin, 2003), 142.

return. Orui's now-unavoidable demise occurs after her frustrated suitor Omura convinces Shinkichi to elope with Ohisa, prompting Orui first to attempt to take Ohisa's life and, when that fails, her own. At the climax of the film Shinkichi and Ohisa flee Edo and by chance stumble upon Kasane's Swamp, where the ghost of Orui tricks Shinkichi into murdering Ohisa in an uncanny repetition of the prologue, in which Shinkichi's father unwittingly killed his mother. Omura then shows up to rob and murder Shinkichi, who meets his end in the waters of Kasane's Swamp, where his own father drowned a generation ago. Uncanny repetition piles upon uncanny repetition.

Nakagawa's meticulous attention to crafting such an intricate, multilayered depiction of uncanny fate restores a true sense of cosmic *osore* to the proceedings that was noticeably lacking in the Daiei films' comparative inattention to narrative detail. Of course, the original nineteenth-century version of the tale by San'yūtei Enchō contained many of the same uncanny narrative elements, and another fundamental motif of the *kaidan* genre, the return of the dead (either as a vengeful wraith or as a half-feline ghost cat), also constitutes a manifestation of Freud's uncanny ("anything to do with death, dead bodies, revenants, spirits, and ghosts").[16] Even the most artless of the Daiei ghost cat films with their spookhouse tricks evoke the uncanny in the mere physical presence of the monster, but in *Kasane* the uncanny assumes a more complex and subtle presence. It takes the obvious physical form of the ghost—first Sōetsu's, then Orui's—but it is also consistently woven into the film's diegesis, from the opening shot to the climax, and finds expression both in thematic and visual repetition.

Nakagawa's turn toward a more thorough, nuanced invocation of the Freudian uncanny, as opposed to what might be deemed the more overtly Todorovian marvelous worlds of the Daiei and Shinkō *kaiki* pictures, constituted a key development of the Shintōhō pictures.[17] While its period setting and its characters' willing acceptance of the existence of ghosts place Nakagawa's *Kasane* in the same marvelous universe as other domestic *kaiki* pictures, one of the film's most effective moments of horror works by suggesting one of the uncanny moments that occurs may in fact have a perfectly mundane explanation, thus creating a more ambiguous reading of the uncanny that invokes in turn a sense

---

[16] Ibid., 148.
[17] It is important to restate that Todorov's "uncanny" is not the same as Freud's usage of the term. Todorov uses the category of "uncanny" for seemingly supernatural occurrences that ultimately receive an unequivocally mundane, rational explanation, in contrast to the ambiguous "fantastic" and overtly supernatural "marvelous." See Tzvetan Todorov, *The Fantastic: A Structural Approach to a Literary Genre*, trans. Richard Howard (Ithaca, NY: Cornell University Press, 1975), 41–2.

Figure 21 The "third teacup" scene in *The Ghost Story of Kasane's Swamp*.

of the Todorovian "pure fantastic"—a narrative containing events that may or may not have a ghostly, otherworldly explanation behind them.

After Orui's death, Shinkichi and Ohisa elope and take refuge in the upper room of a teahouse. When the door to the room appears to open of its own accord, the couple exchange horrified glances. The next shot, however, reveals the teahouse attendant in the entrance, and a seemingly ghostly occurrence receives an indisputably normal explanation. Shinkichi and Ohisa relax, but immediately become unsettled once again when the attendant sets three cups of tea before them, explaining that the third cup is for "the woman who accompanied them upstairs." Once again the adulterous couple exchange looks of dread, and the scene concludes with the camera tilting in for a close-up of the third teacup (Figure 21). Orui's ghost does not manifest herself to confirm the marvelous explanation, and the scene leaves everyone wondering if the attendant made an error, or if Orui's ghost is pursuing the couple. *Kasane* thereby operates in the inverse of many Western horror narratives, which begin with ambiguously fantastic events whose explanations gradually become weighted toward the marvelous.[18] In *Kasane*, we begin with a marvelous setting, into which an interlude of doubt regarding the seeming omnipresence of otherworldly powers is introduced. The uncertainty of the moment unsettles both the characters and the viewer, wavering as it does between two possible interpretations.

Like virtually all domestic *kaiki* films adapted from Edo-period *kaidan* literature, Nakagawa's *Kasane's Swamp* must be classified as a "marvelous" text according to Todorov's schema; however, the teacup scene approaches a "fantastic" reading of its marvelous world. According to the recollections of actor

---

[18] See Carroll's description of Todorov's "fantastic/marvelous" narrative category in *The Philosophy of Horror: Or Paradoxes of the Heart* (New York: Routledge, 1990), 16–17.

Kawabe Jūji, the scene—which does not appear in Enchō's original tale or in the shooting script—was improvised by Nakagawa on-set.[19]

Although Nakagawa claimed he personally was never interested in the horror genre, the scene showcases a masterful understanding of horror tropes that were more typical of Western ghost stories and horror movies than domestic *kaidan* film adaptations. The initial moment when the door appears to be sliding open of its own ghostly accord, only to reveal the maid behind it, recalls the famous and influential "bus" sequence in Jacques Tourneur's *Cat People*, in which the viewer is led to think that a hissing, roaring sound signals the imminent attack of a supernatural panther woman, but is subsequently revealed to be nothing more than the sound of a bus pulling up to a stop. Having dispelled this first ambiguously fantastic moment with a mundane explanation, Nakagawa immediately reestablishes the dissipated uncertainty with the third teacup, for which he refuses to give a conclusive explanation, either marvelous or mundane. He thereby swings the pendulum away from the "pure marvelous" tone of the *kaidan* genre toward the ambiguously fantastic worlds of the Western ghost story, before returning to the marvelous in the climax. However, in reavowing the objective existence of the ghost in *Kasane*'s climax, Nakagawa's film is not out of line with the typical Western horror narrative, in which the monster's existence is confirmed and confronted. Noël Carroll identifies this common structure of the horror genre as Todorov's subcategory of the "fantastic-marvelous," in which the ambiguous events are ultimately given a definitive supernatural explanation.[20] In this manner, *Kasane's Swamp* remains what critic Tada Michitarō happily calls an "orthodox *kaidan*" even while taking on the techniques of Western, fantastic horror.

Bakeneko Redux: *Mansion of the Ghost Cat* (1958)

In the next few years Nakagawa and his crew swiftly brought the domestic *kaiki* genre to its apex, at the same time laying the groundwork for a new style of horror filmmaking in Japan that would eventually see the *kaiki* label retired and replaced by *horā* in the ensuing decades. The unexpectedly positive press *Kasane* had received convinced Ōkura that it was worth investing talent and money in a widescreen, color *kaiki* film.[21] For the 1958 *Obon* season Ōkura put

---

[19] Kawabe, *B-kyū kyoshōron*, 122–4.
[20] Carroll, *Philosophy of Horror*, 16–17.
[21] Shimura Miyoko notes that *Mansion of the Ghost Cat* was one of only two out of the thirty-one pictures released by Shintōhō in the second half of 1958 to be made in color, revealing just how seriously Ōkura considered the *kaiki* genre to the studio's survival. See "'Misemono' kara 'eiga' e," 14.

the color feature *Mansion of the Ghost Cat* into production with Nakagawa once again in charge. Also retained from *Kasane* were assistant director Ishikawa Yoshihiro and composer Watanabe Chūmei, both of whom would eventually make considerable creative contributions to Nakagawa's *Ghost Story of Yotsuya*. Another significant talent to join Nakagawa on *Mansion of the Ghost Cat* was cinematographer Nishimoto Tadashi, who would also film *Yotsuya* for Nakagawa before moving to Hong Kong in 1960, where under the name Ho Lan Shan he would shoot King Hu's *Come Drink with Me* (*Da zui xia*, 1966) and Bruce Lee's *Way of the Dragon* (*Meng long guo jiang*, 1972).

The most important addition to the team was the presence of art director Kurosawa Haruyasu, whose collaborations with Nakagawa on *Mansion of the Ghost Cat*, *The Ghost and the M.P.* (*Kenpei to yūrei*, 1958), *Lady Vampire* (*Onna kyūketsuki*, 1959), *Yotsuya*, and *Jigoku* (1960)—as well as Ishikawa Yoshihiro's solo directorial debut, *The Ghost Cat of Otama Pond* (*Kaibyō Otama ga ike*, 1960)—were deemed the key element to the films' success by Nakagawa himself. According to Suzuki Kensuke, Nakagawa's assistant director on his final film, 1984's *Undead Koheiji* (*Kaidan Ikiteiru Koheiji*), "If you told him [Nakagawa] that *Yotsuya* or *Jigoku* was good, he would tell you it was all due to Kurosawa."[22] Kurosawa had done the art direction for Mōri Masaki's 1956 version of *Yotsuya*, but his innovative work with Nakagawa on pictures like *The Ceiling at Utsunomiya* (*Utsunomiya no tenjō*, 1956) and especially *Poison Woman Takahashi Oden* (*Dokufu Takahashi Oden*, 1958)—which included ambitious set designs allowing interior scenes to be shot from an exterior camera position through the holes in the roof of a dilapidated, weather-beaten dwelling to convey the poverty of its inhabitants—first showcased his potential.[23]

Collectively, Nakagawa's *kaiki* unit represented the studio's top craftsmen, a mixture of seasoned veterans like Nakagawa, who had been directing films since before the war, and newcomers like Kurosawa, who began as an art director in 1955 but brought a wealth of innovative ideas to his work. The assemblage of proven talent along with Ōkura's desire to have *Mansion of the Ghost Cat* filmed in color and widescreen demonstrate that while in generic terms Shintōhō's *kaiki*

---

[22] Author's interview with Suzuki Kensuke, January 15, 2013.
[23] Nakagawa credits the idea entirely to Kurosawa. See *Eiga kantoku Nakagawa Nobuo*, 214–15. Kurosawa states that from *Takahashi Oden* onward Nakagawa treated him as a creative equal, leaving most decision-making in regard to set design entirely up to him. See Kurosawa Haruyasu, "Ki ni naru aitsu: Muma no sake," *Eiga hyōron* 30, no. 12 (1973): 88.

films may have been the brethren of Daiei's ghost cat B-pictures, they were given far more attention to detail—the Shintōhō equivalent of a Kurosawa Akira or Naruse Mikio prestige picture.

In tackling the ghost cat subgenre of *kaiki* cinema, Nakagawa's film adheres to several of the conventions in place since the heyday of Suzuki Sumiko in the late 1930s, but as with *Kasane's Swamp*, they create a film that manages to be "orthodox" in its presentation of traditional material while at the same time innovating new ways to convey more effectively a sense of horror and *osore* for a contemporary audience. The long middle section of the film presents an all-color *jidaigeki* ghost cat tale that deliberately invokes many of the standard, spectacular ghost cat motifs: the cat lapping the blood of its slain master, assuming a humanoid feminine form, performing wire-assisted leaps and bounds while battling multiple samurai, and completing the obligatory *neko jarashi* cat-toying pantomimes with an acrobat doubling for the monster's possessed victim. Kurosawa's art direction takes full advantage of the color filming, and like the same year's *Dracula* from Hammer Films, *Mansion of the Ghost Cat* makes ample use of dripping, bright red blood, which audiences of the time found shocking and transgressive. Shimura Miyoko elaborates,

> In the Shintōhō [ghost cat] films [the color red] is used in places like bloodstained walls, a blood-filled teacup (*Mansion of the Ghost Cat*), blood dripping onto an ornamental hairpin, blood-red ponds of water, and the burned red face of an old woman (*The Ghost Cat of Otama Pond*). Furthermore, it is a fascinating fact that the first color *bakeneko* film, *Mansion of the Ghost Cat*, and the British Hammer Films' monument to classic horror movies, *Dracula* (directed by Terrence Fisher) are both produced in the same year (1958) ... Compared to the American Universal Studios' *Dracula* (1931, directed by Tod Browning), [Hammer's] *Dracula's* candid depictions shocked audiences with scenes like the staking of the vampire's bride and vampire hunter Professor Van Helsing's destruction of Dracula in vivid Technicolor. In response to fierce attacks from critics regarding the film's violence and suggestive sexuality, director Terrence Fisher remarked in later years that the candid scenes in question were the most important parts of the film. *Dracula's* candidness can be thought of as quite similar to Shintōhō's. For example, the image of the [bloodstained] wall can be compared with Daiei's *The Ghost Cat and the Cursed Wall* (*Kaibyō noroi no kabe*, also produced in 1958, directed by Misumi Kenji). In this film the curse of a woman and her dead cat sealed up within a wall causes the image of a large black cat to appear on the wall no matter how many times it is covered over. On the other hand, in *Mansion of the Ghost Cat* red blood drips from a wall that

contains a sealed-up corpse, which conveys a much more directly shocking affect to the audience.[24]

It may seem obvious to say that red, dripping Technicolor blood made both *Dracula* and *Mansion of the Ghost Cat* more terrifying for audiences in 1958 by virtue of its shocking (for the time) presentation of gore, but Shimura's comparison of the same year's black-and-white Daiei release *The Ghost Cat and the Cursed Wall* reveals the import of its presence. *Mansion of the Ghost Cat*'s bleeding wall is no more realistic than *The Ghost Cat and the Cursed Wall*'s black-and-white cat silhouette, and they both symbolically represent the same thing (the *onnen* or cosmic wrath of the murder victim). However, in an example of Carl Plantinga's "direct affect" of cinema,[25] a close-up of red, dripping blood prompts a visceral response in the viewer, while a cat's silhouette elicits no such immediate reaction of its own, inherent accord. The cat may be just as cosmically terrifying if the audience takes the time to consider its symbolic significance, but the blood horrifies on its own, and the uncanny phenomenon of a wall that bleeds compounds the visceral horror with the terror of cosmic *osore*. The scene does not use gore gratuitously, but to make an already *kaiki* moment doubly frightening (Figure 22).

And yet, for all of *Mansion of the Ghost Cat*'s effective use of color in the *jidaigeki* sequence, the black-and-white sections that bookend the picture constitute the film's most innovative and considerable contributions to the development of horror cinema in Japan. The picture begins in the present day with a doctor's wife being haunted by the mysterious spirit of an old woman who appears suddenly in the middle of the night, eventually causing the wife to fall into an unexplained illness. The doctor's visit to a nearby Buddhist temple reveals the old woman is the lingering spirit of the ghost cat that had plagued his wife's ancestors. Rather like *The Wizard of Oz* (1939), the film then moves from our black-and-white everyday world to a full-color fantasy, recounting the origins of the cat's curse in a "pure marvelous" Edo wonderland where characters and audiences alike would expect to find a ghost cat or two. As typical of the genre, in the color sequence the film does not shy away from the spectacle of the half-woman, half-feline monster. Shintōhō's film lacks a former screen beauty like Suzuki Sumiko or Irie Takako in the role of the monster—the cat spirit exclusively inhabits the form of sexagenarian actress Satsuki Fujie. But like

---

[24] Ibid., 18.
[25] Carl Plantinga, *Moving Viewers: American Film and the Spectator's Experience* (Berkeley: University of California Press, 2009), 117. See Chapter 1 for a discussion of Plantinga's theory.

Figure 22 Cursed walls in *The Ghost Cat and the Cursed Wall* (*Kaibyō noroi no kabe*, 1958, above) and *Mansion of the Ghost Cat* (*Bōrei kaibyō yashiki*, 1958, below).

the Shinkō and Daiei pictures, during the *jidaigeki* scenes the camera provides a clear look at her spectacular, monstrous visage, with close-ups in high-key lighting of Satsuki in elaborate makeup inserted among wide shots of her stunt double performing the traditional *neko jarashi* and *tachimawari* battle against armed samurai.

Satsuki also portrays the ghost cat in the contemporarily set *gendaigeki* sequences, but here Nakagawa and cinematographer Nishimoto's filming technique takes a strikingly different approach to the character. Unlike the *jidaigeki* sequence, Nakagawa and Nishimoto keep the camera at a distance from Satsuki, whom they film mainly from behind in long shots, keeping her face obscured from the audience. She does not leap and bound about the frame with the feline agility seen in the *jidaigeki* sequence, but her movements remain unnatural in the creeping slowness of her zombie-like undulations. The filmmakers bring the camera in closer for a tense long take in which the doctor's wife convalesces in the background while the ghost cat rises into frame in the foreground, then slowly creeps toward the fear-stricken woman and briefly strangles her before slinking back out of frame when the doctor enters the room. Even here, the filmmakers deliberately choose to keep the monster's visage hidden from clear view of the audience by keeping Satsuki's hair pulled forward over her face (Figure 23). In other shots they avoid showing Satsuki entirely, consciously evoking the Expressionist use of shadows to imply the lurking presence of the vampire Count Orlock in *Nosferatu* (1922) by casting Satsuki's silhouette onto the walls of the mansion. These shots alternate with subjective tracking shots that replicate the monster's point of view as it slowly stalks the halls of the doctor's renovated dwelling, which doubles as a family residence and a medical office.

Anticipating the often-discussed "Killer's P.O.V." that became a hallmark of the slasher subgenre of horror in the 1970s and 1980s with pictures like *Halloween* (1978), a particularly memorable setup in *Mansion of the Ghost Cat* lets the audience look through the monster's eyes while it approaches the doctor's

Figure 23 Actress Satsuki Fujie as the *bakeneko* in the color *jidaigeki* sequence of *Mansion of the Ghost Cat* (above), and as she appears in the monochrome *gendaigeki* sequences (below).

Figure 24 Expressionistic shadows and point-of-view tracking movement in a series of successive shots from *Mansion of the Ghost Cat*.

receptionist from behind as she obliviously reads a magazine (Figure 24).²⁶ Watanabe's score menacingly swells until the suspense comes to a head when the receptionist looks up and gasps in alarm. The tension recedes as the camera finally cuts back to a medium long shot of Satsuki standing before the receptionist, hunched over with her back to the camera, as the receptionist berates what she assumes to be an ordinary old woman for startling her. The sequence represents a stellar example of how Nakagawa's *kaiki* work sits at the crossroads of global horror filmmaking traditions, using the established international film grammar of German Expressionism to give a modern spin on the culturally particular traditions of the ghost cat while also contributing to the emerging aesthetic of the "Killer's P.O.V.," which would itself become an integral part of global horror movie iconography.

Excepting the color *jidaigeki* sequence, Nakagawa creates a radically new way of portraying a traditional mainstay of domestic *kaiki* cinema. Shimura Miyoko considers this possible in part by the casting of the elderly character actress Satsuki Fujie as the ghost cat, implying that a star like Suzuki Sumiko or Irie Takako would demand a more spectacular, revealing screen presence.²⁷ While

---

²⁶ See Carol Clover's *Men, Women, and Chain Saws: Gender in the Modern Horror Film* (Princeton, NJ: Princeton University Press, 1992) for the most developed discussion of the technique.
²⁷ Shimura, "'Misemono' kara 'eiga' e," 19–20.

it is true that Satsuki cannot perform the wire-assisted acrobatics with the same elaborateness as Suzuki or Irie,[28] *Mansion of the Ghost Cat* does in fact make the usual spectacle of the creature in the color sequence. The drastically different portrayal of the monster in the black-and-white sequences appears to have been motivated purely by aesthetic considerations and, more so than perhaps any other domestic *kaiki* film, provides a blueprint for the portrayal of ghosts and monsters in the J-horror films of more recent years. *Ring* screenwriter Takahashi Hiroshi, who along with director Kurosawa Kiyoshi and fellow screenwriter Konaka Chiaki became one of the J-horror movement's central theorists, describes six ideal techniques for the portrayal of ghosts on film:

1. Don't show the face.
   Show only a fragment of the body or clothes. Or, put it in a long shot so that the details of the face are blurred.
2. Make the standing position or behavior unnatural.
   Human beings have a specifically human sense of space and distance between themselves. Position someone in such a way to defy this sense subtly ...
3. Make its movement non-human.
   Make its movement unrelated to the natural motility of human muscles ...
4. Put it [a body part] in an impossible position ...
5. Use an awesome face.
   There is nothing to add, if the actor's face terrifies. It is an ultimate tour-de-force, an ideal of the ghost film.
6. Show nothing.
   Your weapon is premonition and atmosphere in space and the use of sound. Robert Wise's *The Haunting* (1963) is an exemplary case.[29]

Takahashi's first rule in particular perfectly describes the monster in the *gendaigeki* sequence of *Mansion of the Ghost Cat*, as do most of his subsequent commandments. Although he names Robert Wise's *The Haunting* as the premier example of the technique, Nakagawa's film predates Wise's by five years. While *The Haunting* famously never depicts its ghosts on-camera, making it the

---

[28] Ibid., 18.
[29] Takahashi Hiroshi, *Eiga no ma* (Tokyo: Seidosha, 2004), 27–8. Quoted by Chika Kinoshita in "The Mummy Complex: Kurosawa Kiyoshi's *Loft* and J-horror," in *Horror to the Extreme: Changing Boundaries in Asian Cinema*, ed. Jinhee Choi and Mitsuyo WadaMarciano (Hong Kong: Hong Kong University Press, 2009), 115.

ultimate example of Takahashi's "show nothing" rule, *Mansion of the Ghost Cat* actually fulfills more of Takahashi's criteria than Wise's film.

What was it about the modern-day, monochromatic *gendaigeki* sequences that demanded such a departure in the portrayal of a classic *kaiki* monster? Previous ghost cat films were either adapted from Edo-period *kaidan* and kabuki stage plays (*The Legend of the Saga Ghost Cat*; *The Ghost Cat of Okazaki*) or else deliberate imitations of traditional *kaidan* settings and motifs (*The Ghost Cat and the Mysterious Shamisen*). Significantly, Shintōhō adapted *Mansion of the Ghost Cat* from a 1952 story by science fiction author Tachibana Sotō. Although the film only loosely bases its story on Tachibana's original work, both follow the same novel approach to the ghost cat legend by beginning in the present day. Both book and film rip the traditional cat monster out of her marvelous Edo fantasyland and deposit her in postwar Japan, where her victims are not geisha and samurai who take the existence of monsters for granted, but affluent, urbane modern Japanese. The doctor-narrator in *Mansion of the Ghost Cat* represents the epitome of modernity, beginning the film with the declaration, "Of course I don't believe in ghosts" (*Mochiron watashi wa yūrei nante shinjinai*), but like the rational protagonists of the typical Western horror film, he must ultimately rely on mystical, arcane intervention (the Buddhist priest) to successfully cure his wife of her mysterious affliction, which is caused by the supernatural curse of the *bakeneko*. The act of removing a traditional, premodern monster from its marvelous setting and inserting it somewhere it does not "belong"—rational, postwar Japan—strongly invokes the uncanny as the past invades the present.

As in *Kasane's Swamp*, once again Nakagawa's film relies on this uncanny element to evoke a sense of fear in the viewer. The entirely premodern narrative of *Kasane* achieves this primarily through narrative repetition and visual doubling (father and daughter's facial wounds, the swamp which claims the father in the prologue and the son in the climax). *Mansion of the Ghost Cat*, by virtue of its contemporary opening and closing sequences, evokes an even more directly affective sense of the uncanny for the viewer by depicting a traditional monster that previously had been contained exclusively in the marvelous, premodern past invade the rational, modern present-day world of the audience. Unlike the *shinpi-kaiki* mystery hybrid films, no one reveals the monster to be a criminal in disguise, and both characters and audience must accept its uncanny existence. In the premodern *jidaigeki* sequence, a ghost cat is familiar and knowable, and Nakagawa's film treats it accordingly, depicting it in the direct, spectacular fashion typical of the genre. In the *gendaigeki* sequences the same monster becomes an unknowable anomaly, its presence less spectacular and more abjectly terrifying, and Nakagawa adjusts his filmic portrayal to convey its more mysterious, uncanny, and frightening presence. The ghost cat now embodies both the *osore* of omnipotent karmic retribution—transcending time itself to visit its curse upon the descendants of those who wronged its master—and, for the first time in a Japanese *kaiki* film, fully fulfills the standards of Lovecraft's unknowable "cosmic fear," representing forces beyond the pale of rational human understanding.

Kasane's sense of uncanny is primarily narrative, but *Mansion of the Ghost Cat*'s uncanny works on a more fundamentally cultural level. Being part of Japan's collective cultural consciousness in much the same way the vampire or werewolf functions for Western audiences, the ghost cat is shared cultural shorthand for a monster typically contained in long-long-ago campfire stories. Its appearance in the heart of modern-day and everyday Japan destroys the barriers of safety that previously confined it to the past. Like Nakagawa's formal techniques for depicting this rupture, the thematic motif of a traditional monster of the past invading the present would become one of the central themes of the J-horror movement at the turn of the millennium.

Contemporary *Kaidan:* Vampires, Werewolves, and Beach Bunnies

On the heels of *Mansion of the Ghost Cat*, which *Kinema junpō* prophetically deemed a "new flavor" (*shin-aji*) of *kaiki* filmmaking,[30] Shintōhō produced several *gendaigeki* horror films that further transgressed the boundaries of time and space previously separating the marvelous monsters of period *kaiki* films from the rationally debunked fake monsters of contemporarily set *shinpi-kaiki* mystery hybrids. Nakagawa and his crew delivered two key entries. Just one month after the *Obon* premiere of *Mansion of the Ghost Cat*, the studio released Nakagawa's *The Ghost and the M.P.* (*Kenpei to yūrei*). The picture was a modestly budgeted black-and-white attempt to copy the success of the studio's hit from the previous year, *The M.P. and the Dismembered Beauty* (*Kenpei to bara bara shibijin*), a gruesome but monster-less murder mystery set in the military policemen's barracks of the immediate prewar years. Inspired by the positive commercial and critical reception of the studio's *kaiki* efforts, Ōkura demanded

---

[30] Tada Michitarō, "*Bōrei kaibyo yashiki*," *Kinema junpō*, September 1, 1958, 75.

Nakagawa inject *kaiki* elements into what became *The Ghost and the M.P.*, which told a similar tale of murder among military policemen.

The picture's climax, in which the guilt-ridden killer portrayed by actor Amachi Shigeru stumbles into a graveyard where the ghosts of his victims assault him, can be interpreted as a purely symbolic hallucination on the part of Amachi's character. Unlike their analogues in traditional *kaidan*, the ghosts do not appear to multiple characters, nor do they demonstrate any active agency to influence the "real-world" events of the narrative.[31] In later years Nakagawa referred to the picture's baroque, Grand Guignol final sequence as "embarrassing" (*hazukashii*),[32] but its ambiguous portrayal of the monsters that plague Amachi represented, like *Mansion of the Ghost Cat*, an uncanny rupture of the boundary between the monster-filled, premodern past and the previously monster-free modern era that would characterize the later J-horror pictures.

A film Nakagawa found even more embarrassing was another Tachibana Sotō adaptation, *Lady Vampire* (*Onna kyūketsuki*). It too marked an important step toward the shift from *kaiki* to *horā*, reinterpreting European vampire lore in a Japanese context while simultaneously anticipating later international developments in the vampire subgenre of horror. Japan's first Western-style vampire movie, Ōkura doubtless intended the picture's release in early 1959 to capitalize on the popularity of Hammer's *Dracula*. However, Nakagawa's black-and-white vampire film, featuring Amachi Shigeru as the cape-and-tuxedo-clad eponymous monster (the title *Lady Vampire* refers to the vampire's dining preferences, not its gender), owes more to Universal's horror films of the 1930s and 1940s, mixing the iconography of Bela Lugosi's Count Dracula with Lon Chaney Junior's Wolf Man when the light of the full moon unleashes Amachi's feral, hairy-faced version of a vampire (Figure 25). Despite its shaky understanding of Western horror movie monster taxonomy, *Lady Vampire* expertly adapts what Noël Carroll calls the "complex discovery" plot of the typical Western horror film, with the monster's existence initially revealed only to a select few characters, who must then convince the others that the mysterious goings-on in fact stem from a supernatural force that must be confronted and defeated.[33]

Lady Vampire even foreshadows later additions to the Dracula mythos by making the vampire's primary victim the descendent and physical reincarnation

---

[31] Kawabe suggests this was Nakagawa's way of resisting Ōkura's order to make the picture into an overt monster movie. See *B-kyū kyoshōron*, 118.
[32] *Eiga kantoku Nakagawa Nobuo*, 216.
[33] Carroll, *Philosophy of Horror*, 99–108.

Figure 25 Promotional image for *Lady Vampire* (*Onna kyūketsuki*, 1959) showcasing the contemporary characters and setting plagued by Amachi Shigeru's vampire/werewolf hybrid. ©Kokusai Hōei.

of his long-dead love in a dual performance by glamour actress Mihara Yoko. Today the conceit of portraying either Lucy Westenra or Mina Harker as the spitting-image reincarnation of Dracula's wife has become an oft-repeated trope of *Dracula* adaptations, although it has no analogue in Bram Stoker's original novel and—in a further muddling of Universal Studios monster lore— was probably suggested by Zita Johann's character in *The Mummy* (1932). Given Nakagawa's interest in Buddhism and karma, the idea also likely draws inspiration from traditional Buddhist tales in which reincarnated lovers act out the same roles across multiple lifetimes, which includes the classic Japanese ghost story and frequent subject of *kaiki* film, *The Peony Lantern*. The reincarnated lover motif was first introduced into Stoker's tale in Dan Curtis's television movie *Dracula* in 1973, fourteen years after the release of *Lady Vampire*.[34] Curtis, Francis Ford Coppola, and other Hollywood filmmakers who adopted the conceit were almost certainly unfamiliar with Nakagawa's vampire movie. Nonetheless, *Lady Vampire*'s themes of doomed romance, reincarnation, and

---

[34] Curtis recycled the conceit from his earlier vampire soap opera television series *Dark Shadows*, which aired from 1966 to 1971.

the curse of immortality position it as an early outlier in the twentieth-century romanticization of the Dracula story.

Unlike Hammer's *Dracula*, but similar to Universal's 1931 version, *Lady Vampire* takes place in the present day, but far more so than the Universal film, Nakagawa's vampire picture constantly points to the "now-ness" of its setting. Indeed, many horror fans forget that the 1931 *Dracula* takes place in a world of automobiles, electric lights, and telephones, as the picture downplays these elements in favor of gothic Transylvanian locales with horse-drawn carriages. Even the sequences set in London linger on Victorian drawing rooms and ancient crypts, lending the production the feel of a period piece. By contrast, *Lady Vampire* opens with an automobile driving through the night, alternating close-ups of a gloved hand on a steering wheel with shots of a steadily increasing odometer. Electric headlights pierce the dark of night as the protagonist heads toward a birthday party held by a group of young women sporting the latest contemporary fashion and hairstyles who sing "Happy Birthday" in English to the guest of honor—a quintessentially postwar moment in Japanese cinema. The invasion of the vampire into the urban Tokyo setting of the picture recalls Bram Stoker's original depiction of Dracula penetrating bustling, turn-of-the-century London; but whereas Dracula chose the anachronistically gothic ruins of Carfax Abbey for his metropolitan base of operations, Amachi's vampire resides in a posh Tokyo hotel decorated in of-the-moment late 1950s trappings. The film's most elaborate vampire attack occurs in a downtown Tokyo club, Amachi's victims all trendy postwar socialites.[35]

Apart from a brief flashback that recounts the vampire's origins as a follower of Amakusa Shirō's ill-fated Christian rebellion in the early seventeenth century, it is only in the final sequence, when the hero journalist traces the monster to his centuries-old subterranean dwelling in a remote island off Kyushu, that the film abandons the thoroughly modern setting for the gothic, stylized set design that J-horror creators Kurosawa Kiyoshi and Sasaki Hirohisa identify as a necessary element of the *kaiki* genre. In its insistence on keeping the look of contemporary postwar Japan central to the mise-en-scène, *Lady Vampire* goes even further than *The Ghost and the M.P.* and *Mansion of the Ghost Cat* toward establishing the uncanny invasion of monsters of the past into the present as a theme of the newly emerging aesthetic of Japanese horror film. Despite the groundbreaking

---

[35] Another influence on *Lady Vampire* may have been American International Pictures' films like *I Was a Teenage Werewolf* (1957), which similarly imported classic movie monsters to present-day locales, although Nakagawa's vampire film and subsequent Shintōhō *gendaigeki* horror films lack the overt exploitation of youth culture that characterize the AIP films.

style and subject matter, Nakagawa considered the picture little more than a regrettable consequence of working at Ōkura's Shintōhō. When asked about *Lady Vampire*, he responded to his interviewer, "Ah, the kind of stuff you like. The kind I hate. Mihara Yoko, wasn't it? That was an Ōkura-style thing—those kinds of movies I made."[36]

"Those kinds of movies" went on to redefine the domestic *kaiki* genre, which continued to utilize traditional ghosts and monsters and stylized sets, but brought them into the world of contemporarily set *gendaigeki* productions with the same uncanny affect that Nakagawa pioneered in *Mansion of the Ghost Cat*, *The Ghost and the M.P.*, and *Lady Vampire*. One of Shintōhō's final concessions to the old *shinpi-kaiki* mystery hybrids, in which the ghosts and monsters receive a rational debunking, was 1959's *Diving Girls in a Haunted House* (*Ama no bakemono yashiki*), directed by Magatani Morihei. The film possesses a certain sleazy charm, representing one of Ōkura's more go-for-broke attempts to combine the *ama* pearl diver skin flicks the studio had pioneered in *Revenge of the Pearl Queen* with his profitable *kaiki* fare by showing a sexy heiress (glamour star Mihara Yoko again) and her pearl-diving compatriots wrestle each other in bathing suits on the beach in-between attempts to solve a haunted house mystery and discover hidden treasure.[37] The film ultimately rejects Nakagawa's innovations, however, by revealing the ghosts to be thieves in masks, trying to scare off the bathing beauties so that they can find the treasure themselves. *Kinema junpō*'s review of the picture shows that "real" ghosts were still firmly entrenched in the marvelous past in the popular conscious when it authoritatively states that "because this is a *gendaigeki* story, no 'real' monsters appear."[38]

By the time Ōkura ordered the inevitable follow-up picture, *Diving Girl's Ghost* (*Kaidan ama yūrei*, 1960), Shintōhō had completely overturned the convention that *gendaigeki* could not feature "real monsters." By including the word *kaidan* in the original Japanese title, the film more unequivocally aligns itself with traditional *kaiki* narratives than *Diving Girls in a Haunted House*, although significantly the action does not take place in the Edo period of samurai and geisha, but the contemporary world of scantily clad diving beauties. Further distancing itself from *Diving Girls in a Haunted House*, *Diving Girl's Ghost* presents its ghosts as real entities, not living men in disguise, and despite

---

[36] *Eiga kantoku Nakagawa Nobuo*, 216.
[37] *Kinema junpō*'s review opens with the witty observation that "[the film] stinks, but the title is some kind of genius." Uryū Tadao, "*Ama no bakemono yashiki*," *Kinema junpō*, August 15, 1959, 84.
[38] Ibid.

the modern setting weaves a very traditional *kaidan*-esque tale of murder and revenge from beyond the grave. The picture itself is of dubious quality, technically inferior even to the hokey *Diving Girls in a Haunted House*, but in its importation of not just the iconography but also the themes of the traditional *kaidan* into contemporary postwar Japan, it is emblematic of Shintōhō's revolution of the *kaiki* genre.

A more accomplished grafting of *kaidan* themes onto a *gendaigeki* horror film was director Namiki Kyōtarō's *Vampire Bride* (*Hanayome kyūketsuma*, 1960), the most interesting of the Shintōhō *kaiki* films not made by Nakagawa and his circle of talent. Just as *Diving Girl's Ghost* was a variation on *Diving Girls in a Haunted House* and Ishikawa Yoshihiro's *The Ghost Cat of Otama Pond* an attempt to recycle the success of *Mansion of the Ghost Cat*, *Vampire Bride* recalls shades of Nakagawa's *Lady Vampire*, but Namiki's film represents an even more liberal departure from the iconography of the Western bloodsucker than Nakagawa's vampire-werewolf hybrid. Namiki's vampire, played by actress Ikeuchi Junko, looks and behaves nothing like the suave Victorian bloodsuckers associated with the word. Instead of a jumble of Western movie monster motifs, *Vampire Bride* combines *kaidan* thematic elements with a native Japanese, pseudo-Shintō mysticism in a perfect display of Miriam Hansen's point that non-Western cinemas use Hollywood models to reinterpret local traditions in the cinematic medium.[39]

Ikeuchi's character, like Oiwa and the archetypical suffering heroines of *kaidan* literature and film, finds herself the victim of a cruel plot by jealous rivals, which leaves her face disfigured in the predictable Oiwa fashion. She seeks the help of a mysterious relative, a reclusive mountain witch who practices a profane form of shamanism that has kept her alive for centuries. When the spell to restore Ikeuchi's beauty misfires with fatal consequences, the unfortunate heroine finds herself resurrected and seemingly lovely once more, although now possessed of an uncontrollable thirst for blood that transforms her into a winged, hair-covered beast compelled to hunt down and murder the women who conspired against her. The final act blends the *kaidan* revenge-narrative arc with a plot structure that anticipates the teen slasher subgenre of American horror film in vogue during the 1980s, as the wicked conspirators, now living glamorous lives since disposing of their rival, are murdered one by one. Although remembered

---

[39] Miriam Bratu Hansen, "The Mass Production of the Senses: Classical Cinema as Vernacular Modernism," in *Reinventing Film Studies*, ed. Christine Gledhill and Linda Williams (New York: Oxford University Press, 2000), 341.

today primarily for a film industry rumor that Ōkura Mitsugi forced Ikeuchi to don the heavy, unflattering makeup of the title monster as punishment for spurning his lecherous advances, *Vampire Bride* may be Shintōhō's most creative endeavor to blend the narrative and visual motifs of the native *kaidan* subgenre of *kaiki* cinema with the emerging aesthetic of *horā* filmmaking.

"The Greatest Terror There Is": Nakagawa's *Ghost Story of Yotsuya* (*Tōkaidō Yotsuya kaidan*, 1959)

Ōkura seemed willing to experiment with breaking the rules of the *kaiki* genre in his lower-budget black-and-white pictures, but for the color centerpiece of Shintōhō's 1959 *Obon* "monster cavalcade" release the studio head decided to offer audiences a more traditional, period *kaidan* adaptation. Having outdone Daiei the previous year by producing a widescreen, color, and critically well-received ghost cat picture in *Mansion of the Ghost Cat*, Ōkura next chose to revisit the most famous Japanese ghost story, *Yotsuya kaidan*, and the resulting picture was ultimately released on the same day as Daiei's own color adaptation of the tale. Daiei's update of *The Ghost Story of Yotsuya* (*Yotsuya kaidan*, 1959), directed by Misumi Kenji, drew large inspiration from Kinoshita Keisuke's Occupation-era *The Ghost Story of Yotsuya: A New Interpretation* with its sympathetic portrayal of Iemon (this time played by romantic lead actor Hasegawa Kazuo) and restrained depictions of Oiwa's ghost—indeed it could be considered a color remake of Kinoshita's film. Nakagawa Nobuo, meanwhile, went back to Tsuruya Nanboku IV's original 1825 kabuki script for his *Tōkaidō Yotsuya kaidan* (or "The Ghost Story of Yotsuya along the East Sea Road"), retaining the full version of the play's title not just so audiences could tell it apart from Daiei's version on the theater marquee but also to proclaim its comparative fidelity to the spirit of Nanboku's lurid *kaidan* masterpiece.

Identifying two main strains of *Yotsuya* film adaptations, Yokoyama Yasuko places Misumi's version in the revisionist category also occupied by Kinoshita's film.[40] These pictures, Yokoyama notes, depart from Nanboku in depicting Oiwa as hopelessly in love with Iemon and omit their infant son from the narrative, making the tragedy that befalls the couple a tale of doomed romance rather than the destruction of the family unit. The adaptations in Yokoyama's other, conservative

---

[40] Yokoyama Yasuko. "*Yotsuya kaidan* eiga no Oiwa-tachi: kabuki to wakare, betsu no onna e," in *Kaiki to gensō e no kairo: kaidan kara J-horā e*, ed. Uchiyama Kazuki (Tokyo: Heibonsha, 1997), 154–6.

category, to which both Mōri Masaki's 1956 version as well as Nakagawa's 1959 film belong, retain Nanboku's themes of (dis)loyalty and vengeance that not just mark the sequences involving Oiwa's ghost but also characterize her relationship with Iemon even while alive. Nanboku's (and Nakagawa's) Oiwa stays with the abusive Iemon not out of any professed romantic love, but from a promise that Iemon will avenge her father's murder (unbeknownst to her, Iemon himself is in fact the murderer), remarking at one point in Nanboku's script, "Living in this house is constant torture … But I must remember that Iemon promised to help me attack my father's murderer … If I can just endure this a little while longer, I'll be able to leave this evil man."[41] The infant son—also retained from the kabuki play in Yokoyama's list of "conservative" adaptations—becomes a symbol of Iemon's familial obligations, cast aside when he plots to poison his wife and marry the daughter of the wealthy Itō Kihei.

Although the son receives short shrift in Nanboku's script—being devoured onstage by the ghost of another of Iemon's victims—in Nakagawa's film he serves as a conspicuous and lingering reminder of the father's guilt. For example, during the climax of the picture Iemon is at one point plagued by images of a blood-red mosquito net descending from the sky upon him while Oiwa wails his name, and at one point the baby's cries are clearly heard, recalling Iemon's previous attempt to pawn the mosquito net for cash despite Oiwa's pleas that without it, the baby will be eaten alive. Although the scene has no correlation in Nanboku's script and was apparently an innovation of Kurosawa Haruyasu,[42] it reinforces the themes of familial betrayal central to the kabuki tale.

And yet for all the ways Nakagawa's film draws attention to its roots in Nanboku's play, Horikiri Naota observes that the film abandons much of the kabuki text's preoccupation with worldly evil in favor of emphasizing the otherworldly aspects of the story, omitting plotlines involving prostitution and incest to focus more squarely on Iemon's betrayal of Oiwa and her return from the grave as a vengeful spirit.[43] One could say Nakagawa actually out-*kaiki*s Nanboku's seminal *kaidan* text, drawing out the themes of otherworldly *osore* to a degree not seen before—or since.

While Misumi's film was soon forgotten, Nakagawa's *Yotsuya* swiftly became acknowledged as a classic of Japanese cinema. Kurosawa Haruyasu won a Japan

---

[41] Tsuruya Nanboku IV, "*Ghost Stories at Yotsuya*," in *Early Modern Japanese Literature*, trans. Mark Oshima, ed. Shirane Haruo (New York: Columbia, 2002), 855.
[42] Nakagawa attributes the idea to Kurosawa in his notes that accompany *Kinema junpō*'s publication of the shooting script for the film. See Nakagawa Nobuo, "*Tōkaidō Yotsuya kaidan* enshutsu zakki," *Kinema junpō*, August 20, 1969, 79–94.
[43] Horikiri Naota, "Nakagawa Nobuo arui wa jōya no machieeru," *Eiga hyōron* 28, no. 2 (1971): 100.

Film Technology Award (*Nippon eiga gijutsu shō*) for his art direction on the picture, and *Kinema junpō* placed it on their list of the best films of 1959, an unprecedented honor for the critically ill-reputed *kaiki* genre.[44] For a special issue devoted entirely to "*kaiki* and *kyōfu* (horror)" in 1969, *Kinema junpō* published the complete shooting script for Nakagawa's *Yotsuya* together with a translation of the script for Hammer's *Dracula*, choosing the two films as the exemplary domestic and foreign examples of the genre and inviting Nakagawa to contribute detailed commentary on his memories of the shoot.[45] In 1982 *Junpō* chose it as one of the "Best 200 Japanese Films of All-Time"—the only *kaiki* film to make the list.[46] According to Takisawa Osamu, when Ōkura assigned Nakagawa *Yotsuya* as his fifth *kaiki* project in two years, the director told him, "You have stature as the studio head, but if you appoint me to direct, then I have more stature than you [over this project]," and Takisawa says that there was an implicit understanding among Nakagawa's staff that this would not be just another *obake eiga* monster movie, but an effort to create something special.[47] Nakagawa later recollected that, more so than even their previous *kaiki* productions, the cast and crew put their all into the production, even while the director himself was initially less than enthused about the project.[48]

The film's fidelity to the Edo-period themes and spirit of Nanboku preclude the kind of experimentation with generic tropes seen in pictures like *Mansion of the Ghost Cat* or *Vampire Bride*, which more pointedly anticipate the move away from *kaiki* toward a more contemporary *horā* style. Even the dizzying layers of uncanny repetition that distinguished Nakagawa's other "traditional" *kaidan* adaptation, *Kasane's Swamp*, find comparatively little expression. Instead, *Yotsuya* plays to the hilt the old-fashioned themes of *osore* that were the prized aesthetic of *kaidan* literature, conveyed through the terrifying omnipotence of Oiwa's curse. As I suggest in Chapter 1, when effectively invoked such terror approaches H. P. Lovecraft's "cosmic fear" in its sublime power against which even the gods cannot afford the condemned any protection. Nakagawa's film expertly portrays the unstoppable extent of Oiwa's fury when Iemon seeks refuge

---

[44] Kawabe, *B-kyū kyoshōron*, 133.
[45] *Kinema junpō*, August 20, 1969.
[46] Takisawa Osamu, "Tōkaidō Yotsuya kaidan," in *Eiga-shi jō besuto 200 shirizu: Nihon eiga 200* (Tokyo: Kinema Junpō, 1982), 270–1.
[47] Ibid., 270.
[48] "Kaiki eiga montō," 114. Kyoko Hirano further details the production of the film in "The Rise of Japanese Horror Films: Yotsuya Ghost Story (*Yotsuya Kaidan*), Demonic Men, and Victimized Women," in *Introducing Japanese Popular Culture*, ed. Alisa Freedman and Toby Slade (New York: Routledge, 2018), 204–15.

in a mountain temple, only to have the great gold Buddha statue he cowers before recede into darkness, leaving him to his fate.

In its powerful realization of the themes of *insan* and *osore* that made Nanboku's play the ultimate *kaidan*, and in its culmination of the formal techniques that Nakagawa, Kurosawa, and their crew had perfected over the course of their previous *kaiki* endeavors, *Yotsuya* represents the zenith of domestic *kaiki* filmmaking. The decade that followed its release would alternately see attempts to replicate its success in further *kaidan* adaptations, and further moves away from the period settings and marvelous cosmologies it exemplified. Daiei made yet more adaptations of *Kasane's Swamp* (*Kaidan Kasane ga fuchi*, 1960) and *The Peony Lantern* (*Botan dōrō*, 1968), while Tōei and Tōhō produced respective versions of *Yotsuya* in 1961 and 1965. Shōchiku, meanwhile, which had briefly flirted with *kaiki* material at intervals throughout its history, released modern-day *kaiki* films like Satō Hajime's *Hunchback Ghost Story* (*Kaidan semushi otoko*, 1965) and Matsuno Hiroshi's *The Living Skeleton* (*Kyūketsu dokurosen*, 1968), continuing down the trail blazed by Shintōhō's *gendaigeki* horror films. In a way, Nakagawa's *Yotsuya* marked the beginning of the end of the *kaiki* genre in Japan. Acknowledged as the last word in *kaiki* filmmaking, Japan's horror filmmakers would ultimately seek new horizons of fear beyond the realm of traditional *kaidan* adaptations.

Because of the film's reputation in Japan, Nakagawa's *Yotsuya* has received some small attention from English-language film studies, which have more often tended to overlook popular postwar Japanese *kaiki* pictures in favor of more internationally known art films like Mizoguchi's *Ugetsu* (1953) and Kobayashi Masaki's *Kwaidan* (1964) that deal with ghostly subject matter but ultimately eschew many of the generic conventions of *kaiki* cinema. Colette Balmain devotes part of her book *Introduction to Japanese Horror Film* to a consideration of Nakagawa's *Yotsuya*, in which she offers a sociopolitical reading of the film reflective of the postwar era in which it was produced. Seeing it as representative of the *kaidan* subgenre of *kaiki* cinema—which she deems the "Edo Gothic"—Balmain posits the film in opposition to the *shakaimono* or "social problem film" genre that was also popular in Japan during the late 1950s and early 1960s and critiqued established social institutions: "Edo Gothic films were traditional and tended to reinforce conservative values, with their helpless victims trapped in nightmarish gothic landscapes, articulated through the expressionistic surfaces of a subjective rather than objective reality."[49] Drawing on the work of Japanese

---

[49] Colette Balmain, *Introduction to Japanese Horror Film* (Edinburgh: Edinburgh University Press, 2008), 51.

film historian Isolde Standish, Balmain goes on to suggest that the Edo Gothic films are furthermore

> expressive of a type of "post-defeat victimization" or *higaisha ishiki* (victim consciousness) … embodied within the physical scars of the vengeful ghosts, through which individual and historical trauma becomes displaced from the "self" onto the "other." However, the boundaries between self and other become increasingly problematized, as the external alien turns inward.[50]

Balmain and Standish do not simply invoke the phrase *higaisha ishiki* as a convenient way to describe elements present in the films they examine. The term has entered the Japanese lexicon as a catch-all way of explaining and describing the tendency of much Japanese fiction of postwar era to portray their protagonists as victims of circumstance and the times in which they live, relatively powerless against the forces arrayed against them and capable only of reaction (as opposed to any assertive action).[51]

The most obvious examples of *higaisha ishiki* films deal explicitly with the Pacific War and its disastrous aftermath for the Japanese people, such as Shindō Kaneto's *Children of the Bomb* (*Genbaku no ko*, 1952) and Kinoshita Keisuke's *Twenty-four Eyes* (*Nijūshi no hitomi*, 1954). If, as Balmain suggests, Nakagawa's *Yotsuya* also belongs to the realm of *higaisha ishiki*, the collective postwar experiences of trauma must by necessity be coded and embedded within the imagery and conventions of the *kaiki* genre. However, although I believe Balmain is correct in seeing *higaisha ishiki* manifest in Nakagawa's version of *Yotsuya*, without taking the iconography of the *kaiki* genre and collective Japanese cultural knowledge of an already well-established narrative more fully into account we can arrive at predictable and somewhat unsatisfactory conclusions about how and why the film functions as postwar *higaisha ishiki*.

Balmain sees the wicked, self-interested Iemon as an indictment against American notions of capitalist consumerism that were imported and enforced by the occupation of Japan at the end of the war.[52] While this explains how a particular postwar audience may have collectively read and reacted to the themes presented in Nakagawa's film, the movie places no greater emphasis on Iemon's greed and materialism than Nanboku's early-nineteenth-century kabuki play, nor the many other film versions produced before and after the war. Balmain's

---

[50] Ibid.
[51] Isolde Standish, *A New History of Japanese Cinema: A Century of Narrative Film* (New York: Continuum, 2005), 189–90.
[52] Balmain, *Introduction to Japanese Horror Film*, 56–7.

reading of *Yotsuya*'s central iconic image, the disfigured face of Oiwa's vengeful ghost, is likewise perhaps too grounded in the postwar moment. The right side of her face swollen by the poison she is tricked into drinking, her long black hair disheveled and falling out in bloody clumps, Oiwa is not only the obvious template for contemporary J-horror ghosts like *Ring*'s Sadako but also bears resemblance to photographs of radiation victims from the atomic bombings of Hiroshima and Nagasaki. Seizing on the comparison, Balmain writes,

> While [O]iwa's disfigurement is key to the original folktale, it can also be interpreted as a metaphorical reference to the traumatized and defeated Japan after the Second World War. This is manifest trauma as genetic scar written on the female body, as symbolic of nationhood.[53]

She then quotes a passage from Julie Rauer in *Little Boy: The Art of Japan's Exploding Subculture*: "Twenty-two years after … the atomic bombs dropped on Hiroshima and three days later on Nagasaki on August 9, 1945, monstrous deformities persisted in the Japanese psyche."[54] But the question must be asked, did postwar Japanese audiences see in Oiwa's face the scarred radiation victims of the atomic bombs, and by extension their own collective war trauma? Japanese scholarship on Nakagawa and *Yotsuya* does not make the correlation, and makes little if any reference to postwar attitudes toward collective war trauma in their discussions of Nakagawa's work, from neither the standpoint of auteur theory nor audience reception.[55] Oiwa's disfigured face was an established convention of Japanese representations of the grotesque since kabuki makeup and woodblock prints first made it famous in the late Edo period (Figure 26). Nothing suggests Nakagawa's version of Oiwa's physical appearance was consciously modeled on atomic bomb victims,[56] and if the similarities were noticed by the postwar Japanese audience, it seems too obvious to warrant comment.

While it would be wrong to dismiss the notion that Nakagawa's *Yotsuya* (as well as other postwar "Edo Gothic" films featuring victimized, disfigured ghosts) is part of the *higaisha ishiki* phenomenon, I think it is more fruitful to consider the

---

[53] Ibid., 58.
[54] Julie Rauer, "Persistence of a Genetic Scar: Japanese Anime, Manga, and Otaku Culture Fill an Open National Wound," in *Little Boy: The Art of Japan's Exploding Subculture* (http://www.asianart.com/exhibitons//littleboy/intro.html). Quoted in Balmain, *Introduction to Japanese Horror Film*, 58.
[55] See Ōsawa Jō's and Yokoyama Yasuko's articles in *Kaiki to gensō e no kairo*, 68–94, 146–69, as well as Izumi Toshiyuki's *Ginmaku no hyakkai*.
[56] Interviews with Nakagawa's cast and crew—including Oiwa actress Wakasugi Katsuko—nowhere suggest the makeup was modeled on atomic bombing victims. See Suzuki Kensuke, ed., *Jigoku de yōi hai!: Nakagawa Nobuo, kaidan/kyōfu eiga no gyōka* (Tokyo: Wise, 2000); and Wakasugi Katsuko, *Yōen gensō kaiki jiai Wakasugi Katsuko*, ed. Maruo Toshiō. Famu fataru unmei no joyū shiriizu 1 (Tokyo: Wise, 2000), 164–72.

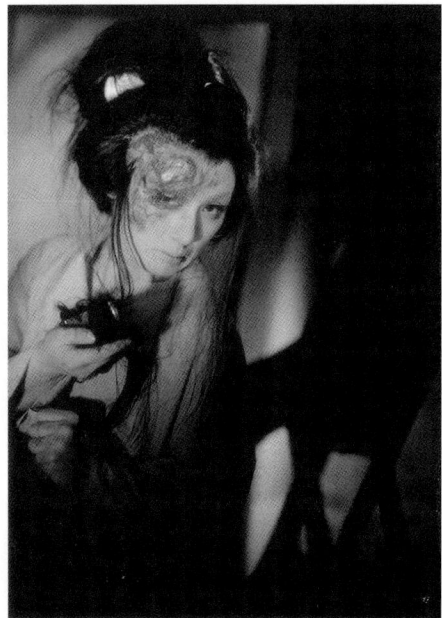 

Figure 26 Left: Publicity image of Wakasugi Katsuko as Oiwa from Nakagawa's *Ghost Story of Yotsuya* (*Tōkaidō Yotsuya kaidan*, 1959). ©Kokusai Hōei. Right: Nineteenth-century woodblock print of Oiwa by Utagawa Kuniyoshi. Courtesy of the British Museum.

film as primarily reflecting the same themes that had characterized the *kaidan* genre since its inception in the Edo period. The collective cultural lode Oiwa mined most strongly for postwar audiences was not Hiroshima and Nagasaki but traditions of *osore*—the aesthetically idealized sense of terror engendered by the wrath of unstoppable cosmic forces. Nakagawa blatantly invokes both the tale's roots in kabuki theater and the traditional themes of omnipotent, undying cosmic fury during the opening credits of the film, superimposed over images of a kabuki stage being prepped for performance while a voice sings an opening *gidayū* chant, "How can you kill one who is yours body and soul, who is bound to you for generations to come? ... O, the fury of a woman maddened is truly like unto the greatest terror (*osoroshisa*—a nominal variant on *osore*) there is!" Two years before the release of Nakagawa's *Yotsuya*, critic Izawa Jun wrote the following in his article "What Is *Kaiki*?":

> More than anyone, I think the great Nanboku lodged "*obake* drama" in the popular imagination. Without him, Oiwa's *kaiki* would not still be appearing on Japanese movie screens. *The Ghost Story of Yotsuya*'s grotesque, decadent, utterly

thorough heartlessness makes it the masterpiece of Japanese ghost stories ... Oiwa has become an icon. Her performance, the *kaiki*-ness of her makeup, these immediately took root in cinema ... Iemon's a thoroughly wicked guy, who can kill without batting an eyelash ... but against Oiwa's ghost he cannot do anything but utterly succumb ... The notion that against such forces one must inevitably succumb comes from kabuki's moralistic bent. We Japanese are suckers for this sort of thing.[57]

Oiwa, according to Izawa, was the ultimate icon of everything that had appealed to Japanese audiences in ghost stories since the heyday of *kaidan* literature and theater in the Edo period. However, apart from Mōri Masaki's 1956 film, postwar audiences had only been given Kinoshita Keisuke's watered-down version of Oiwa's ghost. As noted in the previous chapter, Nakagawa's film, by contrast, restored Oiwa's cosmic wrath by incorporating lines from Nanboku's original play that conveyed the power of the vengeful ghost's *urami* or hatred. Mōri's earlier film adopted this strategy to a lesser extent, but actress Wakasugi Katsuko as Oiwa in Nakagawa's version utters the dialogue with quivering rage, while Sōma Chieko adopts a more wan, melancholic delivery in Mōri's film.

Nakagawa seems to have understood that an emphasis on Oiwa's anger would amplify the themes of *osore* present in the work that lent it its power, and the success of Nakagawa's take on *The Ghost Story of Yotsuya* lies in its ability to convey more strongly than any *kaiki* film before or since the profound terror of the vengeful ghost's wrath, surpassing even Nanboku's original play in certain respects. In a significant departure from Nanboku's script as well as Mōri's earlier film, Nakagawa's Oiwa does not suffer the effects of the disfiguring poison she has imbibed until she learns of her husband's betrayal. Upon receiving the news, Wakasugi immediately clutches her face and screams in pain, as if the knowledge of Iemon's treachery impels her monstrous transformation, rather than the mere physical effects of the poison. To this point in the film Nakagawa and cinematographer Nishimoto have kept the camera at a distance from Wakasugi. Apart from a few expository close-ups, Nakagawa's preferred framing of scenes in long shot predominates the film's portrayal of the living Oiwa. From the moment she begins her hideous metamorphosis into a vengeful ghost, however, the camera favors close-ups of Oiwa's bloody visage (Figure 27). As in *Mansion of the Ghost Cat* and the Hammer horror films there may be a bit

---

[57] Izawa Jun, "Kaiki to wa? Nihon no obake to seiyō no obake," *Kinema junpō*, July 1, 1957, 44.

Figure 27 Nakagawa's film favors long shots for the living Oiwa (above), but brings the camera in close to depict the wrath of her vengeful ghost (below).

of exploitative motivation in lingering on the bright red blood dripping down Oiwa's face, but these shots prove crucial in conveying the anger of Wakasugi's performance, emphasizing the look of hatred in her eyes as she vows revenge even in death upon her unfaithful husband. In his overview of *kaiki* cinema, *100 Horrors of the Silver Screen*, Izumi Toshiyuki's thoughts on the importance of establishing the anger that gives birth to the vengeful ghost's curse support the idea that Wakasugi's performance—and Nakagawa's careful highlighting of it through formal technique—helps to make the film the ultimate example of the genre. Izumi writes,

> If this enmity is not depicted as existing in their mind [while the character is still living], then when their ghost appears, its character becomes vaguely defined, and the impression is severely weakened … the actress's nature is crucial, and naturally goes a long way towards giving the work the proper feel of a *kaidan*.

Emotions like enmity are not generally rare things in this world, but a ghost must be enmity incarnate, something we never wish to casually encounter.[58]

Nakagawa's *Yotsuya* also demonstrates a formal sophistication that goes beyond the disciplined, strategic use of the close-up to depict the wrath of Oiwa's ghost, and proves that—for a director who claimed to be utterly disinterested in the *kaiki* genre—Nakagawa carefully considered the best ways to employ the formal aspects of the cinematic medium to convey suspense, dread, and shock to an audience that was, after all, looking for *kaiki to senritsu* thrills and chills. A comparative look at a pivotal moment in both Mōri's and Nakagawa's respective films, in which the viewer gets their first look at Oiwa's ghastly, poison-disfigured face, demonstrates the superior horrific affect of the latter film.

Mōri stages his reveal in a basic shot-reverse-shot setup. After unwittingly drinking poison, Oiwa clutches her face, moans in pain, and falls to the floor. The camera quickly cuts to a close-up of the startled, horrified reaction of the masseur Takuetsu (whom Iemon has paid to seduce Oiwa), then quickly cuts back to a high-angle reverse shot of the now disfigured Oiwa on the floor, her grotesque deformity plainly revealed by the high-key lighting. Nakagawa's film, conversely, delays the reveal of Oiwa's face to create an atmosphere of dread and suspense, strongly recalling an analogous moment from Mokudō Shigeru's forgotten prewar *kaiki* effort for Shinkō, *The Ghost Story of the Mandarin Duck Curtain*, discussed in Chapter 2. As in Mōri's film, the horrified reaction of Takuetsu anticipates the reveal, but instead of a close-up, Nakagawa frames the moment in a wide shot that includes the figure of Oiwa lying prostrate on the floor in the foreground. Low-key lighting keeps her face hidden from the viewer, and there is no cut as Oiwa slowly, agonizingly crawls to her mirror. Finally the camera cuts to a point-of-view shot of the mirror itself, Oiwa's trembling hand slowly entering the frame to remove the mirror's cover, and the viewer's first glimpse of her hideous face is that of her own shocked, horrified reaction in the mirror. Where Mōri's film takes less than thirty seconds from the time the poison takes effect to reveal its ghastly results, Nakagawa stretches the reveal out over twice as long a period of time.

The initial appearance of Oiwa's ghost is handled in similar fashion. Mōri again gives us a simple shot-reverse-shot in high-key lighting, first of Iemon gazing at his new bride Oume, then a cut to an over-the-shoulder shot in which Oiwa's ghost rises up into the frame from Oume's position. Nakagawa, meanwhile,

[58] Izumi, *Ginmaku no hyakkai*, 47.

employs more nuanced cinematography to achieve a horrific effect in his double reveal of Oiwa's ghost. The first appearance is heralded by her ghostly wailing to Iemon, who sits alone in the frame drinking tea, lit by atmospheric, low-key lighting. As Iemon shrugs off the sound of Oiwa's voice as a trick of the imagination, Nakagawa lets the camera linger on the scene a moment before suddenly and unexpectedly whip-panning straight up to reveal Oiwa's ghost hanging from the ceiling directly above Iemon's head. Nakagawa later replicates the moment in Mōri's film where Oiwa's ghost takes the place of the new bride Oume, improving on Mōri's reveal in which Oiwa rises into the frame behind Iemon's shoulder. In place of the shot-reverse-shot setup, Nakagawa stages the moment in a single take, having Oume demurely drop out of the frame as if lying on the nuptial bed, only to have the hideous Oiwa slowly rise back up into the frame from Oume's place to a menacing crescendo of kabuki drums (Figure 28).

Figure 28 Oiwa's ghost rises into frame in place of Iemon's new bride in a single take.

Here Nakagawa demonstrates that by not cutting to a different shot, the effect of horror may be increased, contrary to the comparatively rapid cutting of Mōri's film.

Nakagawa's film follows up the whip-pans and clever framing of the ghost's initial, startling appearance with a set piece of *obake yashiki* spook-house scares that shamelessly recall Kato Bin's work on Daiei's ghost cat series. Iemon inadvertently slays both his new bride and in-laws while slashing away at the ghosts of Oiwa and Takuetsu with his sword, as gruesome-looking ghouls pop out from behind sliding doors and curtains, then recede, only to be replaced by Iemon's unintended victims. In moments like these, Nakagawa offers concession to generic convention and audience expectations. Reviewing the film during its initial release in 1959, Takisawa Osamu had only one complaint—Nakagawa showed a bit too much of Oiwa's ghost, which he felt lessened the shocking effect of the picture.[59] Takisawa's opinion reflects Takahashi Hiroshi's comments quoted in the previous chapter about the shallowness of the carnival spook-house mode of *kaiki* film. Nakagawa himself later admitted to "showing the ghost too much" in his pictures, but went on to defend the decision:

> I think it's probably a case of excessive fan service, but on the other hand, when you're making these kinds of films, should you make a monster movie in which no monsters appear? Will the audience who came to see a monster movie feel satisfied? Then again, as we've been discussing, monsters that appear too frequently in an opportunistic or exploitative manner have the opposite [intended] effect. However, psychologically speaking if you can emphasize a sense of, "Will it appear? Will it appear?" then the moment when it inevitably *does* appear is effective. I think that's a good method.[60]

Nakagawa's moments of sensational address serve their purpose in giving the audience what they paid to see, but I disagree with Takisawa that they lessen the film's impact. Unlike the Daiei pictures, which offer plenty of momentary scares and startles bereft of careful narrative attention to the themes of *osore* latent in the material, Nakagawa's *Yotsuya* delivers these startling moments as a weighty payoff to the meticulously established wrath of Oiwa's vengeful spirit. As a result of retaining much of Nanboku's original dialogue, Wakasugi's performance, and the manner in which the filmmakers deploy the camera to highlight her burning hatred, the spook-house scares do not merely make the audience jump out of their seats; they provide punctuation for the underlying *osore* of Oiwa's revenge,

[59] Takisawa Osamu, "*Tōkaidō Yotsuya kaidan*," *Kinema junpō*, September 1, 1959, 83.
[60] Nakagawa, "Obake eiga sono hoka/watashi no kiroku eiga ron," 106.

as the ghost makes good on her dying words, "Iemon, you heartless brute, do you think I will leave you with this debt unpaid?!"

Amplifying the film's effective use of the sensational address, Nakagawa and his crew found ways to experiment with the conventional portrayals of ghosts and ghouls on-screen, particularly in the use of montage. The climax of *Yotsuya*, a barrage of quick cuts that depict Oiwa's final assault on Iemon, stands in sharp contrast to the straightforward *tachimawari* fight with the monster that concluded most *kaiki* films to that point. Rather than have the monster physically engage its victim in a choreographed confrontation in the manner of Suzuki Sumiko and Irie Takako, Nakagawa barely even shows Oiwa and Iemon in the same frame. Instead, Oiwa's ephemeral, spectral presence is conveyed via an increasingly rapid montage, suggesting she is at once everywhere and nowhere, making escape impossible for the increasingly unsettled Iemon. Simultaneously pursued by Oiwa's sister Osode and her paramour Yomoshichi, Iemon finally attempts to flee straight toward the camera, only to have Oiwa's ghost suddenly fly in to fill the frame in close-up. The sequence never resorts to the double-exposure technique of filming a see-through ghost, making Oiwa a physical, concrete, and more threatening presence, yet her ghostly status is effectively conveyed via an assault of images on the viewer, rather than a physical assault on her victim.

In her essay "A Study of *Yotsuya kaidan* Films: In a Case of Nobuo Nakagawa's Experimental Expression of Horror," Hirose Ai suggests that it is as if the camera, like Oiwa's wrath, becomes unleashed by her monstrous transformation.[61] From the moment Oiwa drinks the poison and begins the transformation into a vengeful spirit, the number of cuts in the film increases dramatically. The film's opening five-minute sequence, in which Iemon murders Oiwa's father following an argument between the elderly man and his would-be son-in-law, consists of a single uninterrupted take, and subsequent scenes between Iemon and the living Oiwa likewise play out with a minimum of camera movement and cutting. Oiwa's death scene, meanwhile, contains twenty shots in roughly the same amount of time as the single-take opening sequence. The ghostly assault on Iemon at the film's climax consists of more than seventy-five shots—many of them only lasting one or two seconds in duration—in less than five minutes. The briefest shots in the climatic sequence are of Oiwa and her fellow ghost Takuetsu, physically removed from the space of Iemon's battle against Osode and Yomoshichi and

---

[61] Hirose Ai, "Eiga *Yotsuya kaidan* kō—Nakagawa Nobuo no jikkenteki kaiki hyōgen," *Shokei gakuin daigaku kiyōdai* 2 (September 2011): 53–8.

occasionally lit by red or green filtered lighting that heightens the Othered space they inhabit, predating a similar use of extreme color to mark unreal, *kaiki* spaces in the period horror films Roger Corman and Mario Bava would direct in the 1960s. There are a few spook-house moments as well, where for shocking effect Nakagawa alternates the montage effect with in-camera startles, such as having Oiwa's corpse suddenly descend into frame in close-up as Iemon runs toward the camera, but the fast-paced cutting of the entire sequence leaves no feeling of incongruity in these shots. Despite the disparate action of Osode and Yomoshichi's earthly attack cross-cut with Oiwa and Takuetsu's more ethereal assault on Iemon, the film's final set piece flows as a seamless whole.

Yotsuya's greatest achievement, however, may lie in the way in which Nakagawa and his staff deliver another "orthodox" *kaiki* film that adheres to the audience's expectations for a popular genre picture, while mining the material for a nuanced, psychological portrait of its stock characters. Ōsawa Jō attributes much of this to Amachi Shigeru's poker-faced performance as Iemon. Mōri Masaki's 1956 version of *Yotsuya* had distanced itself from Kinoshita's 1949 *New Interpretation* by returning to the notion of Oiwa as a wrathful ghost exacting karmic revenge on her unfaithful husband, but Wakayama Tomisaburō plays Iemon as a nervous, guilt-riddled wreck following the death of his wife, much as Uehara Ken had portrayed him in Kinoshita's liberal remake. In Nakagawa's film, Amachi plays Iemon neither as a nervous repentant nor as a thoroughly conniving villain, but as a stoic who guards his emotions. Even when Oiwa's ghost appears to haunt him, Amachi looks visibly startled and, as the film progresses, increasingly agitated, but never fearful, guilt-stricken, or regretful. Only in the final moments of the picture, when Iemon stabs himself with Osode's sword and shrieks, "Oiwa! Forgive me! I was wrong! Forgive me!" does the audience at last receive confirmation of his true feelings. Since the audience cannot read his emotions, it remains ambiguous to what extent Iemon truly repents of his actions, which Ōsawa argues makes him more psychologically interesting for the viewer than the one-sided, unrepentant sinner Nanboku's kabuki script suggests, as well as the obviously guilt-riddled portrayals of Uehara and Wakayama.[62]

Amachi's performance also has important implications for the presentation of Oiwa's ghost, which allows for a multilayered interpretation of the film's *kaiki* elements. Rather like Suzuki Sumiko's similarly poker-faced villain in the prewar *Ghost Cat and the Mysterious Shamisen*, Amachi's reserved portrayal

---

[62] Ōsawa Jō, "Shintōhō no obake eiga to *Tōkaidō Yotsuya kaidan*: jyanru no fukkatsu tokakushin," in *Kaiki to gensō e no kairo: kaidan kara J-horā e*, ed. Uchiyama Kazuki (Tokyo: Shinwasha, 2008), 80–5.

makes a symbolic reading of Oiwa's ghost as a manifestation of internal guilt possible, but leaves the matter ultimately ambiguous. Uehara's and Wakayama's more obviously repentant takes on Iemon, meanwhile, weight the interpretation of the *kaiki* phenomena toward the metaphorical, and Kinoshita's film all but outright rejects a reading of Oiwa's ghost as anything more than a guilt-induced hallucination. In opposition to the mystery of Iemon's true feelings on the matter of his misdeeds, Nakagawa's film blatantly dwells on the emotions Oiwa makes plain in her speech and actions as an omnipotent, vengeful wraith. In this way Oiwa carries the dramatic import of psychological symbolism while simultaneously existing as a character in her own, terrifying right. What plagues Iemon may be allegorically read as a guilty conscience, but it is also undoubtedly an old-fashioned *kaiki* monster, and it will have its revenge. Blending allegory and symbolism with the spectacular sensibilities of genre cinema, Nakagawa and company have their proverbial cake and eat it too, crafting a pop horror crowd-pleaser that also stands as a serious study in the psychology of men, women, and monsters.

Conclusion

Nakagawa Nobuo is the key transitional figure in the history of the Japanese horror film. Along with Kurosawa Haruyasu and their fellow Shintōhō collaborators, he elevated B-grade *kaiki* film to new levels of artistic expression, garnering accolades from the most demanding of critics while still delivering the crowd-pleasing shocks and startles expected of the genre. But Nakagawa and Shintōhō did not just perfect the classical *kaiki* film. In their experiments with the limits of the genre's content and themes—notably their willingness to move at least some of the action to present-day Japan and its rational world of disbelieving doctors, journalists, and buxom pearl divers—they point the way to a new kind of horror in Japanese cinema. Films like *Mansion of the Ghost Cat* and *Lady Vampire* unveil a dark modern world in which the monsters of the past break free from their marvelous Edo-period wonderlands to invade the present, making them a cognitive threat more closely aligned to the Anglophone horror genre and anticipating a major theme of the globally popular J-horror pictures to come. But even Nakagawa's more traditional *jidaigeki* terrors would go on to inspire the future filmmakers of J-horror with their vividly realized depictions of the *osore* inherent in their psychological dramas of vengeance from beyond the grave.

The appointment of Ōkura Mitsugi as head of Shintōhō in 1955 transformed the struggling studio from an artistic haven for filmmakers to a B-genre factory, churning out lurid crime dramas, erotic exploitation, and *kaiki* pictures. Although cheaply made by the standards of the more financially secure studios, Ōkura treated his *kaiki* films as A-list product. Whereas Daiei continued to hastily produce its annual ghost cat releases as program pictures, Shintōhō's top talent were put to work reintroducing *kaidan* classics like *The Ghost Story of Yotsuya* and *The Ghost Story of Kasane's Swamp* to postwar movie screens. The resulting films often made use of widescreen and color—extravagances the other studios seldom deigned to use on their own *kaiki* B-pictures. Shintōhō's premiere *kaiki* unit, headed by veteran director Nakagawa Nobuo, not only made innovative use of the latest advances in available film technology, they also invigorated the genre with a sophisticated use of the uncanny, earning unprecedented critical acclaim for domestic *kaiki* cinema.

Developing a more mysterious style of filming their monsters by implying rather than showing their presence and keeping their facial features hidden from view, Nakagawa and his crew also anticipated the more contemporary style of Japanese horror filmmaking that would come to be known as J-horror. And yet, the studio's most acclaimed *kaiki* film, Nakagawa's *Ghost Story of Yotsuya*, succeeded by marrying the formal innovations pioneered by the Shintōhō staff with a very traditional take on the themes of *osore* that had distinguished the genre since the premodern Edo period. Following Shintōhō's collapse in 1961, the other studios continued to produce visually innovative *kaidan* adaptations and further pioneer the *gendaigeki* horror picture. However, by the dawn of the 1970s the Japanese film industry began to succumb to a decade-long decrease in attendance, as the rise of television kept families out of the theaters and in their homes for audiovisual entertainment. The coming decades would see the death of the *kaiki* genre, the birth of *horā*, and *kaiki*'s ghastly, partial resurrection in the guise of J-horror.

5

Back from the Grave: The Death of a Genre and the *Kaiki* Legacy of J-horror

The monster always comes back. Ever since Universal's *Bride of Frankenstein* opened in 1935 with the retconned revelation that the mad doctor's creature somehow survived its apparent destruction at the end of the previous film, horror fans have known that a really good monster is only dead until the inevitable sequel or remake. One has only to look at the endless incarnations of Sadako, the iconic J-horror ghost at the center of the *Ring* franchise. Since the original *Ring* series wrapped up in 2000 with *Ring 0: Birthday*, she has returned for *Sadako 3D* and its sequel (2012–13), the *Ju-On* crossover *Sadako vs. Kayako* (2016), and a reboot by the original film's director Nakata Hideo, simply titled *Sadako* (2019).

Yet even in her big screen debut from 1998 Sadako was already in many ways a return, as J-horror resurrected the ghosts of *kaiki* cinema and the sense of *osore* they embodied after decades of dormancy. Equally inspired by Western *kaiki* films like *The Haunting* (1963) and *The Innocents* (1961) and the Japanese pictures that followed in the wake of Nakagawa Nobuo's innovations in domestic *kaiki* cinema, J-horror's creators overwhelmingly looked to the decade of the 1960s when crafting their own works of horror. This is not terribly surprising given that most of the J-horror filmmakers were born in the late 1950s and early 1960s, but the timing could not have been more fortuitous. The 1960s proved to be *kaiki* cinema's final decade. Ten years of robust output, from the Japanese studios' continued production of *kaidan* adaptations to American and European gothic horror pictures along the Hammer model, abruptly ceased by the early 1970s. As a result, the word *kaiki* itself faded from usage, and the English loanword *horā* emerged as a broader way to talk about diverse modes of frightening representation in commercial cinema. The ghost of *kaiki* would return in J-horror, but in splendid horror movie fashion she would not be quite how Japan remembered her … and with terrifying results.

The first half of this chapter sketches an outline of the Japanese *kaiki* film's mature phase in the 1960s, which consists primarily of variations on Nakagawa Nobuo's technique in realizing a more *horā*-esque approach to classic *kaidan* narratives like *Yotsuya*, *Kasane's Swamp*, and *Peony Lantern*. I touch on developments such as the continued influence of Western *kaiki* works—notably Robert Wise's *The Haunting*—on *gendaigeki kaiki* films like Satō Hajime's *Hunchback Ghost Story* (*Kaidan semushi otoko*, 1965) and the late-1960s boom in *yōkai* that created what might be deemed children's *kaiki* films before turning to the reasons and consequences for the genre's sudden decline and death in the 1970s. The chapter's second act demonstrates how the J-horror movement of the past twenty years drew upon the work of Nakagawa and other 1960s *kaiki* filmmakers via a partial resurrection of select themes and formal filmmaking practices to evoke the prized sense of *osore* embodied in the form of the *onryō* or vengeful spirit. Oiwa's uncanny return to Japanese cinema in the persona of Sadako, Kayako, and their fellow "long-haired Japanese ghosts" is seen by many global horror fans today as a tired cliché, but the J-horror ghosts' initial appearance at the dawn of the new millennium terrified Japanese audiences by upending expectations about how the *onryō* operates, deviating from the laws of karmic retribution as they haunt a postmodern world devoid of the cosmologies that previously governed the *kaiki* cinema ghost's behavior.

Twilight: The 1960s, 1970s, and the Death of *Kaiki* Film

The 1960s proved to be the twilight of the *kaiki* genre in Japan, but it was a fertile twilight, as other filmmakers and studios sought to emulate and further develop the modes of visual style and storytelling pioneered by Nakagawa Nobuo and his circle of talent at Shintōhō. While most failed to match the critical acclaim of Nakagawa's *kaiki* work, their employment of his techniques in representing a more horrific style of *kaiki* on-screen left a profound impression on the generation that would grow up to produce the J-horror phenomenon at the turn of the millennium. Kurosawa Kiyoshi explains,

> Nakagawa provided the model, but it wasn't just him who was producing this imagery. The *kaiki* films made in the 1960s were inspired by his example, and they attempted all sorts of things in the effort to portray their ghosts in a scarier fashion. After [Nakagawa's] *Ghost Story of Yotsuya* I think other filmmakers said to themselves, "This is interesting—let's make stuff like this."

We [the J-horror filmmakers] are influenced by the entirety of ghost imagery from that era.[1]

Nakagawa's critical successes were not enough to save the perennially struggling Shintōhō from bankruptcy, but the studio continued to innovate in the arenas of horror filmmaking until shutting its doors for good in 1961. The previous year had seen the resignation of Ōkura Mitsugi as studio executive following a series of scandals and claims of embezzlement, but even prior to Ōkura's exit, the sense among the staff was that Shintōhō's days were numbered.[2] Several of the studio's releases throughout 1960 had a go-for-broke nature to their content and production. No longer concerned about turning a profit, the prevailing attitude seemed to be to use the remaining capital to produce something unique. Nakagawa got approval from the embattled Ōkura to direct an original project, *Jigoku* ("Hell"), which along with *Yotsuya* generally ranks among the director's masterpieces in critical esteem.

Jigoku's first hour recounts a sordid tale of a young college student played by Amachi Shigeru who finds himself mixed up with a variety of unsavory characters, primarily his Mephistophelian coed Tamura (Numata Yoichi). Through an uncanny set of circumstances, the entire cast dies at the same instant, and the film's final sequence is an avant-garde display of gorily realized Buddhist hells. The film remains Nakagawa's best-known work internationally, enjoying cult status among Western horror fans. In Japan, it left an especially profound impression on future *Ring* screenwriter Takahashi Hiroshi. Takahashi recalls watching *Jigoku* multiple times on television as a child in the 1960s and "being blown away" by the unflinching depictions of its characters suffering the torments of Hell: "It was truly incredible … There may have been something like it before, but I don't know for sure. The first time I had ever seen such an intense depiction of terror was in *Jigoku*."[3] Despite the film's hallowed reputation among horror movie fans worldwide, *Jigoku*'s idiosyncratic style and content, although perhaps the purest depiction of *osore* in Japanese cinema to that point, has none of the gothic formal trappings of the *kaiki* genre, making the film a remarkable but rather singular anomaly.

More representative of both the past and future of Japanese horror was *The Ghost Cat of Otama Pond* (*Kaibyō Otama ga ike*, 1960), the directorial debut of Nakagawa's assistant Ishikawa Yoshihiro. Having started with the studio as a

---

[1] Author's interview with Kurosawa Kiyoshi.
[2] "Building the Inferno: Nobuo Nakagawa and the Making of *Jigoku*," *Jigoku*, Criterion, 2006, DVD.
[3] Author's interview with Takahashi Hiroshi.

writer, Ishikawa had only served a few years as an assistant director, but with the studio on the brink of inevitable collapse, Ōkura put Ishikawa in the director's chair for what would be the color centerpiece of the studio's final *Obon* "monster cavalcade." Working with Kurosawa Haruyasu and much of Nakagawa's former crew, Ishikawa's effort matches Nakagawa's work in its technical accomplishment, and if the apprentice falls a little short of the master, it is only because of the recycled feeling of the material from *Mansion of the Ghost Cat*, presenting another tale of a modern-day couple beset by the curse a ghost cat placed upon the young woman's ancestors, related in lengthy flashback by a Buddhist monk. Issues of the convoluted, recycled script aside, *The Ghost Cat of Otama Pond* builds on lessons learned from *Mansion of the Ghost Cat*, notably in its portrayal of the title monster. Nakagawa's ghost cat film had pioneered new ways to depict traditional monsters on-screen, specifically in its limited reveals of the ghost cat's face during the *gendaigeki* sequences. Recognizing the effectiveness of the technique, for *The Ghost Cat of Otama Pond* the decision was made to never show the ghost cat's face at all, even in the *jidaigeki* period sequence. Exemplifying the "less-is-more" aesthetic espoused by Takahashi Hiroshi, Ishikawa's film points, like its predecessor, toward the style and motifs of the J-horror films and their faceless ghosts of the past, which invade the present with their undying curses.

Following Shintōhō's closure in 1961, Daiei and Tōei continued a steady production of *kaiki* films throughout the decade that built on the innovations Shintōhō brought to the genre in their final years of operation. Tōei abandoned the more romantic approach that distinguished their 1950s *kaiki* output with their own lurid adaptation of the *Yotsuya* legend. *The Ghost of Oiwa* (*Kaidan Oiwa no bōrei*, 1961) recalls both Mōri Masaki's 1956 *Ghost Story of Yotsuya* by recasting Wakayama Tomisaburō as Iemon and Nakagawa's 1959 version in its more unsavory, villainous interpretation of the character, along with a mix of old-fashioned, in-frame spook-house tricks and montage to depict the ghostly attacks on Iemon. Oiwa's appearance also receives a more visually startling treatment. For the classic scene in which Oiwa's undead corpse appears nailed to a door floating in a bog, *The Ghost of Oiwa* has the door swiftly shoot up out of the water in a vertical position, Oiwa's undead body standing at attention as it gazes menacingly at Iemon. The setup mimics the correlating scene as it is usually presented on the kabuki stage while also making a kind of inverted callback to Nakagawa's effective whip-pan reveal of Oiwa's ghost on the ceiling.

In 1965 Tōhō distributed their own *Yotsuya* adaptation, a rare foray into *kaidan* for the studio that had previously shunned such material. Directed by Shirō Toyoda and released internationally as *Illusion of Blood*, the film features even more shocking, extreme displays of gore than Shintōhō's most lurid efforts in the genre. In one shot, Iemon hacks at Oiwa's ghost with his sword, slicing the skin off her face, which falls away to reveal the skeleton underneath. Even the comparatively romantic *Peony Lantern* took on a ghastlier, Shintōhō-esque flavor in Daiei's 1968 version, which employed creative makeup and costume effects to make the bones inside the flesh of its female ghost seem to shine through her skin. These films and others deftly honed variations on Nakagawa's technique of realizing classic *kaidan* tales with gruesome, concrete depictions of vengeful ghosts as physically present beings able to give blunt expression to their wrath and become *osore* incarnate.

In addition to a glut of period *kaiki* fare, the 1960s also saw filmmakers develop and innovate the *gendaigeki kaiki* film pioneered in Shintōhō pictures like *Mansion of the Ghost Cat*, *Diving Girl's Ghost*, and *Vampire Bride*, while also absorbing elements from contemporary Western *kaiki* cinema. Director Satō Hajime's *Hunchback Ghost Story* (*Kaidan semushi otoko*, 1965) is the first Japanese horror film clearly influenced by Robert Wise's *The Haunting*, and like Wise's film is held in high regard by the J-horror cadre. *Hunchback* mimics the "show nothing" maxim of *The Haunting* by depicting its ghosts primarily via the sounds of screams, moans, and rapping behind psychically bulging doors. It blends the aesthetics of Wise's approach to the otherworldly with the sensibilities of the European gothic horror films that were also in vogue at the time, particularly in its baroque conclusion featuring actress Hayama Yoko clutching a candelabra as she wanders about the halls and grounds of a haunted mansion clad in flimsy negligee. *Hunchback* combines these formal trappings of 1960s American and European *kaiki* films with a revision of the classic Japanese vengeful ghost narrative in anticipation of the later J-horror pictures. The malevolent spirit at work in the haunted mansion to which the ensemble cast of characters converge proves utterly unstoppable in its wrath. Born out of betrayal and murder just as the ghost of Oiwa and the *bakeneko* are, *Hunchback*'s ghost easily consumes the lives of all who enter its haunted dwelling. In its depiction of unstoppable rage turned on innocents, the film foreshadows the deployment of the *kaiki* tropes of *shūnen* and *osore* in J-horror along more ominous, amoral lines than the more righteous depictions of traditional *onryō* like Oiwa and her ilk, who only haunt those who wronged them in life.

After directing *Hunchback* at Tōei, Satō went on to make the cult classic sci-fi horror film *Goke, Body Snatcher from Hell* (*Kyūketsuki Gokemidoro*, 1968) at Shōchiku, though *Goke*'s psychic, vampiric parasite who arrives in a UFO from outer space places it well outside the boundaries of the *kaiki* genre as it had come to be understood in post-Hammer Japan. Satō's film was part of Shōchiku's sudden but momentary interest in the horror genre, which resulted in a spate of horror and *kaiki* films from the studio in 1968. Along with *Goke*, Shōchiku produced two much more typical *kaiki* works that year. *Cruel Ghost Legend* (*Kaidan zankoku monogatari*) was a straightforward adaptation of the Kasane's Swamp story that owed much to Nakagawa's version while significantly upping the sexual content, while *The Living Skeleton* (*Kyūketsu dokuro sen*) was a *gendaigeki* ghost story that, like Satō's *Hunchback* and the Shintōhō films before it, blended traditional *kaidan* tropes with a modern setting and visual style that betrays both domestic and international influences.

Shōchiku's momentary foray into horror was part of a spike in domestic *kaiki* film releases during 1968 before the genre rapidly dwindled into extinction in the 1970s. Not coincidentally, 1968 also saw a booming interest in *yōkai*, the traditional Japanese goblins that shared a similar place in the cultural consciousness with the ghosts and *bakeneko* who starred in domestic *kaiki* film, and this marked a turn toward a more kid-friendly portrayal of the monstrous in Japanese cinema.[4] Manga author Mizuki Shigeru's beloved *GeGeGe no Kitarō*, which had popularized the image of *yōkai* as subjects for children's entertainment, received the first of many, still-ongoing adaptations to television animation in January 1968. Later that same year the similarly themed anime *Yōkai ningen Bemu* debuted and enjoyed almost equal popularity.

Daiei wasted no time in capitalizing on the phenomenon, and in March released the first of three *yōkai*-themed *kaiki* pictures. *Yokai Monsters: One Hundred Monsters* (*Yōkai hyaku monogatari*) contains an atmospheric recreation of the "100 Ghost Stories" parlor game popular during the Edo period, where many of the representative tales of *kaiki* cinema were first told. An embedded narrative within the film recounts one such tale and features Daiei's former *kaiki* glamour star and "snake actress" Mōri Ikuko as one of the most iconic *yōkai*, the serpent-necked *rokurokubi*. The film's overall tone, however, skews toward the whimsical, the studio clearly aiming at the same young audience who enjoyed Mizuki's friendly and unthreatening take on *yōkai*. Despite this, the themes of karmic comeuppance that lend much *kaiki* cinema its sense of *osore* remain present here as well as in the film's two follow-ups, *Spook Warfare* (*Yōkai daisensō*) and *Along with Ghosts* (*Tōkaidō obake dōchū*, 1969). Comedic

---

[4] See Foster's *Pandemonium and Parade* as well as *The Book of Yōkai* (Berkeley: University of California Press, 2015), 61–5, for a more thorough discussion of Mizuki and the children's *yōkai* fad of the late 1960s.

antics of adorable *yōkai* like the *karakasa* umbrella-monster juxtapose with more typical *kaiki* sequences in which the wicked samurai antagonists find themselves plagued by spectral assaults of *yōkai* depicted in rapidly cut montage sequences familiar to viewers of Nakagawa's *kaiki* classics.[5]

While Daiei attempted to turn *kaiki* film into something more appealing for a younger audience, also adapting the children's horror stories of manga author Umezu Kazuo in the same year's *Snake Girl and the Silver-Haired Witch* (*Hebi musume to hakuhatsuma*), Tōei tapped the genre's past masters for a throwback to Shintōhō's glory days of *kaiki* production. Nakagawa Nobuo and his former assistant Ishikawa Yoshihiro both made a momentary return to feature *kaiki* production in 1968, directing *Snake Woman's Curse* (*Kaidan hebi onna*) and *The Ghost Cat and the Cursed Pond* (*Kaibyo noroi no ike*), respectively. Released together as a double bill, Shimura Miyoko has noted this curiously mimicked Daiei's package release of *The Ghost Cat and the Cursed Wall* and *White Snake Beauty* from exactly ten years prior.[6] The directors' earlier works at Shintōhō had innovated new approaches to *kaiki* cinema's form and content, but here they seem content merely to replicate past accomplishments. *Cursed Pond* retreads the same plot, themes, and iconography of Ishikawa's *Otama Pond*. Nakagawa's snake-themed piece might have been expected to resurrect the erotic *kaiki* villainess embodied by Daiei's Mōri Ikuko, but instead substitutes a snake motif for the more typical *bakeneko* ghost cat form of the victim, whose ghost assumes a scaly, serpentine snake-woman form in place of the more traditional ghost cat, bringing the serpent subgenre of *kaiki* film more in line with Nakagawa's work on *Kasane* and *Yotsuya*.

One year after *Snake Woman's Curse* put a *bakeneko* spin on its material, the original serpent actress, Mōri Ikuko, found herself ironically cast as a ghost cat. On December 20, 1969, Daiei released its final *bakeneko* film, *Secret Chronicles of the Ghost Cat* (*Hiroku kaibyō-den*), ending a run that arguably began when Daiei's predecessor Shinkō debuted *The Legend of the Saga Ghost Cat* in early 1937. *Secret Chronicles of the Ghost Cat* was a hit at the box office, but owed its popularity to the fact that the police arrested Mōri just five days before the film's release for murdering her married lover in a fit of rage. Memories of Daiei's decade-old ad campaign built around the image of the "curiously creepy" Mōri's

---

[5] Shimura Miyoko suggests this was an attempt to simultaneously appeal to children as well as the older, more typical *kaiki* audience. See "Daiei no yōkai eiga: 'yōkai sanbusaku' o chūshin ni," in *Kaiki to gensō e no kairo: kaidan kara J-horā e*, ed. Uchiyama Kazuki (Tokyo: Shinwasha, 2008), 125–44.
[6] Shimura Miyoko, "Kaibutsu ka suru joyū-tachi: neko to hebi o meguru hyōshō," in *Kaiki to gensō e no kairo: kaidan kara J-horā e*, ed. Uchiyama Kazuki (Tokyo: Shinwasha, 2008), 172–4.

supposed snake fetish returned to haunt the actress in the tabloid press and brought *Secret Chronicles of the Ghost Cat* the kind of media attention money cannot buy. Mōri confessed to the crime and there was never any doubt she was the culprit, but the media circus surrounding her trial makes it hard to disagree that she was nonetheless a victim of Daiei's previous effort to sell her as a dangerous and hypersexual woman with a perverse affinity for the macabre. After serving her prison sentence Mōri vanished from the public eye; her ultimate whereabouts and fate remain unknown.

Without the unfortunate circumstances surrounding its star, *Secret Chronicles of the Ghost Cat* would likely have gone relatively unnoticed at the box office. As the 1960s wound to a close, not only the *kaiki* genre but also the whole of the Japanese film industry faced an existential crisis. The rise of television had dealt a brutal blow to ticket sales. With women and families no longer attending the cinema on a weekly basis, by the end of the decade the Japanese studios were targeting their films primarily at a young, single, male audience.[7] As Yanagi Masako's audience research in 1957 showed, young women made up more than half of the audience for the typical *kaiki* film, and as the studios shifted their focus to the production of more supposedly male-friendly genres like *yakuza* crime dramas and softcore pornographic "pink films" (*pinku eiga*), *kaiki* fell by the wayside. The perennial summertime adaptations of traditional Japanese ghost stories moved to television in the early 1970s, where old hands like Nakagawa Nobuo and Ishikawa Yoshihiro directed episodes of anthology series with titles like *Japanese Kaidan Theater* (*Nihon kaidan gekijō*, 1970) and *13 Nights of "Kaiki"* (*Kaiki jūsan ya*, 1971). Nakagawa's adaptation of *The Peony Lantern* for *Japanese Kaidan Theater* was particularly well-received and approaches the level of his Shintōhō *kaiki* work in quality.[8] But on the big screen, *kaiki* was in its death throes. After *Secret Chronicles of the Ghost Cat*, Daiei released its last *kaiki* film, yet another adaptation of *The Ghost Story of Kasane's Swamp* (1970). In 1971 the studio went bankrupt and closed its doors, ten years after Shintōhō had suffered the same fate.

Daiei's collapse brought over sixty years of domestic *kaiki* filmmaking traditions to a conclusion. Tōei had essentially given up on the classical *kaiki* film after their double-bill release of Nakagawa's *Snake Woman's Curse* and

---

[7] Isolde Standish, *A New History of Japanese Cinema: A Century of Narrative Film* (New York: Continuum, 2005), 270–1.

[8] Horikiri Naota, "Nakagawa Nobuo intabyū: Ano yo to no kagawarikata," *Eiga hyōron* 28, no. 9 (1971): 36–40. *Kaidan* anthology series sporadically appeared on Japanese television as late as 2002's *Kaidan hyaku monogatari* and preserve many old *kaiki* filmmaking traditions, but lie outside the scope of this study.

Ishikawa's *The Ghost Cat and the Cursed Pond* failed to replicate the same level of interest as the two's innovative work at Shintōhō, turning instead to director Ishii Teruo and his avant-garde grotesque sensibilities. Like Nakagawa, Ishii had been one of Shintōhō's more prominent filmmakers under Ōkura Mitsugi's tenure, specializing in hard-boiled *yakuza* pictures that featured the studio's in-house glamour stars in what was, for the time, provocative displays of skin and sexuality.[9] Tōei gave Ishii the chance to press the envelope even further while exploring his interest in the *ero-guro-nansensu* or "erotic-grotesque nonsense" genre made famous by author Edogawa Rampo (1894–1965). Inspired by the work of Edgar Allan Poe, Rampo penned many tales that certainly qualify as horrific, but the source of horror lies not so much in its supernatural origin—his "monsters" are invariably human—but in graphically depicted excess of physical deformity and violence. Ishii's homage to the work of Rampo, *Horrors of Malformed Men* (*Edogawa Rampo zenshū: kyōfu kikei ningen*, 1969), amounts to a parade of macabre and grotesque oddities quite far removed from the otherworldly *osore* of the orthodox *kaiki* film. Ishii's *Blind Woman's Curse* (*Kaidan nobori Ryū*, 1970) invokes more traditional *kaiki* iconography, including the ghost cat motif, but as in *Malformed Men* the director's fascination with depicting human physical deformity and grotesqueness marginalizes the *kaiki* elements.

Tōhō, meanwhile, released a trilogy of vampire movies directed by Yamamoto Michio between 1970 and 1974, though they too little resembled anything Japan had produced in the *kaiki* genre to that point. Unofficially known as the "Bloodthirsty Series" (*Chi o sū shiriizu*), Yamamoto's films exhibit the exemplary *kaiki* atmosphere of gothic set design, Expressionistic lighting, and of course bloodthirsty monsters, but draw their inspiration almost exclusively from the Hammer vampire movies they are plainly meant to imitate, rather than traditional *kaidan* adaptations or even the amalgam of Western and Japanese horrific tropes in Shintōhō's vampire films.[10]

Nikkatsu, which had switched over to producing softcore "romantic pornography" (*roman poruno*), mined the erotic elements of *The Peony Lantern*

---

[9] Mark Schilling, *Nudes! Guns! Ghosts!: The Sensational Films of Shintoho* (Udine: Udine Far East Film Festival, 2010), 43–51.

[10] The individual entries are *Haunted House of Horrors: The Bloodthirsty Doll* (*Yūrei yashiki no kyōfu: Chi o sū ningyō*, 1970), *Cursed Mansion: Bloodthirsty Eyes* (*Noroi no yakata: Chi o sū me*, 1971), and *The Bloodthirsty Rose* (*Chi o sū bara*, 1974). The films were released on home video in the UK and United States under the respective titles of *Vampire Doll*, *Lake of Dracula*, and *Evil of Dracula*, despite the series' very tenuous connections to Bram Stoker's character. Marak argues for the presence of traditional Japanese elements in the second film in the series. See Katarzyna Marak, *Japanese and American Horror: A Comparative Study of Film, Fiction, Graphic Novels, and Video Games* (Jefferson, MO: McFarland, 2015), 104–8.

in 1972, though predictably *osore* is not the body-genre emotion it primarily seeks to instill in the viewer. Taking inspiration from Nikkatsu, Tōei brought the ghost cat back for an encore in the tongue-in-cheek titled *The Ghost Cat in the Turkish Bath* (*Kaibyō toruko furo*, 1975), but these erotic detours into *kaiki* tropes were not part of any continuing production schedule of *kaiki* films. By the end of the decade even the occasional "pink" *kaiki* film had ceased to appear. Films dealing with the horrific, ghostly, and monstrous continued to be made in Japan sporadically and include fascinating works like Obayashi Nobuhiko's *House* (*Hausu*, 1977) and Kurosawa Kiyoshi's *Sweet Home* (*Suwiito hōmu*, 1989) that include traces of Japan's *kaiki* film heritage, but sustained horror film production would not return until the rise of J-horror at the turn of the millennium. With the passing in Japan of the studio *kaiki* film and the decline abroad of the gothic mode of horror exemplified by the Hammer studio in the face of drastic changes in the style and content of films like *The Exorcist* (1973) and *The Texas Chain Saw Massacre* (1974), the word *kaiki* itself became relegated to the past, a relic of a bygone era of filmmaking traditions.

Under the newly designated moniker of *horā*, Japanese filmmakers of the 1980s and early 1990s like Miike Takashi drew their inspiration from the graphic gore of American slasher film series like *Friday the 13th* and *A Nightmare on Elm Street* as well as the more outré *ero-guro* work of Ishii Teruo. Miike in particular became infamous as a "gross-out" director for works like *Audition* (1999) and *Ichi the Killer* (*Koroshiya ichi*, 2001), which briefly established Japanese horror cinema's reputation abroad for extreme graphic violence. When the small cadre of filmmakers who founded the J-horror movement at the turn of the millennium desired a return to a more psychological presentation of horror, one of the places they sought it was in the uncanny resurrection of traditional ghosts of the past, along with the themes of karmic omnipotence and *osore* they embodied. In J-horror, the ghosts of *kaiki* cinema returned to haunt the world of the living once again.

Resurrection: J-horror and *Kaiki*

Facing Fears

Screenwriter Takahashi Hiroshi relates the following anecdote about the production of *Ghost Actress* (*Joyūrei*, aka *Don't Look Up*, 1996), retroactively recognized as one of the first J-horror movies:

Figure 29 The ghost's face completely revealed in the climax of *Ghost Actress* (*Joyūrei*, 1996, left) and completely hidden in the climax of *Ring* (*Ringu*, 1998, right).

> When [director] Nakata Hideo and I were making *Ghost Actress* I told him absolutely do not show the ghost's face. Back then, Nakata hadn't yet really developed a sense for that sort of thing. No matter what I said, he thought if we made it like a traditional *kaidan* movie, it would be a success. Nakata had faith in the actress cast in the role, and felt like it was unthinkable to *not* to show her face. So in *Ghost Actress* you can clearly see the ghost's face. Later, when we made *Ring*, I begged him to please follow my advice this time! Since *Ring* was a big-budget movie [compared to *Ghost Actress*], the producers' camp wanted a famous actress to play the part of Sadako. From the producers' standpoint it would be impossible to not show the face of someone like that, but Nakata steadfastly refused. This time he was on my side, insisting the face would not be seen on camera. Unexpectedly everyone agreed, thinking maybe this was the start of something fresh and new.[11]

The debate between Takahashi and Nakata over whether or not to show the ghost's face on camera recalls the decision in 1958 to keep the ghost cat's face obscured for the *gendaigeki* sequences of Nakagawa Nobuo's *Mansion of the Ghost Cat*, which was hailed as "new flavor" of *kaiki* filmmaking rather like the choice never to reveal Sadako's face in *Ring* was felt to be "the start of something fresh." And just as Nakagawa's former assistant Ishikawa Yoshihiro took the technique a step further in *The Ghost Cat of Otama Pond*, never showing the monster's face even in the marvelous *jidaigeki* sequence, Sadako's perpetually hair-obscured visage in *Ring* makes an abstractly terrifying improvement over her counterpart in *Ghost Actress*, whose face the camera finally reveals in the film's climax (Figure 29).

The admittedly underwhelming result of Nakata's insistence that *Ghost Actress* be more like "a traditional *kaidan* movie," might be a latter-day example

---

[11] Author's interview with Takahashi Hiroshi.

of "showing the monster too much," a charge critics levied even at Nakagawa Nobuo's acclaimed *kaiki* films.[12] But the tension between Nakata's desire to return to *kaidan* fundamentals and Takahashi's intuition to deviate from the norm also perfectly encapsulates the manipulation of traditional *kaiki* themes and motifs that in part made J-horror so frighteningly effective for audiences. Like Nakagawa Nobuo and the Shintōhō *kaiki* filmmakers had done forty years prior in films such as *The Ghost Story of Kasane's Swamp* and *Mansion of the Ghost Cat*, the J-horror auteurs created something that was simultaneously orthodox and innovative, taking the traditional ghosts and monsters of Japan's premodern, marvelous past and injecting them with an element of the uncanny, not just in their inventive formal portrayal but also in their uncanny invasion of the modern world.

The term J-horror—or *J-horā* in Japanese—first appeared about twenty years ago in the wake of *Ring*'s unexpected and tremendous international success. Takahashi and Nakata's work on the ultra-low-budget *Ghost Actress* won them the job of realizing the film version of Suzuki Kōji's bestselling horror novel, which combined an urban legend conceit about a cursed videotape with elements of traditional *kaidan* tales of vengeful spirits. While Suzuki's novel and its two sequels—a trilogy that eventually becomes more science fiction than ghost story—concoct a pseudoscientific rationale for the ghost Sadako and the videotape that kills whomever watches it, Takahashi's screenplay offers no explanation for the horrific events beyond Sadako's supernatural wrath.[13] The result met with popular acclaim in Japan, and much like the videotaped chain-letter curse depicted in the film, VHS copies of *Ring* circulated throughout the globe, garnering worldwide interest. Following a 1999 South Korean version,[14] Hollywood produced *The Ring* (2002), a big-budget effort starring Naomi Watts.[15]

---

[12] Criticism of the decision to reveal the ghost's face was also voiced by Nakano Yakushi in "*Joyūrei* ron: Arui wa, eiga no jikogenkyūsayō ni hasamu 'ma' ni tsuite," in *Horā japanesuku no genzai*, ed. Ichiyanagi Hirotaka and Yoshida Morio (Tokyo: Seikyūsha, 2005), 115–30.

[13] Director Iida Jōji's film version of the second novel in Suzuki's trilogy, *Spiral* (*Rasen*), was released simultaneously with *Ring* and retained much of Suzuki's pseudoscience. While *Ring* was a hit with Japanese critics and audiences, *Spiral* was a box office failure. As a result, Nakata directed *Ring 2* (*Ringu 2*, 1999), which ignored the events of *Spiral* and maintained the more supernatural tone of the first film.

[14] Although the filmmakers claimed the picture was an adaptation of Suzuki's original novel and not a remake of the Japanese film, the South Korean version contains several scenes that appear to have been modeled on Nakata's film.

[15] Julian Stinger discusses the "Hollywood folklore" promulgated by the creators of the American *The Ring* around the circulation of bootleg copies of Nakata's *Ring* in the United States and the reputation it accrued among horror fans, prompting the producers to option the film for a remake. As Stringer notes, the story mimics the tale of Sadako's cursed videotape almost to the point of parody. See "The Original and the Copy: Nakata Hideo's *Ring* (1998)," in *Japanese Cinema: Texts and Contexts*, ed. Alastair Phillips and Julian Stringer (New York: Routledge, 2007), 296–307.

The Ring was an even bigger box office hit in Japan than the original, and its critical and commercial success in the United States spurred Hollywood to remake a slew of similarly themed Japanese horror films such as Nakata's *Dark Water* (*Honogurai mizu no soko kara*, 2002), Kurosawa Kiyoshi's *Pulse* (*Kairo*, 2001), Shimizu Takashi's *Ju-On* (2002), and Miike Takashi's *One Missed Call* (*Chakushin ari*, 2003).

It is unclear whether the term "J-horror" originates in Japan or abroad, though the Japanese use of a term comprised of "J" for "Japan" (the foreign designation for *Nippon* or *Nihon*) and the English loanword *horā* conspicuously points to the films' status as cultural and commercial exports to the wider world while also designating them as uniquely "Japanese"—another example of the much-touted soft power of the nation's cultural commodities in the current global marketplace. In the English-speaking world, "J-horror" quickly became a catch-all label for any film made in Japan at any point in history that features horrific and/or supernatural narrative elements. This tendency not only eliminates any distinction between classic *kaiki* pictures and films like *Ring*, *Pulse*, and the *Ju-On* series, it also creates a massively broad classification schema that includes everything from golden-age art house cinema to direct-to-video pornography. For example, an online guide to "alternative J-horror" lists Nakagawa's *Jigoku* alongside Mizoguchi Kenji's 1953 classic *Ugetsu*, Miike Takashi's musical black comedy *Happiness of the Katakuris* (*Katakuri ke no kōfuku*, 2001), and S&M softcore offerings *Guinea Pig 2* (*Ginii piggu 2*, 1985) and *Flower and Snake* (*Hana to hebi*, 2004).[16] A great deal of confusion also surrounds the question of whether or not to include Hollywood remakes of films like *Ring* and *Ju-On* under the rubric of J-horror—an issue made all the more confounding by the fact that the original Japanese directors occasionally helmed the American remakes of their own films. Finally, there is the unfortunate tendency to categorize horror films made elsewhere in Asia like Hong Kong's *The Eye* (*Jian gui*, 2002) and South Korea's *A Tale of Two Sisters* (*Janghwa, Hongryeon*, 2003) as "J-horror" without regard to their country of origin and the unique cultural traditions and filmmaking histories these films invariably incorporate.[17]

Mitsuyo Wada-Marciano cautions that a "loss of filmic context" engendered by newer modes of distribution and consumption such as DVDs and digital streaming results in this kind of categorical confusion, as films such as

---

[16] Zack Davisson, "J-horror: An Alternative Guide," *SeekJapan*, http://www.seekjapan.jp/article-1/765/J-Horror:+An+Alternative+Guide. Accessed November 6, 2010.
[17] See Terrence Rafferty, "Screams in Asia Echo in Hollywood," *New York Times*, January 27, 2008.

Mizoguchi's *Ugetsu*, Shindō Kaneto's *Onibaba* (1964), and even Fukasaku Kinji's *Battle Royale* (2000)—all of which previously had never been marketed, received, or discussed as specimens of the horror genre—were repackaged by Western distributors as precursors to (or relatives of) J-horror.[18] While this trend has even begun to infiltrate Japan, with iTunes Japan listing *kaiki* films like Nakagawa's *Snake Woman's Curse* under the category of *J-horā*, both Wada-Marciano and Chika Kinoshita point out that *J-horā* typically has a more precise definition in its home country, which Kinoshita summarizes as referring to a cycle of relatively low-budget films produced in the last twenty years by a closely knit group of filmmakers, which emphasize atmospheric and psychological fear over graphic gore, and capitalize on urban legends proliferated through mass media and popular culture.[19] The seeds of the movement were laid in direct-to-video productions such as *Evil Spirit* (*Jaganrei*, 1988) and *Scary True Stories* (*Hontō ni atta kowai hanashi*, 1991), both written by Konaka Chiaki, as well as various incarnations of the *Schoolhouse Ghost Stories* (*Gakkō no kaidan*) series that ran between 1994 and 2001 and proved a further testing ground for Konaka, Takahashi Hiroshi, Tsuruta Norio, Kurosawa Kiyoshi, Nakata Hideo, Shimizu Takashi, and other members of the emerging J-horror circle.[20] The movement achieved worldwide success with the release of Nakata's *Ring* and reached its zenith of popularity with the complementary Japanese and American series of *Ju-On/The Grudge* films directed by Shimizu between 2000 and 2006 before eventually descending into repetitiveness and self-parody with titles like *Sadako 3D* (2012) and *Sadako vs Kayako* (2016).

Although J-horror accordingly accounts for only a comparatively small and rather brief moment in the history of Japanese cinema, its transnational popularity and influence on mainstream Hollywood film culture has spurred a profuse body of scholarship on the phenomenon, much of it focused on the mass communication technology that typically provides the vehicle for the J-horror ghost to spread its curse throughout the modern world. Examples of the motif include *Ring*'s chain-mail videotape, the internet chat-room haunting

---

[18] Mitsuyo Wada-Marciano, "J-horror: New Media's Impact on Contemporary Japanese Horror Cinema," in *Horror to the Extreme: Changing Boundaries in Asian Cinema*, ed. Jinhee Choi and Mitsuyo Wada-Marciano (Hong Kong: Hong Kong University Press, 2009), 33–6.

[19] Chika Kinoshita, "The Mummy Complex: Kurosawa Kiyoshi's *Loft* and J-horror," in *Horror to the Extreme: Changing Boundaries in Asian Cinema*, ed. Jinhee Choi and Mitsuyo Wada-Marciano (Hong Kong: Hong Kong University Press, 2009), 104.

[20] Konaka details the creative process of the J-horror circle's early work on *Evil Spirit*, *Scary True Stories*, and *Schoolhouse Ghost Stories* in *Horā eiga no miryoku: fandamentaru horā sengen* (Tokyo: Iwanami Shoten, 2003). For discussion of the *Schoolhouse Ghost Stories* series in English, see David Kalat, *J-horror: The Definitive Guide to the* The Ring, The Grudge, *and Beyond* (New York: Vertical, 2007).

ghosts of *Pulse*, and the death-inducing cell phone messages in *One Missed Call*. In each case a deadly supernatural force spreads contagiously on the back of communications technology, using copied videotapes, the internet, and cell phone address books to reach an exponentially increasing and seemingly limitless number of victims. Colette Balmain analyzes the motif as expressive of fears that mass communication technology actually creates a banal, "dead" society bereft of face-to-face human interaction,[21] sentiments echoed in other readings of J-horror that ascribe its popularity across cultural borders to themes of technophobia universal to postmodern societies.[22] The viral nature of the J-horror ghosts' curse has also inspired studies of the genre as expressing fears of pandemics such as SARS and bird flu that preoccupied much of East Asia and the wider world in the early years of the twenty-first century. Ōshima Kiyoaki, for example, devotes his book-length *A Study of the J-horror Ghost* (*J-horā no yūrei kenkyū*) to a reading of Sadako and her ilk as metaphors for biological viruses.[23]

Balmain's and Ōshima's analyses ground J-horror firmly in horror movie theorist Andrew Tudor's discourse of "paranoid horror," which he identifies as the dominant mode of the global horror film of the past half-century. Tudor argues against universal readings of horror films, insisting that any given horror movie cannot be properly understood outside of the particular sociohistorical circumstances in which it was produced, but of "paranoid horror" he writes, "[It] presupposes a thoroughly unreliable world. In this respect it is popular and pleasurable because its basic codes correlate with our distinctive experience of fear, risk and instability in modern societies."[24] While such readings are certainly valid and undoubtedly go a long way toward explaining the ease with which these films cross cultural boundaries, these early studies of J-horror tend to focus on the vehicle of the curse over the culturally specific supernatural entity behind it, which incorporates a rather different set of fears.

More recent discussions by Valerie Wee and Katarzyna Marak have devoted more attention to the figure of the *onryō* and the ways in which its depiction

---

[21] Colette Balmain, *Introduction to Japanese Horror Film* (Edinburgh: Edinburgh University Press, 2008), 168–87.
[22] See, e.g., Pennylane Shen's "It Came from the East … Japanese Horror Cinema in the Age of Globalization," *Gnovis* 9, no. 2 (Washington, DC: Georgetown University Press, 2009), http://gnovisjournal.org/2009/05/13/it-came-east-japanese-horror-cinema-age-globalization, accessed May 16, 2013. Shen writes, "The recurring J-horror film theme of the destructive and alienating nature of modern technologies, including televisions, cameras, computers, videos, cell phones and the Internet, represents a growing anxiety in urban societies."
[23] See Ōshima Kiyoaki, *J-horā no yūrei kenkyū* (Tokyo: Akiyama Shōten, 2010), 3–5.
[24] Andrew Tudor, "Why Horror? The Peculiar Pleasures of a Popular Genre," in *Horror, The Film Reader*, ed. Mark Jancovich (New York: Routledge, 2002), 52.

in J-horror connects these films to premodern *kaidan* traditions. Positing *kaiki* cinema as the missing link between these two poles, I would suggest that, in addition to Kinoshita's and Wada-Marciano's definition of J-horror, another central ingredient of the formula is the invocation of *kaiki* motifs in a modern, urban setting, specifically the notions of *urami* ("wrath") and *tatari* ("curse"), and their personification in the figure of the *onryō* or vengeful ghost. More so than technophobia or a metaphorical fear of viral pandemics, the vengeful ghost is the fundamental recurring motif of J-horror, and its physical appearance, formal presentation, and thematic import all deliberately invoke the classic image of the vengeful wraith, also the central figure of domestic *kaiki* film. *Ring* provides the textbook example in the figure of Sadako, whose tattered white robe, long disheveled hair, bloody fingernails, grotesque bodily contortions, and insatiable *urami* not only derive from Tsuryua Nanboku's stage directions for Oiwa but were duplicated *ad nauseam* in both domestic and foreign films to the degree that the "long-haired Japanese ghost" has become a worldwide cinematic cliché.

In this way J-horror represents an advanced stage of Hansen's vernacular modernism of cinema, blending the motifs of traditional *kaidan* with a style and story structure influenced largely by American and British ghost movies, and in turn influencing Western cinema via Hollywood remakes of J-horror, which recast Japanese vengeful spirits in the context of American horror films like *The Exorcist*. For example, *The Ring* conceives Sadako's American counterpart, Samara, as more of a demonically possessed child than her misunderstood Japanese prototype. In contrast to Sadako's tragic backstory, Samara is presented as more of an inherent "bad seed" not created by the acts of cruelty that give rise to Sadako's vengeful spirit. *The Ring* even shows Samara's face at the end, in defiance of Takahashi's tastes and revealing a ghastly visage that bears more than a passing resemblance to *The Exorcist*'s possessed Regan (Figure 30).

Figure 30 Left: Regan from *The Exorcist* (1973). Right: Samara from *The Ring* (2002).

While J-horror creators like Takahashi Hiroshi and Kurosawa Kiyoshi name Western ghost story films *The Haunting* and *The Innocents* as their biggest inspiration, they readily admit that the iconography of the ubiquitous J-horror ghost has its origins in the *kaiki* work of Nakagawa Nobuo and his contemporaries. Returning to the issue of "showing the ghost too much," Kurosawa echoes Nakagawa's own sentiments in arguing for the effectiveness of a physically present monster in-frame, noting both Nakagawa's expert use of it and its surviving legacy in J-horror:

> A problem for us J-horror filmmakers is, it's all well and good to have a ghost appear in our films, but to what extent should we show it rushing in and attacking people? In Nakagawa's case, it actually intrudes quite a bit. The ghost will appear to be standing far away softly moaning "I will get you!," then the next thing you know she's so close you can touch her. To be able to pull off having a ghost physically coming at you like that is rather difficult. Nakagawa had several challenges; in his case there weren't old *kaidan* movies in which the ghost flies at the protagonist like that. Beginning with Nakagawa, there were various experiments with this directly-attacking ghost figure … Sadako is like that. She doesn't just vaporously appear, she comes at you violently, clutching and attacking … In the imagery of the ghost they [the Shintōhō *kaiki* films and J-horror] are definitely connected. *Ring* demonstrates that well, the continuum of ghost imagery, though the story is utterly different from classic *kaidan*.[25]

Kurosawa himself made a similar effort to portray the ghost as alternately far-off and ethereal, then corporeally present, close, and threatening in the climax of *Pulse*, in which the protagonist Kawashima confronts one of the multitudes of vengeful spirits that have all but annihilated humanity. Rushing toward the blurry, vaguely defined outline of the wraith that had materialized in the background of the frame, Kawashima reaches out toward the vision, expecting that his hand will pass through the shadowy form and confirm its unreal status. To his horror, his hands make physical contact with the ghost's body. The spirit then says "I am not an illusion" (*Watashi wa maboroshi de wa nai*) in a disembodied voice before approaching the camera until its digitally blurred face occupies the entire frame, whereupon only the eyes come into concrete, clear focus, further confirming the ghost's corporeal reality (Figure 31).

Pulse also demonstrates Kurosawa's attempts to replicate what he calls the impression of "the space between life and death" (*ikiteiru no to shindeiru no no*

---

[25] Author's interview with Kurosawa Kiyoshi.

Figure 31 The ghost as ambiguously ethereal and yet physically concrete in *Pulse* (*Kairo*, 2001).

aida) in Nakagawa's *kaiki* work. As the ghosts' viral curse spreads through the internet to infect all of humanity, characters that have fallen victim to the spectral pandemic begin to gradually turn into *onryō* themselves, their faces drained of color and void of expression save for a vacant, dead look in their eyes. Kurosawa explains how he derives inspiration for scenes like this from Nakagawa's *Ghost Story of Yotsuya*:

> Something I think is really great about [Nakagawa's] *Ghost Story of Yotsuya* is the scene where Oiwa hasn't yet become a ghost and is still alive, but her face is deformed and she's dying—in other words she's in-between life and death, fading, in a liminal state. That scene takes a pretty long time. We understand she's gradually dying, becoming a ghost, but she's not dead yet. Her face has changed but we can't get a good look at it yet. This liminal, weird state, [Wakasugi's] performance, the visuals, all left the strongest impression in my memory. I also have shown ghosts bluntly in my own movies, but this impression of a still-alive person whose existence suddenly changes and they go from the world of the living a little bit towards the world of the dead—when I want to express that feeling in my movies, it's an especially Nakagawa-esque thing, moving dimly a little bit towards the land of the dead, and suddenly the face grows dark and you're unable to see what kind of expression is on it. I use that a lot. That clearly comes from that central scene in *The Ghost Story of Yotsuya*, which had a tremendous influence on me, I think.[26]

Takahashi Hiroshi independently confirmed Kurosawa's comments about the importance of Nakagawa's *kaiki* films in the portrayal of the J-horror ghost, as well as "the space between life and death" depicted in Oiwa's death scene in Nakagawa's *Yotsuya*:

> I'm often watching 1960s Western movies, but for the portrayal of ghosts, Japanese films are important for their worldview of life, death, and the afterlife. Naturally our work has a bit more of that domestic Japanese element, and that frankly comes from Nakagawa Nobuo, I think … Take his Oiwa, and the hair-combing scene. Oiwa's still human; she hasn't yet died, and she's in front of the mirror, combing her hair out in bloody strands, and her wrath against Iemon is gradually coming to a boil. That scene, where she's still human and yet becoming something that's not human, is *The Ghost Story of Yotsuya*'s scariest moment.[27]

---

[26] Author's interview with Kurosawa Kiyoshi.
[27] Author's interview with Takahashi Hiroshi.

In a 1971 interview with Nakagawa, critic Horikiri Naota extolls Oiwa's death scene along much the same lines, praising Nakagawa for crafting a sequence of "living hell" (*ikijigoku*) by blurring the boundaries between the worlds of the living and the dead, though in typically modest fashion Nakagawa once again ascribes all the credit to Kurosawa Haruyasu's production design.[28] The film's protracted portrayal of Oiwa's death leaves such an impression because, as Takahashi's comment suggests, it is not actually a death scene, but a scene of grotesque transformation. Oiwa is "still human, and yet becoming something that's not." As Bakhtin observes, "The grotesque body … is a body in the act of becoming. It is never finished, never completed; it is continually built, created, and builds and creates another body."[29]

Wakasugi's grotesque metamorphosis is not dissimilar to Suzuki Sumiko's own monstrous transformations from twenty years prior. As we have seen in our look at prewar *kaiki* cinema in Chapter 2, much of what Kurosawa Kiyoshi, Takahashi Hiroshi, and Horikiri Naota attribute to Nakagawa Nobuo—namely the physically concrete and threatening vengeful spirit and depictions of characters in the liminal state between living and (un)dead—has antecedent in Mokudō Shigeru's *The Cat of Arima* and *The Ghost Story of the Mandarin Duck Curtain* (and these examples in turn draw on kabuki stage traditions stretching back into the Edo period). Nakagawa's work is the more well-known and arguably the more accomplished presentation of such motifs, but as my study of the *kaiki* genre hopefully illuminates, J-horror draws on over fifty years of popular filmmaking in its formal depictions of the "long-haired Japanese ghost girl" that took the world by storm.

Breaking the Rules

Another debt J-horror owes to the work of Nakagawa and the other Shintōhō *kaiki* filmmakers lies in its presentation of the traditional vengeful wraith plucked out of its marvelous period setting and unleashed into the rational world of modern-day Japan, albeit with crucial modifications to the old formulas that represent the end of a process begun in the late 1950s with Shintōhō films like *Mansion of the Ghost Cat*, *Diving Girl's Ghost*, and *Vampire Bride*. Going a step beyond the Shintōhō ghosts and monsters who showed up in places they were

---

[28] Horikiri, "Nakagawa Nobuo intabyū," 30.
[29] Mikhail Bakhtin, *Rabelais and His World*, trans. Helene Iswolsky (Bloomington: Indiana University Press, 1984), 317.

not expected, the J-horror ghosts broke all the rules of karmic cause-and-effect that had previously governed their behavior.

Wee and Marak both emphasize the role of the *onryō* in establishing a continuity from premodern *kaidan* traditions to contemporary J-horror while conceiving of the vengeful ghost as a stable, unchanging element over centuries. Although I caution against narrow interpretations of traditional material like *The Ghost Story of Yotsuya* as responses to modern historical moments like the bombings of Hiroshima and Nagasaki, ahistorical readings of the *onryō*'s place in Japanese society in statements like "the Japanese have a deep-rooted belief in the supernatural" and making no generic distinctions between something like Ueda Akinari's eighteenth-century literary *kaidan* and contemporary J-horror pictures like *Ring* oversimplify Japanese culture and assume a monolithic attitude toward the otherworldly without variations across time, genre, and media.[30] The power of both the Shintōhō *kaiki* films of the 1950s and the J-horror pictures of recent decades lies not in an unchanged depiction of vengeful ghosts preserved from centuries past but in their "difference in repetition," to cite Stephen Neale's point about the necessity of variation in keeping genres fresh. These films present *onryō* who adhere to enough of tradition to be culturally recognizable and uncannily familiar, while deviating from the formula in ways that took Japanese audiences by shocking surprise.

The Shintōhō films contain many elements that depart from old *kaiki* conventions and point the way toward the development of a more *horā*-esque style, but retain conspicuously *kaiki* touches as well. The stylized set work, period settings, or else an explicitly gothic ambiance all work to suggest the action takes place in some Othered space. The uncanny presence of an old-fashioned vengeful wraith in the high-tech, postmodern landscapes of J-horror evokes the same sense of the uncanny that *Mansion of the Ghost Cat* and *The Ghost Cat of Otama Pond* achieved by displacing the monsters of the past into the present, but J-horror goes a step beyond the Shintōhō ghost cat pictures by wholly removing the monsters from their *kaiki* landscapes. To encounter the uncanny *kaiki* in the contemporarily set Shintōhō films, the protagonists must journey to some suitable *kaiki* locale, such as the old dilapidated dwelling of the wife's ancestors in *Mansion of the Ghost Cat*, a witch's cavern in *Vampire Bride*, or the Victorian-style mansion in *Diving Girls in a Haunted House*. Only in Nakagawa's *Lady Vampire* does the monster first appear in the heart of contemporary Tokyo;

---

[30] Wee, *Japanese Horror Films and Their American Remakes*, Routledge Advances in Film Studies (New York: Routledge, 2014), 30; Marak, *Japanese and American Horror*, 13.

but not only is the title bloodsucker an atypically Western-style monster, the human heroes eventually must trace him to his *kaiki* castle in distant Kyushu for the final confrontation. Conversely, in *Ring* Sadako's haunted well journeys to the protagonists, appearing in their very living rooms via the cursed videotape that brings the monster directly into the heart of everyday existence. The cursed house that stands at the nexus of the vengeful wraith Kayako's curse in the *Ju-On* series is no gothic mansion atop a foreboding mountain, but a nondescript-looking Tokyo home, intentionally made to look like any other house on the neighborhood block.

As directors like Kurosawa Kiyoshi and Sasaki Hirohisa pointed out in Chapter 1's discussion of the formal markers of *kaiki*, these stylistic decisions come in part from practical necessity, as the meticulously crafted sets that created the hyperrealistic, otherworldly locales of *kaiki* cinema now belong to a bygone era of Japanese filmmaking. J-horror uses the limitation to its advantage, however. The location shooting heightens the films' sense of realism, which runs counter to the "super-realism" of the *kaiki* genre's stylized set work, but makes the appearance of a *kaiki* monster like the vengeful wraith even more uncannily frightening, so incongruous is its presence in the mise-en-scène. Shimizu's *Ju-On* series probably best exemplifies the technique, strategically placing its ghosts in the most mundane settings—elevators, public restrooms, apartment living rooms, and other such locations the audience likely encounters on a daily basis.

The realism of the J-horror films' production design aligns them with the new breed of international horror films like *Rosemary's Baby* (1968) and *The Exorcist*, which appeared in the late 1960s through the 1970s and significantly were not labeled as *kaiki* in Japan. These *okaruto* ("occult") films, as they were called, dispensed with the gothic locales of Hammer-style horror—one of the defining markers of the *kaiki* genre—and, like the J-horror films, invoke the uncanny by suggesting primordial monsters yet lurk in our everyday world. But the demonic entities that possess the human characters in *Rosemary's Baby* and *The Exorcist* never manifest directly save for fleeting shots of disembodied faces and out-of-focus visions. In preserving Nakagawa's physically present, "directly-attacking ghost figure" in the mundane mise-en-scène, the J-horror ghost evokes an additional dimension of meta-uncanny. On the level of the film's narrative she is, like the Shintōhō ghost cats, a monster from the marvelous past, uncannily invading the rational present. But the J-horror wraith is also the ghost of *kaiki* cinema itself, a relic returned from a dead genre. The mere act of its return is enough to infuse it with a new potency as a marker of the uncanny.

Like her *kaiki* ancestors before her, the J-horror vengeful ghost also invokes a sense of cosmic *osore* in the way she wields seemingly omnipotent powers of retribution. As we have seen, the typical domestic *kaiki* film drew primarily on Edo-period *kaidan*, either in direct adaptations like *The Ghost Story of Yotsuya* and *Kasane's Swamp* or original screenplays like *The Ghost Cat and the Mysterious Shamisen* or *Vampire Bride*, which retained the themes of karmic vengeance central to the *kaidan* structure. But even in a work with a contemporary setting like *Vampire Bride*, the Japanese *kaiki* monster adheres to the laws of karmic cause-and-effect that govern the traditional vengeful wraith's behavior. A popular notion of karma as a cosmic moral arbiter, in which evil acts are punished, is central to these stories. Traditional *kaidan* justify the hauntings they depict as a form of karmic comeuppance, implying the victims simply get what they deserve. The vengeful spirits of *kaidan* literature and *kaiki* cinema never haunt random victims, but specific targets.

To take the classic example, in *The Ghost Story of Yotsuya* Oiwa only does harm to those who have transgressed against her—namely her wicked husband Iemon and his coconspirators, whom Oiwa tricks Iemon into slaying. As I argue in Chapter 1, the *osore* of *kaiki* cinema is the horror of running afoul of forces against which there is no recourse or protection—for the misdeeds of *kaidan* villains place them beyond the intervention of even the archetypal Buddhist monk, who otherwise wields power over such beings as the vengeful wraith. Recall that near the climax of *The Ghost Story of Yotsuya* (both Nakagawa's film and Nanboku's original play) Iemon seeks refuge in a Buddhist temple, but his sins render the protection of the monks inefficacious as Oiwa's spirit itself becomes an agent of karmic retribution. Nanboku's kabuki script acknowledges the somewhat paradoxical nature of this when the ghost of Oiwa says, "The light of the moon should guide me to Buddha's paradise, but instead it chills like the vengeful face of Oiwa."[31] Moonlight was well-established figurative shorthand for Enlightenment, yet here it is implied that Buddhist law itself compels the vengeful ghost to carry out its curse, which cannot be expurgated by the temple monks because it now operates as the very arbiter of karmic justice. Oiwa's spirit only finds rest once all of those complicit in her undeserved demise have paid with their own lives. The kabuki play alludes to this when, upon slaying Iemon, Yomoshichi exhorts Oiwa to "Find rebirth in Buddha's paradise!"[32] Nakagawa

---

[31] Tsuruya Nanboku IV, *The Ghost Stories at Yotsuya on the Tōkaidō*, in *Kabuki Plays on Stage: Darkness and Desire 1804–1864*, trans. Paul B. Kennelly, ed. James R. Brandon and Samuel L. Leiter (Honolulu: University of Hawaii Press, 2002), 154.
[32] Ibid., 163.

even more unambiguously grants Oiwa peace in the final shot of his film, depicting her ghost no longer hideously deformed, but beautiful as she was in life, cradling her infant son in her arms as she ascends from among the stone stupas of the temple grounds into the heavens.

Like Oiwa and other *kaiki* monsters like the ghost cat, the source of the J-horror ghost's grave-transcending wrath finds root in violent acts of betrayal perpetrated against them by an immediate and usually male family member. In a flashback sequence from *Ring* that recounts the origins of Sadako's ghost, we see her teenaged, living self, who has demonstrated potentially dangerous telekinetic abilities, clubbed over the head and pushed down a well by her father, who fears her powers. Kayako, the vengeful spirit at the center of the *Ju-On* film cycle, parallels Oiwa's circumstances even more directly. While *Ring* hints that Sadako's extrasensory abilities are what enable her to come back from the dead, Kayako—like Oiwa—is a perfectly mundane housewife.[33] Her brutal murder at the hands of her own husband is all that is necessary to transform Kayako into a fearsome wraith, recalling Iemon's betrayal of Oiwa and its ghastly consequences in *The Ghost Story of Yotsuya*. Although film scholar Jay McRoy argues the fractured families in J-horror are another manifestation of the films' modernity that voice contemporary fears of the breakdown of the traditional family unit,[34] their clear antecedent in *Yotsuya*—as well as the variants on the *Kasane's Swamp* legend and other Edo tales in which the ghost is that of a murdered immediate family member—reveals these anxieties were already well established in premodern vengeful ghost narratives.

The J-horror ghost also frightens because she confounds the audience's expectations, adhering to enough of the conventions surrounding traditional depictions of vengeful ghosts to be clearly identifiable as an *onryō* ("vengeful wraith"), but breaking enough of the established rules to make things interesting— and terrifying. For all the ways in which these films draw on traditional *onryō* legends, Buddhism and notions of karmic justice are virtual nonentities in J-horror. Unlike *kaidan* narratives that foreground a cosmological worldview that takes the monster's existence for granted from the outset, J-horror's narrative

---

[33] *The Grudge 2* (2006), the second film in the series of American remakes of *Ju-On*, reveals that Kayako was the child of a Shinto priestess who used her as a medium for containing evil spirits; however, this is not suggested by any of the prior films in the franchise.

[34] See McRoy's chapter on "*Kaidan* and the Haunted Family in the Cinema of Nakata Hideo and Shimizu Takashi," in *Nightmare Japan: Contemporary Japanese Horror Cinema* (Amsterdam: Rodopi, 2008). Despite invoking *kaidan* in the chapter's title, McRoy does not examine traditional *kaidan* narratives in any detail and does not mention that the broken-family motif has precedent in premodern Japanese narratives.

structure often follows Noël Carroll's "complex discovery" category of horror plots. Rational, "normal" people encounter a seemingly supernatural threat that cannot logically be explained. After exhausting rational and scientific avenues of inquiry, the protagonists are forced to confront the unknown head-on.[35] This structure characterizes the opening acts of *Ring*, Kurosawa Kiyoshi's *Pulse* and *Retribution* (*Sakebi*, 2006)—to name but a few—as well as most film versions of *Dracula* and William Friedkin's *The Exorcist*, to give a few Western examples. However, once the monster's supernatural presence has been verified, Western horror movies in this vein typically reinvoke the old traditional religious methods of combating them—think of Professor Van Helsing's wooden crucifixes or Father Merrin's final exorcism in *The Exorcist*. The message seems to be that, having discarded the traditional Christian spirituality of the past, modernity has left the door open for primordial demons to invade the present, and only recourse to the old beliefs will save humanity.

In J-horror, no one ever calls the Buddhist priest once the existence of the ghost has been irrefutably revealed. Reiko, the journalist, single-mother heroine of *Ring*, quickly comes to believe in the curse of Sadako, but instead of visiting a temple or shrine, she seeks the help of her psychic ex-husband Ryūji. Her intention, however, is not to use Ryūji's powers to combat the curse directly, but to do a bit of psychic detective work to decode some hidden meaning in the cursed videotape. Seeking a religious or spiritual means to appease Sadako's ghost is never brought up as a possibility in *Ring* or any of its sequels. On the rare occasions when a monk, priest, or shaman does show up in J-horror, they are either played for laughs, or prove utterly incapable of dealing with the vengeful spirit's curse. In *Ju-On* creator Shimizu Takashi's self-parodying television series *The Great Horror Family* (*Kaiki daikazoku*, 2004), an itinerant Buddhist monk appears uninvited on the doorstep of a modern family's haunted house, having detected an evil presence and offering his services, only to be driven off by the oblivious family, who dismiss him as an anachronistic relic. Attempted exorcisms in *One Missed Call* and *Ju-On: White Ghost/Black Ghost* (*Ju-On: shiroi rōjo/kuroi shōjo*, 2009) end in utter disaster and the deaths of the spiritualists who were foolish enough to attempt them. If Western supernatural horror films like *Dracula* ultimately reaffirm that the old religious methods of combating demons and vampires still hold up, J-horror seems to take a perverse delight in denying this possibility.

---

[35] Noël Carroll, *The Philosophy of Horror: Or Paradoxes of the Heart* (New York: Routledge, 1990), 99–108.

Why are the protagonists of J-horror unable to turn to Buddhist monks in the way that the heroes of Hammer's *Dracula A.D. 1972* seek out the descendent of Professor Van Helsing to defeat Count Dracula with wooden stakes and crucifixes? The implication in these Western horror films is that the Judeo-Christian cosmology remains intact in the modern world, even if society remains perilously oblivious to its perseverance. Vampires might survive into the present day, but so does the traditional Christian framework of good and evil to which they have always been part. In J-horror, a culturally attuned viewer familiar with the *modus operandi* of the traditional *onryō* gets the sense that the *system itself* has vanished, even if its monsters remain.

Although not explicitly stated, this notion is implicitly pervasive in the impersonal, viral nature of the J-horror ghost's curse. As previously mentioned, the circumstances that give birth to the modern vengeful wraith remain mostly identical to their *kaiki* ancestors, but there is no longer any sense that these spirits operate as agents of karmic retribution in the manner of Oiwa or the ghost cat. Sadako, Kayako, and their ilk do not haunt "the right people"—those responsible for their feelings of hatred—but instead turn their anger on humanity at large. The spirits who haunt the spiritually devoid modern cityscapes of J-horror, no longer contained by a traditional cosmology that both regulated their activity and held the power to ultimately abate their wrath, become unfocused and unstoppable. Sadako's ultimate purpose in creating the cursed videotape is not to expose the crime of her own murder, as Reiko and Ryūji mistakenly think for most of *Ring*, but simply to spread her wrath to untold multitudes. Likewise does *Ju-On*'s Kayako employ television, cell phones, and other communicative technology to haunt perfectly innocent people who have nothing to do with her murder at the hands of her husband. Kayako's victims' only sin is coming into contact with the scene of murder—or with someone else who visited the murder site, underlining the viral nature of Kayako's curse. Containment gives way to contagion as the once-focused curse of the vengeful wraith, no longer operating along karmic lines of cause-and-effect, now only concerns itself with consuming as many victims as possible.

We can again see the first steps toward this reconfiguration of the vengeful spirit motif in contemporarily set Shintōhō *kaiki* films of the late 1950s and early 1960s. The modern-day, guiltless victims of the title monsters in *Mansion of the Ghost Cat* and *The Ghost Cat of Otama Pond* unwittingly suffer for the sins of their ancestors, the ghost cats' curses lingering through generations in a contemporary twist on the multigenerational doom that critic Tada Michitarō found so compelling in Nakagawa's take on *The Ghost Story of Kasane's Swamp* in 1957. But even in the Shintōhō ghost cat films, the monster's wrath remains limited, focused upon a select individual. Perhaps more significantly, the guiltless status of the victims allows for the successful intervention of a Buddhist monk in both films, whose prayers put the vengeful spirit to rest and save the young heroines, unlike their doomed ancestors. Against the unfocused rage of the J-horror ghosts like Sadako and Kayako, however, there can be no such recourse.

What can we make of this cosmological vacuum in J-horror, and the juggernaut, all-consuming viral curse that rushes in to fill the void? One possible interpretation is suggested by Marilyn Ivy's anthropological work, *Discourses of the Vanishing*, which examines several modern Japanese cultural phenomena that express a longing for a lost (and largely imagined) traditional Japanese past. Ivy examines a variety of texts, written and otherwise, which express this desire to rediscover authentic Japanese folk traditions in which a pure Japanese spirit can be located and at least partially recovered.[36] J-horror's retention of the fearsome ghosts from classic *kaidan* literature and *kaiki* cinema coupled with its nihilistic lack of karmic justice becomes, in this sense, the nightmare flip side of this longing for the traditional past. Ivy's examination of domestic travel advertising campaigns, Yanagita Kunio's works on rural folk traditions, and spiritual mediums in the remote Tōhoku region all point to a notion that contemporary urban Japanese society has lost touch with its cultural identity and must seek it in remote, rural areas of the country that still remember the old ways. In the case of J-horror, these "old ways" might be conceived of as the missing cosmological system, once an integral part of the *kaidan* narrative that most often takes place in a mythical, romanticized Edo period. In an age when contemporary filmmakers such as Iwai Shunji, Kore-eda Hirokazu, and Miyazaki Hayao reject urban metropolises to seek what they package as the true Japanese spirit in the rural countryside, J-horror addresses the fate of those who remain in the spiritual (un)dead zone of contemporary Tokyo. Those who forget the past are doomed to be destroyed by its vengeful ghosts.

This is, however, a perhaps too-tidy explanation. Like the readings of J-horror as expressive of technophobia and fears of new viral pandemics, it helps explain J-horror's topical appeal, but none of these theories deal directly with the sense of *osore* central to the figure of the vengeful ghost, which has a sublime quality present in both classic *kaiki* films and in J-horror. As expounded upon in Chapter 1, in foreign *kaiki* pictures like *Dracula* or *The Haunting* this

---

[36] Marilyn Ivy, *Discourses of the Vanishing: Modernity, Phantasm, Japan* (Chicago, IL: University of Chicago Press, 1995), 10–17, 63, 243.

osore constitutes a manifestation of H. P. Lovecraft's "cosmic horror," the awe-inspiring existence of entities beyond the pale of human understanding. The marvelous monsters of domestic *kaiki* cinema like Oiwa and the ghost cat may be "knowable" in the fairy-tale context of the films' diegesis, but invoke a similarly awe-inspiring sense of *osore* in their cosmologically licensed, omnipotent power to exact karmic vengeance upon the wicked. For an audience aware of both traditions, the J-horror ghost invokes the former *and* the latter, perverting the karmic rules of domestic *kaiki* cinema by retaining the formal presentation of the vengeful wraith and its rage-fueled *modus operandi*, but eliminating the laws that governed its behavior.

Because the ghosts of *kaiki* films based on traditional *kaidan* operate in a structurally sound cosmology, it is possible for the audience to learn the rules of the system and thereby avoid the terrifying fate of the vengeful spirit's curse. In J-horror there is no system, and therein lies the fundamental terror. This may in part be interpreted as a lament for lost Japanese traditions, but the poststructural *osore* of J-horror perhaps conveys, at a more baseline level, the fear of living in a world that old cosmologies can no longer satisfactorily explain, which brings us back to Tudor's conception of "paranoid horror." J-horror repositions the once knowable old monsters of *kaiki* cinema as perfect specimens of H. P. Lovecraft's cosmic fear—utterly unpredictable and unknowable. The ghosts of traditional culture remain with us, but the old rationales for their existence no longer satisfy. And that is what truly frightens.

Conclusion

Nakagawa Nobuo and the filmmakers who followed his lead throughout the 1960s took the first steps toward the eventual J-horror aesthetic in their refinement of *kaiki* tropes along more *horā*-esque lines, although almost thirty years would lie between the death of the *kaiki* genre in the early 1970s and the advent of the globally successful *Ring* franchise in the late 1990s. When the vengeful ghost of *kaiki eiga* finally reemerged from her well in the guise of Sadako, Kayako, and the myriad other "long-haired Japanese ghosts" that took the world by storm, she owed much of her visual iconography and *modus operandi* to the post-Nakagawa *kaiki* monster. The J-horror *onryō*'s obscured features, its tangible physicality and invasive presence in the mise-en-scène, and its rupture of the marvelous past into the rational present all have their roots in the innovations of Nakagawa and his followers.

But just as J-horror rejects the stylized set work and Othered locales of the earlier *kaiki* genre, so too does it reinvent its ghosts in ways that significantly depart from its predecessors' morality plays of karmic comeuppance. No longer confined to haunting those who wronged them in life, they turn their omnipotent rage on all of us. The J-horror ghost ceases to be an agent of cosmic justice, becoming for the first time in the history of Japanese horror cinema a true embodiment of Lovecraft's cosmic terror: unknowable, unappeasable, and unstoppable. Whether commenting on life in a spiritually bankrupt, twenty-first-century Japan or the "paranoid horror" of postmodern human society in general, J-horror kept the ghost in the well frighteningly relevant into a new era. Her methods and meanings may be starkly different, but the J-horror ghost continues to embody *osore* for contemporary Japanese culture, carrying on a tradition begun centuries ago when her ancestors first crawled out of their wells to haunt Edo-era Japan.

Afterword: The End …?

At the false climax of *Ring*, the protagonists mistakenly believe they have put Sadako's angry spirit to rest by recovering her corpse and exposing her murder. The scene strongly parallels the true climax of Nakagawa Nobuo's *Mansion of the Ghost Cat*, in which an inner wall of the doctor's haunted mansion crumbles during a terrific thunderstorm, revealing the sealed-up remains of the murdered innocent whose wrath gave birth to the titular monster. The doctor and his wife give the bones a proper burial, freeing themselves of the ghost cat's curse. In the final scene the couple, now safely back in modern, urban Tokyo, look back on their ordeal and remark, "Such enmity is a terrifying thing indeed!" (*Sono urami wa osoroshii mono ne!*), using the adjectival form of the word *osore*. More terrifying still is the enmity of *Ring*'s Sadako, who in keeping with the nihilistic themes of J-horror, cannot be appeased as easily as the *kaiki* ghosts of yesteryear. *Ring*'s genuine climax returns to the final image on the cursed videotape that set the film's plot in motion, as a flickering, out-of-focus recording of a well inexplicably appears on the doomed protagonist Ryūji's television screen. Unlike the videotape itself, which abruptly ends with the enigmatic shot of the well, this sourceless imagery continues on to show the ghost of Sadako emerge from the well's depths, crawling toward the screen, then through it into Ryūji's living room.

Sadako's uncanny violation of the television screen breaks down the barrier between present reality and the recorded image and underscores one of the film's central conceits: the mere act of watching is enough to allow its monster to "get" you. The scene's power to instill a sense of terror in the viewer requires no knowledge of the long cultural history of the *onryō* and its manifestations in decades of classic *kaiki* films, borne out by the fact that the American remake *The Ring* replicates the scene virtually unchanged. However, for a viewer aware of these traditions, the image of Sadako crawling out of her well activates the uncanny on multiple levels. Japanese ghosts have been emerging from wells ever since the spirit of the murdered maid Okiku began haunting her master in *The Dish Mansion at Banchō* over two centuries ago. Okiku and her well constitute one of the primal iconographies of Japanese folklore, but until *Ring* the motif had been contained in a Todorovian marvelous past as depicted in prewar and early postwar *kaiki* cinema. Sadako emerging from her own well in the heart of contemporary Tokyo thus serves the same function as Shintōhō's monsters who invade modern-day Japan in pictures like *Mansion of the Ghost Cat*, *The Ghost Cat of Otama Pond*, *Diving Girl's Ghost*, and *Vampire Bride*. The ghosts and monsters of a fairy tale past take on a new, terrifying aspect via their uncanny appearance in the rational present, transgressing the boundaries of the marvelous narratives that safely separate them from our own reality—the monster under the bed made flesh. But Sadako and her J-horror spawn are also the ghosts of *kaiki* cinema itself, a point underscored by the fact that in *Ring* Sadako's ghost is encountered via the same medium through which more recent generations have experienced classic *kaiki* films—home video. Resurrected from her cinematic crypt, the ghost now quite literally reaches through the screen to terrify her victims.

Fittingly, the image of Sadako and her well also harkens back to that precious bit of surviving silent-era footage of Okiku's see-through spirit emerging from the well to haunt her murderer with stop-motion tricks. The title *Ring* ultimately refers to the unbreakable, never-ending cycle of Sadako's curse, but the film's pivotal image makes a ring of its own, circling back to the earliest extant imagery from what might be deemed a Japanese horror film. The *Dish Mansion* footage and other primordial *kaiki* films' emphasis on trick photography may have been intended to dazzle spectators with the uncanny miracle of cinema rather than frighten them with attempts to instill a sense of *osore* in their content, but once audiences grew accustomed to the new medium's potential for special effects, domestic *kaiki* films sought to invoke the same themes of cosmic, karmic terror that distinguished their *kaidan* ancestors in Edo literary and theatrical traditions. The site of spectacle shifted to the body of vamp actresses like Suzuki Sumiko, whose on-screen transformations from a beautiful, sexually appealing woman to a hideous wraith or ghost cat became a focal point for the convergence of domestic, stage-inspired motifs of *kaidan* with the emerging global genre of the horror movie. In her encapsulation of old and new, Suzuki Sumiko and her monstrous performances stand as yet another precursor to Sadako and the postmodern, J-horror ghosts, who likewise combine tradition and innovation.

Following the interim of war and occupation that saw *kaiki* fall victim to a decade-long period of censorship, the ghost was resurrected from her well yet again as Japanese film studios sought to replicate Suzuki's success in a variety of guises. Daiei's attempt to cast first Irie Takao and then Mōri Ikuko as the successor to Suzuki's mantle drew on the old formula of mixing sexuality and monstrosity, while other studios like Tōei experimented with mixing genres themselves in the shape of "romantic *kaidan*." An overriding reliance on "spookhouse" moments of shock characterized these B-picture efforts, which were churned out quickly without much thought to carefully developed screenplays that would depict the themes of *osore* in more psychologically suspenseful terms. Meanwhile, the British Hammer studio's color updates of classic Hollywood *kaiki* films reasserted the gothic formal trappings of the genre at a time when new science fiction monsters like Godzilla seemed poised to replace a conservative definition of *kaiki*. Ōkura Mitsugi's transformation of the Shintōhō studio into a genre factory created the conditions for Nakagawa Nobuo and his staff to bring domestic *kaiki* cinema to the pinnacle of form, retaining the themes of cosmic *osore* that had distinguished the genre while adding a new layer of uncanny by displacing the monsters of the past into the present in a move that even more so than Suzuki Sumiko's prewar films anticipated one of the central themes of J-horror. *Ring* and the globally popular film movement it spawned, like all good genre cinema, built on the conventions and motifs that came before, even if knowledge of such traditions is not necessary to enjoy them. What once thrilled early cinema audiences returned to chill new ones to the bone.

At least for a while.

As the third decade of the twenty-first century dawns, J-horror seems to be suffering from chronic overexposure. Its flagship *Ring* and *Ju-On* franchises have long since ceased to be the products of the small circle of filmmakers working with low budgets and found locations who initially defined the genre. The Japanese studios recognized the J-horror machine as the money maker that it was and responded in kind, flooding the market with imitations, sequels, and spin-offs that inevitably devolved into the self-parodying crossover *Sadako vs. Kayako*. The attendant media blitzes that accompanied these releases made Sadako (and to a somewhat lesser extent, *Ju-On*'s Kayako and Toshio) one of the most recognizable characters in Japan's soft power media landscape alongside Pikachu, Mario, and Hello Kitty. The release of *Sadako 3D 2* in 2013 even came complete with tie-in merchandise of Hello Kitty dressed as Sadako, adorably emerging from an impossibly cute little well. As my own look at *kaiki* cinema has touched upon, horror movie monsters terrify in large part by virtue of their unknown and unfamiliar qualities. Once we become too familiar with the monster, it ceases to be frightening, as reflected in Sadako's (d)evolution into a lovable mascot of Japanese horror who throws out the opening pitch at professional baseball games and enjoys ice cream at local shops in a tourism campaign for her home island of Oshima timed to coincide with the release of *Sadako* (2019).

It is perhaps the inevitable fate of all popular horror monsters in capitalist, consumerist societies to become a parody of themselves, a phenomenon I like to refer to as the "Count Chocula-fication" of horror (what would Bram Stoker think of the children's breakfast cereal hawked by a cartoon version of his demonic bloodsucking vampire?). Even at the height of the J-horror craze in the early 2000s, one of its principal creators recognized its popularity lent itself to parody. In much the same way Universal poked fun at its own groundbreaking horror films in comedies like *Abbot and Costello Meet Frankenstein* (1948), *Ju-On* creator Shimizu Takashi took both J-horror and its *kaiki* ancestors to humorous task in the *Ghosts vs Aliens* series (*Yūrei vs uchūjin*, 2003–7) as well as the television series *The Great Horror Family* (*Kaiki daikazoku*, 2004). The adjective *kaiki* was translated to "horror" for the English-language release of the latter, but the original Japanese title is of course a conscious throwback to the classic films of the postwar era that partially inspired the J-horror movement.

The Great Horror Family concerns the adventures of teenager Imawano Kiyoshi after moving into a haunted house conspicuously similar-looking to the one in Shimizu's *Ju-On* series. The appeal of the show lies in his family's banal, comedically deadpan reactions to the plethora of *kaiki* and J-horror-derived spirits who plague their home. Kiyoshi's father Osamu is the only member of the family unable to see the ghosts and the only one who would appreciate it, being a die-hard fan of the supernatural as attested to by his collection of classic *kaiki* movie posters. Kiyoshi forms an attachment with one ghost in particular, the spirit of a young woman named Asami who haunts his bedroom. Asami is a dead ringer for Sadako, Kayako, and every other "long-haired Japanese ghost" familiar the world over. She creeps, crawls, and contorts about on the floor in-between offering Kiyoshi friendly advice about how to deal with the other spirits who infest the house. Semi-romantic exchanges between the pair are comedically undercut by her habit of vomiting blood at inopportune moments, after which she dutifully cleans up her own mess with a Kleenex. As the series progresses Asami becomes a figure akin to the ubiquitous magical girlfriends in anime, who use their supernatural powers for the benefit of the hapless teenaged male protagonist. *The Great Horror Family* can be seen as a comment on the

J-horror ghost's media oversaturation, a phenomenon that diluted its sense of *osore* and robbed it of its frightening potency. Perhaps one day Sadako and her ilk will recapture the global horror imagination, though as of this writing J-horror continues to be a ghost of its former terrifying self.

Will the genre finally die out completely, much the same way *kaiki* faded from cinema screens for good in the 1970s? Steven T. Brown opens his recent study *Japanese Horror and the Transnational Cinema of Sensations* (2018) with the question "What Was J-horror?," declaratively positioning it as a phenomenon of the past and "already dead, if not buried."[1] Yet J-horror's global reach and lingering place of prominence as one of Japan's most visible pop culture exports continues to inspire new interest from scholars like Brown and Baryon Tensor Posadas, who have moved the discussion of Japanese horror cinema beyond the East versus West binaries and ahistorical, essentialist claims about Japanese culture that characterized much previous work on the subject. Posadas concludes his insightful analysis of the unconventional J-horror ghost in Kurosawa Kiyoshi's *Retribution* (*Sakebi*, 2006)—who violates many of the established J-horror tropes surrounding *onryō* even as the first-generation J-horror ghosts like Sadako and Kayako upended older *kaiki* motifs—by cautioning against the assumption that "'Japanese horror' (with a distinct emphasis on *Japanese*) is a coherent and stable genre that can be distilled into a transhistorical essence."[2]

As I have demonstrated in my own discussion of *kaiki* film, the very idea of horror as a genre of cinema is a relatively recent phenomenon in Japan, arguably only going back as far as the 1980s and the adoption of the English loanword *horā*. Although *kaiki eiga* often gets translated as "horror film" for convenience's sake, I have suggested that "gothic horror" might be a more apt rendering, and Mathias Clasen could just as easily be talking about *kaiki* when he notes that "the Gothic is an historical phenomenon, just one specifically historic incarnation of horror, like the slasher film, whereas horror is a functional designation, one that transcends history."[3] Uncritically lumping premodern *kaidan* literature, B-grade prewar and postwar *kaiki* films, highbrow cinema like Mizoguchi's *Ugetsu*, and something like *Sadako vs Kayako* into the category of "Japanese horror" completely erases the generic distinctions that separated them in Japanese cultural discourse through

---

[1] Steven T. Brown, *Japanese Horror and the Transnational Cinema of Sensations* (Cham: Palgrave Macmillan, 2018), 2.
[2] Baryon Tensor Posadas, *Double Visions, Double Fictions: The Doppelgänger in Japanese Film and Literature* (Minneapolis: University of Minnesota Press, 2018), 190.
[3] Mathias Clasen, *Why Horror Seduces* (New York: Oxford University Press, 2017), 11.

modernization and world wars, economic miracles and recessions, a secure past and a paranoid future.

The East/West binary implicitly created by speaking of "Japanese horror" as a unique tradition or alternative to Hollywood and European horror also obscures the fundamentally transnational nature of popular genre cinema. To quote Lucia Nagib, "World cinema is simply the cinema of the world. It has no centre. It is not the other, but it is us."[4] Rather than conceive of commercial genre cinema from around the globe strictly along Anglophone categorical constructs like "horror" or else in terms of national genres in opposition to Hollywood's hegemony like "Japanese horror," the case of *kaiki* shows us the necessity of considering both the local and the global in any discussion of popular film. The Japanese conceptualization of *kaiki eiga* was not a mere approximation of the English "horror movie." Neither was it created in opposition to the Western horror genre. Across cultural-linguistic divides, we find that popular film genres are at once transnational in their makeup and culturally particular in their conception. *Kaiki*'s temporality and status as an obsolete genre additionally highlights the need to think about film genres not in sweeping, ahistorical terms, but as ways of thinking about popular film at particular moments in time and place. This is as certainly true of musicals in India or action films in China as it is of horror films in Japan.

As we have seen, there was never any real sense in Japan that *Dracula*, *Frankenstein*, or *The Haunting* was generically different from *The Ghost Story of Yotsuya* or a Suzuki Sumiko ghost cat movie, and Japanese *kaiki* film drew as equally upon its Western cousins as it did on premodern *kaidan* and kabuki stage traditions for inspiration. When Western fans and critics embraced J-horror as a revitalizing force in global horror cinema, it was perhaps natural that they seized upon its perceived difference. But the search for J-horror's mysterious Eastern origins caused most to overlook the fact that the creators of J-horror couldn't say enough about the Western films that inspired them. Brown provides a much-needed intervention by highlighting the transnational hybridity that characterizes the work of Japanese horror filmmakers like Kurosawa Kiyoshi and Miike Takashi. He emphasizes screenwriter Takahashi Hiroshi's point that J-horror arose from a combination of traditional Japanese ghost story motifs and Western horror film inspirations, noting, "Contemporary J-horror has been

---

[4] Lucia Nagib, "Towards a Positive Definition of World Cinema," in *Remapping World Cinema: Identity, Culture, and Politics in Film*, ed. Stephanie Dennison and Song Hwee Lim (New York: Wallflower Press, 2006), 35.

characterized by transnational hybridity from its very inception—its origins were already split, already doubled, at the outset."[5] Recognizing that J-horror was transnational not just in its impact but also in its origins is an important step toward understanding the nature of the ghost in the well.

It has been the goal of this work to reveal that this transnationalism does not begin with J-horror but stretches all the way back to the dawn of cinema and the very earliest roots of the horror genre in Japanese film culture. J-horror's transnational hybridity is staggeringly complex when one considers it draws not only on premodern Japanese ghost stories and Hollywood horror movies but also on classic *kaiki* film conventions that were themselves already hybrid traditions. The *kaiki* genre mixed elements of Japan's own venerable history of the strange, grotesque, and otherworldly in literature and theater with the emerging international aesthetics of the horror film—itself a complex hybrid of Hollywood, German Expressionism, and the gothic tradition in Western literature and theater—to create frightening spectacles never previously dreamed of like the sexy, vampish ghost cat embodied by Suzuki Sumiko and her successors, the dizzying use of the uncanny in the films of Nakagawa Nobuo, and the sheer campy delight of something like *Diving Girls in a Haunted House*. The history of the horror film in Japan is itself a bit like a haunted house, full of winding staircases, secret passages, and ghosts of the past who rise from their graves (or wells) again and again with uncanny tenacity. As in the closing moments of *Ring*, we come to know there is no end to Sadako's curse—only an endless ring. The ghost may lie buried for a time, but she always rises again.

---

[5] Brown, *Japanese Horror*, 5–6.

Bibliography

Altman, Rick. *Film/Genre*. London: British Film Institute, 2008.

Anderson, Joseph L. "Spoken Silents in the Japanese Cinema; Or, Talking to Pictures: Essaying the *Katsuben*, Contextualizing the Texts." In *Reframing Japanese Cinema: Authorship, Genre, History*, ed. Arthur Nolletti Jr. and David Desser, 259–311. Bloomington: Indiana University Press, 1992.

Anderson, Joseph L., and Donald Richie. *The Japanese Film: Art and Industry*. 2nd ed. Princeton, NJ: Princeton University Press, 1982.

Andrew, Dudley. "An Atlas of World Cinema." In *Remapping World Cinema: Identity, Culture, and Politics in Film*, ed. Stephanie Dennison and Song Hwee Lim, 19–29. New York: Wallflower Press, 2006.

Bakhtin, Mikhail. *Rabelais and His World*. Translated by Helene Iswolsky. Bloomington: Indiana University Press, 1984.

Balmain, Colette. *Introduction to Japanese Horror Film*. Edinburgh: Edinburgh University Press, 2008.

Barrett, Gregory. *Archetypes in Japanese Film: The Sociopolitical and Religious Significance of the Principal Heroes and Heroines*. Cranbury, NJ: Associated University Press, 1989.

Bordwell, David. *Narration in the Fiction Film*. Madison: University of Wisconsin Press, 1985.

Brown, Steven T. *Japanese Horror and the Transnational Cinema of Sensations*. East Asian Popular Culture. Cham: Palgrave Macmillan, 2018.

"Building the Inferno: Nobuo Nakagawa and the Making of *Jigoku*." *Jigoku*. Criterion, 2006. DVD.

Burke, Edmund. *A Philosophical Enquiry into the Origin of Our Ideas of the Sublime and the Beautiful*. Oxford: Oxford University Press, 2015.

Carroll, Noël. *The Philosophy of Horror: Or Paradoxes of the Heart*. New York: Routledge, 1990.

Carroll, Noël. "Why Horror?" In *Horror, The Film Reader*, ed. Mark Jancovich, 33–46. New York: Routledge, 2002.

Clasen, Mathias. *Why Horror Seduces*. New York: Oxford University Press, 2017.

Clover, Carol J. *Men, Women, and Chain Saws: Gender in the Modern Horror Film*. Princeton, NJ: Princeton University Press, 1992.

Coleridge, Samuel Taylor. "On *The Monk*." In *Gothic Horror: A Guide for Students and Readers*, ed. Clive Bloom, 34. 2nd ed. New York: Palgrave Macmillan, 2007.

Crandol, Michael. "Godzilla vs. Dracula: Hammer Horror Films in Japan." *Cinephile* 13 no. 1 (2019): 18–23.

Creed, Barbara. "Horror and the Monstrous-Feminine: An Imaginary Abjection." In *Horror, The Film Reader*, ed. Mark Jancovich, 67–76. New York: Routledge, 2002.

Crucchiola, Jordan. "The 100 Scares That Shaped Horror." *Vulture*, November 29, 2018. Accessed May 19, 2019. https://www.vulture.com/article/best-horror-movie-scenes.html.

Curti, Roberto. *Italian Gothic Horror Films, 1957–1969*. Jefferson, MO: McFarland, 2015.

D., Chris. *Outlaw Masters of Japanese Film*. New York: I.B. Tauris, 2005.

Davisson, Zack. "J-horror: An Alternative Guide." *SeekJapan*. Accessed November 6, 2010. http://www.seekjapan.jp/article-1/765/J-Horror:+An+Alternative+Guide.

Doane, Mary Anne. "The 'Woman's Film': Possession and Address." In *Re-vision: Essays in Feminist Film Criticism*, ed. Mary Anne Doane, Patricia Mellencamp, and Linda Williams, 67–82. American Film Institute Monograph Series, vol. 3. Los Angeles: American Film Institute, 1983.

"Dr. Jekyll and Mr. Hyde." *New York Times*, March 29, 1920.

"Dracula." *The Film Spectator*, March 28, 1931, 13.

Figal, Gerald. *Civilization and Monsters: Spirits of Modernity in Meiji Japan*. Durham, NC: Duke University Press, 1999.

"Film-Record during April 1914. Guide for Exhibitors and Spectators." *Kinema Record*, May 10, 1914, 21–36.

"Film-Record during July 1914. Guide to Exhibitors and Spectators." *Kinema Record*, August 3, 1914, 17–32.

"Film-Record during October 1915. Guide to Exhibitions and Spectators." *Kinema Record*, November 10, 1915, 24–32.

Foster, Michael Dylan. *The Book of Yōkai: Mysterious Creatures of Japanese Folklore*. Berkeley: University of California Press, 2015.

Foster, Michael Dylan. *Pandemonium and Parade: Japanese Monsters and the Culture of Yōkai*. Berkeley: University of California Press, 2009.

Freud, Sigmund. *The Uncanny*. Translated by David McLintok. New York: Penguin, 2003.

Fujiki, Hideaki. "The Advent of the Star System in Japanese Cinema Distribution." *Jōhō bunkakenkyū* 15 (2002): 1–22.

Fujiki, Hideaki. *Making Personas: Transnational Film Stardom in Modern Japan*. Cambridge: Harvard University Press, 2013.

Gerow, Aaron. *Visions of Japanese Modernity: Articulations of Cinema, Nation, and Spectatorship, 1895–1925*. Berkeley: University of California Press, 2010.

Goldberg, Ruth. "Demons in the Family: Tracking the Japanese 'Uncanny Mother Film' from *A Page of Madness* to *Ringu*." In *Planks of Reason: Essays on the Horror Film*, ed. Barry Keith Grant and Christopher Sharrett, 370–85. Oxford: Scarecrow Press, 2004.

Goldberg, Ruth. "The Nightmare of Romantic Passion in Three Classic Japanese Horror Films." In *Japanese Horror Cinema*, ed. Jay McRoy, 29–37. Honolulu: University of Hawai'i Press, 2005.

Greason, Alfred Rushford. "*Dracula*." *Variety*, February 18, 1931, 14.

Gunning, Tom. "The Cinema of Attractions: Early Film, Its Spectators, and the Avant-Garde." In *Early Cinema: Space, Frame, Narrative*, ed. Thomas Elsaesser and Adam Baker, 56–62. London: British Film Institute, 1990.

Hand, Richard J. "Aesthetics of Cruelty: Traditional Japanese Theater and the Horror Film." In *Japanese Horror Cinema*, ed. Jay McRoy, 18–28. Honolulu: University of Hawai'i Press, 2005.

Hansen, Miriam Bratu. "The Mass-Production of the Senses: Classical Cinema as Vernacular Modernism." In *Reinventing Film Studies*, ed. Christine Gledhill and Linda Williams, 332–50. New York: Oxford University Press, 2000.

Hansen, Miriam Bratu. "Vernacular Modernism: Tracking Cinema on a Global Scale." In *World Cinemas, Transnational Perspectives*, ed. Nataa Durovicova and Kathleen E. Newman, 287–314. New York: Routledge, 2009.

Haraguchi Tomō and Murata Hideki, ed. *Nihon horā eiga e no shōtai*. Tokyo: Heibonsha, 2000.

Hart, Adam Charles. *Monstrous Forms: Moving Image Horror across Media*. New York: Oxford University Press, 2020.

Hasebe Toshio, ed. *'Shihan' Kawai, Daito eiga 2: Kawai eiga danyū joyū*. Tokyo: Takei Kikaku, 1994.

Hayter, Irena. "Mannequins, Movies, and Mass Culture in the 1920s." Paper presented at the annual conference for the Association for Asian Studies, Denver, Colorado, March 21–24, 2019.

Hearn, Marcus, and Alan Barnes. *The Hammer Story: The Authorised History of Hammer Films*. London: Titan, 2007.

Heffernan, Kevin. *Ghouls, Gimmicks, and Gold: Horror Films and the American Movie Business, 1953–1968*. Durham, NC: Duke University Press, 2004.

Hibbin, Nina. "*Dracula*." *The Daily Worker*, May 24, 1958. Quoted in Peter Hutchings, *Hammer and Beyond: The British Horror Film*, 9. New York: St. Martin's Press, 1993.

Hirano, Kyoko. *Mr. Smith Goes to Tokyo: Japanese Cinema under the American Occupation, 1945–52*. Washington, DC: Smithsonian Institute, 1992.

Hirano, Kyoko. "The Rise of Japanese Horror Films: *Yotsuya Ghost Story* (*Yotsuya Kaidan*), Demonic Men, and Victimized Women." In *Introducing Japanese Popular Culture*, ed. Alisa Freedman and Toby Slade. New York: Routledge, 2018.

Hirose Ai. "Eiga *Yotsuya kaidan* kō—Nakagawa Nobuo no jikkenteki kaiki hyōgen." *Shokeigakuin daigaku kiyōdai*, September 2, 2011, 47–62.

Horikiri Naota. "Nakagawa Nobuo arui wa jōya no machieeru." *Eiga hyōron* 28, no. 2 (1971): 93–107.

Horikiri Naota. "Nakagawa Nobuo intabyū: Ano yo to no kagawarikata." *Eiga hyōron* 28, no. 9 (1971): 23–40.

Hutchings, Peter. *Hammer and Beyond: The British Horror Film*. New York: St. Martin's Press, 1993.

Hutchings, Peter. *The Horror Film*. Inside Film Series. Edinburgh: Pearson, 2004.

"Iharo [sic] gana Yotsuya kaidan." *Kinema Junpō*, June 11, 1937, 106–7.

Irie Takako. *Eiga joyū*. Tokyo: Gakufushoin, 1957.
Isobe Masao. *Musei eiga no hana: Yōen Suzuki Sumiko*. Kumamoto: Isobe jidageki eiga kenkyu, 1982.
Ivy, Marilyn. *Discourses of the Vanishing: Modernity, Phantasm, Japan*. Chicago, IL: University of Chicago Press, 1995.
Izawa Jun, "Kaiki to wa? Nihon no obake to seiyō no obake." *Kinema junpō*, July 1, 1957, 44–6.
Izumi Toshiyuki. *Ginmaku no hyakkai: honchō kaiki eiga taigai*. Tokyo: Seidosha, 2000.
"Jidai eiga ni nozomu." *Eiga hyōron*, February 1, 1939, 35.
"Kaiki eiga montō." *Kinema junpō*, October 15, 1974. Reprinted in *Eiga kantoku Nakagawa Nobuo*, ed. Takisawa Osamu and Yamane Sadao, 114–15. Tokyo: Riburopōto, 1987.
Kalat, David. *J-horror: The Definitive Guide to* The Ring, The Grudge, *and Beyond*. New York: Vertical, 2007.
Kamiya Masako. "Shoki nihon eiga no kaiki to torikku." In *Kaiki to gensō e no kairō: kaidan kara J-horā e*, ed. Uchiyama Kazuki, 33–65. Tokyo: Shinwasha, 2008.
Kawabe Jūji. *B-kyū kyoshōron: Nakagawa Nobuo kenkyū*. Tokyo: Shizukadō, 1983.
Kendrick, James. *Film Violence: History, Ideology, Genre*. Short Cuts. London: Wallflower Press, 2009.
King, Stephen. *Danse Macabre*. Gallery Books edition. New York: Simon and Schuster, 2010.
Kinoshita, Chika. "The Mummy Complex: Kurosawa Kiyoshi's *Loft* and J-horror." In *Horror to the Extreme: Changing Boundaries in Asian Cinema*, ed. Jinhee Choi and Mitsuyo Wada-Maricano, 103–22. Hong Kong: Hong Kong University Press, 2009.
Kitamura, Hiroshi. *Screening Enlightenment: Hollywood and the Cultural Reconstruction of Defeated Japan*. The United States in the World. Ithaca, NY: Cornell University Press, 2010.
Konaka Chiaki. *Horā eiga no miryoku: fandamentaru horā sengen*. Iwanami Akutibu Shinsho 86. Tokyo: Iwanami Shoten, 2003.
Kondō Keiichi, ed. *Eiga sutā zenshū 10*. Tokyo: Heibonsha, 1930.
Kristeva, Julia. *Powers of Horror: An Essay in Abjection*. Translated by Leon S. Roudiez. New York: Columbia, 1982.
Kurosawa Haruyasu. "Ki ni naru aitsu: Muma no sake." *Eiga hyōron* 30, no. 12 (1973): 87–9.
Kurosawa Kiyoshi. *Eiga wa osoroshii*. Tokyo: Seidosha, 2001.
Kurosawa Kiyoshi and Shinozaki Makoto. *Kurosawa Kiyoshi no kyōfu no eigashi*. Tokyo: Seidosha, 2003.
Lee, Laura. "Japan's Cinema of Tricks: Optical Effects and Classical Film Style." *Quarterly Review of Film and Video* 32, no. 2 (2015): 141–61.
Lim, Bliss Cua. *Translating Time: Cinema, the Fantastic, and Temporal Critique*. Durham, NC: Duke University Press, 2009.
Lovecraft, H. P. *The Annotated Supernatural Horror in Literature*. Edited by S. T. Joshi. New York: Hippocampus Press, 2012.

Marak, Katarzyna. *Japanese and American Horror: A Comparative Study of Film, Fiction, Graphic Novels, and Video Games*. Jefferson, MO: McFarland, 2015.

Martin, Daniel. "Japan's *Blair Witch*: Restraint, Maturity, and Generic Canons in the British Cultural Reception of *Ring*." *Cinema Journal* 48, no. 3 (2009): 35–51.

McRoy, Jay, ed. *Japanese Horror Cinema*. Honolulu: University of Hawai'i Press, 2005.

McRoy, Jay. *Nightmare Japan: Contemporary Japanese Horror Cinema*. Contemporary Cinema Series, no. 4. Amsterdam: Rodopi, 2008.

Mes, Tom. *Agitator: The Cinema of Takashi Miike*. Godalming: Fab Press, 2004.

Miller, J. Scott. "The Feline as Agent of Karmic Retribution: Poe's *Black Cat* in Japan." Paper presented at the annual conference for the American Comparative Literature Association, Vancouver, Canada, March 31–April 3, 2011.

Misono Kyōhei, ed. *Misono korekushon: Meiji, Taishō, Shōwa eiga shiryōshū taisei*. Tokyo: Katsudō shiryō kenkyūkai, 1970.

Mitford, A. B. *Tales of Old Japan*. 3rd ed. London: Macmillan, 1876.

Miyao, Daisuke. *The Aesthetics of Shadow: Lighting and Japanese Cinema*. Durham, NC: Duke University Press, 2013.

Miyao, Daisuke. "A Ghost Cat, a Star, and Two Intertexts: A Historical Analysis of *A Cat, Shozo, and Two Women* (1956)." *Journal of Japanese and Korean Cinema* 8, no. 2 (2016): 89–103.

Mizumachi Seiji. "*Yotsuya kaidan*." *Kinema junpō*, August 11, 1928, 102.

Mulvey, Laura. "Visual Pleasure and Narrative Cinema." In *The Film Theory Reader: Debates and Arguments*, ed. Marc Furstenau, 200–8. New York: Routledge, 2010.

Murakami Hisao. "*Majin Dorakyura*." *Kinema junpō*, October 21, 1931, 28.

Murakami Tadahisa. "*Arima neko*." *Kinema junpō*, January 13, 1938, 274.

Murakami Tadahisa. "*Kaibyō akakabe Daimyōjin*." *Kinema junpō*, January 14, 1939, 82.

Murakami Tadahisa. "*Kaidan oshidori chō*." *Kinema junpō*, April 12, 1938, 79.

Murakami Tadahisa. "*Saga kaibyō-den*." *Kinema junpō*, February 21, 1937, 118.

Nachi Shirō and Shigeta Toshiuki, eds. *Ayakashi Ōkura Shintōhō*. Tokyo: Wise, 2001.

Nagib, Lucia. "Towards a Positive Definition of World Cinema." In *Remapping World Cinema: Identity, Culture, and Politics in Film*, ed. Stephanie Dennsion and Song Hwee Lim, 30–7. New York: Wallflower Press, 2006.

Nakagawa Nobuo. "Obake eiga sono hoka/watashi no kiroku eiga ron." In *Eiga kantoku Nakagawa Nobuo*, ed. Takisawa Osamu and Yamane Sadao, 106–7. Tokyo: Riburopōto, 1987.

Nakagawa Nobuo. "*Tōkaidō Yotsuya kaidan* enshutsu zakki." *Kinema junpō*, August 20, 1969, 79–94.

Nakagawa Nobuo. "Wa ga nihon eigashi ue no shiranami gonin onna." In *Eiga kantoku Nakagawa Nobuo*, ed. Takisawa Osamu and Yamane Sadao, 126–8. Tokyo: Riburopōto, 1987.

Nakano Yakushi. "Joyūrei ron: Arui wa, eiga no jikogenkyūsayō ni hasamu 'ma' ni tsuite." In *Horā japanesuku no genzai*, ed. Ichiyanagi Hirotaka and Yoshida Morio, 115–30. Tokyo: Seikyūsha, 2005.

Neale, Stephen. *Genre*. London: British Film Institute, 1980.

Ogi Masahiro. "*Kaibyō Arima goten*." *Kinema junpō*, February 15, 1954, 65.

Ōkubo Tomoyasu. "Henshin ningen no tokuisei: Toho 'henshin ningen shiriizu' o megutte." In *Kaiki to gensō e no kairō: kaidan kara J-horā e*, ed. Uchiyama Kazuki, 101–24. Tokyo: Shinwasha, 2008.

Okura Mami. "*Saiko*." *Kinema junpō*, October 15, 1960, 84.

Ōsawa Jō. "Shintōhō no obake eiga to *Tōkaidō Yotsuya kaidan*: jyanru no fukkatsu tokakushin." In *Kaiki to gensō e no kairō: kaidan kara J-horā e*, ed. Uchiyama Kazuki, 67–99. Tokyo: Shinwasha, 2008.

Ōshima Kiyoaki. *J-horā no yūrei kenkyū*. Tokyo: Akiyama Shōten, 2010.

Petley, Julian. "'A Crude Sort of Entertainment for a Crude Sort of Audience': The British Critics and Horror Cinema." In *British Horror Cinema*, ed. Steve Chibnall and Julian Petley, 23–41. British Popular Cinema series. New York: Routledge, 2002.

Phillips, Kendall R. *A Place of Darkness: The Rhetoric of Horror in Early American Cinema*. Austin: University of Texas Press, 2018.

Plantinga, Carl. *Moving Viewers: American Film and the Spectator's Experience*. Berkeley: University of California Press, 2009.

Posadas, Baryon Tensor. *Double Visions, Double Fictions: The Doppelgänger in Japanese Film and Literature*. Minneapolis: University of Minnesota Press, 2018.

Prawer, S. S. *Caligari's Children: The Film as a Tale of Terror*. New York: Da Capo Press, 1980.

Pu Songling. *Strange Tales from a Chinese Studio*. Translated by John Minford. New York: Penguin, 2006.

Radcliffe, Anne. "On the Supernatural in Poetry." In *Gothic Horror: A Guide for Students and Readers*, ed. Clive Bloom, 60–9. 2nd ed. New York: Palgrave Macmillan, 2007.

Rafferty, Terrence. "Screams in Asia Echo in Hollywood." *New York Times*, January 27, 2008.

Raine, Michael. "Adaptation as 'Transcultural Mimesis' in Japanese Cinema." In *The Oxford Handbook of Japanese Cinema*, ed. Daisuke Miyao, 101–23. New York: Oxford University Press, 2014.

Rauer, Julie. "Persistence of a Genetic Scar: Japanese Anime, Manga, and Otaku Culture Fill an Open National Wound." In *Little Boy: The Art of Japan's Exploding Subculture*, http://www.asianart.com/exhibitons//littleboy/intro.html. Quoted in Colette Balmain, *Introduction to Japanese Horror Film*, 58. Edinburgh: Edinburgh University Press, 2008.

Reider, Noriko T. "The Appeal of *Kaidan*, Tales of the Strange." *Asian Folklore Studies*, 59, no. 2, 265–83. Nagoya: Nanzan University Press, 2000.

Saito, Ayako. "Occupation and Memory: The Representation of Woman's Body in Postwar Japanese Cinema." In *The Oxford Handbook of Japanese Cinema*, ed. Daisuke Miyao, 327–62. New York: Oxford University Press, 2014.

San'yūtei Enchō. *Shinkei Kasane ga fuchi*. 2nd ed. Tokyo: Iwanami shoten, 1997.

Satō Tadao. "Kaiki eiga no miryoku." *Kinema junpō*, July 1, 1957, 46–8.
Satō Tadao, Sumigawa Naoki, and Marubi Sadamu, eds. *Shinkō kinema: senzen goraku eiga no ōkoku*. Tokyo: Firumuātosha, 1993.
Schilling, Mark. *Nudes! Guns! Ghosts!: The Sensational Films of Shintoho*. Udine: Udine Far East Film Festival, 2010.
Sharp, Jasper. *Behind the Pink Curtain: The Complete History of Japanese Sex Cinema*. 2nd ed. Godalming: Fab Press, 2008.
Sharp, Jasper. *Historical Dictionary of Japanese Film*. Historical Dictionaries of Literature and the Arts series. Lanham, MD: Scarecrow Press, 2011.
Shen, Pennylane. "It Came from the East … Japanese Horror Cinema in the Age of Globalization." *Gnovis* 9, no. 2 (2009). Accessed May 16, 2013. http://gnovisjournal.org/2009/05/13/it-came-east-japanese-horror-cinema-ageglobalization.
Shigeno Yukiyashi. "Trick Pictures and Illusion Pictures." *Kinema Record*, January 1, 1914, 12–15.
Shimazaki, Satoko. *Edo Kabuki in Transition: From the Worlds of the Samurai to the Vengeful Female Ghost*. New York: Columbia University Press, 2016.
Shimizu Akira, "Kaiki eiga no arekore." *Kinema junpō*, July 1, 1957, 48–9.
Shimizu Chiyota. "*Furankenshutain*." *Kinema junpō*, May 11, 1932, 31.
Shimura Miyoko. "Daiei no yōkai eiga: 'yōkai sanbusaku' o chūshin ni." In *Kaiki to gensō e no kairō: kaidan kara J-horā e*, ed. Uchiyama Kazuki, 125–44. Tokyo: Shinwasha, 2008.
Shimura Miyoko. "Kaibutsu ka suru joyū-tachi: neko to hebi o meguru hyōshō." In *Kaiki to gensō e no kairō: kaidan kara J-horā e*, ed. Uchiyama Kazuki, 171–94. Tokyo: Shinwasha, 2008.
Shimura Miyoko. "Kōgeki no kōzō: *Kaibyō nazo no samisen*, *Kyatto piiporu* o megutte." *Eiga gaku* 16 (2002): 29–53.
Shimura Miyoko. "'Misemono' kara 'eiga' e: Shintōhō no kaibyō eiga." *Engeki eizō* 43 (2002): 13–21.
Shimura Miyoko. "Shinkō Kinema no kaibyō eiga." *Eiga gaku* 14 (2000): 51–63.
"Shinchōrei tai gyōsha mondai." *Kinema Record*, October, 1917, 1–3.
Spadoni, Robert. *Uncanny Bodies: The Coming of Sound Film and the Origins of the Horror Genre*. Berkeley: University of California Press, 2007.
Spalding, Lisa. "Period Films in the Prewar Era." In *Reframing Japanese Cinema: Authorship, Genre, History*, ed. Arthur Nolletti Jr. and David Desser, 131–44. Bloomington: Indiana University Press, 1992.
Standish, Isolde. *A New History of Japanese Cinema: A Century of Narrative Film*. New York: Continuum, 2005.
Stringer, Julian. "The Original and the Copy: Nakata Hideo's *Ring* (1998)." In *Japanese Cinema: Texts and Contexts*, ed. Alastair Phillips and Julian Stringer, 296–307. New York: Routledge, 2007.
Sugiyama Shizuo. "*Kyūketsuki Dorakyura*." *Kinema junpō*, Fall Special, 1958, 120.
Suzuki Kensuke, ed. *Jigoku de yōi hai!: Nakagawa Nobuo, kaidan/kyōfu eiga no gyōka*. Tokyo: Wise, 2000.

Suzuki Yoshiaki. *Shintōhō no hiwa: Izumida Hiroshi no sekai.* Osaka: Seishinsha, 2001.
Tachibana Sotō. *Tachibana Sotō wandārando: kaidan, kaiki hen*, ed. Yamashita Tadashi. Tokyo: Chuoshoin, 1994.
Tada Michitarō. "Bōrei kaibyō yashiki." *Kinema junpō*, September 1, 1958, 75.
Tada Michitarō. "Kaidan Banchō sarayashiki." *Kinema junpō*, September 15, 1957, 68.
Tada Michitarō. "Kaidan Kasane ga fuchi." *Kinema junpō*, September Special, 1957, 91.
Takahashi Hiroshi. *Eiga no ma.* Tokyo: Seidosha, 2004.
Takisawa Osamu. "Tōkaidō Yotsuya kaidan." In *Eiga-shi jō besuto 200 shirizu: Nihon eiga 200*, 270–1. Tokyo: Kinema junpō, 1982.
Takisawa Osamu. "Tōkaidō Yotsuya kaidan." *Kinema junpō*, September 1, 1959, 83.
Takisawa Osamu, and Yamane Sadao, ed. *Eiga kantoku Nakagawa Nobuo.* Tokyo: Riburopōto, 1987.
Tanaka Jun'ichirō. *Nagata Masaichi.* Tokyo: Jiji Press, 1962.
Tezuka, Yoshiharu. *Japanese Cinema Goes Global: Filmworkers' Journeys.* Hong Kong: Hong Kong University Press, 2012.
Todorov, Tzvetan. *The Fantastic: A Structural Approach to a Literary Genre.* Translated by Richard Howard. Ithaca, NY: Cornell University Press, 1975.
Tsuruya Nanboku IV. *Ghost Stories at Yotsuya.* Translated by Mark Oshima. In *Early Modern Japanese Literature*, ed. Haruo Shirane, 844–84. New York: Columbia, 2002.
Tsuruya Nanboku IV. *The Ghost Stories at Yotsuya on the Tōkaidō.* Translated by Paul B. Kennelly. In *Kabuki Plays on Stage: Darkness and Desire 1804–1864*, ed. James R. Brandon and Samuel L. Leiter, 134–63. Honolulu: University of Hawai'i Press, 2002.
Tsuruya Nanboku IV. *Tōkaidō Yotsuya kaidan.* Shinchō nihon koten shūsei, vol. 45. Tokyo: Shinchōsha, 1981.
Tudor, Andrew. "Genre." In *Film Genre Reader III*, ed. Barry Keith Grant, 3–11. Austin: University of Texas Press, 2004.
Tudor, Andrew. *Monsters and Mad Scientists: A Cultural History of the Horror Movie.* Oxford: Basil Blackwell, 1989.
Tudor, Andrew. "Why Horror? The Peculiar Pleasures of a Popular Genre." In *Horror, The Film Reader*, ed. Mark Jancovich, 47–55. New York: Routledge, 2002.
"U Has Horror Cycle All to Self." *Variety*, April 8, 1931, 2.
Uchiyama Kazuki, ed. *Kaiki to gensō e no kairō: kaidan kara J-horā e.* Tokyo: Shinwasha, 2008.
Uchiyama Kazuki. "Nihon eiga no kaiki to gensō." In *Kaiki to gensō e no kairō: kaidan kara J-horāe*, ed. Uchiyama Kazuki, 7–32. Tokyo: Shinwasha, 2008.
Uryū Tadao. "Ama no bakemono yashiki." *Kinema junpō*, August 15, 1959, 84.
Wada-Marciano, Mitsuyo. "J-horror: New Media's Impact on Contemporary Japanese Horror Cinema." In *Horror to the Extreme: Changing Boundaries in Asian Cinema*, ed. Jinhee Choi and Mitsuyo Wada-Marciano, 15–38. Hong Kong: Hong Kong University Press, 2009.
Wada-Marciano, Mitsuyo. *Nippon Modern: Japanese Cinema of the 1920s and 1930s.* Honolulu: University of Hawai'i Press, 2008.

Wakasugi Katsuko. *Yōen gensō kaiki jiai Wakasugi Katsuko*, ed. Maruo Toshiō. Famu fataru unmei no joyū shiriizu 1. Tokyo: Wise, 2000.

Warner, Marina. *Monsters of Our Own Making: The Peculiar Pleasures of Fear.* Lexington: University of Kentucky Press, 2007.

Wee, Valerie. *Japanese Horror Films and Their American Remakes.* Routledge Advances in Film Studies. New York: Routledge, 2014.

Williams, Linda. "Film Bodies: Gender, Genre, Excess." In *Film Theory and Criticism: Introductory Readings*, ed. Leo Braudy and Marshall Cohen, 701–15. 5th ed. New York: Oxford University Press, 1999.

Williams, Linda. "When the Woman Looks." In *Horror, The Film Reader*, ed. Mark Jancovich, 61–6. New York: Routledge, 2002.

Wood, Robin. "The American Nightmare: Horror in the 70s." In *Horror, The Film Reader*, ed. Mark Jancovich, 25–32. New York: Routledge, 2002.

Yamada Seiji. *Maboroshi no kaidan eiga o ōtte.* Tokyo: Yōsensha, 1997.

Yamamoto Ryōkuyō. "*Iroha gana Yotsuya kaidan*." *Kinema junpō*, August 1, 1927, 54.

Yamane Sadaō. "Nakagawa Nobuo no fushigi na asobi no sekai e." In *Eiga kantoku Nakagawa Nobuo*, ed. Takisawa Osamu and Yamane Sadao, 295–307. Tokyo: Riburopōto, 1987.

Yanagi Masako. "Kaiki eiga to kankyaku." *Kinema junpō*, July 1, 1957, 51.

Yokoyama Yasuko. "*Yotsuya kaidan* eiga no Oiwa-tachi: kabuki to wakare, betsu no onna e." In *Kaiki to gensō e no kairō: kaidan kara J-horā e*, ed. Uchiyama Kazuki, 145–70. Tokyo: Shinwasha, 2008.

Yokoyama Yasuko. *Yotsuya kaidan wa omoshiroii.* Tokyo: Heibonsha, 1997.

Zahlten, Alexander. *The End of Japanese Cinema: Industrial Genres, National Times, and Media Ecologies.* Durham, NC: Duke University Press, 2017.

Index

Abbot and Costello Meet Frankenstein 222
Abe Nobuo 69
Akisaku dōrō, see *Autumn Flower Lantern*
Alien 2, 137
Altman, Rick 12, 35, 42
ama films 129, 170–1
Ama no bakemono yashiki, see *Diving Girls in a Haunted House*
Amachi Shigeru 48, 167–9, 185–6, 191
American International Pictures 139, 169 n.35
Anabelle 36
Anderson, Joseph L. 6–7, 129
Andrew, Dudley 26
Aoi hebi buro, see *Blue Snake Bath*
Arai Ryōhei 126–7
Arashi Kanjūrō 78
Arima neko, see *The Cat of Arima*
Audition 34, 198
Autumn Flower Lantern 76
Avenging Corpse, The 31, 89–90

bakeneko 6, 26, 32–3, 46, 57, 78, 135, 193–6, 198
    as agent of karmic vengeance 50, 56–8, 118, 121, 140, 214–16
    connections to J-horror 199, 210, 212
    Irie Takako's portrayals of 15, 121–4, 128
    in *The Ghost Cat and the Mysterious Shamisen* 100–5
    in *The Ghost Cat of Otama Pond* 191–2
    in *Legend of the Nabeshima Ghost Cat* 117–18
    in *Mansion of the Ghost Cat* 128, 159–66, 199
    monstrous-feminine 44, 79
    neko jarashi 95, 124, 126, 159, 161
    postwar criticism of 124–8, 134
    in silent era films 22–3, 66, 68, 71–3
    Suzuki Sumiko's portrayals of 14, 40, 79, 82–5, 90–7, 106, 112, 220

Bakhtin, Mikhail 208
Balmain, Colette 7–8, 46, 175–7, 203
Bandō Tsumasaburō 78, 81
Banchō sarayashiki, see *The Dish Mansion at Banchō*
Bara, Theda 77–8
Barrymore, John 19
Battle Royale 3, 11, 202
Bava, Mario 139, 185
Beast from 20,000 Fathoms, The 28, 61, 136
benshi 67, 70, 81, 147–8
Black Sabbath 139
Blind Woman's Curse 197
Blood and Black Lace 139
Bloodthirsty Series 33, 197
Blue Snake Bath 130–1
body horror 137
Bon, see *Obon*
Bordwell, David 12
Bōrei kaibyō yashiki, see *Mansion of the Ghost Cat*
Botandōrō, see *Peony Lantern*
Bride of Frankenstein 10, 20, 26, 36, 189
Brown, Steven T. 223, 224–5
Browning, Tod 21, 159
Buddhism 4, 175, 191
    and ghosts 28, 45, 99, 211, 212
    impermanence 151
    karmic retribution 28, 99, 211, 212–13
    monks 160, 165, 192, 211, 213–15
    reincarnation 168
    shūnen 45, 99, 211
    temples 38, 99, 160

Cabinet of Dr. Caligari, The 19
Cabinet Propaganda Office 105, 110, 112, 113
Cat and the Canary, The 75
    influence on horror and *kaiki* genres 19, 24, 87
    mystery genre elements 19, 118–19

Cat of Arima, The 25, 91, 92–3, 98, 101, 121, 208
   fight sequence 93–5, 100
   Suzuki Sumiko's performance 85, 93–7, 104, 122
Cat of Okazaki, The (1914 film) 68, 71
Cat People 136, 157
Carpenter, John 33
Carroll, Noël 12–13, 31, 157
   definition of horror 51–3, 136
   definition of monsters 50, 52, 79
   on Lovecraft 58
   thought theory 54–5
   types of horror plots 28–9, 52–3, 167, 213
Ceiling at Utsunomiya, The 150 n.12, 158
censorship 15, 105, 110–20, 129, 140
chambara 91, 92–5, 100, 107, 112
Chaney, Lon 27, 47
Chaney Junior, Lon 167
Chūshingura 113
cinema of attractions 13, 66, 74, 77, 106
Civil Censorship Detachment (CCD) 112, 118
Civil Information and Education Section (CIE) 112–13, 117–18, 120
Clasen, Mathias 12, 55, 59, 223
Clouzet, Henri-Georges 31
Clover, Carol 12, 33, 47
cognitive film theory 12–13, 50–60, 61
Coleridge, Samuel Taylor 59–60, 127
Come Drink with Me 158
Coppola, Francis Ford 168
Corman, Roger 58, 139, 185
Count Dracula 39, 48, 54, 58, 136, 197 n. 10, see also *Dracula*
   Bela Lugosi's portrayal of 20, 95–6, 167
   in Bram Stoker's novel 168–9, 222
   in Hammer films 140, 143, 149, 159, 214
   as representative Hollywood movie monster 27, 79
Creed, Barbara 43–6, 52
Cronenberg, David 137
Cruel Ghost Legend 194
Curse of Frankenstein, The 134, 138–9, 143, 149
Curse of the Inugami 33

Curtis, Dan 168
Cushing, Peter 138–9

Daiei 15, 110, 120–1, 134, 149, 151, 172, 175, 183, 221
   closing of the studio 11, 196
   formation of 111–12
   ghost cat series 41, 71, 95–6, 99, 124–8, 135, 144, 148, 151, 155, 159–61, 187
   and Mōri Ikuko 128–34, 140, 144
   1960s *kaiki* films 192–5
   Occupation era *kaiki* films 118–20
Daitō 85, 88, 111, 118
Dark Water 201
Day the Earth Stood Still, The 27
Diaboliques, Les 31, 60
Dish Mansion at Banchō, The 1, 6, 23, 65, 80, 220
   1911 films 66
   1914 film 23
   1922 film 73, 74
   1937 film 85, 135
   1957 film 135–6
   unidentified silent era film 1–2, 68–70, 75–6, 220
Diving Girl's Ghost 53, 170–1, 193, 208, 220
Diving Girls in a Haunted House 32, 120, 170–1, 209, 225
Doane, Mary Anne 47
Dokufu Takahashi Oden, see *Poison Woman Takahashi Oden*
Don't Look Up, see *Ghost Actress*
Dr. Jekyll and Mr. Hyde 19, 20, 79
Dracula (1931 film) 2, 19–20, 87, 90, 96–7, 169
   as "classic horror" 29
   as *kaiki* film 10, 20–1, 24, 31, 36, 60, 91
Dracula (1958 film) 87, 139, 149, 169, 174
   influence on Japanese *kaiki* film 167
   role in redefining *kaiki* genre 15, 139–40, 144
   violence 140–2, 159–60
Dracula (1973 television film) 168
Dracula (novel) 25, 55, *see also* Count Dracula
   adaptation to film 35, 168–9, 213, 215
Dracula A.D. 1972 214

Earth vs. the Flying Saucers 136
Edo Period 7, 22, 40, 45, 64, 87, 194, 217
  belief in supernatural 53, 61, 215
  "Edo Gothic" 8, 76–8
  and kabuki 7, 64
Edogawa Rampo 34, 197
Edogawa Rampo zenshū: kyōfu kikei ningen, see *Horrors of Malformed Men*
Eiga hyōron 74, 88
Eirin 129
ero-guro nansensu 34, 197, 198
Evening Cherry Blossoms of Saga, The 66, 71
Evil Spirit 202
Execution of Mary Stuart, The 70
Exorcist, The 2, 204, 213
  differences from *kaiki* genre 10–11, 33, 36, 198, 210
Eye, The 201
Eyes without a Face 30–1, 32, 36, 39

"The Fall of the House of Usher" 102
Film Act 13, 129
  suppression of *kaiki* film 24, 75, 92, 105, 110–11
Film Spectator 20, 60
Flower and Snake 201
Foster, Michael Dylan 22
Frankenstein (1910 film) 63
Frankenstein (1931 film) 2, 15, 38–9, 72, 126
  and creation of horror film genre 20, 36, 86–7
  as *kaidan* 25–6, 87, 90
  as *kaiki* film 10, 24, 31, 91, 224
  as science fiction 28, 138
  sound effects 99
Frankenstein (novel) 29, 138
Frankenstein's Monster 27, 50, 58, 79, 136, 149, 189
Freeze Me 3
Freud, Sigmund 53, 54, 154
Freudian uncanny 53, 54–6, 114, 160
  in *The Ghost Story of Kasane's Swamp* 153–5
  in J-horror 198, 200, 209–10
  in *Mansion of the Ghost Cat* 165–6
  in *Ring* 1, 210, 219–20
  in Shintōhō *kaiki* films 16, 167, 169–70, 209–10, 200
Freund, Karl 21
Friday the 13th 2, 34, 198
Fujiki Hideaki 77
Fukusaku Kinji 3, 202
Fushimi Naoe 78, 82

Gakkō no kaidan, see *Schoolhouse Ghost Stories*
GeGeGe no Kitarō 194
gendaigeki 74, 84, 88, 113, 121
  and *kaiki* 119–20, 161–6, 170–1, 175, 187, 190, 192, 193–4, 199
German Expressionism 19, 99, 146, 163, 225
  influence on Hollywood horror 38, 95, 107
Gerow, Aaron 68, 76
Ghost Actress 198–200
ghost cat, see *bakeneko*
Ghost and the M.P., The 158, 166–7, 169, 170
Ghost Cat and the Chicken, The 135
Ghost Cat and the Clockwork Ceiling, The 112
Ghost Cat and the Cursed Pond, The 195, 197
Ghost Cat and the Cursed Wall, The 159–61, 195
Ghost Cat and the Mysterious Shamisen, The 92–3, 100–5, 118, 121, 143
  ambiguity of the supernatural 102–4
  cinematography 114
  screenplay 101, 165, 211
  special effects 101–2
  Suzuki Sumiko's performance 101–2, 104, 185
Ghost Cat at Ōma Crossing, The 41, 124–5, 126
Ghost Cat in the Red Wall, The 85, 105, 121
Ghost Cat in the Turkish Bath, The 198
Ghost Cat of Arima Palace, The (1919 film) 73
Ghost Cat of Arima Palace, The (1953 film) 57, 121, 122, 125
  negative criticism of 41, 126
Ghost Cat of Okazaki, The 39, 47, 125–7, 153, 165

Ghost Cat of Otama Pond, The 37–8, 158, 159
  anticipation of J-horror techniques 192, 199, 209, 214, 220
  similarities to *Mansion of the Ghost Cat* 171, 191–2, 195
Ghost Cat of Sannō, The 68
Ghost Cat of the 53 Way Stations, The 41, 125
Ghost Cat of Yonaki Swamp, The 40, 124, 128, 151 n. 13
Ghost of Oiwa, The 192
Ghost Story of Kasane's Swamp, The 6, 187, 190, 194, 211, see also *The Ghost Story of Kasane's Swamp* (1957 film)
  Mizoguchi Kenji's adaptation 100–1
  1924 film 79, 81, 91
  1960 film 175
  1970 film 196
  Orui's ghost 57, 80, 98, 212 (*see also* Oiwa, *onryō*)
  rakugo 103–4
Ghost Story of Kasane's Swamp, The (1957 film) 4–5, 16, 128, 145–6, 158, 159, 195, 200
  fantastic hesitation in 155–7
  mise-en-scène 152
  positive critical reception of 150–1, 157, 214–15
  prologue sequence 152–4
  and theories of the gaze 48
  uncanny repetition in 153–5, 165–6, 174
Ghost Story of Plover Pond, The 41, 135
Ghost Story of the Mandarin Duck Curtain, The 25, 92–3, 101, 208
  cinematography 98–100, 102, 116, 181
  makeup 98–9, 104, 154
  use of sound 99
Ghost Story of Saga Mansion, The 121, 122–4, 125
Ghost Story of Yotsuya, The 6, 45, 65, 67, 98, 136, see also *The Ghost Story of Yotsuya* (1956 film), *The Ghost Story of Yotsuya* (1959 Shintōhō film), *Ghost Story of Yotsuya: A New Interpretation, Oiwa inari*
  Chūshingura gaiden: Yotsuya kaidan (1994 film) 33
  connections to *Chūshingura* 113
  and definitions of the monstrous 50–1
  fear in 52, 55, 58
  as *horā* 35, 36
  kabuki play 7, 22, 64, 80–1, 178–9, 211
  and *kaiki* 26, 28, 36, 39–40, 87, 90, 109, 224
  karmic vengeance in 28, 73, 211–12
  1911 film 66
  1912 film 23
  1915 film 68, 81
  1921 film 73
  1923 film 74
  1925 film 77
  1927 film starring Matsueda Tsuruko 79–80, 86
  1927 film starring Suzuki Sumiko 24, 76, 84, 86
  1928 films 76, 84, 86
  1937 film 24–5, 149
  1959 Daiei film 172, 173
  1982 film 33
Ghost Story of Yotsuya, The (1956 film) 6, 16, 148–9, 150, 158, 192
  audience interviews 41, 59
  comparison with Nakagawa Nobuo's version 181–3
Ghost Story of Yotsuya, The (1959 Shintōhō film) 4–5, 16, 44–5, 128, 145, 158, 187, 211–12
  accolades 140, 173–4, 191
  adaptation of Nanboku's kabuki script 115, 172–3
  cinematography 99, 100, 116, 179–84
  influence on J-horror 207–8
  influence on 1960s *kaiki* film 190, 192, 195
  and monstrous-feminine 46
  montage 184–5
  as postwar allegory 7–8, 175–8, 209
  psychology of characters 145, 185–6
  and theories of the gaze 48–50
Ghost Story of Yotsuya: A New Interpretation 15, 114–17, 118, 149, 154, 172
Ghost Train 119
Ghosts vs Aliens 222
giallo 139
glamour actresses 128–30, 132, 168, 170, 194, 197
Godzilla 15, 27, 61, 119, 139

differences from *kaiki* film 28–9, 36, 136–8, 143, 221
Goke, Body Snatcher from Hell 193–4
Golden-Tailed Fox 105
gothic horror 79, 169, 197, 209, 225
    affinities with *kaiki* 16, 38–40, 61, 90, 119, 134, 144, 223
    "Edo Gothic" 8, 175–6, 177
    Hammer Films revival 15, 149, 221
    In 1930s Hollywood cinema 36, 149, 169
    In 1960s global cinema 139–40, 189, 193
    versus modern horror 10, 198, 210
    versus science fiction 27, 35, 136
Great Horror Family, The 213, 222–3
Grudge, The 3, 202, 212 n. 33, see also *Ju-On*
Guinea Pig 2 201
Gunning, Tom 13, 66

Halloween 10–11, 33, 162
Hammer Films 38, 167, 169, 197, 214
    decline of 33, 61, 189, 198
    and gothic horror revival 15, 139, 143, 149, 210, 221
    and *kaiki* films 39, 87, 134, 140, 143–4, 174, 194
    violence 140–2, 148, 159, 179–80
Hanayome kyūketsuma, see *Vampire Bride*
Hansen, Miriam 14, 86, 171, 204
Happiness of the Katakuris 201
Hara Komako 78, 82
Hart, Adam Charles 127
Hasegawa Kazuo 172
Hata Kenji 101
Haunted Castle, The 23–4
Haunting, The 58, 164–5, 215, 224
    and *Hunchback Ghost Story* 190, 193
    influence on J-horror 189, 205
Hayama Yoko 193
Hebi musume to hakuhatsuma, see *Snake Girl and the Silver-Haired Witch*
Hell of Oden, The 84, 129
Hello Kitty 221
higaisha ishiki 176–7
Hiroku kaibyō-den, see *Secret Chronicles of the Ghost Cat*
Hirose Ai 184

Hiroshima, atomic bombing of 8, 110, 177–8, 209
Hitchcock, Alfred 2, 29–31, 33, 34 n. 40, 46
Ho Lan Shan, see Nishimoto Tadashi
Hollywood 23, 33, 45, 59, 73, 77–8, 111, 139, 221, 225
    hegemonic position in global cinema 26–7, 224
    horror films as part of *kaiki* genre 10, 21, 24, 25, 87, 126
    horror versus science fiction 134, 136–8, 143, 144
    influence on Japanese *kaiki* films 14, 62, 66, 75, 86–91, 92–3, 95–7, 106–7, 124, 171
    kyōfu eiga 31
    remakes of J-horror 3, 34, 200–1, 202, 204
    slasher films 3, 33–4
Hontō ni atta kowai hanashi, see *Scary True Stories*
Hooper, Tobe 33
horā 11, 42, 56, 187, 198, see also J-horror
    differences from *kaiki* 36–40, 58, 60–1
    etymology 34, 189, 223
    and J-horror 200, 201
    retroactive application to *kaiki* films 21, 35–6, 61, 157
    transition from *kaiki* 107, 147, 167, 172, 174, 190, 209, 216
Horikiri Naota 173, 208
Horror of Dracula, see *Dracula* (1958 film)
Horrors of Malformed Men 197
House 198
House on Haunted Hill 30–1, 32
Hunchback Ghost Story 175, 190, 193–4
Hutchings, Peter 27
hyaku monogatari kaidankai 22, 40, 194

Ichi the Killer 198
Ichikawa Danjurō IX 63, 65
Ichikawa Utaemon 78
Iemon 22, 48, 80, 113 n. 10, see also *The Ghost Story of Yotsuya*, Oiwa
    Amachi Shigeru's portrayal of 185–6
    and Buddhism 174–5, 211
    in *The Ghost of Oiwa* 192

in *The Ghost Story of Yotsuya* (1956 film) 181–2, 186, 192
in *The Ghost Story of Yotsuya* (1959 Shintōhō film) 46, 145, 182–5, 192
in *Ghost Story of Yotsuya: A New Interpretation* 114–17, 186
in *Illusion of Blood* 193
and karmic retribution 58, 211
and Oiwa 46, 52, 56, 172–3, 207, 212
villainous traits 8, 44–5, 50, 52, 55, 176, 179
Ikeuchi Junko 171–2
Illusion of Blood 192–3, see also *The Ghost Story of Yotsuya*
Incredible Shrinking Man, The 137
Innocents, The 189, 205
Inugami no tatari, see *Curse of the Inugami*
Invasion of the Body Snatchers 136
Invisible Man, The 20
Invisible Man Meets the Fly, The 130
Irie Takako 125–7, 128, 130, 149, 153, 160, 163–4, 184
  makeup 71, 96, 122–3, 124, 131–2
  prewar stardom 15, 121–2, 123–4, 133
  as successor to Suzuki Sumiko 15, 121, 221
Iron Claw, The 119–20
Ishii Teruo 34, 197, 198
Ishikawa Yoshihiro 146, 158, 196
  The Ghost Cat and the Cursed Pond 195
  The Ghost Cat of Otama Pond 37 n. 35, 158, 171, 191–2, 199
Ivy, Marilyn 215
Iwai Shunji 215
Izawa Jun 28–9, 138, 178–9
Izumi Kiyoko 76–7
Izumi Kyōka 104
Izumi Toshiyuki 5, 69, 86–7, 180–1
  definition of *kaiki* 28, 53, 120

Jaganrei, see *Evil Spirit*
Japanese Film: Art and Industry, The 6
Japanese Kaidan Theater 196
Jasei no in, see *Lust of the White Serpent*
J-horror 34, 37, 38, 164, 169, 189
  decline of 221–3
  definition 201–2
  Hollywood remakes 14, 34, 200–1, 204
  influence of Western horror on 14, 193, 204, 205, 224

kaiki elements 5, 14, 16, 167, 189–93, 198, 204, 220
  lack of traditional cosmologies 212–16, 217
  Nakagawa Nobuo's influence on 4, 147, 166, 186–7, 205–8, 221
  and *onryō* 177, 190, 204, 208–12, 215–16, 217, 219
  origin of term 200–1
  popularity in the West 2–3, 14, 200–1
  precursors in Japanese film 3–5, 201–2, 225
  scholarship on 3–4, 8, 16, 202–4, 223
  technophobia 202–3
jidaigeki 73, 92, 118, 134, see also *chambara*, *kyūha*, *tachimawari*
  censorship 113
  chambara 93, 107, 112
  and *kaiki* 90, 101, 112, 152, 159, 186, 192
  marvelous approach to the supernatural 160–3, 165, 199
  negative critical perception 88–9
  and vamps 78, 84, 121
Jigoku 4, 146, 158, 191, 201
Jiraiya: The Stormcloud Scroll and the Transformation Scroll 90
Johann, Zita 168
Jokai 82–3
Journey to the West 73
Joyūrei, see *Ghost Actress*
Ju-On 16, 34, 201, 214
  depiction of *onryō* 210, 212
  franchise 3, 189, 202, 221, 222
Ju-On: White Ghost/ Black Ghost 213

kabuki 38, 73–4, 78, 104, 151, 208, 224
  and *bakeneko* 24, 71, 93, 95–6, 124, 165
  and early cinema 22–3, 63–6, 68
  and *The Ghost Story of Yotsuya* 7, 22–3, 64, 68, 80, 115, 176–9, 192
  stage tricks 68, 109, 115
  tachimawari 82 n. 45, 90
  Tsuruya Nanboku IV's script for *Yotsuya* 22, 76, 113 n. 10, 115, 172–3, 179, 185, 211
Kadono Gorō 150
Kaeriyama Norimasa 67–8
kai-i 22, 41

kaibyō eiga 24–5, 87, see also *bakeneko*
Kaibyō akakabe Daimyōjin, see *The Ghost Cat in the Red Wall*
Kaibyō Arima goten, see *The Ghost Cat of Arima Palace*
Kaibyō gojusan-ji, see *The Ghost Cat of the 53 Way Stations*
Kaibyō karakuri tenjo, see *The Ghost Cat and the Clockwork Ceiling*
Kaibyō koshinuke daisōdō, see *The Ghost Cat and the Chicken*
Kaibyō nazo no shamisen, see *The Ghost Cat and the Mysterious Shamisen*
Kaibyō noroi no ike, see *The Ghost Cat and the Cursed Pond*
Kaibyō noroi no kabe, see *The Ghost Cat and the Cursed Wall*
Kaibyō Okazaki sōdō, see *The Ghost Cat of Okazaki*
Kaibyō Ōma ga tsuji, see *The Ghost Cat at Ōma Crossing*
Kaibyō Otama ga ike, see *The Ghost Cat of Otama Pond*
Kaibyō Saga no yosaku, see *The Saga Ghost Cat*
Kaibyō toruko furo, see *The Ghost Cat in the Turkish Bath*
Kaibyō Yonaki numa, see *The Ghost Cat of Yonaki Swamp*
kaidan 31–2, 135–6, 155, 167, 180–1, 211, 220–3
  adaptation to film 10, 77, 109, 142–3, 165, 211, 216, 224
  belief in supernatural 53
  censorship 32, 113, 144
  Dish Mansion at Banchō 85, 135
  Edo period literature 22, 57, 103–4, 107, 179
  and *Frankenstein* 26, 28
  Ghost Story of Kasane's Swamp 151–3, 156–7, 174–5, 187, 190, 211
  Ghost Story of Yotsuya 172–5, 178, 187, 190, 192, 211
  and J-horror 199–200, 204, 205, 209, 212, 215
  and kabuki 22, 65, 92, 179
  and Nakagawa Nobuo 4, 105, 156–7, 193
  1930s film adaptations 86, 88, 91, 98, 135
  1950s film adaptations 32–3, 124, 128, 135, 137–8, 144, 151, 170–2, 187
  1960s film adaptations 187, 189, 194
  Peony Lantern 190, 136
  silent film adaptations 22–3, 36, 64–8, 70, 72–5, 79–81, 91, 106
  as subgenre of *kaiki* 11, 24–5, 31, 87, 90, 175
Kaidan (2007 film) 5, 37
Kaidan ama yūrei, see *Diving Girl's Ghost*
Kaidan chidori ga fuchi, see *The Ghost Story of Plover Pond*
Kaidan: Fox and Tanuki 75–6, 86, 88
Kaidan hebi onna, see *Snake Woman's Curse*
Kaidan honjo nana fushigi, see *The Seven Wonders of Honjo*
Kaidan Ikiteiru Koheiji, see *Undead Koheiji*
Kaidan Kasane ga fuchi, see *The Ghost Story of Kasane's Swamp*
Kaidan kitsune to tanuki, see *Kaidan: Fox and Tanuki*
Kaidan nobori Ryū, see *Blind Woman's Curse*
Kaidan Oiwa no bōrei, see *The Ghost of Oiwa*
Kaidan oshidori chō, see *The Ghost Story of the Mandarin Duck Curtain*
Kaidan Saga yashiki, see *The Ghost Story of Saga Mansion*
Kaidan semushi otoko, see *Hunchback Ghost Story*
Kaidan yonaki iwa 65
Kaidan zankoku monogatari, see *Cruel Ghost Legend*
kaijū 28–9, 138, 139, see also *Godzilla*
kaiki 5–7, 63, 67, 92, 121, 148, 172, 176, 178–81, 192, 222
  censorship 13, 15, 24, 75, 110–11, 113–18, 143–4, 221
  critical reception 15, 40–1, 85, 88, 91, 98, 105, 142, 151, 166, 174
  decline of *kaiki* genre 10–11, 16, 32–4, 61, 189–90, 196–8, 223
  definitions 27–32, 39–40, 42, 53–4
  differences from horror 11–12, 16, 26–7, 35–6, 42, 60–1, 223–4
  and European cinema 9–10, 30–1, 38–9
  etymology 21–2, 71

and fear 40–1, 54–6, 58–9, 72, 81, 160, 166, 220 (see also *osore*)
formal aspects 9, 37–40, 169, 210
and gothic horror 39, 61, 223
and Hammer Films 15, 33, 134, 139–42, 144, 149, 197, 221
and Hollywood 9–10, 14, 20–1, 29–31, 38, 86–91, 95–6, 190, 193, 224–5
and horror film theory 42–50, 52
and J-horror 16, 34, 164, 189–90, 198, 200–2, 204–11, 214–15, 219–20
kaiki to senritsu 24, 30, 117, 135, 181
karmic retribution in 57, 111
and Mokudō Shigeru 90–1, 92, 98–100, 181
and monsters 29, 32, 44–5, 47–51, 165, 186, 211, 216
and Nakagawa Nobuo 5, 7–8, 16, 46–50, 98–9, 105, 145–7, 150, 158, 163, 175, 179, 185–7, 190–1, 195, 216
narrative structure 40, 56, 91, 92–3, 101, 152, 184
obake yashiki mode 109, 125–7, 132, 183
and *osore* 12–13, 59–60, 62, 104, 109–10, 116–17, 127, 134, 140, 144, 145–6, 166, 211, 215–16
and romance 135–6
and science fiction 27–8, 136–8, 221
sexuality 96–7, 128, 130–1, 140, 144, 170
sound 99, 114
special effects 66, 68–9, 73, 81, 94–5, 106, 126
subgenres 11, 24, 87, 107, 123–4, 159, 175
and Suzuki Sumiko 14, 40, 66, 79, 82–5, 91, 97, 112
and Todorov's theory of the fantastic 13, 102–3, 105, 155–6, 220
vamp actresses in 77–8, 81, 106
versus *horā* 11, 34–7, 39, 61, 107, 157, 167, 174, 216
versus *kaijū eiga* 27–9, 138
versus *kyōfu* 31–2, 34–5, 60
and *shinpi* 118–20, 136, 165–6, 170
and *yōkai* 194–5
Kaiki daikazoku, see *The Great Horror Family*

Kaiki jūsan ya, see *Thirteen Nights of Kaiki*
Kairo, see *Pulse*
Karloff, Boris 27, 31, 72, 85, 89
karmic retribution 42, 73, 109–10, 138, 147, *see also* Buddhism
absence in J-horror 190, 212, 214–16
censorship under US Occupation 111, 114–15, 118, 119
in *The Ghost Story of Yotsuya* 28, 145, 185
monsters as agents of 15, 56–7, 61, 91, 92–3, 107, 113, 115, 118, 121, 144, 211
and *osore* 16, 140, 145, 151, 166, 194, 198, 216
Kataoka Chiezō 78
Kato Bin 47, 125–7, 153, 183
Kawabe Jūji 156–7
Kawai studio 76, 82
Kayako 190, 210, 214–15, 216, 221–2, 223
see also *Ju-On*, Oiwa, *onryō*, Sadako
similarities to Oiwa 212
Kenpei to barabara shibijin, see *The M.P. and the Dismembered Beauty*
Kenpei to yūrei, see *The Ghost and the M.P.*
Kill, Baby, Kill 139
Kinema junpō 9, 25, 74–5, 76, 77, 170
"*Kaiki* Films and the Audience" 41
Kaiki to kyōfu special issue 29, 140–1, 174
negative reviews of domestic *kaiki* films 40–1, 79, 85, 91
positive reviews of domestic *kaiki* films 81, 85, 150–1, 166, 174
reviews of foreign *kaiki* films 20–1, 26, 30, 142
"World of *Kaiki* Film" feature 28, 137–8, 144
Kinema Record 68, 71, 74–5, 76, 81
King, Stephen 60
King Kong: Made in Japan 89
Kinmō kitsune, see *Golden-Tailed Fox*
Kinoshita Keisuke 113–17, 118, 154, 172, 185
characterization of Oiwa 114–15, 127, 149, 179, 185, 186
higaisha ishiki 176
Kinugasa Teinosuke 4
Kobayashi Masaki 175
kōdan 22, 124

Kokkatsu 74
Konaka Chiaki 164, 202
Konjaku monogatari-shū 21
Kore-eda Hirokazu 215
Kristeva, Julia 43, 45
Kurihara, Thomas 82
Kuroneko-kan ni kieta otoko, see *The Man who Vanished in the Black Cat Mansion*
Kurosawa Akira 6, 113, 145, 159
Kurosawa Haruyasu 146, 158, 186
   The Ghost Cat of Otama Pond 192
   The Ghost Story of Yotsuya 173–4, 175, 208
   Mansion of the Ghost Cat 159
Kurosawa Kiyoshi 29, 34, 164, 198, 202, 224
   definition of *kaiki* 31, 38–40, 58–9, 109, 169, 210
   on Kurosawa Haruyasu 146
   on Nakagawa Nobuo 5, 190–1, 205–7
   Pulse 3, 201, 205–7, 213
   Retribution 213, 223
Kyoto 82, 86
kyōfu eiga 11, 89, 138, 140, 174
   versus *kaiki* 30–2, 34, 35, 39, 60
Kyōren no onna shisō, see *Passion of a Female Teacher*
kyūha 64, 73, 88, see also *jidaigeki*, Makino Shōzō, Onoe Matsunosuke
Kyūketsu dokurosen, see *The Living Skeleton*
Kyūketsuki ga, see *The Vampire Moth*
Kyūketsuki Gokemidoro, see *Goke, Body Snatcher from Hell*
Kwaidan 175

Lady Vampire 48, 53, 158, 167–70, 171, 186, 209
Lee, Christopher 139, 140–1, 149
Legend of the Nabeshima Ghost Cat 15, 117–18, 147
Legend of the Saga Ghost Cat 40–1, 84–5, 90–1, 121, 165, 195
Life of Oharu 147, 148
Lim, Bliss Cua 12–13
Living Skeleton, The 175, 194
Lord of the Rings, The 52, 56
Lovecraft, H. P. 12, 57–60, 109, 166, 174, 216–17
Lugosi, Bela 19, 20, 27, 85, 95–7, 167

Lumière Brothers 63
Lust of the White Serpent 82

M. Pathe (Japanese studio) 65–6
M.P. and the Dismembered Beauty, The 166
Madam Knockout 84
Maeda Michiko 129, 148
Magatani Morihei 170
Makino (studio) 24, 75–6, 78, 82–3
Makino Shōzō 23, 67–8, 70, 73, 75
Man Who Vanished in the Black Cat Mansion, The 136
Mansion of the Ghost Cat 4, 16, 38, 128, 146, 193, 219
   anticipation of J-horror themes 164, 167, 174, 186, 199–200, 208–9, 214, 220
   blood 159–60, 179–80
   cinematography 145, 162–3
   depiction of *bakeneko* 46, 125, 160–5
   and *The Ghost Cat of Otama Pond* 171, 192, 199
   marvelous versus fantastic (Todorov) 160, 165–6, 169–70, 186
   as Shintōhō "prestige picture" 150, 157–9, 172
Manster, The 139 n. 48
Marak, Katarzyna 53, 203–4, 209
marvelous mode (Todorov) 13, 51–6, 61, 102–5, 170, 216, 220
   in *The Ghost Story of Kasane's Swamp* 155–7, 200
   and J-horror 200, 208, 210
   in *Mansion of the Ghost Cat* 160, 165–6, 186, 200, 208
Matango 137
Matsueda Tsuruko 78, 79–80, 81, 82, 91
Matsuno Hiroshi 175
McRoy, Jay 8, 212
Méliès, Georges 14, 23, 66, 70, 106
Metro-Goldwyn-Mayer 87
Mihara Yoko 168, 170
Miike Takashi 34, 198, 201, 224
Miki Teruko 85
Mill of the Stone Women 39
misemono 64–5, 75
Misono Kyōhei 71
Misora Hibari 135–6, 143, 151
Misumi Kenji 159, 172, 173
Miyagawa Toshiko 85

Miyao, Daisuke 123
Miyazaki Hayao 215
Mizoguchi Kenji 6, 90, 100, 145,
    147, 152
  Ugetsu 3, 82, 104, 175, 202, 223
Mizuki Shigeru 194
Mokudō Shigeru 101, 102, 104, 112,
    114, 118
  The Cat of Arima 92, 93–4, 95, 208
  The Ghost Story of the Mandarin Duck Curtain 92, 98–100, 116–17, 181, 208
  The Ghost Story of Yotsuya (1937 film) 149
  Legend of the Saga Ghost Cat 90–1
Momijigari 63–4, 112
monsters 42, 73, 132, 139, 149, 186,
    189, 212, 214, see also *bakeneko*,
    onryō, *yōkai*
  as agents of karmic retribution 15,
    56–7, 61, 91, 92–3, 107, 113, 115, 118,
    121, 144, 211
  allegorical function 105
  cinematography 100, 101, 147, 162, 164,
    183–4, 187, 192, 199–200, 205
  definition 50–1
  in early cinema 70–1, 106, 109
  and the Freudian uncanny 55–6, 155,
    167, 169, 200, 209–10, 221
  grotesque 60, 130
  in kabuki 64–5, 151
  marvelous versus fantastic (Todorov)
    13, 51–4, 61, 102, 119–20, 157,
    165–6, 212, 216, 220
  in modern horror 10, 16
  monstrous-feminine 44–7
  and narrative structure 40, 91,
    152–3, 167
  obake 11, 24, 106
  obake yashiki 126
  and *osore* 59, 61, 66, 134, 216
  as Other 43–5
  parodies of 222
  revulsion 52, 53
  in science fiction 27–9, 136, 138,
    143, 221
  supernatural origin 28, 29, 31, 32, 52,
    58, 170, 197, 213
  Suzuki Sumiko's portrayals of 82, 84–5,
    90, 97, 101, 104, 160
  and theories of the gaze 47–50

vamp actresses's portrayal of 9, 14, 66,
    77–81, 84, 106
  and violence 140
  yōkai 22, 194–5
Mōri Ikuko 15, 128, 195–6
  Daiei snake trilogy 130–4, 140, 144
  in *Secret Chronicles of the Ghost Cat* 195
  in *Yokai Monsters: One Hundred Monsters* 194
Mori Kaname 74
Mori Kazuo 105
Mōri Masaki 6, 16, 148–9, 158, 173, 179
  filming technique in *The Ghost Story of Yotsuya* (1956 film) 181–3
  and Wakayama Tomisaburō 185, 192
Mothra 28, 139
Mulvey, Laura 47
Mummy, The 20, 91, 168
Murakami Hisao 20–1
Murnau, F. W. 36

Nabeshima kaibyōden, see *Legend of the Nabeshima Ghost Cat*
Nagasaki, atomic bombing of 8,
    177–8, 209, see also Hiroshima
Nagata Masaichi 111–12
  and Daiei 112, 118, 120–1, 144
  and Shinkō 85, 88, 90
Nagib, Lucia 224
Naikaku jōhōkyoku, see Cabinet Propaganda Office
Nakagawa Nobuo 4–7, 9, 16, 46–7, 77, 98,
    105, 127, 139, 145–6, 221, 225
  The Ghost and the M.P. 166–7, 170
  The Ghost Story of Kasane's Swamp 6,
    48, 146, 150–7, 174, 194, 200, 215
  The Ghost Story of Yotsuya 6, 8, 16, 36,
    44, 46, 48–9, 99, 100, 115, 116–17, 140,
    145, 150, 172–86, 192, 207–8, 211–12
  influence on J-horror 4–5, 16, 164–6,
    186–7, 190, 205–8, 210, 216
  influence on 1960s *kaiki* films 147, 175,
    189, 190, 193, 194–5
  innovations in *kaiki* filmmaking 107,
    143, 147, 152, 155–7, 159–66, 184
  and Ishikawa Yoshihiro 191–2, 195
  Jigoku 4, 146, 191, 201
  karma 146, 168
  and Kurosawa Haruyasu 146, 158,
    175, 186

Lady Vampire 48, 167–70, 171, 209–10
Mansion of the Ghost Cat 46, 146, 157–66, 170, 174, 192, 199–200, 219
 on monsters in film 183, 200, 205
 and Nishimoto Tadashi 158, 161, 179
 and Ōkura Mitsugi 147, 150, 170, 174, 191
 The Peony Lantern (*Japanese Kaidan Theater*) 196
 Snake Woman's Curse 46, 195, 196, 202
 The Vampire Moth 119, 120
Nakata Hideo 202
 Dark Water 201
 Ghost Actress 199–200
 Kaidan 5, 37
 Ring 3, 200, 202
 Sadako 189
Namiki Kyōtarō 16, 171
Nana fushigi, see Seven Wonders
Naniwa eregi, see *Osaka Elegy*
Neale, Stephen 7, 209
neko jarashi 95, 124, 126, 159, 161, see also *bakeneko*
Night of the Living Dead 3, 10
Nightmare on Elm Street, A 34, 36, 198
Nihon kaidan gekijō, see *Japanese Kaidan Theater*
Nikkatsu 75, 78, 111, 118, 129, 197–8
 formation of 66
 and Makino Shōzō 23, 67, 73
 proposed merger with Shintōhō 147
nikutai bungaku 129
nikutai joyū 129, see also glamour actresses
Ninja of Osaka Castle 90
Nishimoto Tadashi 146, 158, 161, 179
Noh 3, 98
Nosferatu 19, 36, 95, 162
Numata Yoichi 191

obake eiga 11, 24, 32, 87, 106, 174, see also *kaiki*
obake yashiki 15, 109, 125, 127, 132, 153, 183, see also sensational address
Obayashi Nobuhiko 198
Obon 7, 23, 26, 28, 105, 117
 Shintōhō's annual "monster cavalcade" 149, 150, 157, 166, 172, 192
occupation 8, 176

censorship 15, 110–14, 117–20, 127, 143–4
Oden jigoku, see *The Hell of Oden*
Oiwa 22, 44–5, 50, 51, 57, 109, 119, 124, 139 n. 48, 140, 144, 178–9, 216, see also *The Ghost Story of Yotsuya*, Iemon, *onryō*
 and Buddhism 28, 45, 138, 211
 facial disfigurement 99, 105, 114, 116–17, 154, 171, 177–8
 in *The Ghost of Oiwa* 192
 in *The Ghost Story of Yotsuya* (1959 Shintōhō film) 8, 145, 173, 174, 181–6, 207–8, 212
 in *Ghost Story of Yotsuya: A New Interpretation* 113–17, 172
 and *higaisha ishiki* 8, 177–8
 and Iemon 46, 52, 56, 172–3, 207, 212
 in *Illusion of Blood* 193
 and J-horror *onryō* 190, 193, 204, 207, 212, 214
 kabuki portrayals 80–1, 115, 192
 monstrous maternal 46
 onnagata 68, 80
 Satsuki Nobuko's portrayal of 77
 Sōma Chieko's portrayal 149
 Suzuki Sumiko's portrayals of 79, 85, 96–7, 98
 and theories of the gaze 48–9
 Wakasugi Katsuko's portrayal of 179–80, 207
Oiwa inari 65
Okamoto Kidō 135–6
Okazaki no neko, see *The Cat of Okazaki*
Okiku 1–2, 23, 69, 70, 76, 80, 220, see also Oiwa, Sadako
 Misora Hibari's portrayal 135–6
Ōkura Mitsugi 146–7, 172, 192, 197
 and *ama* films 170
 benshi career 147–8
 and Nakagawa Nobuo 145, 150–1, 157–8, 166–7, 170, 174
 studio policy 148–50, 158, 187, 221
 resignation from Shintōhō 191
Old Dark House, The 99
100 ghost stories game, see *hyaku monogatari kaidankai*
One Missed Call 201, 203, 213
Onibaba 3, 4, 202
Onna kyūketsuki, see *Lady Vampire*

Onna shinju ō no fukushū, see *Revenge of the Pearl Queen*
onnagata 75, 77, 79, 81, 106
Onoe Kikugorō V 63
Onoe Matsunosuke 67–8, 71, 73, 75, 88
   kaidan eiga 23, 65
onryō 44, 149, 193, 219, see also *bakeneko*, Oiwa, Sadako
   in J-horror 190, 193, 203–4, 207, 209, 212–14, 216, 223
Onryō Sakura daisōdō, see *The Vengeful Ghost of Sakura*
Osaka Elegy 104
Ōsawa Jō 87, 185
Ōshima Kiyoaki 203
osore 12, 16, 107, 114, 140, 146, 151, 186, 221
   and actresses's portrayals of monsters 62, 66, 106, 220
   and *bakeneko* 121, 125, 140, 166
   and the Freudian uncanny 154, 155, 221
   in *The Ghost Story of Yotsuya* 145, 173–4, 175, 178, 179, 183, 187
   in J-horror 189, 190, 198, 211, 215–16, 217, 223
   in *Jigoku* 191
   and karmic retribution 16, 61, 104–5, 109, 121, 166, 194, 211, 216
   lack of in postwar *kaiki* films 15, 73, 110, 116–17, 119, 132, 134, 143–4
   and Lovecraft's "cosmic fear" 59, 61, 109, 215–16
   in *Mansion of the Ghost Cat* 159–60, 166, 219
   terror versus horror 60, 127
   and vengeful ghosts 99, 121, 140, 190, 193, 211, 215
   versus cinema of attractions 13, 71, 220
   in Western *kaiki* films 61, 140, 215–16
Ozu Yasujirō 6, 145

Page of Madness, A 4,
Paramount Pictures 20, 87
paranoid horror 10, 203, 216, 217
Passion of a Female Teacher 100–1, see also *The Ghost Story of Kasane's Swamp*
Peony Lantern, The 6, 33, 68, 80, 86, 190
   1910 films 65
   1914 film 23
   1921 film 74
   1930 film 80
   1955 film 135
   1968 film 175, 193
   1970 television film 196
   1972 film 197–8
   origins in Chinese literature 7, 136
   reincarnation in 168
Phantom of the Opera, The 19, 27, 36, 47–8
Pirates of the Caribbean 56
Planet of the Vampires 139
Plantinga, Carl 12, 55, 160
Poe, Edgar Allan 58, 102–3, 139, 197
Poison Woman Takahashi Oden 158
Posadas, Baryon Tensor 8–9, 223
Prawer, S. S. 35
Price, Vincent 58
program pictures 15, 110
   Daiei 121, 125, 128, 132, 149, 187
Psycho 2, 29–31, 32, 33, 34 n. 40, 60
psychoanalysis 12, 45–50, 65, 102–5, 118, 146
   and *The Ghost Story of Yotsuya* 46, 48–50, 114–15, 183, 185–6
Pu Songling 135
Pulse 3, 4, 16, 201, 203, 213
   Nakagawa Nobuo's influence on 205–7
Pure Film Movement 67–8, 73–5, 88, 106, 137

Radcliffe, Anne 60, 127
Raine, Michael 89
Rashōmon 113, 121
Rauer, Julie 177
rensa 69–70, 76
Retribution 213, 223
Revenge of the Pearl Queen 129, 148, 170
Richie, Donald 6–7, 129
Ring 1–2, 5, 16, 189, 210, 219, 225, see also Sadako
   catalyst for J-horror phenomenon 3, 34, 200, 202, 216, 221
   depiction of Sadako 177, 199, 204, 212, 219–20
   influence of *kaiki* film on 205
   and Japanese horror film history 4, 201
   narrative structure 213, 214
   novel series 200

and Takahashi Hiroshi 31, 109, 164, 191, 199
and traditional Japanese culture 1–2, 200, 209
Ring, The (U.S. film) 3, 200–1, 204, 219
Ring 2 200 n.13
Ring 0: Birthday 189
Rodan 28
roman poruno 197
Rosemary's Baby 210
Ruan Lingyu 122

Sadako 1–2, 189, 200, 225, see also *onryō*, *Ring*
  departures from *kaiki* genre conventions 199, 210, 213, 214–15, 219–20
  kaiki eiga influences on 189, 205, 216, 219–20
  and Oiwa 177, 190, 204, 212
  and Okiku 1–2, 220
  overexposure 221–3
  versus Samara 204
  viral metaphor 203
Sadako (film) 189, 222
Sadako 3D 189, 202
Sadako 3D 2 189, 221
Sadako vs. Kayako 189, 202
Saga Ghost Cat, The 85
Saga kaibyō den, see *Legend of the Saga Ghost Cat*
Saga no yozakura, see *The Evening Cherry Blossoms of Saga*
Sakai Yoneko 78
Sakuya the Demon Slayer 33
Sannō no bakeneko, see *The Ghost Cat of Sannō*
San'yūtei Enchō 103–4, 155
Sasaki Hirohisa 37–40, 169, 210
Satō Hajime 175, 190, 193–4
Satō Tadao 96–7, 134, 137–8
Satsuki Fujie 160–4
Satsuki Nobuko 77, 79
Sawamura Shirōgorō 65, 73–4
Scary True Stories 202
Schoolhouse Ghost Stories 202
Schreck, Max 95
science fiction 61, 165, 200
  and horror 2, 10, 15, 27–8, 35, 36, 134, 136, 139, 144

and *kaiki* 15, 27–8, 134, 136–8, 221
Scott, Ridley 137
Second World War 8, 9, 28, 67, 107, 143, 177
Secret Chronicles of the Ghost Cat 195–6
Serpent's Wrath 130
Seven Wonders 72–3, 74, 150
Seven Wonders of Fukugawa 74
Seven Wonders of Honjo
  1922 film 74
  1957 film 73, 150
sensational address 127, 145–6, 153, 183–4, see also *obake yashiki*
Shelley, Mary 138
Shibata Tsunekichi 63–4, 112
Shigeno Yukiyashi 67–8, 71, 87
Shikishima Hanaeda 69
Shimizu Akira 138
Shimizu Chiyota 26
Shimizu Takashi 201, 202, 210, 213, 222
Shimura Miyoko 5, 78, 81, 124, 125, 195
  on Irie Takako 123
  on *Mansion of the Ghost Cat* 149, 159–60, 163
  on Mōri Ikuko 132
  on Suzuki Sumiko 79, 84, 95, 96, 97
Shindō Kaneto 3, 4, 176, 202
Shinkō Kinema 71, 92, 110, 129, 143, 145, 155
  advertising for *kaiki* films 24–5, 104
  and Daiei 111–12, 118, 121, 128
  formation of 86
  jidaigeki 88, 90, 101, 112, 118, 134, 161
  Legend of the Saga Ghost Cat 84–5, 90, 195
  and Mokudō Shigeru 90–1, 112, 181
  and Mori Kazuo 105
  and Nagata Masaichi 88, 90, 111–12, 144
  and Suzuki Sumiko 84–5, 95, 104, 105, 112
  and Tōei 134
  and Ushihara Kiyohiko 92, 104
shinpa 64, 74, 76–7, 82
shinpi 118–20, 136, 165, 166, 170
Shinshaku Yotsuya kaidan, see *Ghost Story of Yotsuya: A New Interpretation*
Shinto 33, 171, 212 n. 33
Shintōhō 4, 16, 41, 73, 87, 89, 128, 140, 155, 158–9, 172, 197

ama films 120, 129, 170
bankruptcy 32, 151, 187, 191, 196
formation of 117–18
gendaigeki kaiki films 136, 166, 170–2, 175, 193
influence on 1960s *kaiki* films, 175, 187, 190, 192–3, 195
and J-horror 200, 205, 208–9, 210, 214–15, 220
Mansion of the Ghost Cat 125, 159–60, 165
and Mōri Masaki 6, 150
and Nakagawa Nobuo 4–5, 16, 98, 105, 107, 139, 143, 145–6, 150–1, 186–7, 195
and Ōkura Mitsugi 146–50, 170, 187, 221
and Watanabe Kunio 117, 119, 150
Shirō Toyoda 192
Shirohebi Komachi, see *White Snake Beauty*
Shōchiku 67, 88, 92, 121
Cruel Ghost Legend 194
The Dish Mansion at Banchō 85, 135
formation 73–4
Ghost Story of Yotsuya: A New Interpretation 114, 117–18
Goke, Body Snatcher from Hell 193–4
kaiki film production 74, 75, 76, 134, 151, 175, 194
Living Skeleton, The 194
and Shinkō Kinema 86
wartime restructuring 111–12
and Yoshino Jirō 73–4, 75
shūnen 45, 59, 99, 193
Shūnen no hebi, see *Serpent's Wrath*
slasher films 3, 4, 43, 162, 171, 223
advent of 10, 33–4
giallo 139
and *horā* 34, 36, 60, 61
Miike Takashi 34, 198
Snake Girl and the Silver-Haired Witch 195
Snake Woman's Curse 46, 146, 195, 196, 202
Sōma Chieko 149, 179
sound 88, 99, 126, 157, 164, 193
Spadoni, Robert 20
Standish, Isolde 176
Stoker, Bram 168, 169, 222

Supreme Command of Allied Powers (SCAP) 111, 117, see also Civil Censorship Detachment, Civil Information and Education Section
Suzuki Kensuke 158
Suzuki Kōji 200
Suzuki Sumiko 14, 66, 82–6, 92, 133, 159, 160, 163
bakeneko performances 14, 71, 84–5, 90–1, 93–7, 118, 122, 125, 132, 224, 225
in *The Cat of Arima* 93–7
in *The Ghost Cat and the Clockwork Ceiling* 112
in *The Ghost Cat and the Mysterious Shamisen* 101–5, 114, 185
in *The Ghost Cat in the Red Wall* 105
in *The Ghost Story of the Mandarin Duck Curtain* 98–100, 154
and Irie Takako 15, 71, 121–2, 160, 163–4, 221
in *Legend of the Saga Ghost Cat* 40, 84–5, 90–1
and Makino Studios 82
monstrous transformations 95, 98–100, 106, 208, 220
and Nagata Masaichi 84–5, 112
as Oiwa 79, 98, 149
sexual appeal 14, 79, 81, 84, 96–7, 122, 124, 129, 132, 221, 225
and Shinkō Kinema 84, 105, 128
stage career 82, 112
tachimawari 82, 84, 91, 93–5, 105, 184
vamp status 78–9, 82, 84, 94, 106
Sweet Home 198

Tachibana Sotō 165, 167
tachimawari 78, 107, 127, 161, 184
Suzuki Sumiko 82, 84, 91, 93–5, 105
Tada Michitarō 125, 151, 157, 214
Takahashi Hiroshi 110, 128, 202
definition of *kaiki* 31, 120
Ghost Actress 198–200
on *Jigoku* 191
on Nakagawa Nobuo 205, 207–8
on the *obake yashiki* mode 109, 125, 127, 183
Ring 199–200
theory of horror film 164–5, 192, 204
on Western horror films 205, 224

Takisawa Osamu 174, 183
Tale of Two Sisters, A 201
Tales of Moonlight and Rain, 82
Tanaka Jun'ichirō 5
Tanaka Kinuyo 85, 135, 149
tanuki 71, 72–3, 75, 88, 150
technophobia 203, 204, 215, *see also* paranoid horror
Teikine 78, 79, 82, 84, 86
television 11, 16, 22, 32, 187, 196
"The Tell-Tale Heart" 102
Tenkatsu 70, 73, 74, 75
Tetsu no tsume, see *The Iron Claw*
Texas Chain Saw Massacre, The 10, 33, 198
Them! 27, 50
Thing from Another World, The 27
13 Nights of Kaiki 196
Tōa 78
Todorov, Tzvetan 12–13, 51, *see also* marvelous mode
  marvelous 155–6, 157, 220
  pure fantastic 102, 105, 155–6
  uncanny 119
Tōei 11, 112, 130, 134–5, 196–7, 198
  1950s "romantic *kaidan*" 135–6, 144, 148–9, 151, 221
  1960s *kaiki* films 175, 192, 193, 195
Tōhō 33, 88, 111–12, 119, 121, 197
  foundation of Shintōhō 117
  and Irie Takako 121–2
  kaijū films 28, 139
  1960s *kaiki* films 175, 192–3
  science fiction 136–7
Tōkaidō obake dōchū, see *Yokai Monsters: Along with Ghosts*
Tōkaidō Yotsuya kaidan, see *Ghost Story of Yotsuya*
Tokyo 63, 74, 82, 169, 209, 219
  in J-horror 210, 215, 220
Tokyo Tsukamoto 32
Tōmei ningen to hae otoko, see *The Invisible Man meets the Fly*
Tourneur, Jacques 157
Transforming Man series 137
trick films 9, 13, 23–4, 66, 68–76, 81, 90, 106, 220
Tsuburaya Eiji 119
Tsuruta Norio 202
Tsuruya Nanboku IV 22, 64, 76, 172–3, 178–9, 185, 211

and J-horror 204
and Nakagawa Nobuo's *The Ghost Story of Yotsuya* 115, 172–3, 174–5, 176, 179, 183
Tudor, Andrew 10, 203, 216

Uchiyama Kazuki 21, 29, 119
Ueda Akinari 82, 209
Uehara Ken 114–15, 185, 186
Ugetsu (film) 82, 104, 175
  classification as "Japanese horror" 3, 4, 11, 202, 223
Ugetsu monogatari, see *Tales of Moonlight and Rain*
Umezu Kazuo 195
Uncanny, *see* Freudian uncanny; Todorov, Tzvetan
Undead Koheiji 150 n. 11, 158
Uninvited, The 58
Universal Studios 38, 99, 111, 119, 136, 167, 222
  Bride of Frankenstein 10, 20, 189
  Cat and the Canary, The 19, 118
  and creation of the horror genre 10, 19–20, 36, 87
  Dracula 10, 24, 36, 19–20, 87, 96, 159, 169
  Frankenstein 20, 24, 36, 87
  Hammer remakes 139, 149
  and *kaiki* genre 10, 14, 20, 24, 86–7, 96
  monsters 27, 91, 92–3, 189
  Mummy, The 20, 168
  Phantom of the Opera 19, 27
  Wolf Man, The 38
Ushihara Kiyohiko 88
  Ghost Cat and the Mysterious Shamisen, The 92, 100–2, 104, 105, 114, 118
Utagawa Kinue 101, 104
Utsunomiya no tenjō, see *The Ceiling at Utsunomiya*

vamp actresses 14, 76–81, 86, 87–8, 106, 220
  Irie Takako 121–2
  Matsueda Tsuruko 78, 79–80, 81
  Suzuki Sumiko 14, 66, 78–79, 81, 82–4, 93–7, 122, 132, 225
Vampire Bride 16, 171–2, 174, 208, 209

and *gendaigeki kaiki* films 171, 193, 211, 220
Vampire Lovers, The 38
Vampire Moth, The 119, 120
Variety 20
Varma, D. P. 60
Vengeful Ghost of Sakura, The 149
vernacular modernism 14, 86, 139, 204

Wada-Marciano, Mitsuyo 26–7, 201–2, 204
Wakasugi Katsuko 178, 179–80, 183, 207, 208
Wakayama Tomisaburō 185–6, 192
Walking Dead, The (1936 film) 31, 89
Warner, Marina 41
Wasei Kingu Kongu, see *King Kong: Made in Japan*
Watanabe Chūmei 158, 163
Watanabe Kunio 149, 150
  Legend of the Nabeshima Ghost Cat 15, 117–18, 127, 147
Watts, Naomi 200
Way of the Dragon 158
Wee, Valerie 8, 53, 203–4, 209
Whale, James 26, 99, 114, 138
Whip and the Body, The 139
White Snake Beauty 130–3, 195
Williams, Linda 47–8, 142
Wise, Robert 164–5, 190, 193
Wizard of Oz, The 160
Wolf Man, The 3, 38
Wood, Robin 12, 33, 43–4, 50
World War II, *see* Second World War

yakuza films 26–7, 129, 148, 196, 197
Yamabuki neko, see *The Yellow Rose Cat*
Yamada Isuzu 85
Yamada Seiji 148
Yamamoto Michio 197
Yamamoto Ryōkuyō 76
Yanagi Masako 41, 57, 196
Yanagita Kunio 104, 215
Yellow Rose Cat, The 85
yōfu 78, see also *vamp actresses*
yōkai 22, 78, 190, 194–5
Yōkai daisensō, see *Yokai Monsters: Spook Warfare*
Yōkai hyaku monogatari, see *Yokai Monsters: One Hundred Monsters*
Yokai Monsters: Along with Ghosts 194
Yokai Monsters: One Hundred Monsters 194
Yokai Monsters: Spook Warfare 194
Yōkai ningen Bemu 194
Yokomizo Seishi 119
Yokota studio 65
Yokoyama Yasuko 80, 172–3
Yomota Inuhiko 5
Yoshino Jirō 73–4, 75–6, 86, 88, 150
Yoshizawa studio 65, 70
Yotsuya kaidan, see *The Ghost Story of Yotsuya*
Yūrei bessha, see *Ghost Train*
Yūrei vs uchūjin, see *Ghosts vs Aliens*

Zahlten, Alexander 26
Zatoichi 93
Zenkatsu 85